Computer-Aided Design of User Interfaces II

Sponsors

**Banque Bruxelles
Lambert**
http://www.bbl.be

Dell Computer Corp.
http://www.dell.be

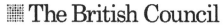

The Bristish Council
http://www.britcoun.org/belgium/

Fonds National de la
Recherche Scientifique
http://www.fnrs.be

Communauté Française
de Belgique
http://www.cfwb.be

ACM Chapter
BelCHI
http://belchi.qant.ucl.ac.be

Institut d'Administration et de Gestion
http://www.iag.ucl.ac.be/iag/

Université catholique
de Louvain
http://www.ucl.ac.be

Official CADUI WWW site: http://belchi.qant.ucl.ac.be/cadui

COMPUTER-AIDED DESIGN OF USER INTERFACES II

Proceedings of the Third International Conference on
Computer-Aided Design of User Interfaces,
21-23 October, 1999, Louvain-la-Neuve, Belgium

edited by

Jean Vanderdonckt
Université catholique de Louvain,
Louvain-la-Neuve, Belgium

and

Angel Puerta
Stanford University,
Stanford, California, U.S.A.

KLUWER ACADEMIC PUBLISHERS
DORDRECHT / BOSTON / LONDON

A C.I.P. Catalogue record for this book is available from the Library of Congress.

ISBN 0-7923-6078-8

Published by Kluwer Academic Publishers,
P.O. Box 17, 3300 AA Dordrecht, The Netherlands.

Sold and distributed in North, Central and South America
by Kluwer Academic Publishers,
101 Philip Drive, Norwell, MA 02061, U.S.A.

In all other countries, sold and distributed
by Kluwer Academic Publishers,
P.O. Box 322, 3300 AH Dordrecht, The Netherlands.

Printed on acid-free paper

Printed in the Netherlands

TABLE OF CONTENTS

Preface–Introduction to Computer-Aided Design of User Interfaces 1
    J. Vanderdonckt and A. Puerta
Program Committee Members 6

Invited speakers

1. Modeling for Component Based Development in UML/Catalysis 7
    A.C. Wills
2. Theory Based Design: From Individual Users and
    Tasks to Collaborative Systems 21
    P. Johnson
3. Evaluating Accessibility and Usability of Web Pages 33
    M. Cooper

Model-Based User Interface Development Environments

4. Model-Based Design of User Interfaces Using Object-Z 43
    A. Hussey and D. Carrington
5. A Method Engineering Framework for Modeling and
    Generating Interactive Applications 57
    Ch. Märtin
6. GIPSE, A Model-Based System for CAD Software 61
    G. Patry and P. Girard
7. Visto: A More Declarative GUI Framework 73
    K. Aerts
8. Beyond Automatic Generation-Exploratory Approach to UI Design 79
    S. Kovacevic
9. Using Application Domain Specific Run-Time Systems and
    Lightweight User Interface Models - A Novel Approach for CADUI 97
    E. Nilsson
10. XXL: A Visual+Textual Environment for Building
    Graphical User Interfaces 115
    E. Lecolinet

Linking and Deriving Models

11. Semi-Automated Linking of User Interface Design Artifacts 127
    S.S. Elnaffar and N. Graham
12. The Teallach Tool: Using Models for Flexible User Interface Design . 139
    P.J. Barclay, T. Griffiths, J. McKirdy, N.W. Paton, R. Cooper, and
    J. Kennedy

13.MDL: A Language for Binding User-Interface Models 159
   R.E.K. Stirewalt

Windows management

14.Vanishing Windows: An Empirical Study of Adaptive Window
   Management 171
   T. Miah and J.L. Alty
15.Adaptive Layout Calculation in Graphical User Interfaces:
   A Retrospective on the A^2DL-Project 185
   S. Stille and R. Ernst
16.Semantic Differences Between User Interface Platforms
   Relevance to Design and Re-Design of User Interface 199
   M.B. Harning

Design Frameworks and Objects

17. A Framework for Management of Sophisticated User Interface's
   Variants in Design Process:
   A Case Study 205
   P. Savolainen and H. Konttinen
18.GRASYLA: Modelling Case Tool GUIs in MetaCases........................ 217
   V. Englebert and J.-L. Hainaut
19.User Defined Objects are First Class Citizen 231
   G. Texier and L. Guittet

Supporting Task-Based Design

20.The Visual Task Model Builder... 245
   M. Biere, B. Bomsdorf, and G. Szwillus
21.Computer-Aided Analysis of Cooperative Applications..................... 257
   G. Ballardin, C. Mancini and F. Paternò
22.Methodological and Tool Support for a Task-Oriented 271
   Development of Interactive Systems
   A. Dittmar and P. Forbrig
23.Modelling Work: Workflow and Task Modelling 275
   H. Trætteberg

Computer-Aided Design of User Interfaces

24. A Generic Framework based on Ergonomics Rules for
Computer Aided Design of User Interface 281
Ch. Farenc and Ph. Palanque
25. CMF: A Coherent Modelling Framework for
Task-Based User Interface Design 293
B. Bomsdorf and G. Szwillus,
26. Towel: Real World Mobility on the Web 305
S. Harper, R. Stevens, and C. Goble
27. Tool-Based Support for User-Designer Collaboration
in Distributed User Interface Design and Evaluation 313
J. Sarkkinen

Computer-Aided Evaluation of User Interfaces

28. An Approach of Computer-Aided Choice of UI
Evaluation Criteria and Methods 319
A. Nendjo Ella, Ch. Kolski, F. Wawak, C. Jacques, and P. Yim
29. Considering Subjectivity in Software Evaluation -
Application for Teachware Evaluations 331
O. Hû, Ph. Trigano, and S. Crozat
30. KALDI: A Computer-Aided Usability Engineering Tool for
Supporting Testing and Analysis of Human-Computer Interaction 337
G. Al-Qaimari and D. McRostie

Preface

INTRODUCTION TO COMPUTER-AIDED DESIGN OF USER INTERFACES

Jean Vanderdonckt[1] and Angel Puerta[2,3]

[1] *Institut d'Administration et de Gestion - Université catholique de Louvain*
Place des Doyens, 1 - B-1348 Louvain-la-Neuve (Belgium)
vanderdonckt@qant.ucl.ac.be , vanderdoncktj@acm.org
Web: http://www.arpuerta.com
[1] *Knowledge Systems Laboratory, Stanford University, MSOB x215*
Stanford, CA 94305-5479, USA
puerta@camis.stanford.edu
[3] *RedWhale Corp., 277 Town & Country Village*
Palo Alto, CA 94303, USA
puerta@redwhale.com
Web: http://www.redwhale.com

Computer-Aided Design of User Interfaces (CADUI) is hereby referred to as the particular area of Human-Computer Interaction (HCI) intended to provide software support for any activity involved in the development life cycle of an interactive application. Such activities namely include task analysis, contextual inquiry [1], requirements definition, user-centred design, application modelling, conceptual design, prototyping, programming, installation, test, evaluation, maintenance. Although very recently addressed (e.g., [3]), the activity of re-designing an existing user interface (UI) for an interactive application and the activity of re-engineering a UI to rebuild its underlying models are also considered in CADUI.

A fundamental aim of CADUI is not only to provide some software support to the above activities, but also to incorporate strong and solid methodological aspects into the development, thus fostering abstraction reflection and leaving *ad hoc* development aside [5,7]. Incorporating such methodological aspects inevitably covers three related, sometimes intertwined, facets: models, method and tools. Today, any sound methodology should propose some method founded on models and supported by appropriate tools [2].

1

Models are intended to capture, to characterise and to abstract real-world information that will lead to a future UI. As every model is built on some abstraction mechanisms, it usually consists in a partial view of the real world with respect to the design problems. Consequently, one or several models may be required. Information is primarily stored into models according to an appropriate format allowing a computer-based system or an automata to so manipulate them, to access them, to retrieve them, to update them, to manage them. Several types of models can be imagined [6,7] (Fig. 1).

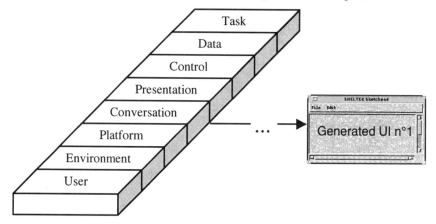

Figure 1. Philosophy of a model-based approach.

A *Task model* is used to describe the tasks the end-user has to perform. Goals in a task model specify when a desired state is met, methods describe procedures to achieve a goal, where atomic methods achieve a goal in one step and composite methods decompose a goal into sub-goals.

A *Data model* is used to abstract the data semantics to be manipulated throughout the UI input/output. It usually consists in a conceptual schema of entities, relationships of a particular design problem or of objects and methods in an object-oriented definition.

A *Control model* is to specify the services an application provides. It is mostly object-oriented; objects capture the state of entities and the operations change the state of objects. It is important that the operations correspond to the atomic methods specified in the task model.

A *Presentation model* specifies the object and operation appearance, the hierarchical decomposition of displays into components, the attributes and layout of each component.

A *Conversation model* is used to describe the human-computer conversation. It describes when the end-user can invoke commands, select or specify inputs and when the computer can query the end-user and presents information.

A *Behaviour model* is sometimes used to specify the input behaviour. The use of a presentation model and a behaviour model allows specifying the layout and the dynamic behaviour of the user interface independently.

A *Platform model* can be used to describe platform characteristics, e.g., input devices, output devices. This type of model is particularly appropriate for CADUI systems intended to produce multi-platform UIs.

An *Environment model* can describe workplace characteristics, e.g., cultural characteristics, environment factors. These models are used in different ways.

A *User model* specifies the end-user characteristics. A user model can be used in order to generate individual user interfaces (adapted to stereotypes), to reconfigure the interface to the end-user, to provide adaptive user interfaces, to provide an appropriate level of help, to actively guide the user during interaction.

Development activities are organised into a structured way called *Method* (the second facet of a methodology) so that they can share common definitions and languages, they can share the same kind of information, they can be reproduced equally and communicated in the same way. A method is generally founded on one or several models. This foundation is referred to in the literature as a *Model-Based Approach* to produce a final UI [5,9]. A model can underlie one particular development activity or be shared among several of them.

Among all these models, the task model has today gained much attention and many acceptances in the scientific community to be the model from which a development should be initiated. In the model-based approach (Fig. 1), one or several models, possibly including a task model, are exploited to reach a final UI, sometimes with variants obtained by varying the considered models parameters (e.g., user profiles, user preferences, design options). Rather, in the *Task-Based Approach*, at least one model, the task model, is exploited to feed in the other models in a particular way that is task dependent or context-dependent (Fig. 2).

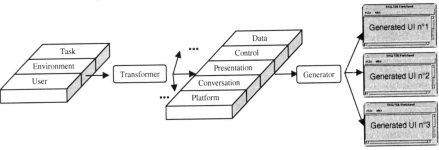

Figure 2. Philosophy of a task-based approach.

The other models (e.g., data model, domain model) are in turn exploited to reach several possible UIs depending on task parameters on one hand and on other parameters on the other. Often, the context covers three facets: the task, the user who is responsible for carrying out the task, and the environment in which the user lives. This environment not only encompasses physical and ergonomic considerations of the workstation (e.g., posture, light, screen distance, ambient noise, and contextual characteristics), but also hardware and software considerations.

The third facet of a methodology are its *Tools*. Computer-based tools are needed to support activities related to the models underlying the method, often along with some automated or semi-automated support for producing code.

The above three facets are commonly used in Software Engineering to develop software in a structured, formal, reproducible, understandable, communicable way. Computer-Aided Software Engineering (CASE) tool is the use of a computer-assisted method to organise and control the development of software, especially on large, complex projects involving many software components and people. Using CASE allows designers, code writers, testers, planners, and managers to share a common view of where a project stands at each stage of development. CASE helps ensure a disciplined, check-pointed process. A CASE tool may portray progress (or lack of it) graphically. CASE tools may also serve in Software Engineering as a repository for or be linked to document and program libraries containing the project's business plans, design requirements, design specifications, detailed code specifications, the code units, test cases and results, and marketing and service plans. Similarly, CADUI tools may also fill this role in the domain of HCI.

In the past, we spoke a lot about specific components like toolkits, libraries, User Interface Management Systems (UIMSs), Interface Builders and other tools [4]. Although these software may be required to produce a UI, they are more devoted to the programming activity itself. In this sense, they can be also considered as CADUI tools. But, in general, CADUI tools are focused on supporting **any** activity, and more specifically the design, the specifications, the modelling and the evaluation of a UI. And not just for programming it.

This book contains the results of the 3rd International Conference on Computer-Aided Design of User Interfaces held in Louvain-la-Neuve (Belgium), 21-23 October 1999. The previous edition, the 2nd International Workshop on CADUI has been held in Namur (Belgium), 5-7 June 1996. Its acronym -CADUI'96- has been chosen to reflect the change of scope from the 1st International Workshop on Computer-Aided Generation of User Interfaces held in Ulm (Germany), 18-19 November 1993.

We do hope that, in the future, tools and techniques for CADUI presented in this volume can evolve, merge and integrate to foster better UI development than ever where [10]

- designers and developers are recognised as more active persons who can see their work supported and aided by software tools;
- designers are more supported by appropriate and powerful CADUI tools;
- a mixed-initiative with human control is proposed to designers rather a than passive role;
- final users are respected in the complexity of their interactive tasks.

This edition of CADUI especially focused on any mean to re-design or re-engineer an existing UI into a more usable one, along with related models. A permanent address on CADUI can be accessed at http://belchi.qant.ucl.ac. be/cadui. Not only the presentations of the contributors of this book but also references on related work are provided. A mirror will be partially accessible at http://www.redwhale.com.

REFERENCES

[1]   Beyer, H., Holzblatt, K., *Contextual Design - Designing Customer-Centered Systems*, Morgan Kaufmann Publishers, San Francisco, 1998.

[2]   Bodart, F., Pigneur, Y., *Conception assistée des systèmes d'information - Méthode, modèles, outils*, 2nd ed., Masson, Paris, 1989.

[3]   Merlo, E., Girard, J.F., Kontogiannis, K. Panangaden, P., De Mori, R., *Reverse Engineering of User Interfaces*, in Proceedings of 1st Working Conference on Reverse Engineering RE'93 (Baltimore, 21-23 May 1993), R.C. Waters, E.J. Chikofsky (eds.), IEEE Computer Society Press, Los Alamitos, 1993, pp. 171-179.

[4]   Myers, B.A., *User Interface Software Tools*, ACM Transactions on Computer-Human Interaction, Vol. 2, No. 1, March 1995, pp. 64-103.

[5]   Paterno, F., *Model-Based User Interface Development*, Springer-Verlag, Berlin, 1999.

[6]   Puerta, A.R., Szekely, P., *Model-based Interface Development*, CHI'94 Tutorial Notes, Boston, April 1994.

[7]   Puerta, A.R., *Model-Based Interface Development*, Kluwer Academic Publisher, Dordrecht, 2000.

[8]   Schlungbaum, E., Elwert, T., *Automatic User Interface Generation from Declarative Models*, in Proc. of 2nd Int. workshop on Computer-Aided Design of User Interfaces CADUI'96 (Namur, 5-7 June 1996), J. Vanderdonckt (ed.), Presses Universitaires de Namur, Namur, 1996, pp. 3-18.

[9]   Szekely, P., *Retrospective and Challenges for Model-Based Interface Development*, in Proc. of 2nd Int. workshop on Computer-Aided Design of User Interfaces CADUI'96 (Namur, 5-7 June 1996), J. Vanderdonckt (ed.), Presses Universitaires de Namur, Namur, 1996,, pp. xxi-xliv. Accessible at http://www.isi.edu/isd/Master–mind/Internal/ Files/DSVIS96/paper.ps.Z

[10] Vanderdonckt, J., *Advice-giving systems for selecting interaction objects*, in Proc. of 1st Int. Workshop on User Interfaces to Data Intensive Systems UIDIS'99 (Edinbourg, 5-6 septembre 1999), N.W. Paton & T. Griffiths (eds.), IEEE Computer Society Press, Los Alamitos, 1999, pp. 152-157.

PROGRAMME COMMITTEE MEMBERS

Chapter 1

MODELING FOR COMPONENT BASED DEVELOPMENT IN UML/CATALYSIS

Alan Cameron Wills

TriReme Corp., Manchester, United Kingdom, alan@trireme.com
Tel : +44-161-225.3240 - Fax : +44-161- 257.3292

Abstract   Component Based Development (CBD) applies the best techniques of object oriented design to the large scale architecture of systems. As in (properly-applied) Object-Oriented Design, separation of concerns, encapsulation, and pluggability make a system extensible and flexible as business needs change. Many of the design principles are therefore very similar. Components are nevertheless different from objects: they cross language and host boundaries; they may be distributed, with consequent robustness and performance issues; they have more sophisticated interfaces than the object's list of messages. This paper will explore some of design methodology for CBD. The ideas will be based on the Catalysis approach.

Keywords: Component Based Development, Object-Oriented Design.

1.   TYPES: BEHAVIORAL SPECIFICATION

The black box. A prominent feature of good design is encapsulation (Fig. 1a): the idea that when one part of a program uses another, it should depend only on what it does, rather than how it works inside. This helps prevent changes in one part of the design from spreading to others; and allows one basic set of requirements to be fulfilled by a variety of different implementations. Modern programming languages, and languages for interconnecting components, therefore provide for interface definitions, in which you can list just what a client (of an object, component, module, ...) will see. One object (etc) may provide several interfaces. Interface definitions list the operations, but don't say what they do. So the client (software designer, user, ...) doesn't know what to expect. To describe properly what the client should expect from the black box, we have to say more (Fig. 1b).

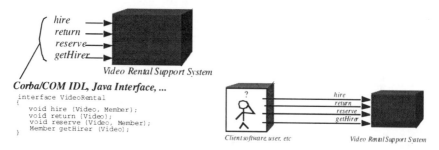

Figure 1. The black box

Black box with label. A Type Spec is a 'label' for an object/compo-nent/system/.... It still says nothing about what goes on inside, but describes the effects of the operations on each other. **\<An implementation\> conforms to \<a type spec\>** means only that any instance of the implementation be-haves as a client using the listed operations would expect from the specifica-tions. In this example, the hire operation links a video to a member; a further hire cannot be done for the same video, until a return of that video is per-formed. We don't care how the operations work, or how the information is recorded in any implementation, provided it meets these expectations.

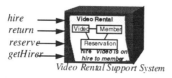

operation hire (video, customer)
postcondition This video is on hire to this customer.
precondition This video is on hire to nobody.
operation return (video)
postcondition This video is on hire to nobody.
precondition This video is on hire to a Cus-tomer.
function Customer getHirer (video)
postcondition returns the customer that this video is on hire to

Figure 2. The black box with label

Models. Certain words and phrases recur throughout these descriptions: *video, customer, is-on-hire-to,...* The spec is about how their relationships change. We can make a picture of them: e.g., any Video is-on-hire-to one or no Customer. The purpose of the model is to provide a vocabulary for de-scribing the operations. It says nothing about the internal structure of the component that performs the operations. It is possible (though not manda-tory) to write the operation specs in a formal language such as OCL.

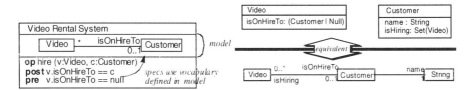

Figure 3. Models.

2.   ABSTRACT MODELS

Attributes and associations. Within a type model (Fig. 4),

- Associations and attributes are different ways of presenting the same information. We use the association style where there is more information to show about both types, and the attribute style (for example with name:String) where there is nothing of interest to add about the target type (usually because it has been defined elsewhere).
- An attribute/association says that the component 'knows' this relationship. It can tell us the name of a Customer and which Customer(s) have a given name, and who has what Video. Because we don't know about the implementation, we don't know how fast or slow looking up this information might be.
- Public attributes/associations imply there is a direct read-only query. Private attributes/associations imply the information is there, but can be observed only indirectly, in its effect on the specified operations.

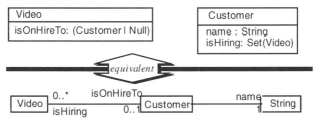

Figure 4. Attributes and associations.

Actions. In an object oriented program, the designer assigns every operation to one object or another: part of the skill of OOD is to distribute the tasks so that any change in requirements tends to affect just a few objects. But in the earlier stages of design, we may know what outcome we want an operation to achieve; but have not yet divided the necessary steps between the affected objects, nor even worked out what those steps might be (Fig. 5):

- Actions provide a pictorial notation linking the affected objects, without saying who does what.
- Postconditions (and preconditions) provide a way to describe something about the outcome of an action, without saying how it is achieved (nor necessarily saying everything there is to say about the outcome).

- A whole series of smaller actions can be summarised by one. For example, 'get cash from bank' with postcondition 'more cash in pocket, less in account' summarises the options of a visit to the bank counter or the ATM, and the sequences & loops of actions (verify identity, choose facility, ...) whereby it's achieved.

Actions are used to express the facilities provided by a component, independently of the dialogue of operations used to achieve it. For example, "extend an existing rental" may be considered to be provided by software, even if it does so only by allowing the video to be nominally returned and re-hired.

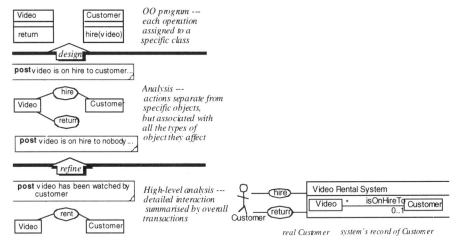

Figure 5. Actions.

3. CONSTRUCTING A MODEL

The kinds of model are the following:

- Business (domain) model: used to describe the concepts and actions that occur in the business.
- System or component model: used to describe the services provided by a piece of hard-ware, software, or a person or business department, to other such components.
- Design model: shows how a service is provided by interactions between smaller objects or components (again, whether hardware, software, or people). Each of the smaller pieces may itself be defined by a component model.
- Model framework: a generalised fragment of one of the above, focussing on one set of relationships or interactions. Can be instantiated and combined with others to make new models.

3.1   Business model

The steps are the following (Fig. 6):

1. Using any description of the business, sketch types, associations, and actions. Concepts → types; static relations → associations & attributes; verbs → actions.

2. Interview or analysis of existing material: cycle around these questions: What happens? Draw actions associated with affected and participating types. For every action you find, write a postcondition (see below); this yields associations/attributes. For every association or attribute you find, ask: What other actions affect or are affected by it? For every type you find, consider whether it has interesting changes of state that can be shown on a state chart. While doing all the above, stick to an appropriate level of detail: in general, a business model should tend towards the abstract. Think 'is this action part of a larger action?' and if so, consider whether to deal at that level instead. Use-case scenarios are a useful input to this process, provided you don't let them lead you into fine detail.

3. Writing a postcondition. Write an informal description of the outcome of the action. Be careful to avoid saying how it happens (what steps, or who does what): just stick to the relationship between before and after. For instance, reserve (customer, title): this customer is now on the waiting list for this title. Draw an instance diagram ("snapshot") of a typical situation before and after this action. You may find you need new associations or attributes to represent the concepts affected and the relationships that have changed. Every changeable fact about the objects should be represented by an attribute or association. For instance, new type Title required, with association 'waitingList' to Customer. Write the postcondition again in terms of changes in the attributes/associations, or new objects created. One can use a formal language like OCL.) For instance, reserve (customer, title): customer has been appended to title.waitingList. Write a precondition.

3. As you find types and associations, write dictionary entries explaining what real-world fact this symbol represents. For instance, Title::waitingList is the set of Customers who have requested and not since hired a Video of this Title.

4. Write business rules in terms of the model. Most rules are invariants. Loops in the type diagram often suggest the necessity for invariants. Some business rules are about permitted changes of state: state charts are useful for this purpose.

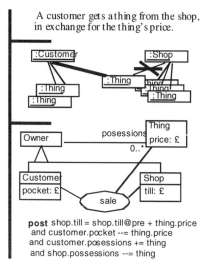

A customer gets a thing from the shop,
in exchange for the thing's price.

Figure 6. Business model.

3.2   Component model

Main principles like that of business modeling; but actions are the interactions between the component and the surrounding world; post/precondi-
tions are about changes in the component's state; types & associations are
those modeling the component's state.

1. A component is always part of some larger design, perhaps how the busi-
    ness organisation works around it. Model this design and see how it re-
    fines the business goals defined in the business model. Some of the ac-
    tions will involve our component; some will not. Avoid detailed actions:
    be precise about the outcomes of high-level actions.

2. Write post/preconditions for the actions involving this component. Just
    write their effect on this component (not any other participants). As con-
    cepts and relationships become involved, borrow types and associations
    from the domain model to represent them. Conversely, do not use types
    and associations that are not required to describe some action. In this
    way, the component model becomes a projection (filtered version) of the
    domain model.

3.3   Design model

The purpose is to show how business-model actions' goals are realised
by a combination of actions involving software components, hardware, people, etc; or to show how a component specification's goals are realised by a

combination of actions involving internal objects or smaller components. The smaller actions may ultimately be object-oriented messages.

1. Decide what your smaller components will be. This will be readjusted later. In a basic OO design, each class will directly represent a type in the model. In a component design, each component will represent some part of the overall system type model. Document how the states of the components represent the overall state (see *Refinement*).

2. Take each higher-level action separately (business action, component interface action).

3. Review the changes of state in an instance diagram (snapshot) showing the two states before and after the action.

4. Invent actions (or messages) between the smaller components (or objects) that will work together to achieve the target change of state. They may operate in a sequence or in parallel (as a pipeline, for example). Use collaboration or sequence diagrams to document the sequence; or state charts, if there are significant loops and branches. Check that the changes of state in the components really do amount (given the retrieval) to the overall abstract system state change.

5. Collect together the tasks of each constituent object or component (the actions it is involved in). Review how well the design is decoupled, and if necessary redistribute tasks.

6. The actions between components may be abstract (rather than specific messages). Refine them to more detailed protocols (for example using a communications protocol; or simply a series of individual messages).

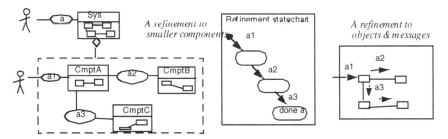

Figure 7. Design model.

4.   REFINEMENT AND CONFORMANCE

Refinement means looking at something in more detail. An interface definition can say exactly what is expected of the implementor, but must leave out how to implement it (since every implementation will be different). Also in the earlier phases of analysis and design, we omit detail (such as how a goal is achieved, and who does what) in favour of the most important issues (what is achieved). It's important to be able to tell whether a particular implementation really does conform to a given abstract description. The main cases fit into two categories: action refinement and component refinement. We use the diamond 'aggregation' symbol to denote a refinement relationship.

4.1   Action refinement

An action represents a goal (pre/postcondition); and in general this is achieved by performing some combination of smaller actions. An action takes a finite period of time. The constituents may happen in sequence, or in parallel (as, for instance, in a pipeline). There are two main cases:

1. **External action refinement** (Fig. 8a): the abstraction is an action between two or more participants; the refinement is between a corresponding set of participants, showing how they achieve the overall effect. Often, the refined layer is already determined and it is not necessary to go further into it. Typical examples: abstraction: a transaction; refinement: the individual operations; abstraction: a message; refinement: the detail of the messaging protocol (for example, CORBA); abstraction: a user's goal such as obtaining cash; refinement: the operations at the cash machine or in the bank. New objects are usually introduced in the model(s) of the participants, because extra information is required to record the intermediate states of the interaction.

2. **Internal action refinement** (Fig. 8b): the refinement shows how one of the participants achieves its part of the overall goal, by actions between its consitituent parts. Typical examples: abstraction: a message sent to an object; refinement: a collaboration of messages between associated objects; abstraction: a user's operation at a client subsystem; refinement: the client's interactions with the server(s); abstraction: a customer's order made with a shop; refinement: the internal workflow that delivers the goods (including some interactions between employees and software). In both cases, you need to show in what combinations the smaller actions can be used. State charts are well-suited to this; alternatives are activity diagrams (with swim lanes); regular expressions; and (worst) sequence charts or collaboration diagrams.

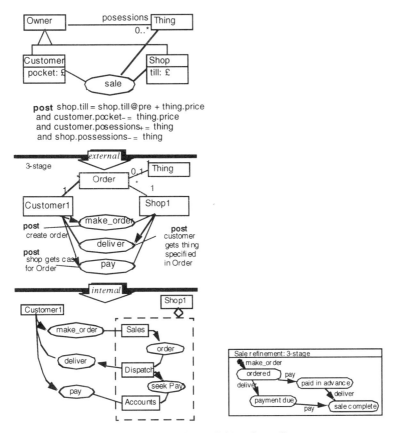

Figure 8. External (a) and internal (b) action refinement.

4.2   Component refinement

Component refinement means that the information held by the system as a whole is divided up between several pieces. They may be objects in an OO program; or distributed components; or linkable modules. Issues that help decide how to divide up a system include: existing assets; separation of individually-variable features; performance; continuity of service (while parts are down); openness (existing components can cope with more types as they come along). There are two basic patterns for distributing information between components:

1. Partitioning: information divided between the components without overlap is good for separation of concerns and openness (each component defines types needed locally);

2. Replication: information is held in more than one component is good for economising on bandwidth (if and only if more queries than changes) and for continuity of service.

4.2.1 Retrievals

Once a partitioning has been decided, it is helpful to document how the business concepts are represented in the implementation (and particularly how they are spread between components). Sketch derivations on models (as dashed lines here). Write up derivation: informally, or in OCL or program code as in example. Examples of retrieval are (Fig. 9): each customer is represented as a Payer in the Accounts system, some customers are also represented in the Despatch system, an Accounts System::Payer's account represents the abstract Customer's account, a DespatchSystem::Customer's orders represent the abstract Customer's orders. If the Customer is not represented in the Despatch System, then the Customer has an empty list of Orders. The OrderTotals in an Account are represented in Accounts System by AccountItems with Code == "Order".

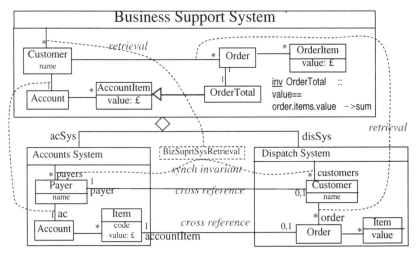

Figure 9. Examples of retrieval.

4.2.2 Synch invariants

Document how info in one component needs to keep up to date with another. Decide what synch is required, leave how until later. Sketch links in model as here. Write up informally or in OCL or code: the name of the Customer in the Dispatch System is the same as the name of the corresponding Payer in the Accounts System. Dispatch System::Customer:: (payer.name==name). Include Business Model invariants that are spread across components: Any Order's accountItem is the sum of the values of its Items - DispatchSystem:: Order :: accountItem.value == item.value→sum

4.2.3 Cross references

A Cross Reference is a handle for identifying an object in one component or domain from within another, e.g. the number on your credit card is an XRef from you to your account. or the link between Customers and Payers would normally be implemented by a key.

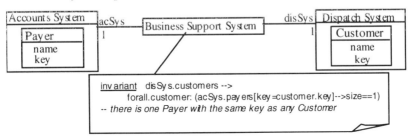

Figure 10. Cross references.

5.   COMPONENT KITS

This example in Fig. 11 shows some key properties of components both in the software and hardware worlds. This assembly is made from a kit of components, designed so that there are many different ways of assembling them. The person who assembles the components to make a product is (like users of Lego and Meccano) assumed to have different skills than the designers of the kit. The rule is therefore that end-products are made by 'wiring' components, but that the internal designs of the components don't change. The benefits include that components are well understood and widely used, and much effort can therefore be put into making them work well. Like Lego, Meccano, and friends, the kit is good for making a certain range of products in a certain style. Like hardware kits, the most successful products are made by choosing members of the same kit, rather than trying to mix technologies, though adaptors can be made.

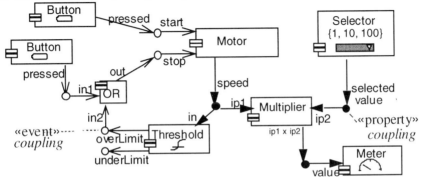

Figure 11. Component kits.

5.1   Connectors

These components are like objects: their internal structure is invisible, they have well-defined interfaces, there are classes and instances (e.g. we can see two instances of Button above). But there are differences from plain objects. An object interface (as in Java, IDL, etc) is a list of function calls: drawings of them show arrows going into the object. These components, however, have arrows coming out (the Button's 'pressed' output, Motor's 'speed', ...). What does it mean, for a component to have an output, and for an assembler to wire it to some input? We can easily envisage an answer, along the lines of 'an output signifies that the component accepts a request to register the interest of the input....' But the fact is that we would rather assemble the components dealing at the level of the connectors, rather than going down to the individual messages all the time. We can plug these components together provided they're all built to the same set of conventions about what it means to plug them together.

5.2   Connector types

There are two types of connector in the example, which we've called <<event>> and <<property>> (corresponding roughly to the connector types in Java Beans). While the <<event>> couplings carry one-off messages, the <<property>> connectors send a continuous update of an integer value (such as the Motor's speed). In kits of larger-scale components, we can invent grander kinds of connector: for example, a <<workobject transfer>>, which negotiates a controlled transfer of a piece of business work from one user to another. In a workflow system, there are many components with this kind of connector.

5.3   Kits

What makes these components so versatile is that there are fewer types of connection than components. The Motor could be wired straight to the Meter, or one of the Buttons straight to the Motor's stop input. This is what makes this bag of components a coherent kit: its members can be plugged together in many different ways. By contrast, chunks of software procured from all over the place would probably need lots of 'glue'.

5.4   Component Kit Architecture

The same principles apply at any scale. In a larger system (Fig. 12), the components will be substantial applications, possibly operating in different machines; and the connectors will be more sophisticated and carry more information. For example, a share-dealer support system produces a stream of deals; these flow through a variety of components. In a component based design, we can separate three activities: (i) Product building: rapid building of products by configuring components, (ii) Component design: implementing a specific component, and (iii) Kit Architecture: defining the connectors.

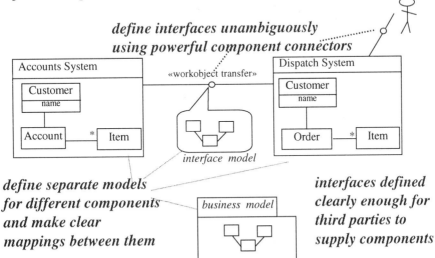

Figure 12. Component kit architecture.

5.4.1 Common models

For larger designs, the information transferred between components is more substantial than just numbers. The architecture therefore includes a model of what flows across the connectors, what the components talk about. This is clearly related to a common business model. Designers of components need to relate their own views back to the common model. For example, Accounts may think of a Customer as something with an account containing a list of debits and credits; Dispatching thinks of a Customer as a thing with an Order containing a list of products. The common model is generally based on the business domain model, and must include information on the business rules that should be adhered to by all components in the kit.

5.4.2 Kit architecture

Component kit architecture means defining a set of connectors that your projects will use, and defining what they achieve and how they work. Some of them can be adopted from existing platforms, for example, Java Beans supplies a mechanism similar to our continuous-update connectors; and CORBA provides a transaction service. The point of the architecture is to de-

Wills

fine what conventions the component designers will stick to, in order to
make the components easy to reconfigure.

REFERENCE

[1]   A.C. Wills, D. D'Souza, *Objects, Components and Frameworks in UML: the Catalysis approach*, Addison-Wesley, Reading, 1998.

APPENDIX

Catalysis = UML ++

z UML + clear techniques + context-flexible process
- OO analysis and design
- Component Based Development
  - rapid development of families of products
- Reuse of models & designs
  - frameworks and patterns
- Process patterns
  - combine appropriate techniques to cover many situations
- Unambiguous specification
  - for high-integrity design and early exposure of important issues
- Traceability spec. through code
  - maintainability, strong quality assurance
- Coherence between UML models
  - strong cross-checking helps consistency and completness

✔ Components

✔ Reuse

✔ Process

✔ Precision

✔ Abstraction

✔ Traceability

✔ Coherence

Chapter 2

THEORY BASED DESIGN: FROM INDIVIDUAL USERS AND TASKS TO COLLABORATIVE SYSTEMS

Peter Johnson
Computing Group, Department of Mathematical Sciences
University of Bath, Bath, BA2 7AY, United Kingdom
·P.Johnson@bath.ac.uk

Abstract   How do we design computer systems so that they are useful and efficient artefacts that improve the quality and productivity of our lives? What explanations can we offer as to why some systems achieve this and others fail? How can we predict which systems or system features are going to be usable and useful and which ones are not? If we knew how to answer these questions then we would be in a better position to design and evaluate computer systems. Moreover, we would be developing an explanatory understanding of HCI and furthering the discipline of computing as a science. This paper provides an example of an explanatory, causal account of HCI that shows how models and principles for HCI can be developed from theory and practice. In particular, the paper considers principles for designing user interfaces to support user tasks. It goes on to consider how further factors need to be considered in the design of collaborative and mobile systems to support healthcare. How these can be modelled to provide an explanatory, causal understanding of relevant aspects of human computer interaction is discussed. The implications of this for further principles of design and evaluation are considered. Examples are provided from current work with theoretical, empirical and design considerations made.

Keywords: Human Computer Interaction, Design Principles, User Tasks, Group Work, Collaboration.

1.   INTRODUCTION

How can we design computer systems so that they are useful and efficient artefacts that improve the quality and productivity of our lives? What explanations might we offer as to why some systems succeed and others fail? How can we predict a priori which systems and system features are going be useful and usable and which ones will not? If we knew the answers to these questions then we would be in a better position to design and evaluate computer systems. Also, we would be developing an explanatory understanding of HCI and computing science. I use the words explanatory understanding to differentiate such an approach from other, alternative, forms that seek purely to describe or to assess interactive systems, without giving any explanatory, causal account of how such interaction might have come about. In recent writings in human computer interaction and software engineering much attention has been given to ethnomethodological studies of human activity as either inputs to design or the analysis of peoples' use of design in the work place or elsewhere. While such approaches are useful, they fail to provide an explanatory, causal account as to how or why designs fail or succeed. Hence, they offer little in the way of guidance or principles for design. It is not the use of ethnomethodological approaches that I am dissatisfied with, far from it, I have long argued for the forms of observation, data collection and analysis that such approaches bring. It is the failure to recognise that a description is not an understanding and that causal explanations are needed to arrive at an understanding of what counts for good design knowledge.

Further problems arise in HCI because of the over emphasis on assessment in evaluation where all that is asked is, "is A better than B" or " is A good for C". Such questions are regularly asked and answered using various degrees of empirical rigour. It is clear that for some purposes, such questions are valid and the accuracy to which they can be answered will, to some degree, depend upon the rigour with which the empirical assessment was undertaken. However, by failing to provide an underlying explanatory, causal account of why "A is better than B" or "A is good for C", HCI is failing to provide a basis for reasoning and reflecting upon the fundamental questions about why some computer systems improve our lives and others do not. Again, I am not against empirical or evaluative approaches, they form an important methodological part of HCI and play a significant role in our search for causal explanations.

In the design and evaluation of interactive computer systems, we must understand what causes some interactions to be seen as good, productive, and useful, and what causes others to fail. Thus, we need an explanatory and causal understanding of human-computer interaction.

Interactions between people and computers occur in many and varied contexts and situations, between many and varied people, for many and varied purposes and with many and varied forms of computers. Moreover, these are all themselves changing over time, as technology, situations, contexts, purposes and people evolve. Consequently, the "complete and absolute truth" about HCI will never be known as there will always be many new and unanswered questions. Hence, HCI researchers will always have new challenges and questions facing them

One aspect of seeking such a causal and explanatory understanding of HCI is that we need to consider the people, computers, tasks, situations and contexts in which the interactions occur, not as individual components but as they come together in HCI. Partitioning up HCI into separate components is going to fail to give a full account since the very nature of the problem to be understood is how they interact. Each component constrains and influences the interaction of the other components. Therefore, we need to be able to construct models of interaction that identify and provide a basis for reasoning about the influences and constraints these components place upon each other.

Most recently, our interaction with computers has begun a further stage in its evolution. With the developments in mobile, distributed and multimedia computing the technologies have made it possible for HCI to occur in the park, in the car, under-water and in many far more varied contexts and situations than before. In the past we have been less concerned with the context and situation than we now need to be because that factor was more or less fixed and less variable than it now is. Therefore, its influences on HCI could be more readily ignored or left unexplained. Similarly, we had far fewer tasks and purposes to understand consequently, we were less affected by having only a descriptive and not an explanatory understanding of HCI in terms of these.

The relationship between theoretical models and the practice of HCI design is not straightforward. Barnard [1] adapts from Long [6] a framework which portrays the relationships between a theoretical science base and 'real world' systems design. Barnard describes 'bridging representations' between the real world and the theoretical scientific representation of the way in which the real world behaves. Bridging representations are required in both directions between scientific theory and the world. More or less formal analysis of the world leads to a 'discovery representation' which simplifies the world according to the researcher's purposes. Scientific theory is then developed based on the discovery representations. Applied science then requires an 'application representation' to serve as a bridge between theory and the application domain.

This paper provides an example of an explanatory causal account in HCI that attempts to overcome the problems of partitioning it into separate components and shows how models and principles for HCI might be developed from such an approach. In particular, the paper considers how user, task, context and situation factors can influence the design of computer systems to support healthcare, and how such factors can be modelled to provide an explanatory causal understanding of the HCI that occurs. Principles for designing user interfaces to support user tasks are offered as a further example of how such accounts can be used to support the software engineering of good HCI.

2.   THEORY BASED DESIGN AND GROUPWARE

Groupware, as software to support collaborative group working has come to be called, has been prolifically produced over the past decade without much in the way of theoretical based models of group activity to support design. There is nevertheless a tradition of designing systems, including collaborative systems, with direct bases in theory. Thus, psychological models of human-human communication have been used a basis for systems design, both when the system is designed to mediate and to support human-human interaction and when human-human interaction is used as a model for human-computer interaction.

Moreover, there have been examples in which the use of a theoretical model to guide system design has resulted in inflexible and ultimately unusable systems. For example, Winograd and Flores' [10] design of Coordinator was heavily based upon speech act theory [9] and had many criticisms for the way it constrained and forced group communication to occur. In the case of Coordinator and speech act theory it would be wrong to conclude that theory based design does not work, or that the theory in question was a poor theory. The mistake that occurred was a failure to recognise that a theory of communication and language use is not an applied theory for the design or evaluation of computer systems. It fails to recognise that the problem domain of computer system design and evaluation is not the same as linguistics. Consequently, what may be a perfectly sound linguistic theory fails to be an applied linguistic theory for HCI. It fails because the scope of phenomena it was originally meant to explain is not the same as that to which it is being applied. Also, it fails because it does not take account of how to apply the constructs, assumptions and predictive base of the original theory to design and evaluation such that the designers and evaluators might know how to interpret and make sense of the theory relative to human computer interaction and computer mediated group work.

It does not follow that design is doomed to fail when it attempts to follow a theoretical model based approach. Design without theory and models is hacking or at best intuitive and experience based and does not result in a discipline of HCI that can pass on a reasoned and causal understanding of what leads to good design and good usability. On the other hand, the lack of applicable theoretical models to support the design and evaluation of group-ware has not prevented systems being produced and some of these may well be highly usable, effective and efficient systems. That is not the point. The point is to know what makes a system good or bad, what causal explanation can be given as to why one design idea works and another one does not.

Without such understanding, design knowledge and the discipline of HCI cannot be established, communicated or developed. Furthermore, designers will have a poor basis for predicting the usability and quality of their de-signs, and good HCI will only be achieved by *post hoc* evaluations of design ideas to find out if they are good or bad. This is unfair and unsatisfactory, both to designers and users alike. There must be a sound theoretical and principled basis for designing collaborative systems that provides explana-tory and predictive models which can be applied to the design and evaluation of groupware to effect good design, good usability and good HCI.

3.   DEVELOPING A THEORETICAL BASIS FOR MODELLING

In previous research [3,4,5], we have developed a theory of Task Knowl-edge Structures (TKS) for the purpose of understanding and explaining the structure of human task activity so as to provide designers of computer sys-tems with a basis for understanding how to design systems to support people in carrying out both existing and new tasks. From this applied theory of tasks we developed a model based approach to user interaction design (ADEPT) and demonstrated how the TKS based models of human activity could be used to inform and facilitate design. More recently , following from the theo-retical work we have been able to formulate four principles of design that have theoretical explanatory basis, provide predictive guidance to designers and that have been empirically shown to produce increased usability.

In summary Task Knowledge Structures encompasses: *roles* (including within and between tasks), *task goal structures* (not restricted to hierarchies), *task procedures* (showing procedural dependency), *taxonomic substructure* (declarative knowledge of the task domain*)*. TKS models actual and required knowledge and has been applied to, complex and creative tasks. It includes a methodology for gathering data, analysing those data, modelling, and appli-cation to design. In the ADEPT model based design environment TKS was used to model existing work task knowledge, proposed work and user inter-face designs to support the proposed work. TKS has also been used as basis for formal modelling of interaction using the process algebra - LOTOS [7]

3.1   Four Principles from TKS

From TKS theory we have developed four principles for design, again in summary form these principles are:

- *Taxonomic Structure*: Objects that are the same or similar will be conceptually grouped together, and actions on the same or similar objects will be carried out together.
- *Procedural Dependency*: Actions which are causally related to each other through a task goal structure will be conceptually grouped together.
- *Conformance*: User interfaces which conform to the users conceptual grouping will be easier to use.
- *Transformation*: transforming a conceptual grouping to accommodate changes in the level or structure of concepts is cognitively expensive.

I do not propose to expand these principles here since the objective in this paper is to go beyond these and begin to develop theoretical models and design principles for supporting collaborative work. However, it is worth stating that these four principles have direct implications for the design of all classes of systems.

3.2   Some implications from TKS principles

- Categorise objects based on object taxonomy and reflect this category structure in the user interface through perceptual properties of the display (such as the spatial grouping of objects).
- Actions should be categorised according to their procedural, sequential causal relations and this should be reflected in the user interface display through the temporal and perceptual properties of the user interface design.
- Users can and do follow the user interface structure to build their own task knowledge structures provided that the user interface supports a task structure.
- Where the user interface does not support a task structure the user will impose their own task structure but this will take longer to achieve and their performance with the user interface will be slower than if the interface reflected a task structure.

The particular scope and form of the original TKS theory was limited to individual users carrying out tasks by themselves. While it accommodated a role perspective on work it did not consider how people work together to perform group tasks or how individual and group tasks interact. To extend this theoretical basis we must consider the nature of group tasks, the nature of collaboration and the interaction between group tasks individual tasks. Moreover, we must approach this from the motivation and for the purpose of informing the design and evaluation of computer supported collaborative work.

4.   EXTENDING THE THEORY AND PRINCIPLES TO COLLABORATIVE GROUP TASK

Much attention has been given to supporting collaboration, through assumptions about sharing data/information, reciprocal views of participants and creating awareness of each group member. Similarly, attempts have been made to base the design around quasi "metaphors" such as "rooms" and "locales" in which group and individual activity is intended to occur. However, these intuitions and assumptions do not provide any insight in to the nature of collaboration or group work. Consequently, computer systems designed to support collaborative work often fail to support any particular form of collaborative group work, and provide little in the way of HCI theory.

In considering the nature of collaborative group work three important activities need to be understood, not as separate activities but as synthesised acts. These activities can themselves be though of in term of tasks in so much that they require cognitive, social and external resources and are purposeful. The three forms of activity that are synthesised in collaborative group work concern: Collaboration Tasks, Group Tasks, Individual Tasks.

For example, consider what may go on when a team of doctors and nurses are engaged in the task of performing an operation in a neuro-surgical operating theatre. Together the group work at the common goal of removing a tumour from a patient's brain. Each member of the team will carry out various acts, some in co-ordination with other member s of the team and others on their own, some of these acts will be part of the team activity and some not. For instance, the consultant surgeon may be accessing and removing the tumour. The senior registrar may have prepared the patient, be assisting and observing the consultant during the removal of the tumour, and subsequently be involved in making good the surgery once the consultant has removed the tumour. The anaesthetist may be involved in monitoring the patient's body state and life support system while the surgery is in progress. The nurses may be involved in keeping everything that is needed during the operation "to-hand" and in ensuring that everything in the operating theatre that comes into contact with the patient is kept sterile at all times.

In this over-simplified example of what is in fact a very complicated collaborative group activity, there are aspects of both group and individual tasks that occur, as in the way the surgeon and the anaesthetist may be working completely independently on tasks that form part of the group activity but of themselves do not require much collaboration. At other times the surgeon may require the anaesthetist to alter the body state of the patient (e.g. the oxygen level) in concert with a particular aspect of the removal of the tumour. At yet further stages in the operation the anaesthetist may have so little to do that they begin to be fill in a cross-word puzzle while monitoring the displays and alarms.

The point is that there are various forms of group and individual task structures involved here. In addition there are tasks of collaboration, as for example how the surgeon signals to the anaesthetist that he wants her to alter the oxygen level. The amount of effort expended and required to do this may vary. Whatever effort is required to collaborate is an additional task and requires additional resources beyond those of the individual and group tasks. The resource load of the various task (i.e. the group tasks, the individual tasks and the collaboration tasks) are all incurred in performing the activity and must be born by the members of the team.

In developing an HCI account of collaborative work that can contribute to the design and evaluation of collaborative systems we must be able to understand the structure of these tasks and how the resource costs involved in such human activity can be affected by computer technologies.

In an attempt to develop a conceptual framework for modelling collaborative group work in HCI we have proposed the following group task modelling framework:

- *Group goals* give the purpose of the group activity, give the responsibilities of the group, and become the focus for attaining 'common ground'.
- *Individual goals* give the purpose of individual activity, give the responsibilities of individuals, and provide the individuals basis for making contributions to 'common ground".
- *Group objects* are artefacts available to the group. They have, properties, relations, states, and can become the content of 'common ground'.
- *Individual objects* are artefacts available to the individual. They properties, relations, states, and are excluded from 'common ground'.
- *Group processes* are patterns of actions available to the group. They have procedural relations.
- *Individual processes* are patterns of actions available to individuals. They have procedural relations.

5. AN EXAMPLE OF COLLABORATIVE WORK ASSESSED MODELLED IN TERMS OF RE-SOURCES

In recent work involving the application of computer technologies to support group work (as part of the EPSRC funded mushroom project) we have been studying how nurses, general practitioners and consultants work together in the management of diabetes. What follow is a small example taken from our studies. Diabetes is a chronic disease that involves patients, clinic nurses, GPs in local surgeries and consultants in regional and district hospitals. The interaction and group work occurs between the medical staff and the patient and between medical staff themselves. The interaction and group working is extended over space and time and it occurs through meetings, postal communication, telephone calls, and through sharing common data and information.

Diabetes patient scenario:
Cath is a chronic diabetes patient with recently developed eye problems.
She visits her local diabetes clinic for a regular check-up, data are collected, checks made and notes taken by the clinic nurse - Cath is then referred to the GP. One week later Cath visits her GP with her friend, data are collected, checks made, notes consulted and taken by the GP and Cath is - referred to Consultant.Six weeks later she visits the diabetes consultant at the district hospital, notes are consulted, and checks are made by the consultant. Cath is, referred to an eye specialist. Letters are given to Cath to take to the eye specialist and her GP.

We can begin to think of the collaboration task resources involved in these activities such as:
- Effort involved in co-ordination of the group process. For example the effort involved in the nurse flagging significant items to the GP .
- Effort involved in establishing common ground between the General Practitioner and the nurse. For example, the GP reading through the notes to build up an understanding of current situation - requires interpretation on part of GP.
- Effort involved in individual processes. For example, the effort involved in transformation of data from the patient's home kept record to the nurses' clinic kept record sheet.

We have found that there are indeed problems in performing the collaborative group tasks that can be attributed to the collaboration tasks and the resources they require at a given time either being to great, not available or in-adequately supported. Here are some examples of those problems found:

The GP may miss flagged items from the shared patient record. For example, on one occasion the GP missed important flagged eye information and consequently had to re-establish this from the patient. This results in a duplication of effort. The GP may not complete task as the nurse expected. For example, on one occasion the nurse expected a certificate to be written but this did not occur. This results in incomplete handling of the patient and requires the making of a new appointment.

The information may be incomplete. For example, the notes did not contain details of a letter. This resulted in extra effort on the part of the GP to find out that consultant had issued a letter.

6.   COLLABORATIVE TASK RESOURCE MODEL-LING FRAMEWORK

In developing the collaborative task modelling framework in terms of re-sources and their requirements in interaction of group task activities we can think of this in terms of the group tasks resources.

Thus, collaborative environments supporting collaborative group work-ing can be assessed in terms of resource costs, contributing to the effort re-quired to achieve: group, individual, and collaboration goals. Where effort is expended in interactions required to perform; group procedures, individual procedures and collaboration procedures. In doing these use can be made of group and individual computational processes. The effects of these will bring about changes to and involve the use of; group and individual objects.

Collaboration requires effort as for example in the effort required on the part of the consultant to interpret and explain current results in the context of the patient's medical history. For example, finding trends in the patient's weight control was difficult because of the format of the data presentation. Furthermore, we can begin to evaluate collaborative work systems in terms of their resource costs.

In developing the collaborative task modelling framework in terms of re-sources and their requirements in group work activities we can think of this in terms of group task resources. Group task resources are what knowledge (both procedural and declarative) the individual and the group as a whole need to carry out the tasks in which they are engaged. In addition , the group-computer interaction resources can be thought of in terms of the above plus what declarative and procedural resources the computer system needs in order to support the group activity.

Clark and Brennan [2] also discuss the "costs of grounding" . These are the additional resources expended for the collaboration to succeed.

In summary we can think of group tasks resources as being composed of different forms of task knowledge modelled in terms of: Group task taxonomic structures; Individual task taxonomic structures; Group task procedural dependencies; Individual task procedural dependencies; and that recruit and utilise Collaboration task knowledge structures.

Hence, we have a basis for designing and assessing collaborative systems supporting collaborative group work in terms of resource costs. These resource costs are incurred in the efforts required to achieve group and individual goals, through the interactions which constitute group procedures, individual procedures, group computational processes and individual computational processes, and in the consumption and use of group objects, individual objects, group data and individual data in those processes.

6.1   Implications for Design Principles

From the earlier work on individual tasks we have identified four principles relevant to Task Knowledge Structures. These are the principles of; Taxonomic Structure, Procedural Dependency, Conformance, and Transformation.

6.2   Collaborative Task Principles

Collaborative tasks require common ground. Common ground derived from taxonomic and procedural knowledge of individual and from group. Resources are expended in: establishing conformance of common ground in the group and performing transformation of individual knowledge to shared knowledge and group knowledge to shared knowledge. As noted above, in order to account for collaborative work, the theoretical basis of TKS needs to be extended to consider group, individual and collaboration tasks. In addition, if the underlying theory is to have a use in HCI design, we must also extend the bridging structures represented by the HCI principles derived from TKS theory. Bridging representations need to be developed which reflect that (i) collaborative tasks require grounding as a necessary overhead, (ii) common ground is derived from taxonomic and procedural knowledge of individuals in the group and from the context in which the collaboration occurs, and (iii) resources are expended in establishing the required levels of common ground amongst the group members relative to the tasks they are performing jointly, and in performing transformations of individual knowledge and information to shared knowledge. The work outlined above has begun these twin processes of extending both theory and design principles.

REFERENCES

[1]   Barnard, P., *Bridging between basic theories and the artifacts of Human-Computer Interaction*, in J.M. Carroll (ed.), Designing interaction: psychology at the human computer interface, Cambridge University Press, Cambridge, 1991, pp. 103–127.

[2]   Clark, H.H. and Brennan, S.E., *Grounding in communication*, in L.B. Resnick, J.M. Levine and S.D. Teasley (eds.), Perspectives on socially shared cognition, APA Books, Washington D.C., 1991, pp. 127–149.

[3]   Hamilton, F., Johnson, P. and Johnson, H., Task related principles for user interface design, in *Proc. of the Schärding workshop on Task Analysis* (Schärding, June 1998).

[4]   Johnson, H. and Johnson, P., *Task knowledge structures: psychological basis and integration into system design*, Acta Psychologica, Vol. 78, 1991, pp. 3–26.

[5]   Johnson, P., Johnson, H. and Wilson, S. *Rapid prototyping of user interfaces driven by task models*, in J.M. Carroll (ed.), Scenario-based design: envisioning work and technology in system development, John Wiley, New York, 1995, pp. 209–246.

[6]   Long, J.B. *Cognitive ergonomics and human-computer interaction: an introduction*, in J.B. Long and A. Whitefield (eds.), Cognitive ergonomics and human-computer interaction, Cambridge University Press, Cambridge, 1989, pp. 4–34.

[7]   Markopoulos, P., Johnson, P. and Rowson, J., *Formal aspects of task based design*, in M.D. Harrison and J.C. Torres (eds.), Proc. of 4th Int. Workshop on Design, Specification and Verification of Interactive Systems DSV-IS'97 (Granada, 4-6 June 1997), Springer-Verlag, Vienna, 1997, pp 209–224.

[8]   Newell, A. and Card, S.K., *The prospects for psychological science in human-computer interaction*, Human-Computer Interaction, Vol. 1, 1985, pp. 209–242.

[9]   Searle, J.R., *Speech acts*, Cambridge University Press, Cambridge, 1969.

[10]   Winograd, T. and Flores, F., *Understanding computers and cognition: a new foundation for design*, Addison Wesley, Reading, 1986.

Chapter 3

EVALUATING ACCESSIBILITY AND USABILITY OF WEB PAGES

Michael Cooper
Center for Applied Special Technology (CAST), 39 Cross Street, Suite 201
Peabody, MA 01960 (USA)
E-mail: mcooper@cast.org *- URL:* http://www.cast.org
Tel: +1-978-531-8555 - Fax: +1-978 531-0192

Abstract   Bobby[SM] is a computer-based tool that supports Universal Design of a specific computer-human interface, the World Wide Web. The notion of a universally designed Web challenges society to think about plurality—to consider all individuals, regardless of age, ability, race, or economic or cultural background—when developing new technologies. Yet at this time, though the Web has much potential for broad inclusion, it often excludes some people from participating in much the same way that a staircase prevents a person in a wheelchair from going in a building's door. In response to this, CAST launched Bobby in August 1996. Bobby teaches Web designers about Web accessibility by displaying accessibility problems directly within the context of the designer's site. Bobby is a teaching tool, helping Web designers (including the rapidly growing number of non-professional designers who are putting up sites) learn skills they can apply later. The more people use Bobby, the more likely they will be to integrate accessibility principles into their way of thinking and their style of Web site design.

Keywords: Universal design, web site evaluation.

1.   INTRODUCTION

The Center for Applied Special Technology (CAST) was founded to study and develop ways technology can be used to enable people with disabilities, especially in educational environments, to participate in the mainstream. In recent years, CAST has refined the concept of *Universal Design,* a term borrowed from architecture. Universal Design of technology refers to software and hardware features that are created with a wide range of users in mind. Universally designed products reduce the need for multiple products targeted to different populations; instead, one product can benefit users with a wide range of needs and preferences.

While developing universally designed software products, CAST found that products using Web pages rely in turn on Universal Design features of those pages. To help authors incorporate those features into their pages, CAST created Bobby[SM] [1]. This free software examines the structure of HTML pages and notes technical or design issues that may present barriers to persons with disabilities who access the site. The tool has helped thousands of users and organizations make significant improvements to their Web sites. These people have in the process been educated about Universal Design principles and now incorporate Universal Design into every aspect of their Web site development.

2.   UNIVERSAL DESIGN FOR LEARNING

Universal Design originated in architecture and product design, where accommodating the widest spectrum of users increases commercial viability. Architects practicing Universal Design create structures that from the outset are intended to be used by all individuals, including those with disabilities. Although Universal Design has it roots in accessible design, it encompasses a philosophy that good design benefits everyone. A product that has not been designed with accessibility in mind may not be usable by a person with a disability, *and* it also may be less than optimally useable by a person without a disability.

Universal Design for Learning (UDL) is an application of these principles to learning environments. The basic premise of UDL is that the learning medium should include alternatives to make it accessible and applicable to students, teachers, and parents with different backgrounds, learning styles, abilities, and disabilities in widely varied learning contexts. The "universal" in Universal Design does not imply there will be one optimal solution for everyone, but rather it underscores the need for inherently flexible, customizable content, assignments, and activities.

2.1   3 Brain Systems

PET scans and other advanced imaging techniques enable neuroscientists to study the learning brain in action. These tools generate images of the brain that distinguish highly active regions from those that are less active. Patterns of regions that become active while an individual is performing different learning tasks generate information about how the brain works as we learn.

Recent neurological findings [2] confirm earlier descriptions of three spatially and functionally distinguishable though interconnected systems in the learning brain. Broadly speaking, one system *recognizes* patterns, one *generates* patterns, and the third determines *priorities*. Recognition systems know *what* and *where* an object is, strategic systems know *how* to do things, and the affective systems know which objects and actions are important.

2.1.1   Recognition

Most of the posterior half of the brain's cortex is devoted to recognizing patterns. Pattern recognition systems make it possible to identify visual, auditory, and olfactory stimuli—to know that a particular stimulus pattern is a book, your dog's bark, the smell of burning leaves. In academic learning, pattern recognition systems are essential for identifying basic patterns such as letters and words, or more complex patterns such as paragraph structure, author's style, or the relationship between a mathematical formula and its graphical representation.

2.1.2   Strategic

The anterior part of the brain (the frontal lobes) comprises the networks responsible for knowing how to do things—holding and moving a pencil, riding a bicycle, speaking, reading a book, planning a trip, writing a narrative. Actions, skills, and plans are highly patterned activities, requiring the strategic brain systems responsible for generating patterns. Strategic systems are critical for all learning tasks, working in tandem with recognition systems to learn to read, compute, write, solve problems, plan and execute compositions and complete projects. Like the posterior brain systems, frontal systems are essential for generating basic patterns such as forming a letter, and complex patterns such as drawing or writing a composition.

2.1.3   Affective

At the core of the brain (the limbic system) lie the networks responsible for emotion. Neither recognizing nor generating patterns, these networks determine whether the patterns we perceive matter to us, and help us decide which actions and strategies to pursue. With the affective systems, we pursue goals, develop preferences, build confidence, persist in the face of difficulty, establish priorities, and care about learning. Recent neurological work shows that the capacity to determining which patterns count is critical to human intelligence and to all learning.

2.2 3 Principles of UDL

These three brain systems form the foundation for CAST's three principles of Universal Design for Learning. Learning requires complex interactions of the recognition, strategic, and affective systems, and no two brains function in exactly the same way. While everyone's brain functions take place in roughly the same areas and work together in roughly the same way, PET scans show that each individual has his or her own activity "signature." Each of us has a different functional allocation of cortex. Some people have larger regions devoted to recognizing patterns, generating strategies, or focusing on particular priorities and these differences seem to be reflected in different configurations of learning style, relative strengths and weaknesses, and varying "kinds" of intelligence.

Thinking about individual differences in light of the three brain systems can help us understand the ways in which curriculum must be flexible to reach all learners. Multiple representations of content can adjust to the recognition systems of different learners; multiple options for expression and control can adjust to the strategic and motor systems of different learners; multiple options for engagement can adjust to the affective systems of different learners.

2.2.1 Multiple Means of Representation

No single representation of information is ideal, or even accessible, to all learners. Some students thrive in lectures; others obtain information effectively from text, while still others learn best through visual media such as diagrams, illustrations, charts, or video. These learning differences reflect variations in neurology, background experiences, and constitution and are manifested along a continuum from slight preferences to profound necessities. For example, one student with a proclivity for art may find an image more comprehensible than a verbal description of an idea; another who is deaf will be shut out completely if only a verbal description is provided.

Universally designed materials accommodate this diversity through alternative representations of key information. Students with different preferences and needs can either select the representational medium most suitable for them, or gather information from a variety of representational media simultaneously.

Unlike the printed page, computers provide the opportunity to present information in multiple media and to provide settings that permit selecting among the offerings. Additionally, computers can often transform information into a medium most appropriate for the user. However, it is not always a straightforward matter to do so. In some cases a direct translation is possible, as in text-to-speech or spoken dialogue to written caption. In other cases, interpretation is necessary, as in image description or text version of a sound effect. Some content cannot truly cross media in a way that most people would agree on: a poem or music, for example. It is essential, therefore, when providing multiple representations, to consider the purpose of the activity, and the nature of the learners themselves.

2.2.2   Multiple Means of Expression

Just as no single mode of presentation suits all learners, neither does any single mode of expression. The dominant mode for expressing ideas and demonstrating learning has long been text on the printed page. Work in multiple intelligences [3] and school reform supports the notion that more options, including artwork, photography, drama, music, animation, and video, open doors for a greater number of students to successfully communicate ideas, knowledge gained, and talents. These ideas apply to students with particular skills and proclivities as well as to students with disabilities that prevent them from using certain media effectively or at all. Universally designed materials offer multiple options for expression and control. Persons with particular preferences or learning needs can find media, supports, and options that enable them to demonstrate their knowledge in the way that is most effective for them.

2.2.3   Multiple Means of Engagement

Reaching to users' enthusiasm and interests is critically important. CAST's third principle of Universal Design proposes that media should support varied skill levels, preferences, and interests by providing flexible options. For any given user, there must be content that is interesting and provides a clear purpose. Digital materials and electronic networks have the potential to provide the flexibility, and developers, researchers, and educators will have to ensure that sound pedagogy guides the development of new digital curricula.

3.   UNIVERSAL DESIGN PRINCIPLES FOR THE WEB

The World Wide Web is a potentially rich learning environment. The notion of a universally designed Web challenges society to think about plurality—to consider all individuals, regardless of age, ability, race, or economic or cultural background—when developing new technologies. Yet at this time, though the Web has much potential for broad inclusion, it often excludes some people from participating in much the same way that a staircase prevents a person from going in a building's door.

The technology now exists to support inclusion of many different types of people in ways that were previously unconsidered, yet that technology is not always used to its maximum benefit. For individuals with visual disabilities, for example, the Web's highly graphical environment poses serious problems. Even with a screen reader, a tool used by individuals with visual impairments to translate written text into spoken text, Web pages can still be inaccessible when screen readers cannot navigate text in columns or recognize images. For individuals who are deaf or hard of hearing, multimedia and audio elements of Web pages are inaccessible without such accommodations as captioning or text descriptions.

Over the last several years, under the leadership of Tim Berners-Lee, inventor of the World Wide Web and Director of the World Wide Web Consortium (W3C), key stakeholders mobilized to move the Web toward universal accessibility. This increased focus led, in April 1997, to the W3C's establishment of the Web Accessibility Initiative (WAI) to lead the Web to its full potential by promoting a high degree of usability for people with disabilities. In coordination with other organizations worldwide, the WAI is pursuing accessibility through development of technology, guidelines, tools, education and outreach, and through research and development.

An important piece of the WAI's work has been the development of a document called the Web Content Accessibility Guidelines [4] which brings together all of the previous efforts in this area and provides many new ideas. Within this larger international movement, CAST has identified a critical need to provide practical support to Web developers in implementing the guidelines.

3.1   Supporting the Authoring of Universally Designed Web Sites

Applying the principles of Universal Design to a web site requires awareness of and commitment to the issues. Equally importantly, it requires enough applied understanding of these issues to create effective universally designed web sites. That is, an author must know the design principles that make a web site universally designed, and the author must know technically how to realize those principles on the web site. To help bring this awareness about, CAST launched Bobby in August, 1996. Bobby is a free interactive tool offered on CAST's web site that analyzes an HTML page with respect to the WAI's Web Content Guidelines, and translates them into instructions for improving its accessibility. After typing in a URL, Bobby delivers a full report within seconds. This report optionally includes the original page, with "Bobby-hat" icons (Figure 1) that visually show the location of errors.

Figure 1. A page evaluated by Bobby. (a) the original page. (b) the page with visual notification of accessibility errors. Clicking on the "hat" provides a more extensive description of the error.

Bobby then explains the factors that limit the site's use and recommends ways to fix those problems. In the report, the factors are presented as a list of error types. For each type, the parts of the page on which it is found is indicated, this time by showing the HTML source. An extended explanation of the cause of the error and means of repairing it is available by clicking on the error title. The errors are organized by three levels of priority—Priority 1 issues are the most important to address for accessibility. Within the priority levels, the report is also grouped into items that it can evaluate automatically, and descriptions of items that require human judgment to determine an appropriate response. While any web page will require an amount of subjective determination, Bobby is able to address many of the most numerous access issues.

Now in version 3.1, Bobby has been continually enhanced to provide better support for the guidelines. Many of its recommendations are for alternate representations of media, such as text alternatives and extended descriptions for images; others help authors avoid problems encountered by persons using access aids or non-standard browsers. Bobby can test most of these guidelines. In some cases the test involves detecting the presence or absence of certain features e.g., text alternatives that are included with specific HTML constructs like the ALT or LONGDESC attribute of media elements. In other cases, Bobby examines the way certain elements are used, such as color, size, or hierarchical organization.

Bobby is designed to be an educational tool that teaches Web designers about Web accessibility. As Web designers use Bobby, they not only learn how to address problems within their own site, they also learn skills that they can apply to site design in the future. Bobby offers concrete design suggestions and is linked to other sites that discuss access issues. The more one uses Bobby, the less likely one is to need it in the future, as accessibility issues and their solutions become integrated into one's Web design at the outset.

In order to serve as an effective model of accessibility and good interface design, Bobby employs the latest technological innovations in its own design. Bobby is now written in 100% Java, and has two forms: the online server, and a downloadable version that uses the same page evaluation code and offers both a graphical and a command-line interface. Since it is written in Java, this version can run on many different hardware platforms. Bobby uses Java's most current accessibility features, which allows the program itself to be accessible to users with disabilities. Many access aids are built into the interface, and it has the requisite code to allow third party access aids to communicate with it effectively.

3.2   Universal Design of the UDL Tool

A product that supports the development of universally designed computer-based products should be universally designed itself. Through the development of Bobby and other CAST products, the application of UDL principles has been continuously refined. Additionally, the technology is constantly evolving and opening up new opportunities for improvement. In the past, the accessible version was the server version that was provided on an accessible web page. The first version of the application was not accessible to all users because of limitations in the Java language at that time. Java has now evolved and Bobby takes full advantage of its features to provide an accessible interface.

Thus, universal design as it relates to physical accessibility of the product has now been largely achieved. The next level of universal design is its cognitive accessibility, or its usefulness to a wide range of audiences. This requires a transformation of the reports Bobby presents to users. Current Bobby reports are appropriate mainly for expert HTML authors who are comfortable editing source code. Much web design is now done by people using authoring tools who may not what understand the HTML errors presented, or how to solve them. Providing information appropriate to these users will make its benefits available to a wider audience and improve its ability to influence positively the design of web pages worldwide.

The quality and thoroughness of page examination will be enhanced to give Bobby a more complete view of a web page. As Bobby is enhanced, new types of optional checks will be added to Bobby to expand its role as a Universal Web Page Design Evaluation tool. Some check types under consideration include spell checking, page readability, and site layout and visual design. Some of these are topics related to human-computer interaction principles about which a larger understanding is now reaching the Web development community. Analysis and validation of these issues will become as important as accessibility evaluation in the near future.

Another important component of Universal Design in the modern world is internationalization and multiculturalism. Already, Bobby has been in the position of providing English-only reports for non-English web pages from around the world. It is important that Bobby be able to examine non-English pages in a manner appropriate to the language, and provide reports in that language (or another language of the user's choice). Multiculturalism of the tool means that it must be usable, from the opening interface to the final report, by people with different assumptions, experiences, and educational backgrounds. A first step to achieving these goals will be the creation of an international version that allows users to switch languages on the fly.

Bobby will also broaden the context of its use by providing a complete API that will allow other developers to integrate Bobby into their products. This will be of value to developers of page authoring programs who will be able to incorporate Bobby's features directly into their product. This will also allow the development of products that use Bobby's core functionality to accomplish different goals; for example, Bobby is currently expected to be integrated with an interactive repair tool that steps the user through the process of fixing problems that Bobby itself has merely identified and explained.

3.3   Impact

Bobby teaches Web designers to correct access problems in a simple and inviting way. Users type in the URL they want to analyze and Bobby tests the page, highlights problems, gives an accessibility rating, and explains any access problems found. Bobby also gives links to other sites that discuss access issues. Seeing how their sites look to people with disabilities gives Web developers an understanding of the sometimes subtle barriers "hidden" within their sites.

Because Bobby is a teaching tool, Web designers (including the rapidly growing number of non-professional designers who are putting up sites) learn skills they can apply later. The more people use Bobby, the more likely they will be to integrate accessibility principles into their way of thinking and their style of Web site design. Hundreds of thousands of visitors have come to the Bobby Web site, and many of them report using the program to test their sites. Overall, Bobby is testing more than 3 million Web pages a month and is referenced from more than 2800 sites.

4.   CONCLUSION

Universal Design is an important approach to addressing accessibility issues in technology. Bobby was created to encourage universal Web page design by checking pages for potential problems and teaching authors how to resolve them. Many developers learn about accessibility issues when they use Bobby to validate their HTML for various browsers and use Bobby's graphic download time assessment. The tool was used by CAST as it developed its new model, universally designed Web site. CAST continues to use the venue of its Web site, combined with the success of Bobby, to support and encourage other developers to produce universally designed technology.

REFERENCES

[1] *Bobby Version 2.0, HTML Web analyzer*, Center for Applied Special Technology (CAST), National Universal Design Laboratory, Peabody, Massachusetts, 1997. Accessible at http://www.cast.org/bobby.

[2] Cytowic, R.E., *The neurological side of neuropsychology*, MIT Press, Cambridge, 1996.

[3] Gardner, H., *Frames of Mind: the theory of multiple intelligences*, BasicBooks, New York, 1983.

[4] WAI Accessibility Guidelines – Page Authoring, Web Accessibility Initiative, World Wide Web Consortium, Geneva, 1998. Accessible at http://www.w3.org/TR/1998/WD-WAI-PAGEAUTH-0203, http://www.w3.org/TR/WAI-WEBCONTENT.

Chapter 4

MODEL-BASED DESIGN OF USER-INTERFACES USING OBJECT-Z

Andrew Hussey and David Carrington
Software Verification Research Centre
Department of Computer Science and Electrical Engineering
The University of Queensland
Brisbane, Qld, 4072, Australia
{ahussey,davec}@svrc.uq.edu.au

Abstract   Model-based tools enable developers to produce prototype user-interface designs from a model of the system. However most existing model-based tools do not enable a developer to work from an abstract specification of the system to produce a prototype design. Instead, the model of the system that is provided to the tool is at a low level of abstraction. Consequently, much design work focuses prematurely on the concrete visual appearance of the user-interface. To address this issue, this paper discusses a model-based design process that commences from an abstract specification.

Keywords: Model-based design, user-interface design, Object-Z.

1.   INTRODUCTION

Most existing methods and tools for developing user-interfaces focus the developers' attention prematurely on the visual appearance of the system [9]. The user-interface must provide appropriate access to the abstract information and operations described in the system's functional requirements. Focusing initially on appearance rather than function, can corrupt the architecture of the system, diminish usability and require that work be abandoned. The objective of this paper is to discuss model-based design methods that are amenable to tool support and that help developers avoid such wasted design effort.

In an object-oriented interactive system design, some objects are presented to users. Each such object and its presentation (including user interactions

43

required to invoke operations) together define an "interactor" [2]; the object provides the abstract specification of the interactor.

In Section 2. we discuss the need for improved methods for model-based design. Section 3. presents the Interface-Adapter pattern for augmenting interactive system specifications to produce user-interface designs. A pattern is a description of a recurring structural or behavioural solution [4]. Our approach is based on the adapter design pattern described by Gamma et al. [4]. We summarise the complete pattern, which is given in [6]. Section 4. gives an example of model-based design commencing from an interactive system specification and applying the Interface-Adapter pattern. Section 5. considers future work that would apply our method as the basis of a model-based design tool.

2.   MODEL-BASED DESIGN

Lauridsen [7] argues that many of the problems in user-interface development are caused by the low level of abstraction at which design decisions are made, resulting in lack of overview in the design process. Instead a stronger connection is needed between the interactive system specification and the user-interface design.

User-interface designs in which each interactor is trivially presented in terms of one or more "widgets" can be derived from abstract system specifications [6]. A widget is any widely used interactor such as a button, scrollbar or list. A design may reuse widgets from a library. Operations on the specification interactors are invoked indirectly by user-interaction with widgets, and the state and outputs of specification interactors are presented by widgets.

There has been much research of mechanisms for tool-assisted selection of widgets based on functional specifications [7]. Tools that assist the user-interface development process, using models of the interactive system, are "model-based" [11]. Model-based tools have not been widely accepted in industry [11] because they lack customisability, do not support complex relationships between widgets and in most cases the resulting implementations are slow because they are interpreted. Most developers use interface builders, toolkits and a programming language. Further, most existing tools do not assist developing widget-based implementations (i.e., implementations constructed using widgets) from an abstract specification. In particular, they do not enable progressive development of a concrete specification in terms of widgets from an abstract specification.

In [6], we advocate using an abstract system model as the *basis* for task decomposition, avoiding the need to produce the model following task decomposition. For most model-based tools, the initial specification of the user-interface that must be provided to the tool is at a low level of abstraction. Our approach is similar to the approach used in UIDE [10], because like UIDE, the design is derived by manipulation of an abstract system model. However we ensure that the transformations are correctness preserving (a design derived by transformation is compatible with the original abstract specification). To enable demonstration of correctness of transformations, our models are expressed in terms of Object-Z [3], a formal, object-oriented specification language. Our approach does *not* automate design of the user-interface for a system. At each stage of the development process, it is the responsibility of the designer to choose the transformations that will be performed.

By commencing from an abstract model of the system, attention is focused on providing support for the tasks expressed in the abstract model. Our method ensures that every such task is expressed as a concrete task in the user-interface design: each operation of the specification can be expressed as a combination of operations of the user-interface design.

3.   INTERFACE-ADAPTER

We summarise a pattern for producing user-interface designs from interactive system specifications. Our summarised pattern, Interface-Adapter, consists of two parts: the *Context* that describes the circumstances in which the pattern can be applied, and the *Solution* that describes the effect of applying the pattern.

Context. The Interface-Adapter pattern is used when an operation of a specification class produces output or updates the state of an interactor. Because almost all interactive systems will either produce output or update state, the Interface-Adapter pattern is widely applicable.

Solution. In the Interface-Adapter pattern, an *adapter* interactor is interposed between the user and a *core* interactor. Input to the core interactor and/or output from the core interactor are handled by the adapter interactor. The Interface-Adapter pattern corresponds to task decomposition.

Although Interface-Adapter produces a potential architecture for the system, its primary purpose is to derive user-interface designs. The architecture derived by Interface-Adapter is deliberately simple; other more complex user-interface architectures such as PAC [1] and MVC [8] can be readily derived from the architecture produced by Interface-Adapter [5].

The interactors that are added to a specification using the Interface-Adapter pattern provide mechanisms for performing the abstract tasks defined by interactors in the abstract specification. The tasks supported by the system following application of the Interface-Adapter pattern are the same as prior to applying the pattern, except that the action sequence to perform tasks that now involve the adapter interactor has been decomposed (i.e., the system following application of the pattern is compatible with the original system).

The **Interface-Adapter** pattern is depicted in Figure 1.1 using Rumbaugh's object model notation as described in [4]. We assume that the *core* interactor writes data that is to be presented to the user in the variable *outData*, while the *adapter* interactor receives data from the user in the variable *inData*.

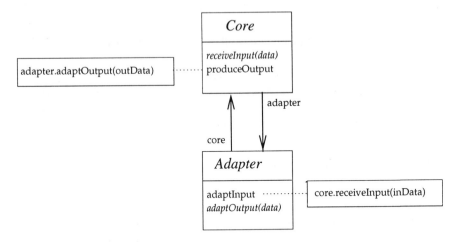

Figure   1   The **Interface-Adapter** pattern

4.   CASE STUDY: THE VOTING SYSTEM

We use a simple example to demonstrate how the **Interface-Adapter** pattern is used to transform an abstract Object-Z specification. For simplicity, because our primary concern is to illustrate principles, the example that we present in this paper is deliberately "toy" sized. A larger web browser case study is presented in [5].

4.1   ABSTRACT SPECIFICATION

The purpose of the voting system user-interface is to allow the user to construct a vote consisting of an ordered list of candidate names. Such a system would be useful for automating an optional-preferential voting system. The user-interface provides a list of available candidate names that cannot be altered by the user. No candidate name is duplicated. The vote has no duplicates, contains any number of candidate names from the list of candidates and is initially empty. We declare a given set *CANDIDATE* that describes the set of all possible candidates.

In an Object-Z specification, a class is defined by a named box encapsulating state and, optionally, initialisation and operations. The state schema in the class is un-named and contains attribute declarations and a constraining invariant. The class *Candidates* initially describes the candidates with which the user is supplied. The initialisation schema is labelled *INIT* and defines the initial state of instances of the class.

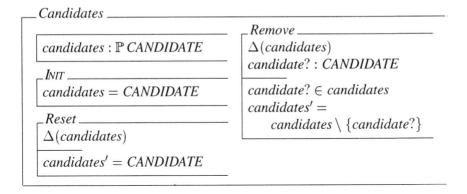

An operation schema is divided into two parts. The upper part defines the context of the operation including inputs and outputs. The Δ-list defines those state attributes that are altered by an operation. State variables not listed in the Δ-list are unchanged by that operation. The lower part defines a predicate relating the initial and final states of the operation. The decorations ? and ! indicate input and output attributes respectively.

The class *Vote* represents a single vote as a list of candidate identifiers (without duplicates) in decreasing order of preference.

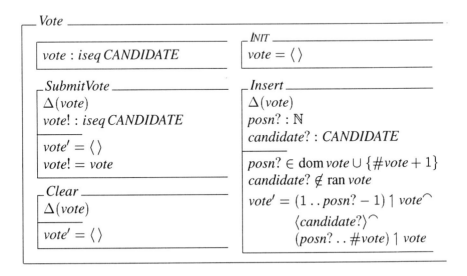

The system is defined by the instantiation of the *Candidates* and *Vote* interactor classes.

```
┌─ VotingSystem ─────────────────────────────────────────────────
│  ┌──────────────────────────┐  ┌─ INIT ─────────────────────
│  │ candidates : Candidates  │  │ candidates.INIT
│  │ vote : Vote              │  │ vote.INIT
│  └──────────────────────────┘  └────────────────────────────
│  ┌──────────────────────────────────────────────────────────
│  │ candidates.candidates ∪ ran vote.vote = CANDIDATE
│  └──────────────────────────────────────────────────────────
│  AddToVote ≘ candidates.Remove ∧ vote.Insert
│  ClearVote ≘ vote.Clear ∧ candidates.Reset
│  SubmitVote ≘ vote.SubmitVote ∧ candidates.Reset
└──────────────────────────────────────────────────────────────
```

The operation *AddToVote* removes the user's selection from *candidates* and inserts the candidate in *vote* (the *candidate*? attributes in the interface for each operation of the conjunction are unified). Both *ClearVote* and *SubmitVote* reset the system to its initial state, with *SubmitVote* also outputting the completed vote.

4.2   REDEFINITION IN TERMS OF WIDGETS

We redefine the *Candidate* and *Vote* classes using the **List** class. The **List** class specifies a list widget and provides the presentation for the redefined *Candidate* and *Vote* classes. Widget classes are distinguished from other Object-Z classes because they have an associated presentation to which their state and operations can be mapped. In [5] we provide a complete version of **List** that has operations to select elements, but in this specification the selection operations are not used.

```
┌─ List[X] ──────────────────────────────────────────────────────
│  ┌──────────────────────────┐  ┌─ INIT ─────────────────────
│  │ elements : seq X         │  │ elements = ⟨⟩
│  │ selection : ℙ ℕ          │  │ selection = ∅
│  └──────────────────────────┘  └────────────────────────────
│  ┌──────────────────────────┐
│  │ #selection ≤ 1           │
│  │ selection ⊆ dom elements │
│  └──────────────────────────┘
└──────────────────────────────────────────────────────────────
```

The *Candidates$_{list}$* class transforms the attribute *candidates* in the *Candidates* class (denoted by *candidates$_{original}$*) using the coupling invariant ran *candidates* = *candidates$_{original}$*, and transforms the interface for *Remove* using the coupling invariant *candidate*? = *candidates(posn?)*. The interactor class *Candidates$_{list}$* extends **List** to allow the candidate at a chosen numeric index in the list to be removed using the *Remove* operation. The *Remove* operation takes a position as input, rather than using the selection, because the operation models direct manipulation of the list widget. The addition of *candidate*! to the interface of *Remove* ensures that the effect of the system operation *AddToVote* on the system state is unchanged (see *VotingSystem$_{library}$* below).

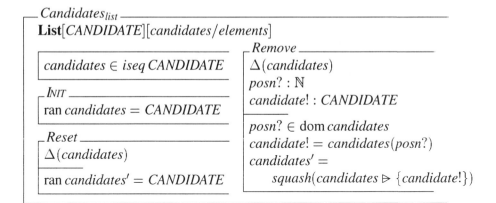

Similarly, we replace the class *Vote* by *Vote$_{list}$*, using the **List** library class. For brevity, we elide the redefinition of the *Vote* class.

We use buttons to invoke the operations to submit the vote and clear the vote (i.e., we apply the **Interface-Adapter** pattern). Buttons offer a *Click* operation that normally occurs in association with an operation of a specification interactor. The **Button** class specification and presentation (including executions required to invoked operations) is defined in [5]. The *Click* operation for each button is promoted only in conjunction with operations on *vote* and *candidates*.

The *VotingSystem$_{list}$* class is defined in terms of *Candidates$_{list}$* and *Vote$_{list}$*.

___*VotingSystem$_{list}$*_____

    candidates : *Candidates$_{list}$*   ___*INIT*_____
    vote : *Vote$_{list}$*   *candidates.INIT*
    submit, clear : **Button**[*Text*]   *vote.INIT*
    _____   *submit.INIT*
    submit.label = "Submit"   *clear.INIT*
    clear.label = "Clear"

    AddToVote $\widehat{=}$ *candidates.Remove*[*posn1?/posn?*] $\|$ *vote.Insert*[*posn2?/posn?*]
    ClearVote $\widehat{=}$ *clear.Click* $\wedge$ *vote.Clear* $\wedge$ *candidates.Reset*
    SubmitVote $\widehat{=}$ *submit.Click* $\wedge$ *vote.SubmitVote* $\wedge$ *candidates.Reset*
_____

We indicate the active interactor for the operations *ClearVote* and *SubmitVote* by underlining. The active interactors for an operation are the interactors with which the user must engage to invoke the operation.

4.3   INTRODUCTION OF DRAG-AND-DROP

To demonstrate the correctness of a drag and drop design formally, we apply the Interface-Adapter pattern, interposing a buffer between the candidate and vote lists into which a candidate is inserted during a drag and from which it is removed when the consequent drop occurs. The drag and drop buffer receives output from *candidates.Remove* and provides input to *vote.Insert*. The class *DragDrop* presents the candidate identifier that is currently the subject of a drag operation. Operations of the *DragDrop* class are not directly accessed by the user; rather they are invoked by interaction with objects of other classes in the system. *DragDrop* does not constrain the location of the drop; such constraints are dealt with in the specification of the interactors that use *DragDrop*.

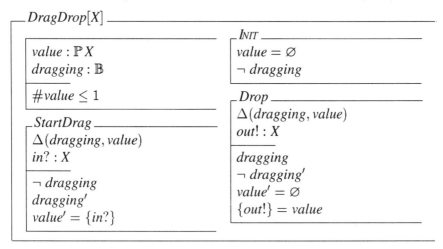

We extend the *Candidates$_{list}$* and *Vote$_{list}$* interactor classes to use an instance of the *DragDrop* class to move a chosen candidate from the candidates list to the vote list; dragging a candidate is modelled by the operation *ChooseCandidate*. The operation *Remove* is subsumed by the operation *ChooseCandidate* and is removed from the availability list (denoted by ↾).

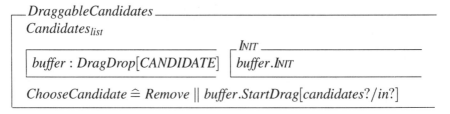

The *ChooseCandidate* operation models a "drag". The operation is invoked by pressing or clicking a mouse-button with the mouse cursor over the candidates list and then using the mouse to move the candidate that is being dragged.

We define the *DroppableVote* class by inheritance from $Vote_{list}$. For brevity we elide its definition.

We give the completed system class for the widget-based specification as $VotingSystem_{dragdrop}$. The class $VotingSystem_{dragdrop}$ provides a user-interface design for the voting system because the presentation has been completely defined. We indicate the active interactors for each operation.

┌─ *VotingSystem*$_{dragdrop}$ ─────────────────────────────
│ ┌─────────────────────────────┬─ *INIT* ──────────────
│ │ *candidates* : *DraggableCandidates* │ *candidates.INIT*
│ │ *vote* : *DroppableVote*   │ *vote.INIT*
│ │ *buffer* : *DragDrop*[*CANDIDATE*] │ *buffer.INIT*
│ │ *submit*, *clear* : **Button**[*Text*] │ *submit.INIT*
│ ├─────────────────────────────┤ *clear.INIT*
│ │ *submit.label* = "Submit"   └──────────────
│ │ *clear.label* = "Clear"
│ │ *candidates.buffer* = *buffer*
│ │ *vote.buffer* = *buffer*
│ └─────────────────────────────
│
│ *AddToVote* $\hat{=}$ *candidates.ChooseCandidate* $\,^\circ_9\,$ *vote.InsertCandidate*
│ ..
└──

Because the drag and drop interface-adapter has been introduced and handles communication of candidates between the candidate and vote lists, the operation *AddToVote* is redefined. The redefined operation passes selected candidates to the vote list via the drag and drop buffer; this is achieved by sequentially composing operations to choose a candidate from the candidates list and insert that candidate into the vote list.

The redefined *AddToVote* operation (denoted in our discussion by $AddToVote_{concrete}$) has the same effect on the state of the *candidates* and *vote* interactors as did the original *AddToVote* operation (denoted by $AddToVote_{abstract}$) for the class $VotingSystem_{list}$ but also manipulates the state of the *buffer* interactor. In behaviours of the original system, we replace the $AddToVote_{abstract}$ operation by the $AddToVote_{concrete}$ operation to obtain behaviours of the transformed voting system (defined by $VotingSystem_{dragdrop}$). All the behaviours of the original system are represented by behaviours of the transformed system.

Figure 1.2 shows the presentation for the voting system, using Tk widgets.

5.   CONCLUSIONS

By transforming from an abstract specification to a widget-based prototype using Interface-Adapter, the developer can be sure that their implementation provides mechanisms to perform required tasks. Formal transformations help achieve conformance of a widget-based design to an original (abstract)

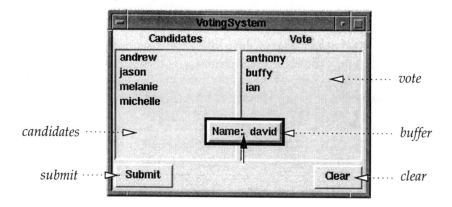

Figure 2   Tcl/Tk implementation of the voting system

interactive system specification. However, applying transformations is time consuming; hence the technique, used manually, is likely to be feasible only for safety-critical or small systems. Since formal methods are commonly acknowledged to be of most benefit for larger scale systems, developers need tools to assist them in using formal approaches for large or commercial scale user-interface development.

Our future work will investigate how to provide such tool support for transforming abstract formal interactive system specifications to prototype widget-based user-interface designs. The intent is to develop mechanisms for model-based user-interface development suitable for industrial use. A tool for assisting formal development of user-interfaces would assist developers applying patterns for transforming an abstract user-interface specification to a widget-based specification, would guide transformations (e.g., by identifying suitable widgets corresponding to a specification) and would permit association of design information (such as presentation and widget layout) with resulting widget-based specifications. The tool would support a philosophy of iterative redesign, user testing and analysis. Adapter components could be plugged and unplugged to and from core interactors as required, and core interactors could be redefined in terms of different widgets if necessary, with the tool performing necessary correctness checks for the designer.

With tool support, we believe our method offers significant advantages over conventional user-interface development techniques. By concentrating the developers' attention on the abstract system specification, the correctness of the user-interface (satisfaction of abstract tasks) is enhanced. The developer is free to focus their attention on usability issues concerning the design rather than less creative but time consuming issues of conformance to the abstract specification. Further, by focusing on abstract tasks initially, developers may avoid premature design effort before abstract tasks have been properly formulated. With our approach, prototyping is used judiciously (because it is an expensive activity) only after significant requirements analysis has been done and never simply to verify that the prototype design conforms to the abstract requirements.

References

[1] J. Coutaz. Architectural Models for Interactive Software. In S. Cook, editor, *European Conference on Object-oriented Programming - ECOOP '89*, pages 382–399. Cambridge University Press, 1989.

[2] J. Coutaz, L. Nigay, and D. Salber. Agent-Based Architecture Modelling for Interactive Systems. Technical Report SM/WP53, LGI-IMAG, Grenoble, April 1995. ESPRIT BRA 7040 Amodeus-2.

[3] R. Duke, G. Rose, and G. Smith. Object-Z: A Specification Language Advocated for the Description of Standards. *Computer Standards and Interfaces*, 17:511–533, 1995.

[4] E. Gamma, R. Helm, R. Johnson, and J. Vlissides. *Design Patterns: Elements of Reusable Object-Oriented Software*. Addison-Wesley, 1994.

[5] A. Hussey. *Object-Oriented Specification and Design of User-Interfaces*. PhD thesis, Department of Computer Science and Electrical Engineering; The University of Queensland, February 1999.

[6] A. Hussey and D. Carrington. Which widgets? Deriving Implementations from Formal User-Interface Specifications. In *5th Eurographics Workshop on the Design, Specification and Verification of Interactive Systems, DSV-IS '98*, pages 239–257. Springer-Verlag, 1998.

[7] O. Lauridsen. Generation of User Interfaces using Formal Specification. In K. Nordby, P. Helmersen, D. J. Gilmore, and S. A. Arnesen, editors, *Human-Computer Interaction - INTERACT '95*, pages 325–330. Chapman and Hall, 1995.

[8] ParcPlace Systems Inc. *VisualWorks User's Guide*. ParcPlace, 1994.

[9] K. Schneider and A. ander Repenning. Deceived by Ease of Use. In *DIS'95 Symposium on Designing Interactive Systems: Processes, Practices, Methods and Techniques*, pages 177–188. ACM Press, 1995.

[10] P. Sukaviriya, J. D. Foley, and T. Griffith. A Second Generation User Interface Design Environment: The Model and the Runtime Architecture. In *INTERCHI '93 : Bridges between Worlds*, pages 375–382. ACM Press, 1993.

[11] P. Szekely. Retrospective and Challenges for Model-Based Interface Development. In F. Paterno, editor, *Interactive Systems: Design, Specification and Verification – 1st Eurographics Workshop*, pages 1–27. Springer-Verlag, 1994.

Chapter 5

A METHOD ENGINEERING FRAMEWORK FOR MODELING AND GENERATING INTERACTIVE APPLICATIONS

Christian Märtin
Fachhochschule Augsburg – University of Applied Sciences
Department of Computer Science, Baumgartnerstraße 16, D-86161 Augsburg
maertin@informatik.fh-augsburg.de

Abstract   This paper reviews model-based design environments for interactive software systems. The expressiveness and flexibility of such environments can be raised by using a method engineering approach for tailoring object-oriented design methodologies that meet project-specific requirements. Applying artefacts such as software patterns to computer-aided user interface construction can further improve the resulting interactive applications.

Keywords: Model-based design environments, *AME*, *OBJECTWAND*, method-engineering, software life cycle, development approach, artefacts, patterns, UML.

1.   INTRODUCTION

Over the last couple of years new requirements for application software have emerged: richer interactive functionality, enhanced usability, multimedia support, Web integration, client-server organization, high reliability, maintainability and extendability.

Model-based design environments for *interactive software systems (ISSs)* can help to cope with these complex requirements. Such systems consequently apply a modeling paradigm (e.g. object-oriented, declarative, ER-based, etc.) to represent the structure and behavior of the user interface and its relationships to the application's domain functionality. Two main categories of model-based environments for designing ISSs can be distinguished: *model-based specification systems* and *model-based generators*.

Some recent systems have demonstrated that a combination of both interactive specification techniques and automatic generator components makes sense. In *AME* [7] and its successor *OBJECTWAND* [9] a life cycle driven approach was chosen to coordinate intelligent automated tools and flexible interactive tools for specifying and designing prototypical ISSs for the business domain. Models are represented by an object-oriented scheme that is based on a set of modeling classes. These classes, their role in a model specification, the life cycle activities and tools that refine a given model specification into a more detailed one are formally described in [8]. Related work on model-based ISS design environments is covered in [12].

In the following chapters an evolutionary and synergistic approach for tailoring more individual ISS design methodologies is discussed. This approach is a preliminary result of *SALC (Software Automation Life Cycle)*, a project set up to explore hierarchy levels and activities in generic software processes with respect to their automation potential.

2.   METHOD ENGINEERING FOR CADUI

Method engineering is the "coordinated and systematic approach to establishing work methods" and therefore "produces methodologies" [10]. To facilitate the development of individual computer-aided design environments for interactive applications we propose a meta-model of *ISS design methodology*. It defines the meta-structure and possible elements of individual model-based ISS design methodolgies. It can also be used as a framework for building ISS design environments.

2.1   Meta-model purpose

The meta-model is shown in Figure 1 in *UML* notation. It will help to clarify the notion ISS design methodology and allows us
- to define specific methodologies for individual ISS projects,
- to define life cycle driven tools that support development activities,
- to build a repository for methodology elements and meta-level CASE tools for ISS method engineering, and
- to re-engineer existing ISS design environments for other contexts.

Most existing ISS design environments impose a life cycle with a fixed number of predefined activities on each new project. Life cycle activities are directly associated with development activities and tools that generate or aid to create the UI and couple it to the domain parts of an application. This is not so different from the view taken by designers of modeling techniques like UML [1]. They propose *one* life cycle, e.g. the *Rational Unified Process,* that typically comes together with the modeling technique.

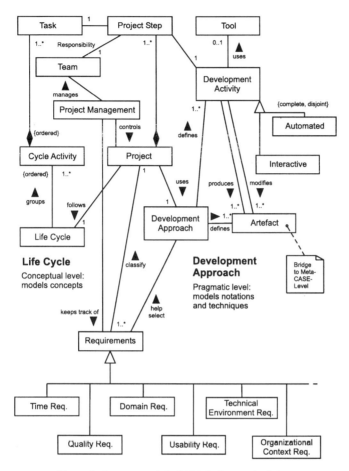

Figure 1. A meta-model of ISS design methodology

However, in general the project-specific and organization-related requirements vary too much, to be mirrored by one process alone. A given life cycle cannot be flexible enough to be applied to the whole spectrum of real life development projects. Specific requirements of ISSs, e.g. user participation, organizational context, integration of new media and conformance to HCI standards further complicate the situation.

Therefore, we suggest to use method engineering based on meta-models, to gain project- and domain-oriented insights into ISS design. Each ISS design project may require an individual life cycle. See [3, 11] for related work on life cycle meta-modeling. Our studies have also been influenced by *Evolutionary Fusion* [6] and *Catalysis* [4].

2.2   Meta-model structure

A *project* is composed of project steps. Each step is associated with a semantic *task* to be accomplished during the development life cycle and with a *development activity* that implements the task. *Project managment* manages the development *team,* schedules *project steps* and keeps track of the various *requirements* of a specific project. The development team is responsible for executing the steps (sequentially, overlapping, or in parallel). A project may follow an existing *life cycle* (top down) or compose a new life cycle from given and/or new *cycle activities* (bottom up). A life cycle activity (e.g. analysis) is composed of one or more life cycle tasks.

Different *development approaches* may be required for different projects. A project uses the selected development approach with its set of defined *development activities.* Development activities for ISS design may be *interactive* (e.g. designing a class diagram) or *automated* (e.g. generating the layout for dialog box with given interaction objects). They mirror the techniques and notations of the development approach. A major difference between the meta-model and most existing model-based design environments is that here a *tool* can be *associated* with a development activity but *is not identical* with the development activity. The activity specifies input, output and effects of the tool. A tool *implements* a development activity. The development approach also specifies the set of artefacts, produced and modified by development activities. The class *artefact* defines all elements needed for modeling and generating ISSs. All components of ISS models as well as data and knowledge resources applied by development activities in order to refine a model are collected in this class. An environment like *AME* is as an instance of the meta-model and an example ISS design methodology for business-related GUI applications.

3.   DESIGN ARTEFACTS

Artefact classes in our meta-model are structured as shown in Figure 2. Our attention is mainly focussed on artefacts like patterns and structural relationships which can improve future ISS modeling and generator tools.

3.1   Exploiting patterns

In AME structural patterns in OOA/D diagrams were parsed in order to automatically generate the window and dialog box hierarchy for GUI applications. In addition source code templates for generating the behavior of standard interaction objects and dialog boxes were used. Recently tools that generate code from design patterns [5] have emerged, at least for adapting design patterns to specific contexts (see e.g. [2]).

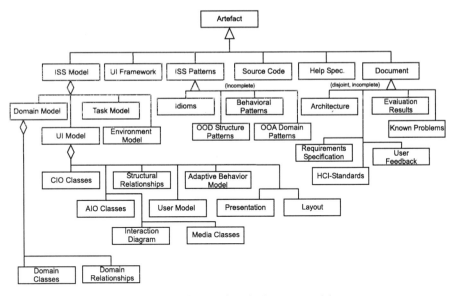

Figure 2. Design artefacts in the meta-model.

3.2 Applying patterns to ISS modeling and generation

In *SALC* a prototypical modeling tool *(MDT)* was developed for applying software patterns to automated ISS design beyond the scope available in AME. *MDT* consists of a graphical editor and an extensible graphical library of software patterns. The editor is used for constructing UML class diagrams for ISSs from primitive modeling elements, adaptable design patterns from the library, and *Java*-based UI frameworks.

MDT can also be used to create new OOA domain patterns and graphically specify their mapping to detailed OOD structures and behavior. This feature allows to represent the mapping of non-standard relationships between domain classes – e.g. associations with domain-specific roles – to reusable individual UI class structures. It also allows to specify the related source code for expanding the pattern within a specific context.

4. CONCLUSION

In this paper a method engineering approach for defining ISS design methodologies was presented. Meta-model-based approaches like this will enable us to adapt existing model-based ISS design environments to project-specific requirements.

Some aspects for applying pattern artefacts were highlighted. In SALC we currently examine the use of concrete patterns in ISS design environments. We have developed a Web-based stock trading agent using Java-based development tools. Some generic patterns were extracted and represented as UML class diagrams. We now identify those parts of the application windows and their elements which are strongly related to the patterns and look for efficient ways to make them reusable by ISS generators.

5.   ACKNOWLEDGEMENTS

The author acknowledges the contributions of Stefan G. Renz, Markus Heyking and Marcus Nerf to SALC. Special thanks go to Andreas Kirchhofer for his structuring hints and for drawing the meta-model figures.

6.   REFERENCES

[1]   Booch, G., Rumbaugh, J., and Jacobson, I., *The Unified Modeling Language User Guide*, Addison Wesley, Reading, 1999.

[2]   Budinsky, F.J., Finnie, M.A., Vlissides, J.M., and Yu, P.S., *Automatic Code Generation from Design Patterns*, IBM Systems Journal, Vol. 35, No. 2, 1996.

[3]   Daniels, J., *Object Method: Beyond the Notations*, Object Expert, January/February 1997, pp. 36-40.

[4]   D'Souza, D.F. and Wills, A.C., Objects, *Components and Frameworks with UML- The Catalysis Approach*, Addison-Wesley, Reading, 1998.

[5]   Gamma, E., Helm, R., Johnson, R., and Vlissides, J., *Design Patterns. Elements of Reusable Object-Oriented Software*, Addison-Wesley, Reading, 1995.

[6]   Malan, R., Letsinger, D., and Coleman, D., *Object-Oriented Development at Work – Fusion In the Real World*, Prentice Hall, Englewood Cliffs, 1995.

[7]   Märtin, C., *Software Life Cycle Automation for Interactive Applications: The AME Design Environment*, in [12], pp. 57-73.

[8]   Märtin, C., *Model-based Software Engineering for Interactive Systems*, in R. Albrech (ed.), Systems: Theory and Practice, Advances in Computing Science Series, Springer Verlag, Berlin, 1998, pp. 187-211

[9]   Märtin, C. and Humpl, M., *Generating Adaptable Multimedia Software from Dynamic Object-Oriented Models: The OBJECTWAND Design Environment*, in Proc. HCI International'97, M.J. Smith, G. Salvendy, and R.J. Koubek (eds.), Advances in Human Factors/Ergonomics, Vol. 21B, Elsevier, Amsterdam, 1997, pp. 703-706.

[10]   Odell, J.J., *Method Engineering. In: Advanced Object-Oriented Analysis and Design Using UML*, Cambridge University Press, Cambridge, 1998, pp. 205-218 .

[11]   Renz, S.G., Modellierung objektorientierter Software-Entwicklung, Offene Systeme, Vol. 7, 1998, pp. 73-81

[12]   Vanderdonckt, J. (ed.), *Computer-Aided Design of User Interfaces*, Proc of 2nd Int. Workshop on Computer-Aided Design of User Interfaces CADUI '96 (Namur, 5-7 June 1996). Presses Universitaires de Namur, Namur, 1996.

Chapter 6

GIPSE, A MODEL BASED SYSTEM FOR CAD SOFTWARE

Guillaume Patry and Patrick Girard
LISI / ENSMA, Téléport 2, 1 Avenue Clément Ader
BP 40109, 86961 Futuroscope Chasseneuil Cedex
{patry, girard}@ensma.fr
Tel : (33/0) 5.49.49.80.70 - Fax : (33/0) 5.49.49.80.64

Abstract   We describe in this paper GIPSE, a model based system that is specialised in CAD systems. GIPSE facilitates the design and the development of applications using structured dialogues. From a functional core and some initialisation files describing the user interface properties such as the tasks, their structuration and the presentation, GIPSE allows the online construction of self-running applications.

Key words: Model-Based Systems, CAD, User Interface, CADUI

1.   INTRODUCTION

User interface and dialogue control are a large part of any software. They are hard to implement, to debug and to maintain [11]. The problem grows much worse when the application dialogue extends, or when it follows some dialogue strategy where relations between user tasks are not well defined. Such is the case in CAD systems. The user must be able to express a lot of geometrical relations between entities, leading to a structured dialogue where parameters of tasks may be given by the way of a (possible huge) number of subtasks.

A lot of tools have been created in order to facilitate designing user interfaces. These tools range from toolkits and application frameworks to model based systems. In the latter ones, the desired user interface is automatically generated from a specification made of declarative models. However, few of these tools address the problem of structured dialogues.

Our goal in this paper is to describe GIPSE, a model based system specialised in applications where this dialogue form is usual. In the subsequent section, we explain more precisely the particularities of our main domain, CAD software. A natural decomposition of structured dialogue in a general task structure follows. Then we describe GIPSE, our specialised model based system, and give some example of its use.

2.   DOMAIN

Technical design is a domain where construction constraints are largely used. In order to be helpful for end users, Computer Aided Design (CAD) software have to facilitate the expression of these constraints. Graphical applications do not usually ask the user for carefully positioning objects. On the contrary, CAD systems require the user to strictly define the geometrical entities that make up technical objects. So, systems offer a wide range of methods for constructing these entities. A software from the former type may allow the construction of an ellipse with two mouse interactions, and then may allow its modification by the way of direct manipulation. On the contrary, CAD systems allow the creation of these entities in terms of centre, radius, axis, or allow the use of constraints such as tangency or coincidence. Moreover, these parameters can themselves be defined by the way of numerical or grapho-numerical expressions. Circle creation, for example, can use a subtask that returns the projection of a position on a line to define its centre, and then use another subtask to calculate the distance between two entities as the radius. The dialogue associated with a task is recursively including dialogues associated with subtasks allowing the realisation of intermediate goals.

This kind of dialogue is called a structured one [15]. On the one hand, it gives to the user a very powerful way of expressing constructs constraints. On the other hand, using these dialogues requires specific software architecture, to reduce the combinatorial explosion of subtask calls. Some examples of these architectures may be found [4, 10, 18].

Nevertheless definition and implementation of these dialogues is very difficult. Current user interface development systems lack the ability to describe them. These systems, such as JANUS [1], MASTERMIND [20] TRIDENT [2] or MECANO/Mobi-D [16, 17], may be used in fields where the user's tasks are well defined. Examples of such fields are database manipulation (JANUS), or stock management (Mobi-D). In such systems, the number of tasks allowed to the user at any point of the session is limited. In contrast, structured dialogues give the user many ways of expressing his/her needs: any (sub)task able to produce a parameter from a currently waited kind must be available.

3. STRUCTURED DIALOGUES

Structured dialogues may be seen as a set of producers and consumers. Some tasks consume data produced by some other tasks. In our previous example, the "Create Circle" task gets data from two others tasks, "Projection" and "Distance", which produce respectively one position and one real value.

Tasks may be decomposed in three categories: terminal tasks, production tasks and opportunistic tasks.

- Terminal tasks use data, but do not produce[1] them. They are used to modify the application (mainly geometrical) model. Some examples are tasks allowing entity creation, destruction or modification. These tasks are the main reason for the existence of CAD systems. At any moment, only one terminal task may be active. One can not create a circle while creating a line. Two dialogue strategies may apply: either the expression of a new terminal task is forbidden (by disabling menu components), either this expression replaces the current one, which is then cancelled, with all its subtasks.

- Production tasks consume data in order to produce another data that will be transmitted to another tasks. These subtasks exist solely in the context of another task, either a terminal task or a production (sub)task. If no terminal task is in use (i.e. the user is not currently modifying the model), then no production task must be available, as there is no one to transmit data. It is the existence of such tasks that define structured dialogue. Production tasks are defined by the result they give, and not by their client (to which task they give it). The "Centre" task gives a position, and may be used to define the extremity of a line or the centre of an ellipse. Last, production tasks do not modify the application model. They may extract some information from their parameters ("Centre"), or they may calculate some value ("Distance"), but they do not create, modify or destroy any entity while doing so.

- Opportunist tasks are the third kind of tasks in structured dialogues. These are the tasks that neither modify the model, neither produce information for other tasks. These tasks allow end users for asking for a modification of the system to allow better realisation of tasks. An example of

---

[1] Be careful that we are interested here in dialogue. So, when we claim that terminal tasks do not produce anything, it is in the sense of dialogue: they do not produce any data (dialogue token) for other tasks. Obviously, they produce entities in the CAD system model.

this kind of task is the translation of the visible content of a window. Opportunist tasks modify the presentation of data, but do not change them. These tasks may be used at any moment, without cancelling the currently active terminal task. The former temporarily replaces the latter, until it is completed. The terminal task then resumes as if no interruption had ever been done. In our previous example of a circle construction, the user may, at any moment, ask for a zoom, define the position that delimits the zoomed area, and then resume his/her construction.

4.   GIPSE: A MODEL-BASED SYSTEM

GIPSE is a model-based system specialised in software that use structured dialogues. Its main goal is to provide a basis than can be extended later to provide additional capacities. One of the stated goals was to allow for fast modification of the dialogue.

GIPSE does not generate code. It is composed of a software component that links itself with the application in order to manage the dialogue. It acts as the dialogue controller for the whole application. As the application starts-up, specifications of the dialogue properties and functional core functionalities are loaded from textual models. From this point, GIPSE manages the dialogue until the end of the session with the application.

This structure has several benefits. First, as the model is directly used by the system, there is no recompilation time whenever there is a change in the dialogue structure. Second, as the dialogue is itself a data structure, in opposition to hard coded dialogue, it is possible to dynamically modify it. The user may be allowed to remove unneeded functionnalities, or to add new ones, created by the way of Programming by Demonstration (PbD) [3]. This leads to the possible extension and specialisation of a system by the end user himself/herself [14]. Third, it is possible to integrate verification tools in the software itself. Some works have already been done on that subject [9]. This ability to examine the software dialogue, even during run time, comes handy when the end user is able to modify the dialogue. Inconsistency or incorrect dialogue structures may be notified.

In this paper, we do not focus on the PbD features of GIPSE, which is a purely interactive tool that allows developing interactive applications by extension/specialisation [6, 13, 14]. We only deal with declarative models that are used by GIPSE to manage the interactive system

4.1   Task structuration in GIPSE

GIPSE uses an architectural model called H^4 [7], which was designed specifically for CAD systems. In the H^4 model, the dialogue controller is composed of a hierarchical set of agents, named dialogue **interactors**, relatively to the theory of Interactors ([8, 12]). Each of them corresponds to a task level: they group and structure system **tasks** in a hierarchical fashion. They are defined by the nature of information they accept as input, and produce output information, which is the result of the task. Usual dialogue interactors in drawing applications include *designation* (picking graphical entities), *information* (giving information such as centre or extremity of entities), *calculus* (projection, distance), and *creation*. Communications between interactors are automatically managed by a **Monitor**. Interactors may accept information from any other interactor that is lower in the hierarchy, without knowing who produced it. The communication unit is a typed element, named **Token**, which may either be a command (order to initiate an action) or data (parameter of actions). The monitor transmits tokens to the next interactor in the hierarchy that waits for such typed data.

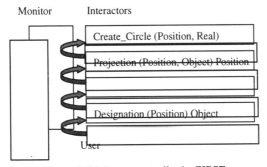

Figure 1. Dialogue controller in GIPSE.

This model of dialogue controller allows for a great deal of independence between tasks. The monitor manages communication between separate task levels. Possible interactions between tasks of the same level are managed by the interactor that manages this level. Each task can be defined independently from each other. The same thing can be said about interactors. Each one is independent from the other, and manages the tasks at its own level. The number of other interactors able to provide or consume data does not matter. An interactor provides data to and consumes data from the monitor, and transmits theses data to any active task via the monitor. One consequence of that structure is no need for complex task and dialogue models (see section 4.2). It should be noticed that this model is focusing on dialogue control. Presentation of model objects is out of its scope. CAD entities are highly structured and relational. Their presentation on the screen is therefore left to the functional core, using some specialised software component.

4.2   Specification of CAD software with GIPSE

A system, in the H^4 model, can be specified from three components: tokens (communication unit between tasks), tasks (communication unit between user and system) and interactors (task structuring unit). The monitor
can be derived from the interactors order.

The description of these components, along with a description of the
presentation, allows for the complete specification of the application dialogue. The token specification is akin to the object model, whereas tasks
specification constitutes the task model, interactors specification represents
the dialogue model and presentation specification states for the presentation
model.

4.2.1   Object model

Tokens are objects that communicate user's intention. They may contain
data (references to model objects, or values), or commands initiating tasks.
Commands, and some data such as string or numerical value, exist in any
application. Most of them, however, are application-dependent and refer to
model objects.

Tokens are a communication unit, allowing tasks to freely exchange data.
The exact structure and value of these objects are of no importance to other
dialogue controller objects. The interactor that manages a given task does
not care what is the value of a position. What is important is the nature of the
transmitted data, as it allows it to know when the task may be called (i.e.
have received all parameters).

```
-- Tokens
Rectangle
Line
Point
Arc
Unbounded_Line
Circle
-- Groups
Support_Object    {Unbounded_Line, Circle}
Drawing_Object    {Rectangle, Line, Point, Arc}
Graphical_Object  {Support_Object, Drawing_Object}
```

Figure 2. Object model example.

The object model of the dialogue controller contains the list of application-dependent token types, and provides for a structuring mechanism (Figure 2.). This structuring mechanism (groups) allows for concision in task description, as we will see in the next section.

4.2.2 Task model

Thanks for the H^4 architecture, tasks may be defined individually, without any connection between them. A name, a list of input parameters and one (optional) output parameter define each task. This specification allows the system to automatically disable any task that cannot give any parameter of the waited kind. As it has been said, it defines the tasks in terms of what it takes and what it produces.

Some help line may also be added to the description. This is used by the system to provide the user for dynamic help. Figure 3 shows an example of task description. In the second case, we can see the use of structuring: only one task description is required for all the graphical entities (every entities in our small example).

```
-- Terminal task
Task{
    Create_Circle (Position, Real)
    Help {Circle creation by center and radius}
    Parameter {Position, "Center"}
    parameter {Real, "Radius"}
}
-- Production task
Task {
    Center {Graphical_Object} Position
    Help {give an Object's Center}
    Parameter {Graphical_Object, "Give an object"}
}
```

Figure 3. Task model example

Other characteristics of the task may be added for PbD purpose (see later). Such characteristics are, for example, the reaction of the task when macro-recording is on. Some tasks may be ignored (that is, not recorded), while others are strictly forbidden ("save" for example).

4.2.3 Interactor Model

The Interactor model defines the dialogue. Each interactor defines the dialogue at its own level, while the hierarchy of interactors gives an implicit rule on which task may use which other tasks. A task from a given interactor can use any task from a lower level interactor, given that, this lower task is able to produce data that are waited by the higher one.

Interactors define the dialogue at their level using a MAD-like approach [19]. Tasks are structured with Alternative (ALT) and Sequence (SEQ), possibly repetitive (ALT* and SEQ*).

For example, the "Creation" interactor definition may look like this:

```
Interacteur Creation {
  Seq {
   Alt {
     Task {New}
     Task {Open}
   }
   Alt {
     Alt* {
      Task {Create_Circle     (Position, Real)}
      Task {Create_Rectangle (Position, Position)}
      Task {Create_Line     (Position, Position)}
     }
     Task {Close}
     Task {Quit}
   }
  }
}
```

Figure 4. Dialogue model example.

The end user must begin by either creating a new document or opening an existing one. It then can either create an indefinite amount of objects (the Alt*), or finish the session by closing the document or exiting the application. Other interactors are defined in the same way. Most of them are composed of a simple alternative between multiple tasks. The language constructs are very few; the communications between interactors and the behaviour of the monitor (described in 4.1) extend automatically the possibilities of the language.

This description defines the static constraints on dialogue: what is eventually available at any given moment. Dynamic constraints are managed by the system at run-time: in the set of available tasks, only tasks that produce expected data are effectively available. Others are disabled (greyed out) by the system. This is completely automatic.

The description of the dialogue in independent chunks, themselves composed of structured tasks, and linked by explicit rules, allows for an easy description of the whole dialogue. Adding a new task to the system implies only the modification of the interactor that will manage it, to have this task fully integrated with the whole application dialogue. The same description, realised via a state-transition diagram, would be unmanageable, as the number of possible transitions between tasks is exponential. The adjunction of a new task would, in this case, imply the creation of one transition from any task able to consume the produced data, and to any task able to produce waited data.

4.2.4   Presentation Model

Presentation of a CAD system may be boiled down to one (or more) visualisation space and some way to express commands and data to the system. The former does not concern us, as it is under the control of the model itself. The latter are composed of menus and dialogue boxes that allow entering specific data, such as strings, or numerical values.

The presentation model we use is based on tasks, and concentrates on ways of initiating them. We use menus and submenus as containers for labels or pictures that, when used by user, activate the corresponding tasks.

```
Menu Objet {
   Label Line    {Create_Line (Position, Position)}
   Label Circle    {
       Create_Circle (Position, Reel)
       Create_Circle (Position, Position)}
   Label Rectangle {Create_Rectangle (Position, Position)}
   Menu Modification {
       Label Color {Modify_Color (Object)}
       Label Style {Modify_Style (Object)}
   }
}
```

Figure 5. Presentation model example.

As shown by the "Circle" label (Figure 5), a label may be associated with more than one task. The only restriction is that these tasks should be in the same interactor. When the user selects this label, both tasks are initiated. The system then allows unrestricted use of any task that give a parameter for any of these two tasks. A parameter is transmitted to any task that waits for it. A parameter that is accepted by one task and not by the other automatically cancels the second one. For example if the user clicks on "Circle" (initiating both tasks) and then gives a numerical value, then the task he/she is asking for is the one with the numerical parameter. The other one is then silently cancelled.

4.2.5   Example of use

We will present in this section an example of system modification. We suppose that a new functionality, defined by (and associated to) its specification "Intersection (Object, Object) Position" has been added to the functional core. From this point, we add to the textual task model the information associated with this task.

```
...
Task {
   Intersection (Graphical_Object, Graphical_Object)
                                          Position
   Help {return the nearest intersection of the two object }
   Parameter {Graphical_Object, " First Object "}
   Parameter {Graphical_Object, " Second Object "}
}
...
```

We then add the task to an interactor. As it is a production task (it returns a "position"), that calculates its response from the parameters (in opposition to extracting information of these parameters), we place it in the "Calculus" interactor.

```
...
Interacteur Calculus {
  Alt {
    Task {Centre    (Graphical_Object) Position }
    Task {Distance (Position, Position) Real}
    Task {Intersection (Graphical_Object, Graphical_Object)
Position}
  }
}
...
```

and we add a label in a menu to allow the end user for using the task.

```
Menu Calculus {
  Label Centre    {
     Create_Line (Position, Position)}
  label Distance {
     Create_Circle (Position, Reel)}
  label Intersection {
     Intersection (Graphical_Object, Graphical_Object) Po-
sition }
  }
```

From this point the new task is fully usable in the system. The user may use it as a subtask for any higher task asking for a position. In the same way, any task producing a Graphical_Object and belonging to a lower interactor may be used to give its parameters.

We describe here a purely textual way to accomplish this modification. As we stated upper, it is possible with GIPSE to do the same modification in a purely interactive way, using PbD possibilities of GIPSE. The only thing we cannot do interactively is modifying the object model, which is a work that has been conducted in our laboratory [21].

5.   RELATED WORK

GIPSE is a specialised model based system (MBS). It is specialised in an application domain that presents some very specific characteristics, which influence the required dialogue structure. The main difference between GIPSE and other existing MBS lies therefore in its dialogue management system. Most MBS, as we have already stated, have few or no support for structured dialogues. They are adapted for the conception of forms applications, but are unusable for the design and conception of CAD systems.

GIPSE has some common points with SACADO [5, 10], another development environment oriented towards CAD systems. Both use the notion of hierarchical level of dialogue tasks. However, the model used and the assertion made by the system on the application are different. SACADO makes it necessary for the developer to define the set of relations between tasks: any function that may be used while creating a circle to produce a parameter must be explicitly given. On the contrary, the hierarchical decomposition described in the dialogue model of GIPSE gives an implicit set, whose exact content has not to be defined by the developer.

6.   CONCLUSION AND FURTHER WORKS

As a model based system specialised in CAD systems, GIPSE facilitates the conception and development of applications using structured dialogues. Using a functional core and some initialisation files that describe the dialogue properties (the tasks, their structuring and the presentation), GIPSE allows the online generation of dialogue and the execution of the application.

GIPSE is a very flexible system, which allows the modification of the dialogue without any recompilation, by the modification of human-readable text files. Current works aim to extend this flexibility in several ways. End-user programming, that allows adding and removing user-produced tasks, has already been integrated in the system. The creation of new category of objects and associated tasks is actually in study. Another currently studied extension is the ability to mix structured dialogue and direct manipulation, allowing the user to choose his/her interaction depending on his/her goals [13]. Last, we are now integrating validation and verification tools in the system, to warn or prevent the user for creating non functional dialogues [9]. These additions will allow GIPSE to become a full CAD software development environment, an actual CADUI product.

REFERENCES

[1]   Balzert, H., *From OOA to GUI : The JANUS-System*, in Proc. IFIP TC13 Human-Computer Interaction INTERACT'95 (Lillehammer, 27-29 June, 1995), Chapman & Hall, London, 1995, pp. 319-324.

[2]   Bodart, F., Hennebert, A.-M., Leheureux, J.-M., Provot, I., B. Sacré and Vanderdonckt, J., *Towards a systematic building of software Architectures : the Trident Methodological Guide*, in Proc. Eurographics Workshop on Design, Specification, and Verification of Interactive Systems DSV-IS'95 (Bonas, June 1995), Springer-Verlag, Vienna, 1995, pp. 262-278.

[3]   Cypher, A., *Watch What I Do: Programming by Demonstration,* The MIT Press, 1993.

[4]   Fekete, J.-D., *Un modèle multicouche pour la construction d'applications graphiques interactives.* PhD Université Paris-Sud, Orsay, 1996.

[5]   Gardan, Y., Jung, J.-P. and Martin, B., *An End-User oriented approach to design man-machine interface for CAD/CAM*, in *Proc. IEEE Internationel Conference on Systems,*

Man and Cybernetics (Le Touquet, 17-20 October 1993, 1993), IEEE Computer Society Press, Los Alamitos, 1993, pp. 525-530.

[6]   Girard, P., Patry, G., Pierra, G. and Potier, J.-C., *Deux exemples d'utilisation de la Programmation par Démonstration en Conception Assistée par Ordinateur*, Revue Internationale de CFAO et d'informatique graphique, Vol. 12, No. 1-2, 1997, pp. 169-188.

[7]   Guittet, L., *Contribution à l'Ingénierie des Interfaces Homme-Machine - Théorie des Interacteurs et Architecture H4 dans le système NODAOO*, PhD Université de Poitiers, 1995.

[8]   Harrison, M.D. and Duce, D.A., *A review of formalisms for describing interactive behaviour*, University of York, January 7, 1994.

[9]   Jambon, F., Girard, P. and Boisdron, Y., *Dialogue Validation from Task Analysis*, in Proc. Eurographics Workshop on Design, Specification, and Verification of Interactive Systems DSV-IS'99 (Minho, Portugal, 2-4 June, 1999), Springer-Verlag, Vienna, 1999, pp. 201-221.

[10] Martin, B., *Contribution pour une nouvelle Approche du dialogue Homme-Machine en CFAO*, PhD Université de Metz, 1995.

[11] Myers, B.A., *User Interface Software Tools*, ACM Transactions on Computer Human Interaction, Vol. 2, No. 1, 1995, pp. 64-103.

[12] Paternò, F., *A Theory of User-Interaction Objects*, Journal of Visual Languages and Computing, Vol. 5, No. 3, 1994, pp. 227-249.

[13] Patry, G., *Contribution à la conception du dialogue Homme Machine dans les applications graphiques interactives de conception technique : le système GIPSE*, PhD Université de Poitiers, 1999.

[14] Patry, G. and Girard, P., *From Adaptable Interfaces to Model-Based Interface Development: The GIPSE Project*, in Proc. ERCIM Workshop on User Interfaces for All (UI4ALL'97) (Obernai, 3-4 november, 1997), INRIA Lorraine, 1997, pp. 127-133.

[15] Pierra, G., *Towards a taxonomy for interactive graphics systems*, in Proc. Eurographics Workshop on Design, Specification, Verification of Interactive Systems DSV-IS'95 (Bonas, June 7-9, 1995), Springer-Verlag, Vienna, 1995, pp. 362-370.

[16] Puerta, A., *The MECANO project : comprehensive and integrated support for Model-Based Interface development*, in Proc. Computer-Aided Design of User Interface CADUI'96 (Namur, 5-7 June, 1996), Presses Universitaire de Namur, Namur, 1996, pp. 19-35.

[17] Puerta, A.R., *A Model-Based Interface Development Environment*, IEEE Software, Vol. 14, No. 4, 1997, pp. 40-47.

[18] Qiang, L., Wei, L., Ke, X. and Jiaguang, S., *An Event-Driven and Object Oriented FrameWork for Human Computer Interface of CAD System*, in Proc. CAD & Graphics'97 (Shenzen, 2-5 Dec., 1997), International Academic Publishers, Volume 1, 1997, pp. 42-45.

[19] Scapin, D.L. and Pierret-Golbreich, C., *Towards a method for task description : MAD*, in *Working with display units*, Elsevier Science Publishers, North-Holland, 1990, pp. 371-380.

[20] Szekely, P., Sukaviriya, P., Castells, P., Muthukumarasamy, J. and E. Salcher. *Declarative interface models for user interface construction tools : the MASTERMIND approach*, in Proc. IFIP TC2/WG2.7 Working Conference on Engineering for Human-Computer Interaction EHCI'95 Grand Targhee Resort, USA, 14-18 August, 1995), Chapman & Hall, London, 1995, pp. 120-150.

[21] Texier, G. and Guittet, L. User defined objects are first class citizens, in *Proc. Computer-Aided Design of User Interface (CADUI'99)* (Louvain-Neuve, Belgique, 1999), Kluwer Academic Publishers, Dordrecht, in this book.

Chapter 7

VISTO: A MORE DECLARATIVE GUI FRAMEWORK

Kris Aerts and Karel De Vlaminck – (*Kris.Aerts@kc.kuleuven.ac.be*)
Katholieke Universiteit Leuven, Flanders, Belgium

Abstract   By inverting the widget - call back relationship and by providing selectors, a suitable abstraction for concrete widget choices, Visto provides a more declarative approach to defining user interfaces, building on the declarativeness of the lazy functional language Haskell.

1.   CONTEXT

The functional programming research community has always paid a special interest in declarativity. Although there exists no water proof definition of what a declarative system is, a system can be called more declarative than another if it focuses more on *what* should be done instead of on *how* it should be done.

The Haskell [4] *quicksort* definition below can therefore be considered far more declarative than the equivalent Pascal or Java procedure, because the latter extensively spells out *how* the ordered sequence is to be calculated (through various variable manipulations), whereas the Haskell program simply says *what* to do: append the ordered sequence of smaller elements before the ordered sequence of larger elements.

$$quicksort\ [] \quad = []$$
$$quicksort\ (x:xs) = quicksort\ [y \mid y \leftarrow xs,\ y < x]$$
$$++ (x : (quicksort\ [y \mid y \leftarrow xs,\ y > x]))$$

Typical GUI programming is *not* declarative. It focuses on the *how* in 2 ways:

- first one chooses a particular kind of widget (a button, a menu or a key short cut, ...) instead of providing suitable abstractions,

- thereafter one adds a call back function to the widget to provide the desired functionality. In this sequence one first chooses *how* something is to be invoked (through which widget) and afterwards adds *what* is to be done (which call back function) instead of vice versa.

Visto is a prototype result of research in the functional community focused on finding a more declarative user interface definition. To this purpose we provide abstractions over widgets and insist that the GUI ('widget') is added to the functionality ('call back').

Because Visto finds its roots in textual programming, no graphical design tools have been implemented yet, although some are planned for future stages.

2.   VISTO'S MENTAL MODEL

Most GUI systems consider the user interface as a collection of widgets totally independent from the application. Their programming language provides widget combinators or they implement a tool for drawing and positioning the widgets. Adding functionality is typically accomplished by attaching call back functions to the widgets. Changing the user interface then becomes a difficult task, requiring not only replacing the widgets, but also defining new call back functions, as their type depends on the widget.

Instead of adding behaviour and functionality to a user interface, Visto insists that a user interface is added to the defined functionality.

The traditional technique is also potentially dangerous: the drawn user interface may look good, but if it doesn't offer all the desired functionality, it's no good user interface. Only if we clearly identify the desired functionality of the application and know which functions should be present in the user interface, we can constitute a good interface. Visto does precisely that.

The objects in Visto and their methods describe the functionality of the application. This is the start basis of any Visto project. In a second phase the programmer identifies which methods are to be called from within the user interface. To that purpose he associates GUI invokers, such as buttons, key presses and menu items with methods. A selected method can be associated with any number of invokers to allow alternatives in the interface and to please both expert and non expert users. This also allows for easy modification: just change, add or remove some invokers and recompile!

Another requirement of any user interface is consistent information display. Visto offers support for that too. If objects wish to display information, they have to define a **draw** method. If they do so, Visto takes care that this **draw** method is applied every time the object receives a message. The development of the Visto objects is therefore automatically centred around the visualisation of information.

3.   STAGES OF DEVELOPMENT

In this section we present the suggested itinerary for developing a proper Visto application. After all, Visto is more a design methodology then an advanced tool.

3.1   FUNCTIONAL APPLICATION CODE

Visto is designed for the implementation of a graphical user interface on top of (existing) Haskell programs. Its design philosophy therefore inherits many functional features, such as the requirement that every Visto methods returns a return value and the use of a single state variable per object. These matters are no key issue for this conference and will be abstracted away in this paper.

We haven chosen a functional source language because of its distinct declarative nature. This offers many advantages such as provable correctness, strong typing and concise, readable and maintainable code [2]. Haskell, the standard lazy functional language, was the natural choice.

Although the GUI of the finished application will be event-driven, the Haskell code of the application layer doesn't have to take this into account. It can be safely developed using traditional software methodology techniques.

3.2   VISTO OBJECT DEFINITION

Visto – for VISual State Transforming Objects – is a prototype based object oriented system [5] with special features for deriving objects from objects and for the model-view relationship. The visual aspect of Visto is important as we expect the programmer to define objects that correspond to visual *user* entities. In a word processor the *visual* model uses texts, whereas the application layer may prefer to use paragraphs, undo buffers and other logical entities hidden for the user.

We do not expect the user to work with these logical entities, but rather with *visual* objects. The Visto programmer will define a set of objects, and, for each of these objects, a number of methods for actions on the objects. These methods constitute the complete set of actions the user interface can use. Screen refreshes are automatically performed using the **draw** method.

3.3   CHOOSING INVOKERS

Objects typically communicate through messages, thereby invoking each others' methods. In Visto methods can be invoked both by objects sending messages and by the GUI itself.

The methods defined in the previous stage constitute the complete set of actions that the GUI may invoke. The next stage is choosing which actions will effectively be present. This is done by associating invokers with methods. Note that we have first considered which actions on the different objects may be needed and only afterwards decided which ones will be present in the GUI.

Because we start from the methods, it is easier to ensure that the application provides all the needed functionality and not just a nice looking interface.

The programmer can associate a single method with *any* number of invokers. This allows different alternatives to be addressed in a simple way, e.g. a menu item and a button for the first time user or a key short cut for the expert user.

Changing the user interface then becomes quite simple, like replacing a button invoker with a menu invoker. This is quite different from the traditional approach where the type and parameter count of the call back function depends on the widget used. So changing a widget may incorporate quite some work.

Following the example of J. Johnson [3] we provide an abstraction for the actual widgets, called selectors [1]. In this technique we focus on the declarative aspect of the widgets: selecting the appropriate data. Examples of selectors are:

- Selecting a single value from a range or from a discrete set,

- Selecting a specified number of values,

- Selecting between n_1 and n_2 values,

- Special interest selectors such as currency, time, ...

This stage offers two steps with an enhanced declarativity: focusing on the functionality over the widgets by adding invokers to methods and not vice versa, and abstracting away from the actual widgets by through selectors.

3.4   CREATING THE FINAL GUI: LAYING OUT AND INSTANTIATING INVOKERS

This final stage will be performed in a (not yet implemented) tool for directly drawing the user interface using direct manipulation. The tool will first analyse the Visto program and collect all the used invokers. These invokers will then constitute the precise set of things the programmer has to put in the user interface. It can be compared with a puzzle where the puzzler has all the pieces in front of him and assembles them together until all pieces fit, while being assured of the completeness of the result. The same applies to Visto. Once all the selectors have been instantiated and inserted in the interface design, the programmer is assured that the interface provides all the desired functionality. This is different from traditional tools where the programmer has little or no guidance on which widgets to use. Such an interface may then look good, but miss some essential functionality.

When placing the selectors on screen, the programmer chooses between various visual instances, such as for example an entry, a slider bar, button rows and columns, key short cuts, ... A time can be selected by combining such range selectors for hour, minutes and seconds or by manipulating the hands of a clock, ...

A different user interface with identical functionality can then be created by instantiating the selectors differently or by drawing other combinations. Changing the functionality of the user interface is accomplished by adding, removing or changing some invokers in the previous stage.

This way the semantically different changes in the user interface (changing outlook or functionality) have to take place in different stages of development, which is always a desired feature of a methodology: keeping separate decisions separate.

4.   A SHORT EXAMPLE

Tradition dictates the counter example. Although this example combines many features in one object, such as state and behaviour, visual representation and invoker, which in real life should be better separated, it can still be used to clarify the framework.

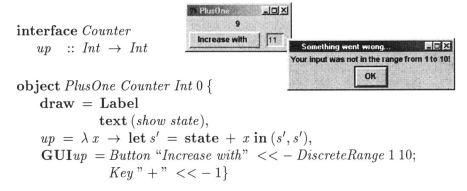

interface *Counter*
    up   :: *Int* → *Int*

object *PlusOne Counter Int* 0 {
    draw = **Label**
               text (*show state*),
    up = λ *x* → **let** *s′* = **state** + *x* **in** (*s′*, *s′*),
    GUI*up* = *Button* "*Increase with*" << − *DiscreteRange* 1 10;
         Key " + " << − 1}

The **interface** simply states which methods an object has to provide in order to be a *Counter*: *up* which takes an *Int* with which to increase the counter.

PlusOne is a *Counter* with a state of type *Int* with inital value *0*. This object supplies a **draw** method, so the state of the object is shown on a label.

GUI*up* gives two invokers for the *up* method: after clicking the button "Increase with" the counter is increased with the value selected by the *DiscreteRange* selector (selecting a number between 1 and 10[1]), or by pressing the key '+' in which case the counter is increased by 1.

These invokers have been defined completely separate from the methods. To change the user interface we don't have to mess with call back functions, but only have to redefine the **GUI***up* body.

If we consider the object *PlusOne* as the model (with already a view present in its own definition – to make the first example self-contained –), we can define another view using the **expand** derivation.

---

[1] In the screen shot we can see that a requester is displayed because the input *11* was not in the proper range.

expandInterface *CounterView* **from** *Counter*
  _up
expand *Plus One View CounterView String* "*Dutch*" **from** *PlusOne* {
  draw = **Label**
    let counter = **superState**
    text (*translate state counter*) }

As a view should not change its model, we remove the *up* method. This can be done in Visto by preceding with an underscore the method name in the derived interface. The view object *PlusOneView* only defines a **draw** method, which simply displays the number in textual form. We use the keyword **superState** to gain access to the model's state. Note that the view object can have a state on its own. Although we haven't defined a method to change that state here, *PlusOneView* contains the language in which to translate the number. The (self defined) Haskell function *translate* takes a language and a number and returns the value in textual form.

5.   CONCLUSIONS

The Visto methodology of concentrating on the visual objects, defining methods for manipulating that (displayed) information and supplying GUI-invokers for the methods opens a brand new perspective on user interface design. Especially the move from call back functions to GUI-invokers is an important shift.

Although Visto has not reached an entirely mature phase, this fresh declarative approach deserves further research.

References

[1] K. Aerts, K. De Vlaminck: *A GUI on top of a functional language (abstract)* Proceedings of ACM SIGPLAN International Conference on Functional Programming, 1997, p.308

[2] P. Hudak, M.P. Jones: *Haskell vs. Ada vs. C++ vs. Awk vs. ... An Experiment in Software Prototyping Productivity* Available from *http://www.haskell.org/papers/NSWC/jfp.ps*, 1994, 16 pages

[3] J. Johnson: *Going Beyond User-Interface Widgets.* CHI'92 Proceedings, 1992 , 273-279.

[4] S. Peyton Jones, J. Hughes (editors): *Haskell 98: A Non-strict, Purely Functional Language* Report on the Programming Language Haskell 98, Available from http://www.haskell.org/.

[5] W.R. Smith: *Using a Prototype-based Language for User Interface: The Newton Project's Experience* In ACM Sigplan Notices, OOPSLA, (1995), Vol. 30, no. **10**, 61-72

Chapter 8

BEYOND AUTOMATIC GENERATION – EXPLORATORY APPROACH TO UI DESIGN

Srdjan Kovacevic
Aonix, 5040 Shoreham Place, San Diego, CA 92122
Tel: +1-619-824-0214 - Fax: 619/824-0212
srdjan@acm.org

Abstract   Automatic generation of user interfaces holds a promise of improving productivity by working at a higher level of abstraction. However, UI design is a creative activity and cannot be fully automated. It is critical that a design tool provides adequate support for exploration. The paper presents a model-based approach to UI development that combines automatic generation of user interfaces with design transformations. Design transformations are platform and language-independent abstractions for exploring alternative designs. The paper presents how this approach is validated in TACTICS, which integrates a compositional model of user interfaces and a transformational model of the UI design space. The paper gives examples of design transformations and illustrates them using design patterns.

Keywords: model-based user interface, task model, automatic generation, design transformations, design patterns.

1.   INTRODUCTION

The growing complexity and importance of user interfaces increases demands on UI designers and developers. At the same time, there are not enough skilled UI designers and developers to meet this demand. What they need are better tools to improve their productivity by allowing them to focus on creative aspects of their work, and automating the mundane ones.

Automatic generation of user interfaces holds a promise of speeding up implementation and improving productivity by working at a higher level of abstraction. It can also improve the quality of design by utilizing knowledge about UI design guidelines and graphical design (e.g., [4]).

Automatic generation of user interfaces is already in widespread use, by millions every day. Every time one opens a web page, a browser automatically generates it from an HTML specification. The issue is not whether automatic generation is feasible and practical, but how effective it can be. While declaratively specified (HTML-based) user interfaces are still limited and more sophisticated web applications require plug-ins or procedural (Java) code, it is not inherent limitation of the automatic generation, as demonstrated by research in model-based user interfaces [3, 7, 10, 12, 15, 16]. It is more due to the underlying model. HTML uses a simple model and that limits the range of user interfaces it can describe and their capabilities. By using a richer model and specification language, advanced UIs can be described (and generated) as well.

The real problem is therefore not in automatic generation of user interfaces in itself, but how it can be most effectively used for UI design. UI design is a creative activity and cannot be fully automated. It is critical that a UI design tool provide adequate support for exploration. That means not only supporting a wide range of UIs, but equally important is support for exploring and changing designs – how one can chose among all different possible UI designs.

At any point, a designer must have ownership and full control over the design. While the goal is to work at a higher level of abstraction and spare the designer of low-level implementation details, the tool must allow the designer to control how the high-level specification is mapped onto a UI. Yet, the designer should not be forced to specify every little detail. This balancing of productivity and flexibility is one of the issues UI tools must resolve.

In this paper I discuss a model-based approach to UI development that combines automatic generation with design transformations. Automatic generation produces a working UI from a high level specification, captured in a model. It is used to produce quickly and easily a starting point for exploration and to automate mundane parts of UI development. Design transformations provide (high-level) abstractions for exploring alternative designs.

This approach has been validated in TACTICS (*Transformation- And Composition-based Tool for Interface Creation and Support*). TACTICS integrates a compositional model of user interfaces and a transformational model of the UI design space. The TACTICS model is compositional because it views a user interface as a collection of primitives structured based on the application and on the desired dialogue style; the model identifies user interface components and structuring principles for assembling components into a coherent interface. This is a base for automatic generation. The behavior and the look-and-feel of a UI are explained in terms of properties of UI components and the way they are structured. The model is transformational because it views the UI design space as a grid and defines a set of transformations for moving along the grid lines that connect different UI designs. Transformations modify UI structures to achieve a different look-and-feel, making it easy for a designer to generate and try alternative designs. The model also integrates additional knowledge for providing assistance in this process.

The automatic generation of UIs in TACTICS is discussed in [7, 9]. Here I focus on the transformation part and how it complements automatic generation. The paper is organized as follows. The next section describes the UI development process supported by TACTICS. Section 3 overviews the automatic generation and presents design patterns driving the UI generation from a task model. Section 4 discusses design transformations, principles behind how they work, and examples illustrating their use, including transformed design patterns. Sections 5 and 6 contain further Discussion and Conclusions.

2.   GENERATING AND EXPLORING USER INTERFACES IN TACTICS

Figure 1 illustrates the UI development process supported by TACTICS. It distinguishes two distinct steps: (1) describe application semantics, including user tasks and domain model, and (2) specify UI details specific to a desired look and feel. Each step can be repeated, as needed for iterative and incremental development.

This decomposition takes advantage of the fact that each user interface is a product of two sets of requirements: (1) application information requirements and (2) look and feel requirements. To fully define a UI, we need to specify both.

The primary role of a user interface is to serve its underlying application. It must meet all its information requirements, both in terms of its inputs and outputs. A user interacting with an application must be able to specify what action to perform and all input values for action parameters. The application must also be able to present all relevant information back to the user. These are mandatory requirements for any user interface – if they are not satisfied, the application may not be fully functional (i.e., parts of it may not work, either because it is not possible to specify all required parameters or results cannot be presented to the user).

Typically, there are many different ways the application information requirements can be satisfied. For instance, different interaction techniques can be used to specify input value, or values can be specified in varying order.

Which particular user interface is selected is determined by the look and feel requirements. These requirements are optional in a sense that even if they are not fully satisfied (e.g., there is no desired interaction technique available on a target platform and a different technique must be used), the application will still be functional. The look and feel requirements affect the application usability and not its functionality.

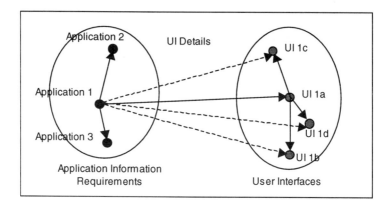

Figure 1. TACTICS approach to user interface development.

Approach: generate + transform. Figure 1 illustrates that each application can be mapped onto more than one UI. If we change some of the application requirements, we map it to a different set of interfaces. Furthermore, the mapping can be decomposed into two or more steps. The first step (the solid arrow from Application$_1$ to UI$_{1a}$) maps an application to default UI that meets all its information requirements. The subsequent steps apply different look and feel requirements, mapping a given UI to different designs (e.g., the solid arrow from UI$_{1a}$ to UI$_{1d}$). This is equivalent to transforming a UI to another UI while preserving aspects derived from the application information requirements. Design transformations allow exploration of different UI designs in a model-based UI environment. More details on design transformations can be found in [2, 5].

This approach brings several advantages. It simplifies the mapping rules performing the automatic generation.as they do not have to accommodate all possible combinations of UI settings. Adding new variation points is also made easier as it does not require changes to the mapping rules. Furthermore, a designer does not have to specify all UI details up front to get to a working UI. Yet, the designer can do it by specifying "UI hints" that get translated into design transformations needed to get to the desired UI [7]. For instance, the designer can go "directly" from Application$_1$ to UI$_{1b}$ by specifying up front that the default UI (UI$_{1a}$) should be immediately transformed into UI$_{1b}$.

Iterative, incremental development. The TACTICS approach fully supports iterative, incremental development. The designer not only does not have to specify all UI details to get a working UI, but all application details do not have to be there either. The mapping rules will generate a UI for a partial application specification. As the application is changed by adding new entities or changing or removing existing ones, these changes are propagated to its UI. Any conflicts caused by the changes (e.g., an entity used as a parameter is deleted) can be detected by consistency and completeness checks. The designer controls how each conflict is resolved (e.g., redefine the parameter as well). Since all transformations are associated with the elements they have been applied to, the designer does not have to reapply them. Therefore, it is possible to specify an application and its interface using incremental, iterative approach.

Effectiveness – UI Model and Architecture, For this approach to be effective, we need to decouple UI features from application functionality and have full control over UI features without affecting application functionality. This requires an adequate model and underlying architecture. While traditional UI tools focus only on input and output communication tasks, the TACTICS model goes beyond that by identifying a layer of components that manage UI-related context of an application. More specifically, in addition to communication components, TACTICS identifies a set of buffering components that store the UI context and a set of control components that maintain and utilize the contextual information.

As a result, a UI is no longer limited to performing only the communication tasks (facilitating information exchange between a user and the application functional core), but it takes on two additional tasks: buffering, and managing information flow. This simplifies the application functional core and at the same time increases reusability and flexibility of a UI. For instance, the functional core no longer has to deal with UI details such as the order in which parameters are specified, whether there are default values etc. Its UI will take care of such details – store input parameters until they are used, get default values if there are any etc. The increased flexibility of a UI enables design transformations to control look-and-feel of a UI without affecting the application functionality (i.e., the functional core).

3.   AUTOMATIC GENERATION

How TACTICS automatically generates a UI is discussed in detail in [5, 7, 9]. This paper focuses on transformational support for design exploration. More specifically, we concentrate on the behavioral aspects of a UI. Visual aspects of a UI have received more attention elsewhere (e.g., [15, 4, 16]), as well as by commercial tools (interface builders, although they are limited to design time constructs – e.g., see [14]), whereas behavioral aspects have been mostly neglected. Therefore, I focus on the "wiring" infrastructure that controls the "feel" of a UI. Of course, this cannot be entirely separated from the presentations, especially in direct manipulation interfaces, and TACTICS addresses these issues as well, but that is beyond the scope of this paper. Handling of the presentation aspects in TACTICS is discussed in [5, 7].

3.1   Design Patterns

Automatic generation and transformations are explained in terms of design patterns. *Figure 2* is derived from *Figure 1* by narrowing our focus from an application as a whole to task components.

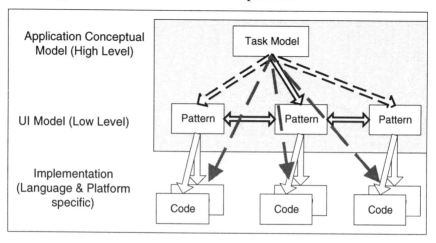

Figure 2. Mapping tasks to different UIs via design patterns.

For each task, a number of different user interfaces can be implemented by applying different design patterns. These patterns are expressed in terms of the TACTICS UI components, showing how they are structured and the message flow between them. Each design pattern can in turn be implemented in a specific language, for a target platform. Details of the mapping from a pattern to code are beyond the scope of this paper, but it is important to note that the applicability of this approach is not limited to the TACTICS model, since each design pattern can be replaced by its implementation, as shown in *Figure 2*.

Each task can be mapped to different user interfaces by applying different patterns. Each pattern represents a set of underlying implementations, which are platform and language specific, but each delivers the same look and feel reprersented by their pattern. A task is mapped to a pattern by binding its elements to pattern roles. Applying a different platform, e.g., a pattern P_2 instead of P_1, is equivalent to transforming P_1 into P_2, where P_2 must have the same set of roles as P_1.

3.2   Example

A starting point for UI generation is the application task model. In TAC-TICS, each primitive task (a task that is not decomposed into other tasks, but is an action that has a corresponding operation in the functional core) is bound to a design pattern that defines how to instantiate a UI for the task (action). In *Figure 3*, the action *Move* with two parameters and pre- and post-conditions is bound to the *Action Pattern*. Using the UML notation [17], it shows a design pattern as a collaboration symbol with four different roles (Action, Parameter, Precondition, and Postcondition). Note how two parameters (*Object* and *Position*) are bound to the same role. This is allowed because the *Parameter* role has cardinality "*" (i.e., ANY).

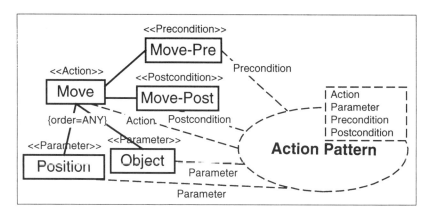

Figure 3. Task binding to a design pattern.

A default pattern used for automatic generation (before any transforma-tions are applied) is shown in *Figure 4*. Besides classes corresponding to the predefined roles (shown bold), the pattern includes classes that are instanti-ated as part of automatic generation. *Action-Context* is a buffering primitive storing the action-specific context during and between action activations. *Select-Action*, Cancel-Action, and Invoke-Action are three control primitives that are instantiated for each action, with their respective pre- and post-conditions. *Figure 4* does not show all pre- and postconditions, but only those related to the corresponding collaboration roles – *sa-prec* "inherits" all original action preconditions (e.g., the Move command has one: {Object ex-ists}); *ia-post* similarly inherits the original postconditions. All pre- and postconditions are shown in *Table 1*.

For each element bound to the parameter role, a *Parameter-Value* primitive is instantiated. It is a control primitive that gets a value for the parameter (either from a user, via an interaction technique, or from other sources, as will be discussed later) and stores it in the Action-context primitive. By default, all other elements require that the action be selected first (see *Table 1*). Invoke-Action also requires that all parameters have their value. Once all values are there, a user can confirm the action, which triggers this primitive to execute the operation defined in the Action role. The interface *Operations* exports the operations defined in the *Functional Core* that the UI needs to access. Depending on implementation, each control primitive can run in a separate thread[1]; hence messages use sequence numbers with thread names.

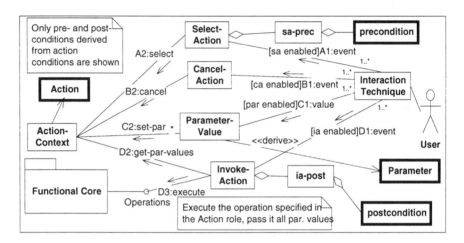

Figure 4. Standard (default) Action Pattern used for automatic generation.

The pattern shows both the structural aspects (UI building blocks and their relationships) and the message flow between them. For instance, when a user generates an event to select an action, an interaction technique will call the Select-Action primitive only if it is enable (i.e., its precondition *sa-enabled* is true).When Select-Action receives the event, it notifies the Action-Context that the Action is selected. To keep the figures simple, not all constraints that drive the generation process are shown. For instance, interaction techniques are selected based on a type of values that a control primitive requires.[2]

---

[1] TACTICS supports a blackboard architecture, where each control primitive can act as a knowledge source and buffering primitives are parts of a blackboard, facilitating integration of different modalities [6].

[2] However, this is a necessary, but not sufficient condition – the selection process should also ensure that there are no conflicts leading to ambiguous inputs; in TACTICS, this is handled by the completeness and consistency checking rules.

Table 1.

Component	Preconditions	Postconditions
Select Action	{NOT action selected} Inherit action's prec.	{action selected}
Cancel Action	{action selected}	{NOT action selected}
Invoke Action	{action selected} for each par. P: {P Has Value}	{NOT action selected} for each par. P.: {NOT P Has Value} Inherit action's postc.
Parameter Value	{action selected}	{Parameter Has Value}

4. TRANSFORMATIONS

Transformations are platform and language independent abstractions for manipulating UI properties. They establish a transformational model of the UI design space, defining how certain properties of a UI can be changed in terms of modifying properties of UI components and the underlying UI structure. Transformations encapsulate knowledge about related changes in the UI structure and perform all those changes automatically. They allow a designer to specify desired changes at a higher level of abstractions. For instance, to modify a UI design to use default values, instead of modifying individual primitives comprising a UI by adding new slots, modifying the existing ones, and changing wiring between components, it suffices to specify values to be used as defaults and specify parameters or object attributes they apply to. A designer can thus change a UI without writing any code, e.g., simply by filling a dialog box with required values.

Transformations allow designers to focus on *what* has to be changed, not *how*. This is analog to the way we format documents. Instead of writing and embedding individual formatting commands in the text, we can select the text and apply a style, which in turn translates into a combination of possibly large number of formatting commands controlling font and paragraph properties, tabulation, etc. We can change the style easily, by selecting the same text again and applying a different style.

A very important feature of transformations is that they preserve the internal interface toward the functional core. Therefore, exploring UI designs by using transformations does not require changes in the functional core. For instance, if we transform the default design shown in *Figure 4*, we do not have to change the interface *Operations* of the package *Functional core*. We can achieve a different look and feel while preserving the application functionality.

While transformations have been used in software engineering for generating "functional" code for a target program and performing optimizations [1], UIDE [2] was the first to apply the transformation approach to UI design. TACTICS improves on UIDE in two aspects. It features a separate UI representation capturing UI specifics at a finer level of details than UIDE. Whereas UIDE keeps UI details together with the application conceptual model that is interpreted at run time, TACTICS generates a separate object-oriented structure implementing the application UI. Different UIs are produced by configuring individual components and relationships among them, allowing for finer control over UI features than is possible in UIDE. The second improvement is a wider range of transformations.

A UI is transformed by altering the primitives forming the UI structure and/or changing the way the primitives are related to each other. Each primitive forming a UI has a set of properties that control its behavior. In TACTICS, a predefined set of primitives is used to compose UIs. A UI is implemented by fully instantiating all necessary primitives properly configured. It is therefore possible to change their behavior even after they are instantiated, which is what transformations do. The simplest transformation is to modify one or more properties of a primitive to change its behavior. Transformations can also add new primitives to the structure, delete existing primitives or replace a subset of primitives with another subset. Representative UI (sub)structures can be represented as design patterns, like the one shown in *Figure 4*. Transformations modify one or more of these patterns, depending on the transformation scope and extent

4.1   Transformation Examples

Next we look at examples illustrating the use of transformations. As a starting point, we can use the pattern shown in *Figure 4* to instantiate the following UI for the *Move* action, by attaching appropriate interaction techniques to each control primitive. The command is selected from a menu (the *Menu Item* interaction technique attached to Select-Action), object and position are selected by pointing (the *Pointing-Mouse-click* interaction technique), the command can be completed by pressing return or clicking OK on a confirmation box that pops up when both parameters are provided, and the action can be cancelled by pressing Esc at any point while it is selected and not completed. Now, let's look at several transformations we can apply to change this UI.

Make Confirmation Implicit. The first change we will consider is to eliminate the need for explicit confirmation. To accomplish that, we simply use a transformation that makes a given control primitive implicit, in this case *Invoke-Action.*We do that by changing its *Info-Kind* property to *im-*

plicit. Table 2 shows a subset of properties of the *Action-Event* Primitives (which include Select-Action, Cancel-Action, and Invoke-Action). As a result, the Invoke-Action primitive will "fire" immediately when all of its preconditions are satisfied. Consequently, there is no need for an interaction technique to trigger the event and the transformation would remove any interaction technique linked to Invoke-Action. The pattern in *Figure 4* would be changed with the one without the corresponding link.

Table 2. Subset of configurable properties of Action-Event Primitives.

Property	Description
Name	External name of the IFC primitive
Info-kind	Controls whether input values must be explicitly provided (explicit, implicit, optional)
Link-to-ITec	Rel. linking IFC to interaction techniques that can deliver the required information
Bundled-in	Rel. linking (bundled) IFC to its bundle
Controls-state	Interaction objects whose state depends on the state of this IFC primitive
Accept-Values	Values that will trigger event

Make Selection Implicit. Next, we want to eliminate the need to explicitly select the Move action from a menu. The simplest way to accomplish this is to apply the *Bundling* transformation to the Select-Action and Object parameter primitives as shown in *Figure 5*. The changes from the standard pattern are highlighted in the diagram. Now, selecting an object will pass a value (the selected object) to the bundle that than does two things: first sends an event to the Select-Action primitive, and then sends the value to the Parameter-Value primitive corresponding to the bundled parameter. As a result, a user of the transformed UI no longer has to separately select the action; it is selected by providing a value for the parameter bundled with the Select-Action primitive. The resulting UI supports the following scenario: a user selects an object by pointing (the system "knows" that the user wants to move it), then selects a position by pointing, and the objects "jumps" to the new position (note that we have already made confirmation implicit).

What happens if we try to apply the same transformation to another action, such as *rotate*, that works on the same type of object – how will the system know whether to move or to rotate the object? This is ambiguous design and the rules checking consistency will detect this. The solution is to either use a different *pointing* interaction technique for each command, or to use key modifiers or different mouse keys (if using the mouse). The possibility to detect design conflicts is an important advantage of model-based UI design tools over traditional tools such as interface builders.

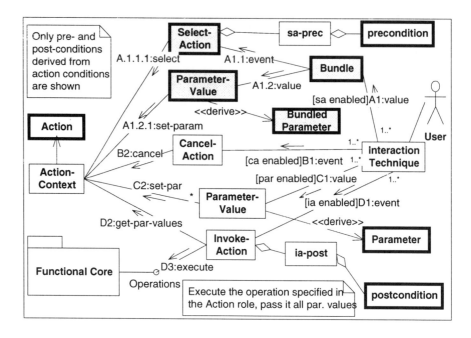

Figure 5. Action Pattern using the *Bundling* transformation.

Direct Manipulation Interface. We now further transform the design to give it a direct manipulation feel, where a user can simply drag an object. We will add the position parameter to the bundle and use the *dragging* interaction technique to provide values for the bundle. *Figure 6* shows relevant changes to the Action Pattern. Note that this requires a special interaction technique, configured to start on a mouse-down event over an object instance of a given type (this select the action and provides a value for the object parameter), followed by mouse moves. This provides a stream of new positions, but these intermediate values are not passed to position parameter until the stop event is detected (mouse up). Updates of the presentations are handled by the technique (e.g., drag a shadow or a special icon, or an object itself).

When such a technique is not available, we need to apply additional transformations. If the technique sends the intermediate values to the *Position* parameter, that would set the parameter value and (since the only other parameter, *Object*, already has the value) trigger the confirmation – remember that we have made it implicit earlier. To handle this, we need to make the confirmation explicit again and trigger it on a mouse-up event.

It the technique cannot provide the feedback needed to show the object at new positions, we can apply the *Dynamic Feedback* transformation, which configures UI to automatically update the selected object(s) whenever a parameter (in this case Position) obtains a new value. Since the object parameter is the only other parameter and it is always selected first when the Dragging interaction technique is used, that satisfies the syntactic requirements of the dynamic feedback transformation (all other parameters must have their values before the parameter with the dynamic feedback). For detailed discussion of the Dynamic Feedback and other transformations see [5].

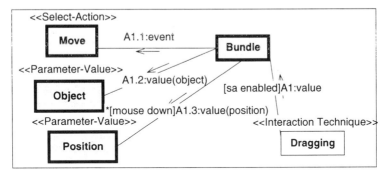

Figure 6. Result of bundling

Through a sequence of transformations, we have changed the original design into a one with direct manipulation feel. It is also possible to automate this process and apply the Direct Manipulation transformation directly – it's a high level transformation that will identify the changes required to go from one style to another based on captured knowledge about differences between different dialogue styles [5].

5.   DISCUSSION

The transformational approach to UI development relies on identifying and reusing common patterns of UI design. It enables quick and easy exploration of the design space. However, the design space reachable via transformations is not continuous, but is more like a grid on which a designer can move. It is therefore important to have an adequate set of transformations allowing fast and easy navigation without unduly constraining the design space.

By using patterns, a designer/developer can zoom-in and analyze different designs. They are expressed in terms of the TACTICS UI primitives, or building blocks, that have properties that can be modified by transformations. A UI is implemented by instantiating all necessary generic primitives properly configured. It is therefore possible to change their behavior even after they are instantiated, which is what transformations do. Two main alternatives are to either (1) interpret a model at run time, instead of instantiating a stand alone UI, or (2) generate code directly corresponding to different patterns, implementing the primitives configured only for a particular design. The first alternative introduces run time overhead of having to constantly interpret the model. The second one is the most efficient, but the least flexible at run time. The TACTICS approach adds a small run time overhead by using generic primitives, with properties and behavior that may not be needed, but is better suited for design time exploration. Changing properties is very fast and easy in TACTICS because each primitive has a well-defined set of properties and their valid values. If we were to generate and compile source code (i.e., translate design patterns directly to code), the changes would be more complex, requiring re-generating portions of the UI model. Furthermore, TACTICS allows run time customization by end user and adaptive UIs.

What this means is that even though the transformation-based approach may appear tightly associated with the compositional capabilities of TACTICS, it is not necessary to have TACTICS and design patterns expressed in terms of the TACTICS UI building blocks to use transformations. As *Figure 2* illustrates, it is possible to map transformations directly to code. Moreover, whether we apply transformations with or without the TACTICS compositional model, it can be transparent to users (UI designers) since they don't have to work at the code level, nor even the level of TACTICS building blocks. They can apply transformations interactively, in the same manner they can use interface builders (which also generate code behind the scene.

Transformations can be used for exploration, applying them during design process interactively. They can also be batched – specified in a specification, applied automatically as part of UI generation process (effectively change a default UI). For instance, once we have decided on certain aspects of a UI, we can include the transformations that will realize that UI in a specification, up front; there is no need to go through the process of generate/transform for those details.

The high-level specification as well as design transformations are platform independent. Platform specificity is handled by the generation rules. Transformations are optional and a UI designer uses them only to override the outcome of the automatic generation and to control UI features at a desired level of details.

An important benefit of the transformational approach is that it gives designers flexibility to control UI look and feel without having to modify the source code directly. By having designers stay within the model-based environment, we enable real iterative, incremental development and eliminate discontinuity between the models and different artifacts derived from the model, including the UI implementation, documentation that may be generated, help, etc. Otherwise, predictive evaluation and formal analysis, including completeness and consistency checks performed on the model would not be viable.

Implementation. Two different systems were implemented based on TACTICS, both supporting automatic generation of UIs, but in different contexts and for different purposes. The original implementation was an interactive design environment prototype that integrated support for generating UIs, evaluating/critiquing designs and interactively changing designs by means of design transformations. It was implemented in ART Inference Corp's and Common Object Lisp System (CLOS) and is described in [5, 6].

The second implementation was as part of an intelligent tutoring system for Web-delivered training, reported in [7] and was done in C++. Transformations were supported, but not interactively; instead, they were embedded as hints in the high-level specification used to generate a UI.

6. CONCLUSION

The paper presented a model-based approach to UI development that combines automatic generation of user interfaces with design transformations as applied in TACTICS. Transformations complement the TACTICS composition (generation) rules and are a crucial part of our approach to generating UIs. They enable support for a wide range of UI designs, as well as easy navigation – changing one design into another – while keeping the generation rules simple. The transformational approach to UI development relies on identifying and reusing common patterns of UI design; the paper illustrates several such design patterns related to select design transformations. The focus was on behavioral aspects, the wiring behind the scene.

There are several areas requiring further attention. One is a more formal treatment of transformations. UI transformations are abstractions relating changes of UI properties to changes of UI components and the underlying structure. These abstractions form a transformation model of the UI design space. Dimensions of this space are defined by manipulable UI properties, but we have not formally defined these dimensions or formal properties of transformations. Having a formal treatment of transformations and their properties (e.g., commutativity, associativity) will enable their use in formally describing and comparing different designs. Another issue is balancing of complexity of UI design with control that a designer has. TACTICS has addressed this problem by providing a combination of low-level transformations (giving more precise control over UI look and feel) and high-level transformations that are more powerful, but less precise. Again, a formal definition of the design space would facilitate analysis and combination of transformations, including their interdependencies. Another big issue, although not unique to this approach, is whether a tool can learn and adapt to new technologies, accommodate new designs (i.e., patterns) and integrate them with existing transformations?

To make this approach truly effective, even before the above issues are resolved, there are two critical areas. One is the usability of the transformational approach – we need a study to evaluate whether the UI design patterns captured in transformations are adequate for real-world UI designers. What aspects of a UI should be malleable, what are the variation points that UI designers would like to use – are some of the questions to be addressed. Another is integration of the model-based UI development and the mainstream OO development. A major obstacle in adopting model-based UI tools is a perceived overhead in specifying a model. At the same time, modeling is already being extensively used for non-UI development. For instance, tools supporting UML [17] already capture most of the information required by TACTICS, but do not utilize it for UI development. The transformational approach is particularly suitable for such integration because UI designers can explore different designs without requiring changes to the internal interface toward the functional core. Therefore, they can share the info with OO developers and avoid stepping on each other's toes. My goal is to integrate TACTICS with a full-fledged OO modeling tool, such as StP/UML [8, 13]

REFERENCES

[1]   Balzer, R., *A 15 year perspective on automatic programming*, IEEE Transactions on Software Engineering, Vol. SE-11, pp. 1257-1267, 1985

[2]   Foley, J., Kim, W.C., Kovacevic, S. and Murray, K., *UIDE — An Intelligent User Interface Design Environment*, in "Architectures for Intelligent Interfaces: Elements and Prototypes", J.W. Sullivan and S.W. Tyler (eds.), Addison-Wesley, New York, 1991, pp. 339-384.

[3]   Johnson, P., Wilson, S., Markopoulos, P. and Pycock, J., *ADEPT – Advanced DEsign Environment for Prototyping with Task Models*, in Proc. of ACM Conf. on Human Aspects in Computing Systems INTERCHI'93 (Amsterdam, April 1993), Addison-Wesley, New York, 1993, pp. 55-56.

[4]   Kim, W.C. and Foley, J.D., *Providing High-level Control and Expert Assistance in the User Interface Presentation Design*, in Proc. of ACM Conf. on Human Aspects in Computing Systems INTERCHI'93 (Amsterdam, April 1993), Addison-Wesley, New York, 1993, pp. 430-437.

[5]   Kovacevic, S., *A Compositional Model of Human-Computer Interaction*, DSc dissertation, The George Washington University, 1992.

[6]   Kovacevic, S., *TACTICS – A Model-Based Framework for Multimodal Interaction*, in Proceedings of the AAAI Spring Symposium on Intelligent Multi-Media Multi-Modal Systems, 1994.

[7]   Kovacevic, S., *Flexible, Dynamic User Interfaces for Web-Delivered Training*, in Proceedings of the 3rd International ACM Workshop on Advanced Visual Interfaces AVI'96, ACM Press, New York, 1996.

[8]   Kovacevic, S., *UML and User Interface Modeling*, in Proceedings of the 1st International Workshop UML'98 – Beyond the Notation (Mulhouse, June 3-4, 1998).

[9]   Kovacevic, S., *Model-Driven User Interfaces Development*, in Proceedings of the 10th International Conf. On Software Engineering and Knowledge Engineering SEKE'98, 1998.

[10] Lonczewski, F. and Schreiber, S., *Generating User Interfaces with the FUSE System*, TUM-I9612, Technische Universitaet Muenchen, Muenchen, 1996.

[11] Luo, P., *A Human-Computer Collaboration Paradigm For Bridging Design Conceptualization and Implementation*, in "Interactive Systems: Design, Specification and Verification", Proc. of the 1st Eurographics Workshop on Design, Specification, and Verification of Interactive Systems DSV-IS'94, F. Paternò (ed.), Springer-Verlag, Berlin, 1995, pp. 129-147.

[12] Puerta, A., *Model-Based Development Environment*, IEEE Software, Vol. 14, No. 4, July-August 1997, pp. 41-47.

[13] *StP/UML - Software through Pictures/Unified Modeling Language*, Aonix, September 1997.

[14] Szekely, P., Luo, P. and Neches, R., *Beyond Interface Builders: Model-Based Interface Tools*, in Proc. of ACM Conf. on Human Aspects in Computing Systems INTERCHI'93 (Amsterdam, April 1993), Addison-Wesley, New York, 1993, pp. 430-437.

[15] Szekely, P., P. Sukaviriya, P. Castells, J. Muthukumarasamy, and Salcher, E., *Declarative interface models for user interface construction tools: the Mastermind approach*, in "Engineering for Human-Computer Interaction", L. Bass and C. Unger (eds), Chapman & Hall, London, 1996.

[16] Vanderdonckt, J. and Bodart, F., *Encapsulating Knowledge For Intelligent Automatic Interaction Objects Selection*, in Proc. of ACM Conf. on Human Aspects in Computing Systems INTERCHI'93 (Amsterdam, April 1993), Addison-Wesley, New York, 1993, pp. 424-429.

[17] The Unified Modeling Language, OMG, http://www.omg.org.

Chapter 9

USING APPLICATION DOMAIN SPECIFIC RUN-TIME SYSTEMS AND LIGHTWEIGHT USER INTERFACE MODELS
A NOVEL APPROACH FOR CADUI

Erik G. Nilsson
SINTEF Telecom and Informatics, P.O. Box 124, Blindern, N-0314 Oslo, Norway
Erik.G.Nilsson@informatics.sintef.no - Tel: +47 22 06 78 85 - Fax: +47 22 06 73 50

Abstract   This paper presents an application domain specific run-time system using a lightweight user interface model to combine advanced user interfaces with flexible configuration mechanisms. The system is called the VUIM – VRP User Interface Module, and is a generic user interface run time system for vehicle routing applications. It balances between being a very general, model-based, non-application domain specific UI development tool and being a turn-key application (ready to use, but with very limited abilities to be adapted to specific needs). The VUIM includes a class library with a set of generic, but application domain-specific UI building blocks. These building blocks are on a higher level than simple UI controls, but more generic than a dialog box or a window in an application. The class library is augmented with a run time system (generic application), that "interprets" a UI model. The VUIM exemplifies a novel approach for CADUI.

Key words: Model-based user interface systems, application domain specific run-time systems, visualisation of vehicle routing problems.

1.   INTRODUCTION

Most of the research done on model-based user interface (UI) tools [16, 21, 22] is criticised [15, 21, 24] for bringing out too simplified user interfaces and of being restricted to limited interaction styles[1]. In this paper a new

---

[1]   Usually forms-based front-ends to data base applications.

and different approach is presented. The UI is generated (more exactly, a UI model is interpreted at run time to generate the running UI), but the generated UI is both graphical, highly interactive (e.g. utilising drag and drop), and configurable. This combination is achieved by having an application domain specific, but nevertheless generic UI model with a connected run time system. The approach allows for a certain degree of control over the UI by the application / UI developer.

This paper draws most of its experience and examples from a project called GreenTrip [9]. The goal of the GreenTrip project has been to produce a generic, cost-effective tool to optimise routing of vehicles, that takes into account multiple business constraints, permits efficient (re)configuration, and integrates easily in existing IT infrastructures. To achieve this goal, the GreenTrip Generic Toolkit (GGT) has been developed.

The GGT [4] consists of a set of tools (see below) that eases the development of complex VRP (Vehicle Routing Problem) applications. This includes a modelling tool (VAMT) and a generic VRP User Interface Module (VUIM). The VUIM is what is focused in this paper.

The VUIM consists of a set of Java classes that generates a number of graphical and forms based user interfaces towards the rest of the GGT. The user interface generation is based on a VRP model (which includes a UI model) described through the VAMT. The graphical user interfaces include map based and time based (Gantt) visualisations, while the forms based user interfaces include tabular and tree based presentations.

In the rest of this paper, we give a short overview of the GGT, take a closer look at the VUIM, and discuss how this approach may be used more generally. Finally, we relate this work to other research, and give some concluding remarks.

2.   OVERVIEW OF THE GGT

The GreenTrip VUIM is a part of the GreenTrip Generic Toolkit, developed in the GreenTrip project. The GGT is a set of tools that eases development of applications addressing Vehicle Routing Problems.

In *Figure 1*, the components constituting the GGT and their connections are presented.

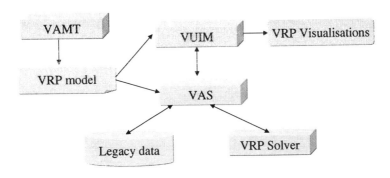

Figure 1. The components of the GGT.

The VAMT (VRP Application Modelling Tool) is a modelling tool that is used to describe complex VRP applications. The VAMT user (usually an application developer) does this by making choices, changes and additions to the predefined VRP conceptual model (see below).

The VRP application server (VAS) uses the VRP model described in the VAMT, to generate (interpret) the functional part of a running VRP application. This includes initiating the VRP Solver and connecting to relevant legacy systems. The VAS is able to serve a number of VUIM instances. The VRP Solver [8] gives optimised solutions to the VRP problems. The VRP solver runs in parallel with the VAS, and thus facilitates continuous optimisation, independently of user actions. The VUIM is the generic VRP User Interface Module, which is described in detail in the next section. A VRP application usually depends on communication with existing applications (like an order handling system). Thus, there is a need for interfaces to legacy systems.

As described above, the GGT uses a predefined conceptual model (see *Figure 2* for a UML [5] class diagram). A Plan tells which Visits a Vehicle serves. A Visit is a stop at a certain geographic location to pick up or deliver a part of an Order. Alternative sets of Visits serving an Order may be described using OrderExecutions. A set of Visits served by one Vehicle is called a Tour. The Visits that are not served by any of the Tours in the Plan, are called Unallocated Visits. A Driver may drive different Vehicles (over time), and different Drivers may share a Vehicle (e.g. when working shifts). When referring to the conceptual model in the running text, concepts from the model is Capitalised.

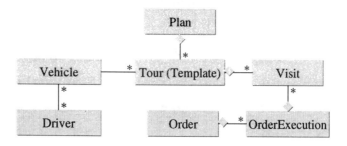

Figure 2. The VRP conceptual model used in the GGT.

The VAMT user may configure the model, by omitting some object types (Driver, Vehicle, Order Execution and Tour Template), he has a lot of choices regarding what kind of functionality and attributes that should be included or excluded, and he may add new attributes. How the model configuration affects the user interface is described in the next section.

In essence, developing an application using the GGT consists of defining the appropriate model in the VAMT tool, and configuring connections to external applications that the VRP application should connect to (legacy systems, map and topology modules). Regarding the map and topology modules, simple implementations of these (conforming to the required interfaces) are included in the GGT.

The GreenTrip project has focused on the industrial needs of the end users. As a result, the GGT has been broadly tested by end-users, and different parts of the GGT are being marketed commercially by the technological partners.

3.   THE VUIM

The VUIM is a generic visualisation system, which presents the VRP information in various ways to the end user. Most of the presentation mechanisms are predefined in the VUIM code or given implicitly by the VAS-relevant choices made in the VAMT. In addition, the VAMT user may specify a number of UI specific details regarding if and how attributes are to be presented, and which attributes that are to be used as identifiers in different parts of the visualisations.

3.1   Approach

The VUIM was developed to balance configurability and user interface functionality. On the one hand, it is not possible to specify a *single* user interface that is ideal for all VRP application. On the other hand, it was a clear user requirement to have graphical, highly interactive user interfaces, not just simple forms based ones.

This dichotomy is handled by identifying a set of *user interface types* (see below), i.e. a limited set of ways to present and manipulate VRP data – and to make these UI types as configurable as possible. In identifying the UI types, much effort was put into studying user needs. This work was a combination of collecting requirements from the end users in the project and studying existing solutions [6]. The study of existing solutions was done with a broad scope – covering anything from solutions already being used by the end users, through existing VRP turnkey solutions, to UIs used in related domains (e.g. in scheduling in general [26]).

During the development of the VUIM, it was tested by the end users. Based on their feedback, the VUIM was changed and extended – all the time obeying the rule that no "special needs" for any single user or user subgroup should be standard functionality in the VUIM. Instead, a tailoring mechanism making it possible to configure the VUIM to cover the special needs was introduced.

3.2   Functionality

3.2.1   User interface types

The user interface type identification work concluded that the most important user interface types were forms based, tabular, browser, map based and time based presentations.

Not surprisingly, traditional *forms based* presentations are needed. These UIs are laid out automatically, and single occurrence versions exist for all VRP object types in the VRP conceptual model. In addition, two parent-child (or master-detail) presentations are included, highlighting the most important one-to-many associations in the VRP conceptual model, i.e. Plans with connected Tours, and Tours with connected Visits. The child part is presented using a tabular presentation. In most cases the forms based presentations are used as part of a browser UI, but in some cases separate windows for single occurrence presentations are generated (e.g. when the user double-clicks on an icon). In the top part of the right pane of the browser type interface presented in *Figure 3*, a forms-based UI for Tour is included.

To see all details about the occurrences of a VRP object type, *tabular* presentations of all occurrences of one of the VAMT object types are included. Again, the UIs are laid out automatically, and versions exist for Tours, Visits, Orders, Vehicles and Drivers. The versions showing all occurrences are presented in separate windows – or all of them together in one window using tab folders. In addition, there is one special tabular presentation, showing all unallocated visits. This presentation may also be viewed as a parent-child presentation where the parent part is only the heading "Unallocated Visits". As mentioned above, the tabular presentation is also used in the child part of the forms-based parent-child presentations. The right pane in the browser type interface presented in *Figure 3* exemplifies such a parent-child presentation using a tabular presentation in the lower part.

To visualise structure and details simultaneously, *browser based* presentations of hierarchical subsets of the VAMT object model are included. The "VUIM browsers" consist of one pane with a tree-based visualisation of VRP objects and their connection, and another pane showing details about objects selected in the tree pane. The VUIM includes browser based presentations of two given hierarchical subsets of the VRP conceptual model. One version shows the composite object including all related instances starting from Plan, the other shows the same starting from a collection of all Orders. The presentations in the details-pane use one of the UI types just presented. Different icons are used in the tree pane to indicate which type each object is an instance of. An instance of the VUIM browser is shown in *Figure 3*.

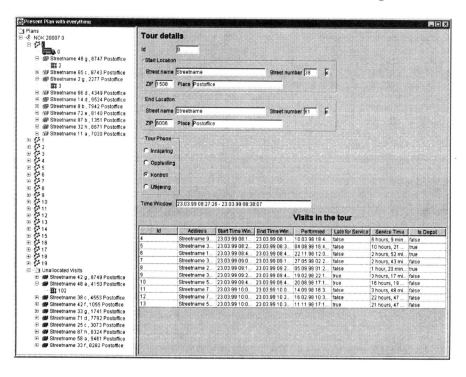

Figure 3. The VUIM Browser.

Using application domain specific run-time systems and
lighweight user interface models
103

As the geographic aspects of a Plan are very important, *map-based* presentation of a given hierarchical subset of the VAMT object model is included. The map-based presentation lets the user choose a subset (or all) of the Tours in a Plan, and presents them as overlays on a map background. Visits are shown as icons placed at the geographic location where the Visit takes place, while the Tour is represented as straight lines between the icons. Each Tour has a (user configurable) colour. The GGT supports positional feedback from an external system (e.g. through a GPS[2] based system). If such support is used, the Vehicle is also shown in the map-based presentation, at its current location. As all icons (except the optional Vehicle icon) indicate Visits, additional semantics are coded into the Visit icons. Currently, the form of the icon indicates whether it is an ordinary Visit, a Visit at a depot, or an unallocated Visit. Furthermore, the colour of the icon tells whether the Visit is delayed or not. The latter requires live feedback on the progress of the Tours, which is part of the positional feedback mechanism. An instance of the map-based presentation is shown in *Figure 4*.

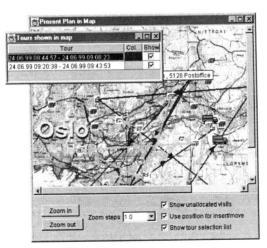

Figure 4. The map-based presentation.

To see how the Plans are distributed over the planning horizon, *time-based* presentation of a given hierarchical subset of the VAMT object model is included. The time-based presentation lets the user choose a subset (or all) of the Tours in a Plan, and presents them as a detailed Gantt diagram. In this Gantt diagram, main bars are shown for each Tour. Within each main bar, sub-bars are shown for each Visit. These sub-bars are split into a green part

---

[2] GPS: Global Positioning System - a satellite-based system for determining geographical position.

showing time window for arrival and a red part showing time window for departure. The colours of the main bars are the same as the corresponding Tour colours in the map-based presentation. An instance of the time-based presentation is shown in *Figure 5*.

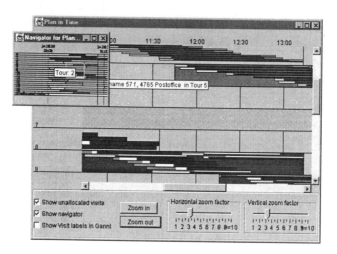

Figure 5. The time-based presentation.

To augment the visual presentations, tool-tips are extensively used to present details about the various visual elements. The user may open multiple occurrences of all the important presentations.

As the VAMT user may tailor the number, type and sequence of attributes (see below), the layout of the forms based presentations must be generated automatically. This is done by a simple algorithm, which task is primarily to ensure that there is room enough horizontally for the widest attributes, and that the attributes are aligned properly. Choices of actual UI elements to be used for each attribute are left to the VAMT user – who may choose among a predefined set of UI elements. The available choices – and the defaults – depend on the data type of the attribute. In this way, the VAMT user may not choose inappropriate UI elements, and if he does not make explicit choices, the element choices will nevertheless be appropriate.

In addition to the optional positional and Tour progress feedback mentioned above, the information shown in the VUIM changes regularly, partly as the basic data from the legacy systems changes (e.g. new Orders or changes in existing Orders), and partly as the VRP Solver finds new and better solutions. Furthermore, the end users may do changes to the plan (see below). All changes are handled by the VAS, and reported to all VUIM clients regularly, so that the different presentations are updated. This change propagation mechanism also gives a surprising benefit. As the VRP Solver works in parallel with the rest of the GGT, the VUIM may be used to visualise how the VRP Solver works. By opening a map-based presentation when the solver is started (and all Visits are unallocated), the user gets a very good visual picture of how the Plan is gradually built up. In fact it acts as a "visualiser" for the VRP Solver.

3.2.2   Interaction

In the truly graphical presentations (the map- and the time-based ones) the end user has some basic, generic interaction mechanisms. He may select Tours or individual Visits, and by double clicking, forms based windows with details about the chosen object are shown. In the graphical presentations, there are also context sensitive pop-up menus; both connected to the presentation as such and to the different objects in the presentation.

Both the maps and the Gantt diagrams may include large amounts of information. For the user to be able to grasp details zooming mechanisms are needed (and as zooming in makes the visualisation larger, scrolling is also needed). The map presentation support standard zoom functions while the time-based presentation offers mechanisms for zooming horizontally and vertically independently. This facilitates to focus either on a small number of Tours or on a short period of time (or a combination). Zooming very closely in the Gantt presentation may cause the user to "get lost". To aid the user, both in knowing where he is focusing and to change focus, a miniature version of the Gantt diagram is used. Within this miniature version, a rectangle indicates which part of the whole Gantt chart that is shown in the full view. The rectangle may also be manipulated by the end user to change the view (supplement to scroll and zoom).

As mentioned above, the GGT is intended to work in close connection to existing administrative applications handling e.g. orders, vehicles, drivers and customers. To minimise the risk of introducing inconsistencies, none of the input data to the plan generation and management may be change through the VUIM. The results from the VRP Solver (i.e. the Plans), on the other hand, may be adjusted by the end user through the VUIM. Both the generated Plans and any manual changes on them, are possibly communicated to connected administrative applications (e.g. the applications handling driving lists for the drivers).

Changing a Plan in the VUIM means changing which Visits that belongs to which Tours, including allocating unallocated Visits to a Tour, and unallocating already allocated Visits. Also, the sequence of Visits within one

Tour may be changed. In addition, the end user may perform certain other changes, like changing the Tour phases[3].

These Plan changes may be carried out in the map- and time-based presentations. In the map based presentation, changes are done by dragging Visit icons onto the lines representing the Tour, or redirecting a Tour leg line to include a Visit by dragging it. The direct manipulation is supplemented by pop-up menu functions. In the time-based presentation, changes are done by dragging Visit bars between Tour bars (including a special bar containing all unallocated Visits).

As mentioned above, the user may open multiple occurrences of all the important presentations, and the user may open forms-based windows to view details from the map- and time-based presentations. Opening the different presentations are done from a generic main window. All these dialog dynamics are predefined, and may currently not be influenced through the UI model.

3.3   The user interface model

Similar to [1, 12, and 17], the user interface model in the VUIM is an integral part of the VRP conceptual model, both seen from the VAMT user and in the implementation. The information in the VAMT model may be divided into three parts:

1. Model information that is only interesting for the other parts of the GGT than the VUIM. This includes e.g. constraints, goal function, and specifications regarding interfaces to legacy systems.
2. Model information that is interesting both for the VUIM and for other parts of the GGT. This includes e.g. VRP object types to exclude, additional attributes, names, data types etc. for attributes, address formats, enumeration values for enumerator type attributes, and Tour phases.
3. Model information that is only interesting for the VUIM. This includes e.g. which UI element type to use in forms based presentations, maximum number of characters, whether an attribute should be suppressed in the UI, the sequence in which the attributes should be shown in the presentations, which attribute to use as "label" in the trees, maps and Gantt presentations

Regarding the data types, the GGT defines both a set of simple data types such as integer, real, string and boolean, and some compound data types such as enumeration, address and co-ordinates, duration, time and time window. For some of the compound data types, like address and time window,

---

[3]   A Tour phase is the state for a Tour (planned, locked, loaded, in progress, etc.). Whether Tour phases should be used or not may be specified in the VAMT.

specialised compound UI elements are available. This means that the VAMT user specifying an attribute of the type "time window", may choose between having the attribute presented as a "Time window" or as a "Text field".

Regarding the "label" attributes that must be specified for each VRP object type, this information is used whenever appropriate. So e.g. if the VAMT user chooses to identify Tours in the time-based presentations by the registration number of the connected Vehicle, the registration number values are used both in the dialog box where the user chooses which Tours to include in the Gantt diagram, and in the tool tip texts for the Tour bars both in the main Gantt window and in the miniature version. Furthermore, the label is also used as window title in Forms based pop-up windows opened from the time-based presentation.

3.4   Implementation

Figure 6 shows how the VUIM is built up internally.

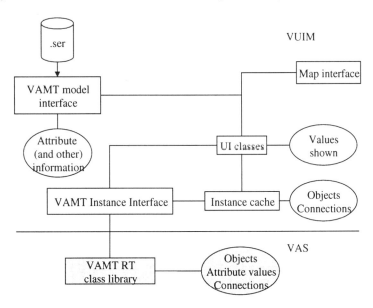

Figure 6. The different parts of the VUIM

Logically, the VUIM consists of five parts, the VAMT model interface, the map interface, the VAMT instance interface, the instance cache, and the UI classes. The VAMT model interface is responsible for reading and storing the VRP model containing the meta-information about the application. Much of the code for this part is shared with the VAMT. The VRP model

(including the UI model) is represented as a set of Java classes, which are se-
rialised between the VAMT and the VUIM. The VUIM representation is optimised for fast access to the UI model part the VRP model.

The map interface is responsible for communication with the map module. The responsibility of the map module is to provide background pictures
to be used in the map-based presentations. Based on an input rectangle, the
map module supplies meta-information about maps covering the area. Based
on the meta-information, the VUIM chooses the most appropriate map to use
as background. The communication between the VUIM and the map module
is done using standardised, geographical co-ordinates utilising UTM [25]
and WGS84.

The VAMT instance interface is responsible for communication with the
VAS. This module collects the actual application data (instances and attrib-
ute values). The instance cache is responsible for keeping a local store of the
VRP object instances from the VAS and their connections. This cache is
needed both for performance reasons, and to be able to handle changes in the
VAS. In this part, only the key is stored for each VRP object.

The UI classes are the core of the VUIM. In this part, all the user interface code is situated. It also does some local storage of attribute values
(purely for performance reasons). The user interface is implemented using
the Swing set class library, which is part of the Java Foundation Classes
[19].

The "interpretation" of the UI model is done partly in the VAMT model
interface, but primarily in the UI classes. Most of the UI model information
influencing the appearance of the different UI types may be – and are indeed
– handled when the UIs are generated. This causes the opening of the different UIs to be slowed down a bit, but it also makes the performance when the
user interacts with the different UIs comparable to "compiled" UIs.

3.5   Future extensions and enhancements to the VUIM

The VUIM may be extended and enhanced in a number of areas. Enhancements may be categorised into enhancements to the generic run time
functionality in the VUIM, and enhancements to the configuration mechanisms available in the VAMT.

Possible run time enhancements include visualising Tours along actual
road tracks (not as straight lines), enhanced manipulation (e.g. drag and drop
between visualisations and manipulation of time windows in the Gantt
chart), and new visualisation types (e.g. iconic views, 3D visualisation, time
and distance charts, etc.).

Possible configuration enhancements include possibilities for the VAMT
users to define dialog dynamics like user interface actions (e.g. to define that

double-clicking a Tour in the browser should open a map-based view of that Tour), and like defining pop-up menus with acitons, to design their own icons, and to define which icons to use depending on attribute values. E.g. if the VAMT user defines an enumeration attribute called visitType, with the values *pickup, delivery* and *combined,* he could have the possibility to define different Visit icons to be used depending on the values for this additional attribute.

4. APPLICATION DOMAIN-SPECIFIC LIGHT-WEIGHT USER INTERFACE MODELS

The development of the VUIM and the GGT draws on principles that may well be generalised and applied to other application domains. On a continuum with tailored, specialised, non-configurable applications in one end and general systems development tools (including most model-based UI development tools) in the other, an application domain specific development tool like the GGT would lay somewhere in-between. This is shown in *Figure 7.*

Figure 7. Application domain specific development tools compared to turn-key applications and development tools.

The GGT, with relatively limited tailoring possibilities, would be situated closer to application than the development tool side, but other tools could be designed to lay closer to a development tool.

In general, tools situated to the left are less configurable, but also easier to configure than tools on the right side (having fewer and more usable configuration mechanisms). As indicated in the figure, this also influences whom the configuration mechanisms are targeted at, and what kind of "actions" the person doing the configuration uses.

The generality and flexibility obtained on the right hand side, often has a price: the developer must do very much work to develop an application. To reduce the development work needed, different approaches are used. Some tools – like the traditional 4GL approach, gives special support to development of database applications. This can be viewed as a degree of specialisation, but not to a specific application domain. Another approach – conducted by most model-based UI development tools – is to automate or support the UI design task. Both the 4GL and the model-based approach trades the reduced development work for possibilities in the UI – in most cases the tools only support forms based UIs.

The application domain specific development tools approach tries to combine some of the flexibility of the general-purpose development tools with a further reduction of development work that is obtained by general model-based tools and still having a user interface comparable to the turn-key applications.

The VUIM has not found an ideal combination of these benefits. One obvious area where it could be improved is the tailoring mechanisms. As it is now, this can only be done through the UI model part of the VRP conceptual model – both being very data oriented. The existing configuration mechanisms and the possible enhancements to them (discussed in the previous section) requires just a small amount of development· work, but offers limited flexibility. Alternatively, different configuration mechanisms could be envisioned:

One possible configuration mechanism is to have a plug-in architecture. This is an approach used in a number of desktop applications (word processors, web-browsers, media players, etc.) which leaves the developer free to enhance the application in certain domains, using whatever development tools he likes, as long as the resulting plug-in conforms to the rules set up by the application. This mechanism is flexible, but it usually requires much development work.

Another possibility is to use a specialised language for defining the configuration. This is similar both to scripting mechanisms available in most productivity applications such as word processors and spreadsheet tools and to high-level languages used in systems development tools (e.g. many model-based UI development tools [e.g. 2, 3, 7, 11, and 14]). This mechanism is relatively flexible, and requires moderate amounts of development work.

A third possibility is to use sub-classing for specialising the run-time system of the application domain specific tool. This approach would only work if the run-time system is implemented using an object-oriented programming language, and is designed so that specialisation by sub-classing is manageable. A similar approach is used in some user interface development tools. The sub-classing approach is flexible, and given an appropriate design of the class structure of the run-time system, it only requires moderate amounts of development work.

Using application domain specific run-time systems and
lighweight user interface models
111

5.   RELATED WORK

The approach presented in this paper differs from most published work on model-based user interface development in the sense that the GGT tools are specialised for a restricted application domain. Although being general, most other approaches [e.g. 1, 2, 10, 12, 18, and 20] are implicitly or explicitly restricted to certain application or user interface *types* or *styles* [11]. It is most common to restrict to forms based UIs towards a data base application, but also tailoring to application types like tourist information systems [23] exist.

The presented approach may also be compared to end user productivity applications with configuration options (like the Office products from Microsoft [13]). These tools differ both with regards to how and whom the configuration mechanisms are targeted at, and with regards to what type of changes that may be done. Most such tools only offer mechanisms facilitating changes to the user interface towards a 100% predefined domain model. In the GGT, also the model may be changed and extended.

As mentioned above, the solution used in the GGT by including the UI model as an integral part of a general conceptual model is similar to some model-based tools [1, 12, and 17]. Despite this, it should be mentioned that the conceptual models of these tools are very different from the VRP conceptual model used in the GGT.

6.   CONCLUSION

A central topic in the discussion groups at CADUI '96 [15,24] were the choice between automatic generation of user interfaces and only assisting the UI developer in the design work. The approach presented in this paper solves this conflict by restricting the applicability of the tools to a certain application domain, and predefining the presentation types to be used. By offering a number of easy configuration mechanisms, the user may still configure the tool to his needs. Combining this, the result is a tool that combines advanced graphical and interactive user interface with flexible configuration options.

Although the functionality of the GGT is restricted to VRP applications, the user interface types in the VUIM are less VRP specific. All the interface types in the VUIM may be applied to other and wider application domains. Most of the interface types may be viewed as stereotypes or complex user interface components. One could well envision a more generalised tool offering user interfaces like the ones presented in this paper working towards a much more generalised development tool and run time system.

ACKNOWLEDGEMENTS

The production of this paper was supported by the GreenTrip project, a research and development undertaking partially funded by the Esprit Programme of the European Commission as project number 20603. The partners in GreenTrip were Pirelli (I), ILOG (F), SINTEF (N), Tollpost-Globe (N), and University of Strathclyde (UK). The author would like to thank colleagues at SINTEF for valuable comments and suggestions, both during the development of the VUIM and on this paper.

REFERENCES

[1]   Balzert, H., *From OOA to GUI - the JANUS System,* in Proceedings of the 5th IFIP TC13 Conference on Human-Computer Interaction INTERACT'95 (Lillehammer, 25-29 June 1995), K. Nordbyn, P.H. Helmersen, D.J. Gilmore and S.A. Arnesen (eds.), Chapman & Hall, London, 1995, pp. 319-324.

[2]   Balzert, H., Hofmann, F., Kruschinski, V., and Niemann, C., *The JANUS Application Development Environment – Generating More than the User Interface,* in Proceedings of the 2nd International Workshop on Computer-Aided Design of User Interfaces CADUI'96 (Namur, 5-7 June 1996), J. Vanderdonckt (éd.), Presses Universitaires de Namur, Namur, 1996, pp. 183-207.

[3]   Bauer, B., *Generating User Interfaces from Formal Specifications of the Application,* in Proceedings of the 2nd International Workshop on Computer-Aided Design of User Interfaces CADUI'96 (Namur, 5-7 June 1996), J. Vanderdonckt (ed.), Presses Universitaires de Namur, Namur, 1996, pp. 141-157.

[4]   Bouzoubaa, M., Hasle, G., Kloster, O. and Prosser, P., *The GGT: a Generic Toolkit for VRP Applications and its Modelling Capabilities,* in Proc. of the 1st International Conference and Exhibition on The Practical Applications of Constraint Technologies and Logic Programming PACLP99 (London, April 1999).

[5]   Booch, G., Rumbaugh, J., and Jacobson, I. *The Unified Modeling Language User Guide,* Addison-Wesley, Reading, 1998.

[6]   L. Bodin and L. Levy: *Visualization in Vehicle Routing and Scheduling Problems,* ORSA Journal on Computing, vol. 6 no. 3, pp. 261-268, 1994

[7]   Copas, C. and Edmonds, E., *Declarative Interaction through Interactive Planners,* in Proceedings of the 2nd International Workshop on Computer-Aided Design of User Interfaces CADUI'96 (Namur, 5-7 June 1996), J. Vanderdonckt (ed.), Presses Universitaires de Namur, Namur, 1996, pp. 265-284.

[8]   de Backer, B., Furnon, V., Kilby, P., Prosser, P. and Shaw, P., *Solving vehicle routing problems with constraint programming and metaheuristic,.*submitted to *Journal of Heuristics,* special issue on constraint programming.

[9]   The GreenTrip Consortium, *Efficient Logistics via Intelligent Vehicle Routing Systems,* European Conference on Integration in Manufacturing IiM 97 (Dresden, 24-26 September 1997).

[10] Harning, M.B., *An Approach to Structured Display Design – Coping with Conceptual Compexity,* in Proceedings of the 2nd International Workshop on Computer-Aided Design of User Interfaces CADUI'96 (Namur, 5-7 June 1996), J. Vanderdonckt (ed.), Presses Universitaires de Namur, Namur, 1996, pp. 121-138.

[11] Lonczewski, F. and Schreiber, S., *The FUSE-System: an Integrated User Interface Design Environment,* in Proceedings of the 2nd International Workshop on Computer-Aided Design of User Interfaces CADUI'96 (Namur, 5-7 June 1996), J. Vanderdonckt (ed.), Presses Universitaires de Namur, Namur, 1996, pp. 37-56.

[12] Märtin, C., *Software Life Cycle Automation for Interactive Applications: The AME Design Environment,* in Proceedings of the 2nd International Workshop on Computer-Aided Design of User Interfaces CADUI'96 (Namur, 5-7 June 1996), J. Vanderdonckt (ed.), Presses Universitaires de Namur, Namur, 1996, pp. 57-73.

[13] Microsoft, *Microsoft Office 2000 Resource Kit,* Microsoft Press, Redmond, 1999.

[14] Puerta, A., *The MECANO Project: Comprehensive and Integrated Support for Model-Based Interface Development,* in Proceedings of the 2nd International Workshop on Computer-Aided Design of User Interfaces CADUI'96 (Namur, 5-7 June 1996), J. Vanderdonckt (ed.), Presses Universitaires de Namur, Namur, 1996, pp. 19-35. Accessible at http://www.arpuerta.com/pubs/cadui96.htm.

[15] Puerta, A., *Work Group Report: Issues in Automatic Generation of User Interfaces in Model-Based Systems,* in Proceedings of the 2nd International Workshop on Computer-Aided Design of User Interfaces CADUI'96 (Namur, 5-7 June 1996), J. Vanderdonckt (ed.), Presses Universitaires de Namur, Namur, 1996, pp. 323-326.

[16] Puerta, A., *A Model-Based Interface Development Environment,* IEEE Software, Vol. 14, No. 4, July/August 1997, pp. 41-47. Accessible at http://www.arpuerta.com/pubs/ieee97.htm.

[17] Roberts, D., Berry, D., Isensee, S., Mullaly, J., *Designing for the User with OVID: Bridging User Interface Design and Software Engineering,* Macmillan Technical Publishing, 1998.

[18] Schlungbaum, E. and Elwert, T., *Automatic User Interface Generation from Declarative Models ,* in Proceedings of the 2nd International Workshop on Computer-Aided Design of User Interfaces CADUI'96 (Namur, 5-7 June 1996), J. Vanderdonckt (ed.), Presses Universitaires de Namur, Namur, 1996, pp. 3-17.

[19] Sun Microsystems: *Java Foundation Classes: Now And The Future – White Paper,* Accessible at http://www.javasoft.com/marketing/collateral/foundation_classes.html, 1999.

[20] Szekely, P., Sukavikiya, P., Castells, P., Muthukumarasamy, J. and Salcher, E., *Declarative Interface Models for User Interface Construction Tools: the MASTERMIND Approach,* in Proceedings of the 6th IFIP TC 2/WG 2.7 Working Conference on Engineering for Human-Computer Interaction EHCI'95 (Grand Targhee Resort, 14-18 August 1995), L. Bass and C. Unger (eds.), Chapman & Hall, London, 1995 pp. 120-150. Accessible at http://www.isi.edu/isd/Mastermind/Papers/ehci95.ps.

[21] Szekely, P., *Retrospective and Challenges for Model-Based Interface Development,* in Proceedings of the 2nd International Workshop on Computer-Aided Design of User Interfaces CADUI'96 (Namur, 5-7 June 1996), J. Vanderdonckt (ed.), Presses Universitaires de Namur, Namur, 1996, pp. xxi-xliv.

[22] Vanderdonckt, J., *Current Trends in Computer-Aided Design of User Interfaces,* in Proceedings of the 2nd International Workshop on Computer-Aided Design of User Interfaces CADUI'96 (Namur, 5-7 June 1996), J. Vanderdonckt (ed.), Presses Universitaires de Namur, Namur, 1996, pp. xiii-xix.

[23] Wiecha, C., Bennett, W., Boies, S., Gould, J., and Green, S., *ITS: A Tool for Rapid Developing Interactive Applications,* in "Readings in Intelligent User Interfaces" (originally published in ACM Transactions on Information Systems, July 1990).

[24] Wilson, S., *Work Group Report: Reflections on Model-Based Design: Definitions and Challenges,* in Proceedings of the 2nd International Workshop on Computer-Aided De-

sign of User Interfaces CADUI'96 (Namur, 5-7 June 1996), J. Vanderdonckt (ed.), Presses Universitaires de Namur, Namur, 1996, pp. 327-333.

[25] Worboys, M.F., *GIS – A Computing Perspective,* Taylor & Francis, 1995.

[26] Zweben, M. and Fox, M.S. (eds.), *Intelligent Scheduling,* Morgan Kaufmann Publishers, 1994.

Chapter 10

XXL: A VISUAL+TEXTUAL ENVIRONMENT FOR BUILDING GRAPHICAL USER INTERFACES

Eric Lecolinet

Ecole Nationale Supérieure des Télécommunications & CNRS URA 820

Dept. INFRES, 46 rue Barrault, 75013 Paris, France

elc@enst.fr - http://www.enst.fr/-elc

Abstract   This paper presents XXL, a visual+textual environment for the automated building of graphical user interfaces. This system uses a declarative language which is a subset of the C language and can either be interpreted or compiled. It includes an interactive builder that can both handle graphical and non-graphical objects. This tool makes it possible to create highly customized interfaces by visual programming or by "sketching" early interface ideas that are automatically interpreted by the system to produce executable GUI objects. This builder is based on the concept of textual+visual equivalence and is able to re-edit and modify any legible source code, not only the code it itself produced. This environment is thus a truly open system that can cooperate with higher-level tools.

Keywords: User interface design, interface builders, visual / textual equivalence, sketching, model-based interface development, specification languages.

1.   INTRODUCTION

As noted in [9], the paradigm of model-based interface development has attracted a high degree of interest. However, despite its potential, this technology has not yet reached the marketplace and still remains limited to laboratory tools. On the contrary, "classical" interactive interface builders (GUIBs) are now quite widespread tools that are currently used by programmers and interface designers in spite of their well-known limitations. A possible reason for explaining this situation is that:

- Interactive builders make it possible to create highly customized GUIs that make use of quite a large set of GUI primitive elements (i.e. the "widgets" or "controls" that are provided by the underlying GUI toolkit.)

- Interactive builders are rather easy and intuitive to use because they are based on a direct manipulation paradigm (generally referred to as "Visual Programming".)

This paper does not present a high-level model-based approach but a textual+visual development tool, called **XXL**, that could be seen as the "missing link" between interactive GUI builders and high-level model-based environments. The core idea of this system is to unify textual programming (by using a specification language) and visual programming (by using an interactive GUI builder.) User interfaces can thus either be made through textual or visual programming or a free combination of both modes. Thus, as other interactive GUIBs, the XXL builder makes it possible to create highly customized interfaces by visual programming. The resulting source code is either interpretable or compilable by a standard C or C++ compiler. Most of this code follows a declarative style.

But unlike classical tools, the XXL system is also able to deal with preexisting source code. This code must just follow the (C language compatible) XXL syntax and can be produced by any means. It can for instance be directly written by a programmer or it can result from automatic code generation from another tool. By opposition with other systems, the XXL builder is thus able to re-edit and modify any legible source code, not only the code it itself produced. This property has important consequences:

- It avoids the usual strong separation between the encoding of the presentation and the interactive part of the GUI. Most interactive builders deal with both aspects in a completely different way: they make it easy to set presentation through visual programming, while they generally provide little help for specifying the GUI interaction (which usually require writing C or C++ source code). The XXL system provides several ways to integrate both aspects in a unified framework, as will be explained in the next sections.

- It allows for a truly iterative development scheme. It is for instance possible to create a GUI prototype by using the interactive builder, then to encode very specific behaviors textually in C/C++ language (for instance for dealing with variable amounts of data or data that changes dynamically at run time), then to re-edit interactively the graphical part of these textual specifications with the XXL builder in order to refine the GUI presentation, and so on. So, the interactive builder can be used at any stage of the development process because the generated source code can be freely modified without preventing further interactive modifications by using this visual programming tool.

■ Because it is based on a generic and declarative textual specification language, the XXL environment can be seen as a truly open system that can cooperate with higher-level tools. This point is especially interesting and effective because the system is based on the concept of visual and textual equivalence. One could for instance consider the following scheme:

- standard XXL specifications could be produced by a high-level model-based system,
- these specifications could be interactively modified by using the XXL builder in order to refine the GUI presentation and make them perfectly fit the user needs,
- the resulting code could then either be feed back to the model-based system, or be enriched textually by adding specific dynamical behaviors, etc.

These three phases could take place at any time during the development cycle, and be mixed in any order until the final GUI is obtained.

The next section describes the underlying concepts of the XXL system and the properties of the interactive builder. Section 3 presents an extension of the system that makes it possible to create GUIs from "rough drafts". This module can be used at the first stages of the prototyping phase in order to produce an executable GUI from a "preliminary drawing" that helps designers conceive how the interface could look like. At last we will compare XXL with related work and we will conclude.

2.   THE XXL MODEL

The XXL system is based on a generic Object Oriented Model that tends to integrate and make work together several programming modes that are usually dealt with separately. Besides its own "inner function", each XXL object must implement data and methods that makes it possible:

■ To deal interactively with a graphical representation of this object in the XXL builder,

■ To produce the corresponding textual representation of this object in XXL/C language source code,

■ To retrieve and to decode its corresponding textual representation in a XXL/C source file.

This architecture implies several interesting characteristics that are detailed in the next subsections.

2.1   THREE VIEW EDITION

This model makes it possible to associate a visual representation with *any* object, including non-graphical objects. This point is especially important and is a major difference with classical point-and-click direct manipulation interface builders. These tools are generally based on a WYSISYG paradigm and can only display the "widgets" or "controls" that compose the GUI. But they are generally unable to represent (and to let the user interact with) the non-graphical objects that may be part of the UI.

This point can be seen as a consequence of the "concreteness" of WYSISYG representations. On the one hand, moving and manipulating widgets directly by using the mouse pointer is quite convenient and intuitive, especially for novice programmers. But this concreteness implies a corollary drawback: the inability to represent and modify "immaterial" behaviors, abstract specifications or GUI parameterizations in a simple and coherent way.

The XXL model provides an integrated way to represent and interact with any kind of object. The interactive builder provides three views of the interfaces that are being developed: the *graph view* (Fig. 1), the *text view* (Fig. 2) and the *widget view*. The text view shows the corresponding descriptions in the source code. The graph view is an iconic representation that is equivalent to the text view. These two views constitute the dual (textual and visual) "abstract" specification of the UI while the widget view can be seen as the "result" of this specification. These views are *linked together* and are *incrementally updated* whenever the UI is modified interactively by using the builder. There is a one to one correspondence between the various representations of a same object. For instance, control-clicking on an object representation in any view will highlight its other available representations in the other views.

This three-view model makes it possible not only to show and control the graphical aspects but can also represent the "hidden abstract parts" of the UI. This can be seen as an attempt to let the designer see "what is behind the curtain" and provide the kind of "indirect manipulation" defined in [7] as the ability to "directly manipulate an abstraction that controls the behavior or appearance of the actual objects".

2.2   TEXTUAL + VISUAL EQUIVALENCE

Textual + Visual Equivalence is another consequence of the system architecture. Textual specifications of XXL interfaces can either be interpreted or be compiled by using a standard C or C++ compiler. In both cases, the interactive builder will be able to establish the reverse correspondence between the dynamical objects that it manipulates and their textual descriptions in the original source files. The builder is thus able to deal with preexisting source code and let the user modify the corresponding objects dynamically (even if this source

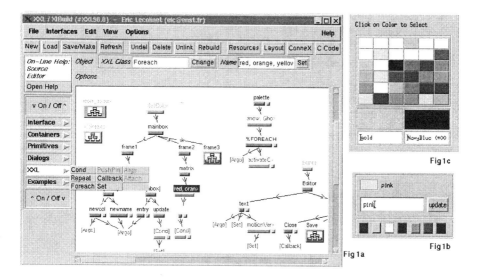

Figure   1   The graph view and two GUI examples.

code is C compiled). This source code must just follow the XXL syntax. It can be produced by any means and does not have to be necessarily generated by the XXL builder.

Moreover, XXL objects can dynamically modify their own external representation at run-time (i.e. their textual specification in the XXL/C source code). As a consequence, the original source code is modified in an incremental way by the builder and these modifications can even be made *while the application is running*. This property results from the XXL OO model as all objects are intrinsequely able to control their own representations when created, deleted or modified.

It is interesting to notice the XXL/C source code is post-interpreted from the internal representation of the objects that have been previously created. We call this "reverse-interpretation" as the parsing of the source code is guided by the run-time process (which actually results from the compilation of the same source code). In other words, XXL can be seen as a (C compatible) compilable language that is able to post-interpret its own source code dynamically at run-time in order to establish the reverse correspondence between the internal (i.e. binary) and external (i.e. textual+visual) representations of the produced objects.

2.3   GRAPHICAL, GENERIC AND IMMATERIAL OBJECTS

The current version of the system includes four main categories of objects:

- *Graphical objects* that have a physical representation in the resulting GUI (that is to say the "widget view').

- *Control objects* that specify control statements such as repetitions, conditions or embedded pieces of code such as call-back functions.

- *Structuring objects* whose aim is to decompose the interface into homogeneous and reusable components.

- *Property objects* that parameterize the appearance and behavior of the actual GUI.

All objects are represented in the text and in the graph views. Programmers can not only interact with graphical components but also with the "immaterial" objects that enforce more abstract specifications. Objects have different representations in the graph view, depending on their actual type. The graph view is not a mere "widget tree" but a direct oriented graph (DAG) of various specification objects.

The *graphical objects* encapsulate the graphical widgets of an underlying toolkit (the current implementation of the XXL system being based on the X-Window / Motif 1.1 toolkit.) These objects handle three different representations (in the text, the graph and the widget views). The widget view is always active and can also be handled with in a direct manipulation style.

A graphical object does not necessarily correspond to a single specific widget of the underlying toolkit. The system also provides contextual "generic" objects that make it possible to handle actual graphical components with a higher level of abstraction. Such objects are dynamically instantiated into different actual widgets according to their structural and functional context. Moreover, object classes can be changed interactively when using the XXL builder. These changes are then recursively propagated to the children of the modified objects. This conception scheme makes it possible to hide many low-level details to the designer and remodel GUIs after their initial creation in quite an efficient way. For instance, a box containing a set of buttons can immediately be changed into a radio box, a dialog box, a menu bar or a menu by only changing the type of the container object. The actual corresponding widgets (and child widgets) are automatically changed in order to match the generic specification.

Implicit behaviors are automatically added when combining certain objects. A menu (or a dialog box) can for instance be specified as a button child. This menu (or this dialog) will then be automatically popped up when its button parent is pressed (or clicked in second case.) Moreover, the type of the actual menu widget will also depend on context: this menu will be a "pull-down" menu if its button parent is part of a menu bar and a contextual "pop-up"menu in other cases. Thus, presentation and interaction are often implicitly deduced

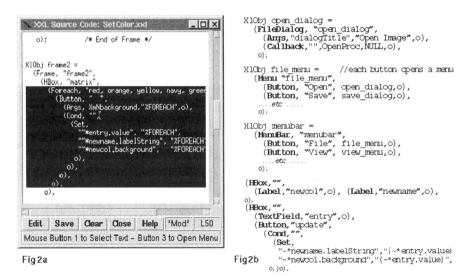

Figure 2   Text view and textual specifications.

from context. Error checking is performed in real-time in order to detect possible incoherences and to warn the user in an appropriate way.

This features tries to solve a classical drawback that interface builders are usually blamed for: they require taking decisions that fix the presentation too early in the conception process [13]. The XXL builder allows for "second thoughts" by letting programmers modify their initial decisions and deeply change the structure, behavior or presentation of the UI at any stage of the iterative design process.

2.4   THE XXL SPECIFICATION LANGUAGE

The XXL system is based on an underlying specification language which is designed to be compact and reasonably easy to understand. The main interest of this language is that it is not "yet another programming language": in spite of its very specific form, it is actually a subset of the ANSI C language. This means that XXL descriptions can be freely included into C or C++ functions or other constructs and can be compiled as any other C statement. XXL interfaces can thus make use of the whole power of a standard programming language. This point is especially important when designing complex interfaces that deal with variable amounts of data or that evolve dynamically at run time. To paraphrase a quotation from [12], this means that we can both benefit from the intuitiveness - but (relatively) low expressivity - of interface builders and the low intuitiveness - but high level of expressivity - of standard programming languages.

Various behaviors can be specified in a declarative way thanks to a feature called Conditional Evaluation. This mechanism makes it possible to reevaluate a subpart of an XXL specification when a certain condition is satisfied (for instance when a certain event occurs on a graphical object on when an active value is changed). It is thus possible to specify object creation, modification or deletion in a declarative style. Fig. 1b illustrates a basic example of this mechanism (the corresponding code is at the bottom of Fig. 2b). This interface changes the color and the label of the two top widgets by reading a string that is entered by the user in a text field. When the user clicks on the update button, the sub-expression that is included in the *Cond* statement is reevaluated. This sub-expression specifies an assignment that gets the string value that was entered in the entry widget, converts it to the appropriate types and changes the string label and the background color of the appropriate objects. This mechanism can be seen as a way to specify call-back functions in a declarative way.

More sophisticated behaviors or constructs can also be specified. For instance, the *Foreach* abstract object makes it possible to iterate an XXL sub-expression. The simple color palette shown on Fig. 1c is created by using this feature: there is only one color button specification (Fig. 2a) that is iterated for several color names. Several actual widgets are thus generated but they all correspond to a single XXL graphical object. The behavior of these objects is also specified in a declarative way by means of a *Cond* statement which is itself included in the *Foreach* statement.

XXL specifications can also constitute interface models that can be instantiated several times. For instance, the five icons that are included in the interface shown in Fig. 3a result from five successive realizations of the same XXL sub-interface This example also shows the use of behavior objects that implement dynamic manipulations techniques. The icon interface specification (Fig. 3b) includes a *MoveHandle* object that automatically makes the icon instance movable by grabbing it interactively with the mouse. These icon instances are linked together with *DLinks* graphical objects. These links (that are materialized by arrows on the screen) will automatically follow the objects they are related to (that is to say the actual realizations of the icon specification) when these objects are moved.

As said before, XXL specifications can be included in C or C++ programs and be compiled "as it". They can also be interpreted by using a special-purpose Unix shell or by loading them dynamically from a C program. This feature can be used for testing new interfaces at the beginning of the prototyping phase. It also makes it possible to *exchange* XXL Interfaces dynamically between separate (and possibly remote) programs: XXL specifications are then sent through the network by using sockets and are interpreted at run-time by the receiving program. This mechanism can also be used for modifying objects or calling functions that reside in remote programs.

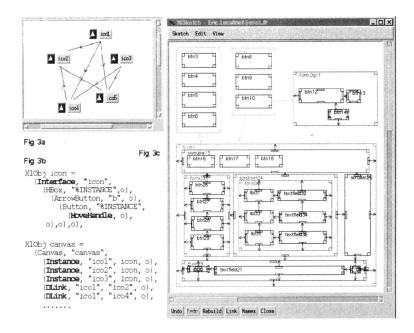

Fig 3a

Fig 3b

Fig 3c

```
XlObj icon =
  (Interface, "icon",
    (HBox, "%INSTANCE",o),
      (ArrowButton, "b", o),
        (Button, "%INSTANCE",
          (MoveHandle, o),
        o),o),o),

XlObj canvas =
  (Canvas, "canvas",
    (Instance, "ico1", icon, o),
    (Instance, "ico2", icon, o),
    (Instance, "ico3", icon, o),
    (DLink, "ico1", "ico2", o),
    (DLink, "ico1", "ico4", o),
    .......
```

Figure   3   Interface and instances (a, b); The sketch view (c)

3.   SKETCH DRAWING

This section presents an extension of the system that makes it possible to create GUIs from "rough sketches". This module provides a separate interactive way of designing interfaces at the early stages of their conception. It makes it possible to create an executable GUI from a "preliminary drawing" that helps designers conceive how the interface could look like. The idea is to let them draw early interface ideas in the same way as they would do on a piece of paper. But this electronic sketch will also produce a fully operational interface.

The Sketch View (Fig. 3c) lets designers conceive a first draft of the GUI by drawing a sketch on the screen. This drawing is dynamically interpreted by the system in order to produce an executable GUI. Actual XXL objects are implicitly "deduced" from the sketch and the resulting widget view is produced in real time so that designers can immediately see the result of their drawing and correct it iteratively (the system providing full undo capabilities). The graph view and the text view are made available to the designer once the sketching stage is over. Visual and/or textual edition can then be performed to refine the GUI, add call-back functions, etc.

These various views are mostly used at different steps of the development process. The sketch view let designers focus attention on the global layout of the GUI without having to take care of implementation details. The graph view makes it possible to refine the presentation and to deal with immaterial objects that represent abstractions, while the text view is mostly used for dealing with implementation details or with the dynamical management of user interfaces (when GUIs must handle variable amounts of data or data that changes at run time). So, the XXL system tries to integrate high-level design as well as low-level implementation details into a unified framework.

3.1   SKETCH INTERPRETATION

Graphical objects are created by drawing rectangles at a certain location in the sketch. The first rectangle drawn in the sketching area is implicitly considered as a "main box" (that will not necessarily be the actual main window of the final application but can be included into another object at a later stage). Then, an included horizontal rectangle, located at the top of this main box will automatically be seen as a menu bar by the system (Fig. 3c). Drawing enclosed rectangles inside this menu bar will generate menu bar buttons. Menus (and dialog boxes) are created by drawing vertical (or horizontal) rectangles outside the main box. Menus and dialogs are attached to the button that will open them by drawing a link between these components.

Other rectangles (drawn in the main box, the menus or the dialog boxes) will be first interpreted as button objects. Buttons are then automatically transformed into intermediate container boxes if another rectangle (i.e. a button) is drawn inside them. Object type can also be explicitly set by the designer (for instance for transforming a button into a text area or whatever.)

The system proposes default rules for lay out management. Objects are automatically aligned but this default layout can be changed interactively. Graphical constraints are automatically computed by the system. These constraints are materialized by arrows on the drawing (fig 3c). Constraints can be set in a direct manipulation style by moving objects with the mouse or by attaching or detaching the corresponding arrows.

This way of designing GUIs favors the use of spatial topological constraints instead of fixing absolute x, y coordinates by moving and resizing widgets directly with the mouse. This leads to a more flexible representation that can evolve dynamically at run-time when the final user resizes the windows or customizes the application (for instance by specifying larger fonts). The use of such constraints is rather easy and natural here because they are either deduced from the drawing, or explicitly drawn in a simple way. Thus, it is interesting to notice that the drawing performed by the user is not a WYSISYG but a logical representation of the GUI. The actual GUI will not exactly look exactly the same as the drawing but will follow the logical constraints specified by the designer. It is up to the graphical system to adjust and lay out the corresponding widgets in an appropriate way.

The sketching module is based on a set of contextual rules that implicitely transform the user drawing into structural or topological constraints. These rules are encoded in an object oriented style. Drawing a new component produces a new sketching object that is managed by its own container. The combination of the rules defined in both objects will control the graphical aspect of these two sketching objects and will also implicitly produce XXL objects of an appropriate type (or modify existing objects in an appropriate way.)

4. RELATED WORK

The XXL system is related to the three following domains: interface builders, model-based interface development and sketch drawing. Similarly to standard interface builders (a comprehensive survey can be found in [8]), the XXL builder makes it possible to create highly customized interfaces by visual programming. However, the underlying model is quite different: the system can handle generic and immaterial objects, it uses a declarative language (which is a subset of the C language) and it is based on a textual+visual equivalence paradigm.

Promising approaches have been proposed in the field of model-based interface development [13], [12], [2], [14], [11], [9]. However XXL is not a high-level model-based approach but a visual+textual environment for the automated building of UIs. In that sense, it could be compared to certain aspects of other systems that can generate user interfaces from partial models such as Janus [1], or Mobi-D [10], that includes an interactive tool.

Interface sketching is a rather new approach and there are very few systems that implement this idea. For instance, the SILK system [3] provides an interactive tool that allows designers to quickly sketch an interface by using an electronic pad and stylus. By opposition, the XXL system uses a "faked metaphor" (designers draw sketches as they would do in "reality", by not in the same "material" way) in order to prevent users from pattern recognition errors to ease interaction with ordinary pointing devices, and thus, to avoid the use of specific hardware.

5. CONCLUSION AND FUTURE WORK

This paper presents an hybrid approach which tries to mix several aspects of interactive GUI builders, model-based systems and interactive sketching. This new system lets designers produce generic interface specifications in an interactive way, either by textual or visual programming or by constrained sketching. The conception process is fully iterative and is consistent from the very early stages of design to the realization of the final application. The full system provides four different views of the GUI that correspond to various stages of the conception process (or to the various level of expertise of the designers involved in this task).

The system has been fully implemented and relies on the X-Window system and the Motif toolkit. The XXL builder has been used for realizing various tools and students' projects at our institute. The XXL environment has also been used for creating and refining the interactive builder itself. The system is freely available at URL: `http://www.enst.fr/~elc`.

We are now developing a new GUI toolkit called **Ubit** that is based on a "brick construction game" metaphor [6]. Such a model is especially well suited for visual programming tools and should offer new perspectives when combined with the XXL builder.

References

[1] Balzert H., Hofmann F., Kruschinski V., Niemann C., *The JANUS Application Development Environment-Generating More than the User Interface.* In Jean Vanderdonckt, Ed., CADUI'96, Presses Universitaires de Namur, pp. 183-206, 1996.

[2] Bodart F., Hennebert A-M., Leheureux J-M., Provot I., Sacre B., Vanderdonckt J., *Towards a Systematic Building of Software Architecture: The Trident Methodological Guide.* Workshop on Design, Specification, Verification of Interactive Systems, pp. 237-253, 1995.

[3] Landay J., Myers B., *Interactive Sketching for the Early Stages of User Interface Design.* Proc. of the CHI Conference, 1995.

[4] Lecolinet E., *XXL: A Dual Approach for Building User Interfaces.* Proc. ACM UIST, pp. 99-108, Seattle, USA, Nov. 1996.

[5] Lecolinet E., *Designing GUIs by Sketch Drawing and Visual Programming.* Proc. Int. Conf. on Advanced Visual Interfaces (AVI). ACM Press, pp. 274-276, 1998.

[6] Lecolinet E., *A Brick Construction Game Model for Creating Graphical User Interfaces: The Ubit Toolkit* Proc. INTERACT'99.

[7] Morse A., Reynolds G., *Overcoming Current Growth Limits in UI Development.* Communications of the ACM, Vol.3 6, No. 4, April 1993.

[8] Myers B.A., *User Interface Software Tools.* ACM Trans. on Computer-Human Interaction, Vol. 2, No. 1, pp. 64-103, 1995.

[9] Puerta A., *The MECANO Project: Comprehensive and Integrated Support for Model-Based Interface Developement.* In Jean Vanderdonckt, Ed., CADUI'96, Presses Universitaires de Namur, 1996.

[10] Puerta A., Cheng E., Ou T., Min J., *MOBILE: User-Centered Interface Building.* Proc. of the CHI Conference, 1999.

[11] Schlungbaum E., Elwert T., *Automatic User Interface Generation from Declarative Models.* In Jean Vanderdonckt, Ed., CADUI'96, Presses Univ. de Namur, pp. 3-17, 1996.

[12] Szekely P., Luo P., Neches R., *Beyond Interface Builders: Model-Based Interface Tools.* Proc. INTERCHI'93, pp. 383-390, 1993.

[13] Wiecha C., Bennett W., Boies S., Gould J., Greene S., *ITS: A Tool for Rapidly Developing Interactive Applications.* ACM Trans. on Information Systems, Vol 8, No. 3, July 1990.

[14] Wilson S., Johnson P., *Bridging the Generation Gap: from Work Tasks to User Interface Designs.* In Jean Vanderdonckt, Ed., CADUI'96, Presses Univ. de Namur, pp. 77-94, 1996.

Chapter 11

SEMI-AUTOMATED LINKING OF USER INTERFACE DESIGN ARTIFACTS

Said S. Elnaffar and T.C. Nicholas Graham

Department of Computing and Information Science

Queen's University, Kingston, Ontario, Canada K7L 3N6

{elnaffar,graham}@cs.queensu.ca

Abstract   User centered design involves the creation of design artifacts such as task and architecture models, typically by people with different backgrounds using inconsistent terminology. Communication between user interface designers can potentially be improved if the viewpoints represented by these design artifacts can be correlated. This research demonstrates how different design artifacts can be linked semi-automatically. We illustrate this technique using Adligo, a computer-based tool for generating links between the User Action Notation (UAN) task model and the Clock architectural model. Our results show that in two case studies, we were able to generate 90% of possible links with error rate of 0% to 12%, with limited human assistance.

Keywords: User Interface Design Artifacts, Linking User Interface Viewpoints

1.   INTRODUCTION

Numerous design activities contribute to the usability of an interactive system [Brown et al., 1998]: the production of *task models* helps to record the human activities that a computer system is meant to support, *scenarios* and *task-oriented specifications* record how users perform these tasks via a particular user interface, while *software architectures* provide a high-level view of the system's implementation.

A trend in processes for interactive system design has been to use information from each of these design activities to support the others. For example, task-oriented specifications can be used to automatically generate user interface architectures [Paterno et al., 1997] and user interface dialogue specifications [Palanque et al., 1995], or to completely generate user interfaces [Johnson et al., 1995; Szekely et al., 1995].

Even when the relation between design activities is not this explicit, it is helpful for designers carrying out one activity to have access to information from others. For example, Cockton and Clarke have shown the importance of explicitly linking documents capturing context of use of interactive systems to design documents [Cockton and Clarke, 1999]. In our earlier work with the Vista environment [Brown et al., 1998], we showed how linking behavioural design artifacts (such as task models and task-oriented specifications) to constructional artifacts (such as code) can help relate the differing points of view of HCI designers and software engineers. In Vista, users simultaneously see up to four styles of design docuemtent in a visual browsing environment. Clicking on part of one document highlights related parts of other documents. This allows developers to answer questions such as, what tasks may be impacted by the modification of a particular architecture component, or whether two similar action sequences in a UAN specification [Hartson et al., 1990] are implemented by the same mechanism. Brown and Marshall have since extended this work to link user interface scenario documents to implementation design documents [Brown and Marshall, 1998]. Linking approaches therefore help in relating information that may be presented from different points of view, allowing information from different design documents to be more easily used by other designers and developers.

The difficulty with linking approaches is that they typically require large numbers of links to be specified manually. For example, Vista is capable of automatically linking artifacts grouped exclusively within the behavioural or constructional domains, but requires a user to provide links that bridge the gap between these two points of view. Cockton and Clark's approach requires links to be explicitly made using an LD Relationship Editor [Cockton and Clarke, 1999]. Hand-specifying links is tedious, time-consuming and error-prone. For example, in the two case studies presented in section 5., approximately 100 links in each needed to be coded by hand using the Vista system. Furthermore, as design artifacts evolve throughout the life cycle of the interactive system, links continually need to be changed, again by hand. In order for link-based approaches to be practical, therefore, some kind of automation of the process of finding and maintaining links is required. Automating the generation of links is challenging, however, as different design artifacts are typically developed by different people, perhaps using incompatible terminology, and perhaps involving informal components such as English language text.

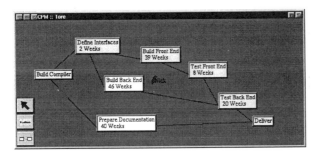

Figure   1   UI of a groupware critical path planning application [Graham, 1997].

This paper presents a mechanism for the semi-automated generation of links between task-oriented specifications in the User Action Notation (UAN) [Hartson et al., 1990] and architecture models expressed in the Clock architecture style [Graham and Urnes, 1996]. A user must provide a small set of rules to guide the link generation process. As shown in section 4., these rules are presented in a simple tabular format called a *dictionary*. This approach has been implemented in *Adligo*, a tool which inputs a UAN specification, a Clock architecture and a dictionary, and outputs a set of links suitable for browsing with the Vista environment. As shown in the case studies of section 5., when provided with fewer than ten user-specified rules, Adligo was capable of generating 90% of links found by a human, with an error rate of 0% to 12%. With 16 rules, 100% of links were found, with no errors.

This paper is organized as follows. Section 2. presents an example application, and motivates the utility of developing links. Section 3. introduces Adligo's rule-based solution to link generation, while section 4. discusses Adligo's implementation. Finally, section 5. reports on the results of two case studies used to evaluate the effectiveness of Adligo.

2.   EXAMPLE: CRITICAL PATH PLANNING

In order to motivate the problem of link generation, we will use the example of a groupware critical path planning application [Graham, 1997]. Using this application, we will informally discuss some of the difficulties of automatically generating links. We will then use the critical path planner to illustrate Adligo's dictionary, allowing semi-automatic generation of these (and other) links.

Several design artifacts (collected in [Graham et al., 1996]) contributed to the development of the critical path planner. The system is based on a task model adapted from Dilworth [Dilworth, 1993]. Planners carry out two basic tasks – breaking up the project into a network of job steps ordered by their dependencies, and allocating resources to these job steps. Figure 1.1 shows a system supporting these tasks.

A UAN task-oriented specification was developed to show how each of the planning tasks can be carried out using the interface of figure 1.1. Figure 1.2 shows one of the tables from this UAN specification, describing the task of repositioning one of the job step nodes in the critical path network. In order to reposition a node, the user first moves the mouse pointer over the node, clicks on it, drags the mouse, and releases. As the mouse is moved, the node follows the mouse pointer. As the node is moved, it is *locked*, so that none of the other users can move the node at the same time. Locked nodes are shown with red text on other users' displays, so that the other users can see that they are not permitted to move that node. The full UAN description contains 18 such tables [Graham et al., 1996].

Figure 1.2 also shows a view of the software architecture of the critical path planner. The architecture is based on the Clock architecture style [Graham and Urnes, 1996], a layered extension of the Model-View-Controller (MVC) architecture [Krasner and Pope, 1988]. In this architecture, the system is decomposed into *components*, responsible for I/O at some point of the display, and *ADT's* responsible for maintaining system state. The links shown in the figure reveal the relation between the architecture and the system it implements.

For example, the mouse click actions (Mv/M^) that start and end the movement of a node are handled by the `mouseButton` method of the `browseNode` component. Similarly, the movement of the node itself (~[x,y]) is handled by the `relMotion` method. Locking of the node is handled by the methods of the `Lock` ADT. Modifying the position of the node (nodePosition:=(x,y)) is handled via the `setNodePosition` method of the `NodePosition` ADT. The current position of the mouse pointer ((x,y)) is obtained via the `MousePosition` ADT.

These links can be visually browsed using Vista [Brown et al., 1998], helping developers to associate task-oriented specifications with user interface implementations. However, it is clear that such links are highly tedious to generate by hand. It is not feasible to derive such links completely automatically – the developers of the UAN specification and of the software architecture have used different terms to describe the same parts of their artifacts, and the UAN specification contains informal English prose that is not amenable to automatic processing.

The next section shows how Adligo provides a simple rule-based mechanism that allows links to be semi-automatically derived. As will be shown in section 5., 90% of the 108 links that a human found in the CPM example were derived using only 8 rules in the Adligo dictionary.

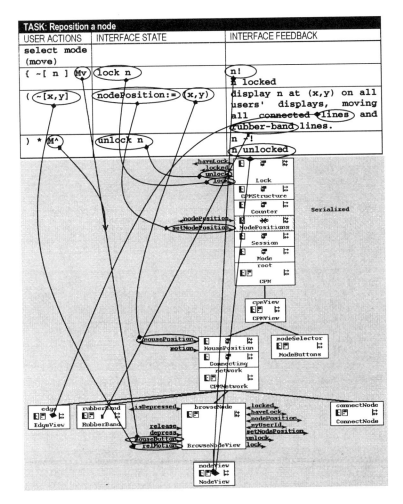

Figure 2 Example links derived by Adligo.

3.   SEMI-AUTOMATED GENERATION OF LINKS

The key to being able to find links between the behavioural task-oriented specification and the constructional user interface architecture is to bridge the difference in point of view of the two forms of specification. A single component might contribute to the implementation of several tasks; similarly, a single task may be carried out through the use of multiple components.

The basic approach to generating links is to provide a set of *linking rules* in a dictionary. Figure 1.3 shows a subset of the rules used with

DICTIONARY: Standard

Rule #	RULE SCOPE	UAN PATTERN	CLOCK ARCHITECTURE PATTERN
S2		Mv	mouseButton
S3		M^	mouseButton
S6		~[$(x), $(y)]	motion | relMotion
S21		$(obj)+=1	increment$(obj) \| inc$(obj) | increment
S26		currentPos	mousePosition
S27		(x,y)	nodePosition | userPosition
S28		$(anyVar) :=	set$(anyVar)

DICTIONARY: The CPM Planner

Rule #	RULE SCOPE	UAN PATTERN	CLOCK ARCHITECTURE PATTERN
C1	Create a new node	select mode	Network
C2		mode	button
C6	Reposition a node	n	nodeView->browseNode
C9		currentMode:=	setMode
C10		mode	Mode
C11		connect $(obj1) to $(obj2)	setConnectionTarget
C12		lines	edge.view
C13		rubber-band	rubberBand.view
C14		solid line from n1 to n3	edge.lineFrom

Figure 3 Selected rules extracted from the standard and custom dictionaries used to link design artifacts in the critical path planning application.

the critical path planning application. The rules are divided into a *standard* dictionary which is included for every application, and a *custom* dictionary, which provides rules specific to a particular application.

Rules establish a correspondence between parts of a UAN specification and parts of a Clock architecture. For example, rule S2 in figure 1.3 establishes that the pattern Mv in a UAN specification corresponds to the method mouseButton in a Clock architecture. This rule states that whenever the Mv user action is encountered in a UAN specification, there should be some mouseButton method in the architecture that implements this user action. This is a *rule* since the correspondence applies whenever the Mv symbol is encountered. As shown in figure 1.2, rules S2 and S3 generate links showing that in the *Reposition a Node* task, the Mv and M^ user actions are handled by the mouseButton method of the browseNode architecture component.

3.1   MULTIPLE TARGETS

Sometimes, a pattern in a UAN specification may correspond to different locations in a Clock architecture, depending on implementation choices made by the developer. For example, motion events in Clock may be treated as absolute or relative to the current position, handled either by a `motion` or `relMotion` method. Therefore, rules must permit a UAN pattern to match a set of possible architecture patterns.

As shown in rule S6, multiple architecture patterns may be combined using a disjunction ("|") symbol. The UAN pattern specifies that the general form in UAN for moving to a new screen location is `~[x,y]`, where x and y are some identifiers. In this rule, the symbols `$(x)` and `$(y)` represent variables that may be matched to arbitrary identifiers in the UAN specification. The architecture pattern establishes that mouse motion user actions may be handled by `motion` or `relMotion` methods.

In figure 1.2, rule S6 generated the link between `~[x,y]` to the `relMotion` method implemented by the `browseNode` architecture component.

3.2   RULES WITH VARIABLES

Very powerful rules can be written using variables. For example, a common pattern of correspondence between UAN specifications and Clock architectures is that assignment to some value in UAN is implemented via a *set* method in the architecture. For example, in figure 1.2, the UAN `nodePosition := (x,y)` is implemented via the method `set-NodePosition` in the `NodePositions` ADT.

Rule S28 searches for correspondences of this general form: the UAN pattern `$(anyVar):=` is matched to a method in the architecture of the form `set$(anyVar)`. Variables in the UAN and architecture patterns must be unified in finding a match.

Similarly, rule S21 identifies a common correspondence case, showing how incrementing a value may be matched to any of a set of increment methods.

This ability to use variables, unification, and multiple architecture patterns allows simple rules in the standard library to identify common usage patterns, generating many links without requiring any custom rules at all.

3.3   CUSTOM RULES

The standard rules described above help provide links for built in user actions of UAN (such as user actions corresponding to mouse and keyboard input), and for commonly observed usage patterns in specifications. However, real specifications normally require additional rules, primarily to resolve inconsistencies in terminology between the UAN designer and the user interface implementer.

For example, rule C11 in figure 1.3 shows how the English text `connect` x `to` y corresponds to the method `setConnectionTarget`. Such correlations are not difficult for a human to provide, but would be difficult to find automatically.

Sometimes, such correspondences must be scoped to a particular task. For example, in the UAN task *Reposition a Node* (figure 1.2), the symbol n refers to some node in the critical path network. It would be dangerous to establish a global rule stating that n always refers to a node, since this may not be true for every task specification, and might lead to the generation of incorrect links. Rule C6 of figure 1.3 shows how a rule establishing this correspondence can be scoped to apply only to a specific task.

Similarly, rules may be scoped to apply to a particular method or component in the architecture. For example, rule C14 explicitly specifies that `solid line from n1 to n3` corresponds to the `lineFrom` method of the `edge` component. Similarly, rule C6 explicitly specifies the location of the target component in the architecture (i.e., the component `nodeView` is specified to be a child of the component `browseNode`.)

Restriction of the scope of rules can have the effect of creating rules that are so specific that they generate only one link. Such rules can be useful in specifying explicit links when the generality of the rule-based approach is not appropriate.

4.   IMPLEMENTATION

We now briefly describe how the Adligo tool uses the dictionary described in the last section to generate links. For an in-depth description of Adligo's algorithms, see [Elnaffar, 1999]. The generation of links includes the following steps:

1. Find a *match* for one of the rules in the UAN specification;

2. Find the *context* for the match;

3. Starting from the context component, find the best match for the architecture pattern.

The notion of a context component is key to the generation of links. A context is a part of the user interface to which user actions are applied. The standard UAN mechanism for changing a context is the user action `~[c]`, which specifies that the user moves his/her pointer into the context of screen region c. Following a context change, Adligo assumes that subsequent user actions are applied to the new context.

Consider for example the sequence `~[n] Mv` of figure 1.2, as interpreted using the rules shown in figure 1.3. The following sequence of

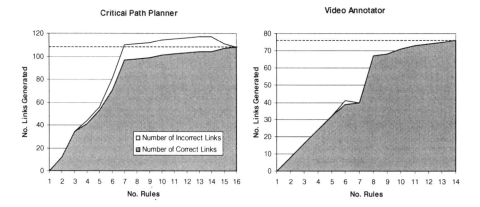

Figure 4 Results of CPM and Video Annotator case studies. The dashed horizontal line shows the number of links found by hand.

rule applications leads to the generation of a link to the `mouseButton` method of the `nodeView` component:

1. The user action `~[n]` changes the context. `n` matches the rule C6, setting the context to the component `nodeView->browseNode`.

2. The user action `Mv` matches rule S2. Adligo attempts to match a method `mouseButton` within the context of the `nodeView-> browseNode` component.

3. The parent of the `nodeView` component implements the `mouseButton` method; the link is therefore generated to the method `browseNode. mouseButton`.

5.   EVALUATION

In order to evaluate the effectiveness of our semi-automated technique for linking user interface artifacts, we performed two case studies on existing applications. These applications are the critical path planner [Graham, 1997] described in section 2., and a groupware video annotator tool [Graham and Urnes, 1997], both designed and developed prior to this work with Adligo. Both case studies involved over 100 lines of UAN, divided into approximately 20 tables. The implementation architectures of the examples consist of 13 and 30 components, containing over 100 methods. Therefore, the examples are small enough for us to derive links by hand for purposes of comparison, but large enough to expose how well Adligo functions.

In order to create a correct set of links against which to compare Adligo's performance, we derived by hand a set of links between the UAN task-oriented specification and the Clock architecture. We then ran Adligo to mechanically derive a set of links. Through this process, Adligo's dictionary was tuned to successively improve the links generated. Finally, we compared the hand-derived links to Adligo's links. For each case where the links differed, we either decided that the hand-derived links were incorrect and updated them, or decided that the generated links were incorrect, and recorded an error.

Figure 1.4 shows the number of correct and incorrect links generated by Adligo as rules were successively added to the dictionary. In both examples, adding eight rules was sufficient to generate approximately 90% of available links, while 16 rules was sufficient to generate 100% of the links found by hand.

The percentage of generated links that were incorrect ranged between 0% and 12% in the two applications, finally dropping to 0%. As the number of rules increases, the error rate initially increases (as the number of generated links increases.) As rules are added, the error rate then decreases as the rule set becomes more precise.

5.1   ANALYSIS

These results show that, at least for these two examples, Adligo is highly successful at generating links. With a small number of rules, in excess of 90% of available links can be automatically generated, with an error rate within approximately 10%. Creating rules to this level of accuracy appears to be relatively little work. Rules are easy to write, as they are syntactically presented as a dictionary, in which correspondences are written directly using the UAN notation. Further studies with external users will be required to determine how willing developers will be to create linking rules.

The simplicity of the dictionary format carries a cost of expressiveness – only simple control over scoping of rules is provided, and only simple patterns based on variables are allowed. The examples we have performed to date allow us to tentatively conclude that these restrictions are not problematic in practice. In cases where the dictionary language is not sufficiently expressive, rules can be added to the dictionary that either explicitly add links or explicitly rule out error cases. In our examples, when such rules are added, coverage rates climb to 100% while error rates drop to 0%. This shows that if Adligo users wish to invest the time to refine their rule sets, very accurate performance can be obtained.

The Adligo approach is most successful if the UAN specifier is methodical in the use of UAN. For example, if the ":=" symbol is used consistently to indicate change of interface state, standard rules related to assignment will be invoked. If the same names for tasks and contexts are used consistently, then custom rules will be more likely to generate correct results. For example, many of the custom rules in the critical path planner dictionary specifically deal with the use of poor names in the UAN specification such as n, n1, n2, etc. to refer to nodes in the network. While the requirement of consistency and use of clear naming conventions adds an extra burden on UAN designers, such conventions also lead to specifications that are easier for humans to read.

The rule-based approach has the potential advantage of being robust to changes in the underlying design documents. As new tasks are added or reworded, or as architecture components are modified and repositioned, it is likely that existing rules will continue to apply. Further experimentation will be required to demonstrate the extent to which rules are robust to evolution in design documents.

6.   CONCLUSIONS

This paper has shown that it is practical to partially automate the generation of links between user interface design artifacts, even when these artifacts are developed by different people and when the artifacts involve informal English prose. Users must provide a small set of rules in a simple dictionary format. From the rules, the Adligo tool derives links between task-oriented specifications and user interface architectures.

We plan to continue investigating the effectiveness of the rule-based approach, and plan to carry out experiments tracking the robustness of rules as design artifacts evolve.

Acknowledgements

This work was partially supported by the Natural Science and Engineering Research Council (NSERC) and by Communications and Information Technology Ontario (CITO). Greg Phillips provided helpful feedback on earlier drafts of the paper. Tim Wright was very helpful in connecting Adligo to Vista.

References

Brown, J., Graham, T., and Wright, T. (1998). The Vista environment for the coevolutionary design of user interfaces. In *Proc. CHI '98*, pages 376–383.

Brown, J. and Marshall, S. (1998). Sharing human-computer interaction and software engineering design artifacts. In *Proceedings of OZCHI'98*.

Cockton, G. and Clarke, S. (1999). Using contextual information effectively in design. In Sasse, A., Tauber, M., and Johnson, C., editors, *Proc. INTERACT '99*. Kluwer.

Dilworth, J. (1993). *Production and Operations Management: Manufacturing and Services, Fifth Edition*. McGraw Hill.

Elnaffar, S. (1999). Semi-automated linking of user interface design artifacts. Master's thesis, Queens University at Kingston, Canada.

Graham, T. (1997). GroupScape: Integrating synchronous groupware and the world wide web. In *Proc. INTERACT '97*, pages 547–554. Chapman and Hall.

Graham, T., Damker, H., Morton, C., Telford, E., and Urnes, T. (1996). The Clock Methodology: Bridging the Gap Between User Interface Design and Implementation. Technical Report CS-96-04, York University, Canada.

Graham, T. and Urnes, T. (1996). Linguistic support for the evolutionary design of software architectures. In *Proc. ICSE 18*, pages 418–427. IEEE Press.

Graham, T. and Urnes, T. (1997). Integrating Support for Temporal Media into an Architecture for Graphical User Interfaces. In *Proc. ICSE 19*. IEEE Press.

Hartson, H., Siochi, A., and Hix, D. (1990). The UAN: A user-oriented representation for direct manipulation interface design. *ACM TOIS*, 8(3):181–203.

Johnson, P., Johnson, H., and Wilson, S. (1995). *Rapid Prototyping of User Interfaces Driven by Task Models*. John Wiley & Sons.

Krasner, G. and Pope, S. (1988). A cookbook for using the Model-View-Controller user interface paradigm in Smalltalk-80. *JOOP*, 1(3):26–49.

Palanque, P., Bastide, R., and Senges, V. (1995). Task model – system model: Towards a unifying formalism. In *Proc. HCI International*, pages 489–494. Elsevier.

Paterno, F., Mancini, C., and Meniconi, S. (1997). Engineering task models. In *Proc. IEEE Conference on Engineering Complex Systems*, pages 69–76. IEEE Press.

Szekely, P., Sukaviriya, P., Castells, P., and Muthukamarasamy, J. (1995). Declarative interface models for user interface construction tools: the MASTERMIND approach. In *Proc. EHCI '95*, pages 120–150.

Chapter 12

THE TEALLACH TOOL: USING MODELS FOR FLEXIBLE USER INTERFACE DESIGN

Peter J. Barclay[2], Tony Griffiths[1], Jo McKirdy[3], Norman W. Paton[1], Richard Cooper[3], Jessie Kennedy[2]

[1]*Department of Computer Science, University of Manchester, Oxford Road, Manchester M13 9PL, UK.*
Email: { griffitt, norm } @cs.man.ac.uk

[2]*Department of Computing Studies, Napier University, Canal Court, 42 Craiglockhart Avenue, Edinburgh EH14 1LT, UK.*
Email: { pjb, jessie} @dcs.napier.ac.uk

[3]*Department of Computing Science, University of Glasgow, Glasgow G12 8QQ, UK.*
Email: { jo, rich} @dcs.gla.ac.uk

http://www.dcs.gla.ac.uk/research/teallach/

Abstract   Model-based user interface development environments aim to provide designers with a more systematic approach to user interface development using a particular design method. This method is realised through tools which support the construction and linkage of the supported models. This paper presents the tools which support the construction of the Teallach models in the context of the Teallach design method. Distinctive features of the Teallach tool include comprehensive facilities for relating the different models, and the provision of a flexible design method in which models can be constructed and related by designers in different orders and in different ways.

Keywords: Model-based, User Interface Development Environments, Flexible User Interface Design, Methods, User Interface Design Tools..

1.   INTRODUCTION

The development and maintenance of user interface software is challenging. Although interface development environments provide facilities that allow individual components within an interface to be constructed without recourse to programming, the behaviour of user interfaces is generally implemented by complex, hand crafted software systems. Although design patterns can be used to provide an organisational framework for interface software, it is still the case that user interface software is intrinsically complex, and that changing an existing interface to reflect changing requirements and to take account of user feedback is a laborious and often somewhat ad-hoc process.

Model-based user interface development environments (MB-UIDEs) have been developed with a view to providing a more systematic approach to user interface development, building in particular on abstract models of different aspects of user interface functionality (e.g., TADEUS [11], FUSE [7] and MOBI-D [10]). Typically, a MB-UIDE will include domain, task, dialogue and presentation models. The benefits that it is hoped will arise from the use of MB-UIDEs include the generation of interface software based on the abstract models, and more seamless integration of the interface design and implementation processes.

However, although MB-UIDEs have a range of promising characteristics for easing user interface development, they introduce a number of new challenges. The development of effective tools for the construction and linking of a collection of abstract models is itself a substantial challenge, which must be addressed in the context of a design method that directs the interface developer in the construction of a coherent collection of models. This paper seeks to address these two issues – tools for model construction and tool support for a design method – in the context of the Teallach MB-UIDE [6]. Distinctive features of the Teallach tool include comprehensive facilities for relating the different models, and the provision of a flexible design method in which models can be constructed and related by designers in different orders and in different ways.

The paper is structured as follows. Section 2 sets the scene by introducing the Teallach system. Section 3 describes a case study that will be used throughout the paper. Section 4 outlines the flexible design method supported by Teallach, and which must be accounted for in the tool. Section 5 describes the facilities provided by the tool for editing and relating the Teallach models. Section 6 presents some conclusions.

2.   TEALLACH BACKGROUND AND MOTIVATION

The Teallach MB-UIDE is primarily concerned with constructing user-interfaces to object oriented databases. The Teallach user is the designer of interfaces to database applications, not the end-user of these interfaces. In order to meet the needs of such design efforts, Teallach provides three models: a domain model, a task model, and a presentation model. These models are described in detail in [6].

The presence of underlying models gives some advantages to an interface-building tool, such as a clear semantics for the interface under construction, and facilities for the automatic checking of consistency in the models (and hence in the resulting interfaces), together with support for 'help' and 'undo' functionality. However, we have identified a number of weaknesses in existing MB-UIDEs. Some of these are described below; for more details, the reader is referred to [4].

- Some systems impose a rigid methodology on the interface-designer.
- Most systems do not provide the facilities to work with database-specific concepts, such as transactions.
- Many systems have a fixed set of widgets from which interfaces can be constructed, thereby disallowing the use of application specific widgets which may be required in some domains.
- Few systems have a clear method for representing flow of state information within the interface to be generated.

One of the goals of the Teallach project is to develop models that address some of these shortfalls, and to build a prototype tool that illustrates our solutions. In particular, we do not wish to impose a particular style of working on the interface designer. For example, one designer may wish to proceed from specifications to implementations, whereas another may wish first to sketch forms to be used in the interface, and then connect these to application functionality. Both these approaches, and others, are allowed by Teallach. This is achieved by 1) treating all of the models in an even-handed manner, and 2) performing consistency checking as late as possible, so that the designer is free to work through 'inconsistent' designs towards consistent ones. In particular, automatic generation of model components may be used as the designer desires: it is possible to generate large parts of the interface automatically (and optionally modify these generated components), or to 'wire together' user-built substructures with no use of automatic generation.

Teallach's interfaces are realised as compiled Java applications, giving the efficiency of compiled code while running on any major platform. The widgets used are taken from Java's Swing widget set [2], but additional user-supplied widgets may be added to the toolkit and used at any time. Access to database-specific concepts is supplied through Teallach's ODMG-style [1] domain model.

3.   CASE STUDY

To provide a tangible explanation of the manner in which the Teallach tools operate and are used, subsequent tool discussion will be conducted in relation to a case study, which is a library database application – the UML class diagram of this is shown in Figure 1.

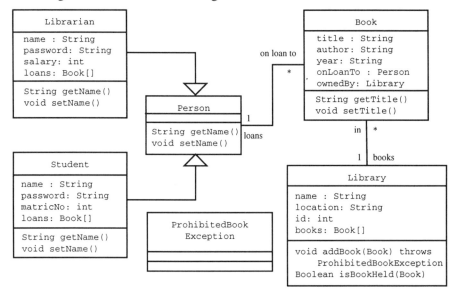

Figure 1. The Library Database Schema..

For brevity, consider a single task that the user of a library application might perform – that is *searching for a book*. Using the application, the user indicates that a search is to be performed, and subsequently specifies a collection of search parameters which constitute the attributes on which the search is to be based – for example, a search based on a named author. The user then initiates the search (amounting to the running of a query parameterised by the specified information) and is presented with the resultant information. Assuming one or more books were returned, the user can browse through them. The remainder of this paper demonstrates, in terms of one possible traversal of the Teallach method using the tools, how a designer might construct a user interface to support this task.

4.   THE TEALLACH METHOD

One of the principle aims of Teallach is the provision of a flexible design method such that designers using Teallach are not restricted to a single developmental strategy. Although some might question this approach given the more rigid methods promoted by other MB-UIDEs [4], the methodological stance adopted by Teallach arose from the following observations. Firstly, there is little evidence to support the notion that the less flexible methods forwarded by other MB-UIDEs are indeed the best (or only) approaches; forcing designers along a linear developmental path appears overly restrictive and does not support the characteristics of the software development life cycles that designers often favour. For example, one could indicate that TADEUS [11] operates by successively refining a task model through a dialogue model and a number of interaction tables. Secondly, Teallach recognises that if it is to be adopted as a means of user interface development, then it needs to observe the developmental habits of software developers who often work in iterative cycles of development where various aspects of their artefacts are developed in parallel or in an interleaved manner [8]. Through its flexible methodology, Teallach aims to support (as far as possible) the observed working practice of software developers.

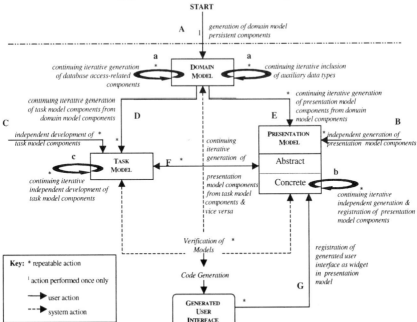

Figure 2. The Teallach Method.

Figure 2 shows the flexible methodological structure proposed by Teallach and which is subsequently realised in the Teallach tools. Due to the number of potential routes through the method – made possible by its inherent flexibility – it is not feasible to discuss each. Instead, the interactivity and dependencies between the steps in the method will be discussed at a high level, with the intention that the discussion provides a feel for the developmental freedom available to the designer. Later discussion of the actual Teallach tools, by which the method is realised, will demonstrate one possible path through the method.

Teallach refers to a design effort as a *project* – that is, a collection of models which contribute to the development of a specific user interface. Projects can be saved during the course of development, and components of one project can be imported into another to facilitate reuse. The remainder of this discussion will assume that the developer is creating a new project. It should be noted that the aim of this section is to outline the Teallach method – the *means* by which the actions may be performed using the tools is discussed in section 5.

Teallach has been developed to facilitate the design of user interfaces to pre-existing object oriented databases (OODBs). There is therefore a basic assumption that the schema and classes for the underlying database must exist prior to user interface development. The Teallach tool therefore permits one entry point to the developmental cycle (as shown in Figure 2). This allows the structure of the underlying database application to be established within a project in the form of the *persistent* components of a project-specific domain model (step A). Having determined the persistence capability of the application, the developer is then free to design each of the individual Teallach models.

At *any* stage in the design of a user interface, each of the models can be independently developed. Consider first the domain model. As required, the developer can create components to facilitate access to the underlying database (database connectivity components) and can import information about auxiliary data types which may be required for the runtime operation of the application – see the steps labelled (a) in Figure 2. It should be noted that the domain model also provides the facility to view and utilise the types provided by the Java API – a subset of the auxiliary information available to Teallach. The inclusion of these components is a one-off action which can be performed at any stage during development.

Consider now the task model. Independently of the other Teallach models, components (and hierarchies of components) within the task model can be created, manipulated, and deleted – as shown by steps (C) and (c) in Figure 2. Similarly, the developer can, independently of the domain and task models, create, manipulate and delete components (and hierarchies of components) within the presentation model and can register new widgets (steps (B) and (b) in Figure 2). Each of these activities can be performed at any stage during user interface development.

At any point during development the designer can either associate components from distinct models (thus linking the models to generate a cohesive user interface design) or can generate new components in a model from a component previously constructed in another model. Such activities are represented by steps (D), (E) and (F) in Figure 2 (and also labelled in the actual tool shown in Figure 3). These activities can be performed repeatedly and in any order.

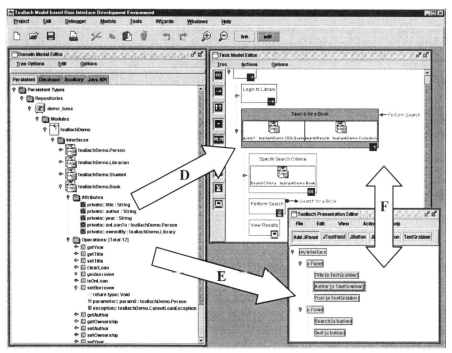

Figure 3. The Teallach Tool and Possible Inter-model Operations.

Consider first step (D), which shows the association of task model components with domain model components. The designer can use a domain model structure to automatically generate an initial task hierarchy, or can link components in the two models through the use of state objects. A state object is the means by which the task model represents constructs imported from the other Teallach models. Greater detail of these associations is given in section 5. Step (E) supports a similar scenario where the domain model components are used to automatically generate a presentation. Further details of these associations are also given in Section 5.

In Teallach, the task model is not tied to a specific visual representation of a user interface. This maxim is realised in the tool by linking task model components to high-level abstractions of concrete presentation model constructs (termed the *abstract* presentation model). In step (F) components in the abstract presentation and task models can be linked together, or can be used to automatically generate a new component in the other model. In all such operations, the designer will create a state object in the task model to represent the linked presentation model component.

At any stage during design, the developer can choose to verify the various models; a step which determines the consistency and completeness of the models with respect to one another. Assuming model verification has succeeded, the designer can automatically generate a user interface as described by the models. The developer can either choose to accept the generated interface, or can return to the various models and continue the design process in an iterative cycle. The designer can choose to register any generated user interface as a self-contained "black-box" widget within the presentation model (see step (G)), thus facilitating a bootstrapping process of development and reuse of generated components.

From the above discussion it can be seen that, with the exception of step (A), provided that the required components exist within each model, any of the discussed steps can be performed in any order and any number of times. Hence designers are given the freedom to work in the manner most suited to themselves and their projects, and are not restricted by an overly prescriptive developmental strategy.

5.   THE TEALLACH TOOL

5.1   General

The Teallach tool has been implemented using Java 2.0 and the Swing GUI tool-set. This tool-set has provided us with a rich library of GUI primitives that facilitate design using the model-view-controller pattern; our experiences with both this tool-set and Java in general have been mainly favourable. It has been designed so that Teallach itself, and the interfaces it generates which are also implemented in Java, will run on all major hardware and OS platforms. Teallach interacts with the underlying application (typically an OODB) through its domain model, which provides an interpretation of the contents of the application through the concepts of ODMG. In the current prototype Teallach has been designed to interact with the Poet OODBMS [9].

As shown in Figure 3, the tool provides separate editors for each of the three models, implemented using a desktop metaphor. In addition, the presentation model provides further, free-floating windows, such as a preview of the interface under construction, and a palette of widgets the designer can use. Model constructs can be exchanged between the editors either by drag-and-drop or by cut-and-paste metaphors using a single system clipboard.

The semantics of inter-model associations are described in more detail below, but the basic scheme is as follows: when a fragment of one model is dropped into the editor of a different model, some new structure is generated in the target editor, derived from the source model (drag-and-generate). It is also possible to 'link' components from different models, for example to show that a particular widget is to be used to perform a particular task. This is achieved by switching the tool into *link* mode and drawing arcs between the associated components (click-and-link). The large arrows in Figure 3 show the possible ways in which the three Teallach models can interact.

5.2   The Domain Model Editor

A project-specific Teallach domain model reflects the structure and functionality of the underlying application, database connectivity, and auxiliary data types such that they can inform and link into the user interface. To provide a measure of platform independence, the domain model represents these factors using constructs derived from the concepts specified in the ODMG object database standard.

The domain model editor within the Teallach tool comprises four independent panels, representing: persistent data components, imported auxiliary classes, auxiliary classes derived from the Java API, and the database connectivity aspects of an application. A domain model serves purely as an information source (as shown in Figure 2), and as such the domain model tool is not concerned with receipt of information from the other models. Instead, its role is to make available information to the other models in a uniform manner such that the persistence of the data is transparent.

Upon start up of the Teallach development environment, as mentioned in Section 4, a model of the persistent data related components of the application is generated. This is done automatically through an analysis of the schema of the underlying database. The domain model editor shown in Figure 3 shows the persistent data components of the domain model that represent the schema described in the case study.

There are also two panels concerned with the representation of auxiliary data types, that is, data structures which are not database classes, but which provide functionality required for the runtime operation of the application. The first of the two auxiliary data panels provides the designer with the means to import, as required, any user-defined classes or packages that provide additional functionality. To import a package or class, the designer must simply specify its fully qualified name. The screen shot in Figure 4 shows an auxiliary class that has been imported for use in the case study. It provides the facility for authentication of a string as a valid year. Once again, the designer is able to copy or drag this domain model component and paste or drop it into one of the other models so that its functionality can be exploited. The second of these panels represents the data types in the Java API.

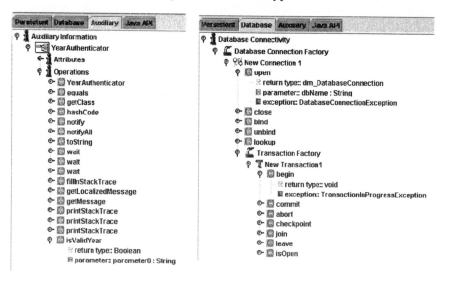

Figure 4. Importing Auxiliary Information   *Figure 5.* Database Connectivity Panel.

The final panel within the domain model editor concerns the establishment of components to support database connectivity. Once again, such components are modelled in terms of the appropriate ODMG concepts. Within this panel, the developer can instantiate database connections and therein transactions. Similarly, the developer can create OQL queries that can be run over the underlying database. Once established, the developer can treat database connectivity components in the same manner as other domain model components. Figure 5 shows the representation of a database connection and transaction required for the *search for book* case study. Having established the connectivity with the database, the developer would then be required to build the query using this same panel in the domain model editor.

5.3   The Presentation Model Editor

Teallach provides both a *concrete* presentation model (CPM) and an *abstract* presentation model (APM). The CPM contains real widgets such as those available in Swing, and user-supplied custom widgets. For example, the widget JPasswordField (for capturing users' passwords) is available from Swing, whereas the widget TextGrabber (for inputting text) is a user-supplied widget. Arbitrarily complex Interactors, such as 3D molecule-viewers, may be used as concrete widgets provided they have been registered with the presentation model tool.

Teallach's APM extends the light-weight presentation model described in [3]. This model defines abstract categories of widgets, designed to offer a particular functionality. An abstract category may be realised by many different concrete widgets. For example, the category *Inputter* represents anything which may capture the user's input; both a JPasswordField and a TextGrabber may serve as realisations of Inputter.

The designer may use either concrete or abstract presentation objects, and intermix these freely. Of course, where abstract interactors are used, a decision must be made as to which possible realisation will be used in the final interface; a default is always available, so a valid interface is defined at all times. Details of how abstract categories are realised by concrete widgets are recorded in a *style*, so that consistency of look-and-feel can be achieved, and differing interfaces can be easily generated which support the same functionality.

5.3.1   An Overview of the Presentation Model Tools

The interface designer interacts with Teallach's presentation model through a collection of related tools. The presentation model editor allows the designer to construct presentation fragments, whether by hand or automatically; the widget palette provides access to the components which may be used for building interfaces; and the presentation meta-editor allows the designer to edit the meta-model of the presentation, as described below.

5.3.2   Constructing Interface Fragments by Hand

The designer may construct presentations by hand, by explicitly assembling components. An example can be seen in Figure 6, where the designer is constructing the form to be used when specifying the criteria to be used when searching for a book. From the presentation model's widget palette, the designer has selected three *TextGrabber* components, to capture the title, author, and year fields for the book sought. These components have been placed within a JPanel, which is a (usually invisible) container provided by Swing for grouping together related items, and ensuring that they behave as desired when the window is resized. An ancillary class, from the domain model, may be employed to ensure that the format of the text entered into the year field can represent a valid year.

The designer has then added a second JPanel to the search window, grouping two buttons that allow the user either to confirm the search criteria and proceed to performing the search (*search*), or to quit from this window, if desired (*quit*).

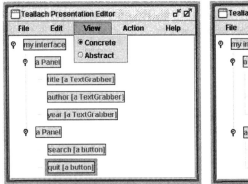 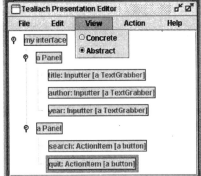

Figure 6. Constructing Presentation Model Elements.

Once constructed, this interface fragment can be used in a variety of ways: 1) it can be 'shrink-wrapped' for later use in this and other applications; 2) it can be linked to constructs in the domain and task models to form part of the final user-interface; or 3) it can be dropped into the task model to automatically generate task structures corresponding to the activity of searching for a book.

In addition to the tree-structured view provided by the presentation editor, Teallach also provides a preview of the end-interface under construction. For example, an automatically generated preview of the search form is shown in Figure 7; this allows the designer to see an immediate result when altering properties of the presentation such as colour, font, and layout.

Figure 7. The Presentation Model Preview Window.

5.3.3   Editing the Presentation Meta-model

Teallach's presentation meta-editor allows the designer to modify the abstract presentation model. The meta-editor is shown in Figure 8. This tool has both a *categories* tab and a *register* tab. The categories tab allows new abstract categories to be defined and added to the presentation model; once defined, they become available for use in the abstract widget palette. Figure 8 shows part of the definition of the category Inputter, derived from the category Item; this has a method getValue() returning an object (of any type) which has been input by the user of the widget.

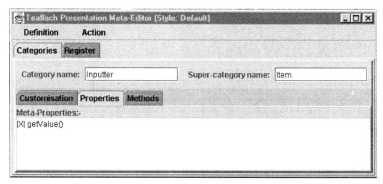

Figure 8. The Presentation Model Meta-Editor.

The register tab allows new concrete widgets to be registered within existing categories. Once registered, a widget becomes available for use in the concrete widget palette. This allows the designer to use custom-built and third party widgets in an interface.

The meta-editor uses the meta-data it collects to automatically write Java code implementing the newly defined meta-objects. This code is then compiled reflectively, so that the new objects can become available in the system without need for interpretation.

5.4   The Task Model Editor

The Teallach task model tool provides an environment for constructing and editing hierarchical task models, the semantics of which have been presented in [5]. A hierarchy constructed using the task model tool is a temporally ordered representation of the goals and subgoals a user wishes to achieve in the developed interface. The Teallach task model is novel in that it provides a designer with the ability to declare local state and associate this with a task, and subsequently to indicate how this state information is initialised and utilised within a task.

To realise the task model for the case study, our designer constructs a high-level specification of the task they intend application end-users to perform through the modelled interface. To achieve this, the designer drags a task of the required type from the task model's palette of task types (shown in Figure 3) and drops it at the required location in the task model construction area.

At the lowest level in the task hierarchy, the designer creates *interaction* and *action* tasks which represent how the application processes information, and how the end-user and the application participate in the task. These tasks may have links to domain or presentation model functionality which is realised and invoked through a suitably initialised state object (as described in section 5.5.1).

5.5   Establishing Model Interaction Using Link Mode

At any time during the model development process, the designer may create links between components specified in any of the Teallach models. By creating a link, the designer is stating, for example, that a widget is to be used to perform a particular task, or that an action task corresponds to an invocation of an operation on an application class. Links between the Task and Presentation models are also used to describe dialogue dynamics. This section will show how, through the use of state objects representing both domain and presentation model constructs, the task model tool provides the facility to bind together the concepts in the three Teallach models.

5.5.1   Creating and Using State Information in the Tool

A state object is the means by which the task model tool maintains references to constructs from the other Teallach model tools, and is constructed through either a *paste as state* menu option, or as a side-effect of Teallach automatically generating a task construct from another Teallach model construct. A state object refers to a named instance of either a domain or abstract presentation model class, and is realised as a uniquely named rectangle within the scope of a non-primitive task.

Once a state object has been created it can be utilised in several ways. For example, one of the state object's methods can be invoked (equivalent to invoking underlying application or widget functionality), or one (or more) of a state object's public attributes can be read from or written to (equivalent to specifying the flow of information between the user and the underlying application).

For the purposes of our case study, the designer needs to specify that the search criteria provided by the end-user should be stored in a named object of type `Book`, and that a named query should be invoked on the database with this `Book` object as the search parameter. The designer therefore copies the `Book` persistent domain class from the domain model tool and pastes in into the *specify book information* non-primitive task selected in the task model tool using the *paste as state* option from the Edit menu. Similarly, using the Database Connectivity editor pane, a state object corresponding to a new OQL query is copied from the domain model to the *Search for a Book* task. The designer will also need to create state objects representing the database session and transaction in which the OQL query will be performed. Once the designer has provided a suitable name (e.g., `currentBook`), new state objects are created at the required locations. In Figure 3, the task model editor shows that the Search for a Book task contains two state objects corresponding to `searchResults:Collection` and `query1:OQLQuery`.

The following sections illustrate *some* of the ways in which state objects can be used to link constructs in the three Teallach models using both the link and generate mechanisms.

5.5.2   Linking Task and Domain Model Constructs

Once our designer has created the necessary state objects, they can link action or interaction tasks with them. For example, the designer needs to show that the *Perform Search* action task invokes the `execute()` method on the `query1:OQLQuery` state object. This is achieved by the designer selecting the *link* toggle button on the main toolbar to switch to link mode, and subsequently clicking on the *Perform Search* action task and `query1:OQLQuery` state object – an extending arc is drawn between the two constructs to give the designer visual feedback.

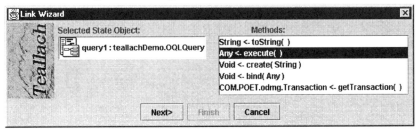

Figure 9. Assigning Method calls to an Action Task Using the Link Wizard.

If the link operation is successful, then Teallach invokes its *Link Wizard* to guide the designer through the potentially complex task of creating the link. As shown in Figure 9, the Link Wizard recognises that the designer is creating a link between an action task and a state object, and asks the designer to choose which of the selected state object's methods they wish to invoke by providing them with a list of possible methods from which to choose. Once a method has been selected, the Link Wizard checks if the selected method requires any parameters, or if it has a return value. In either case it asks the designer which state objects will provide the information for the parameters, and optionally, which state object will be used to store the return value. For both of these questions the Link Wizard will provide a list of suitable alternatives to the designer. An example of this is shown in Figure 10, where the Link Wizard is enquiring where the collection of Objects (i.e., Books) returned by the `query1.execute()` method will be stored; the designer selects the `foundBooks:Collection` state object within the *Search for a Book* task.

Figure 10. Handling return Values Using the Link Wizard.

If the chosen domain method raises an exception (i.e., an IllegalOperationException), then the task model editor will display a red circle next to the action task for each exception that it raises. The designer is then free to specify what should happen if the exceptional circumstance arises; the task model editor can be used to specify that if the `query1.execute()` method (as utilised by the *Perform Search* action task) raises an exception, then the *Search for a Book* task should be performed again – this is shown in Figure 3.

5.5.3   Linking Task and Presentation Model Constructs

If the designer wishes to declare that an interaction task is to be realised by a particular widget (e.g., that the *Get Author Name* interaction task corresponds to a particular Swing JTextField widget in the CPM), then in a similar manner to the previous section, the designer will create a state object corresponding to the JTextField widget in the required location within the task model editor. It should be noted that it is actually the APM construct which corresponds to the CPM widget that is used. If the link operation is accepted, then the Link Wizard will once again be activated.

Since the semantics of this link operation are different to that discussed in the previous section, the Link Wizard will ask the designer a different set of questions. For example, if the designer   creates a link between the *Get*

Author Name interaction task and the `author:Inputter` state object (realised by a JTextField widget in the CPM), then the Link Wizard will ask if the task is receiving or outputting (or both) information, and will proceed with a dialogue which will ascertain the type of the information being processed, and which state object(s) will provide this information.

By linking task and presentation model components the designer is also specifying the dynamics (dialog) of the interface. This is achieved by the semantics of non-primitive task model nodes (i.e., sequential, concurrent, etc.) being applied to the non-primitive presentation model nodes to which they are linked.

5.6   Establishing Model Interaction Using Generate Mode

To assist the designer in the process of constructing a consistent set of models, Teallach provides a drag-and-generate mode. This mode is invoked by dragging a fragment of one model into a suitable location within another. As a result of this operation a new model structure is created in the target model. Since the domain model is immutable, it cannot act as a target model. When the target model is the task model, Teallach creates appropriate state objects in addition to the newly constructed task hierarchy (i.e., domain classes or presentation widgets), and automatically creates links between these state objects and any action or interaction tasks.

For example, our designer may decide to drag the `Book` class into the task model editor to create a new first child of the *Search for a Book* task: this will create an order-independent task called *Edit Book*, with an action task child corresponding to each of the class's methods, and interaction tasks corresponding to each of the class's public attributes. The designer is then at liberty to edit the new constructs required. In this case the designer will simply remove any unwanted action or interaction tasks, and will rename the top-level task *Gather Search Criteria*.

Once this task has been constructed, the designer can then drag the new task construct into the presentation model to create a default form to represent the required task.

6.   SUMMARY

This paper has presented the flexible design method forwarded by the Teallach MB-UIDE, which is realised through a rich set of tools that support the construction of the Teallach models. In particular the Teallach method and its supporting tools remove the rigid methodological constraints imposed by other MB-UIDEs, providing user interface designers with a method and design environment that more closely meets their modes of working.

This inherent flexibility has posed many challenges for the Teallach design team, as a flexible design method requires often complex control facilities. We have therefore concentrated on providing a core set of design primitives (e.g., building models individually using no automatic generation, providing a simple *paste as state* operation for inter-model linking), and subsequently providing higher-level design functionality (utilising the core primitives) which supports a more rapid design method (e.g., automatically generating model constructs from the information modelled in another Teallach model). The often complex process of inter-model linkage has also been greatly simplified through the use of a Wizard metaphor.

ACKNOWLEDGEMENTS

This work is funded by UK's Engineering and Physical Sciences Research Council (EPSRC), whose support we are pleased to acknowledge. We also thank our partners on the Teallach project for their contributions to the development of the overall Teallach system. They are Carole Goble, Phil Gray, Michael Smyth and Adrian West.

REFERENCES

[1] Cattell, R.G.G. et al., *The Object Database Standard: 2.0*. Morgan Kaufmann Publishers, Inc., 1997.

[2] Eckstein, R., Loy, M., and Wood, D., *Java Swing*, O'Reilly & Associates, Sebastopol, 1998.

[3] Gray, P., Cooper, R., Kennedy, J., McKirdy, J., Barclay, P., and Griffiths, T., *A Lightweight Presentation Model for Database User Interfaces*, in Proc. of 4th ERCIM International Workshop on User Interfaces for All (Stockholm, 19-21 October 1998), C. Stephanis and A. Waern (eds.), ERCIM. Accessible at http://www.ics.forth.gr/proj/at-hci/UI4ALL/UI4ALL-98/gray_ps.zip.

[4] Griffiths, T., McKirdy, J., Forrester, G., Paton, N., Kennedy, J., Barclay, P., Cooper, R., Goble, C., and Gray, P., *Exploiting Model-Based Techniques for User Interfaces to Databases*, in Proceedings of VDB-4, Chapman & Hall, London, 1998, pp. 21-46.

[5] Griffiths, T., Paton, N.W., Goble, C., West, A., *Task Modelling for Database Interface Development*, in Proc. of the 8th Int. Conf. on Human-Computer Interaction HCI International'99 (Muncih, 22-26 August 1999), H.-J. Bullinger and J. Ziegler (eds.), Vol. 1, Ergonomics and User Interfaces, Lawrence Erlbaum Associates, Mahwah, 1999, pp. 1033-1037.

[6] Griffiths, T., Barclay, P.J., McKirdy, J., Paton, N.W., Gray, P.D., Kennedy, J., Cooper, R., Goble, C.A., West, A. and Smyth, M., *Teallach: A Model-Based User Interface Development Environment for Object Databases*, in Proc. 1st Int. Workshop on User Inter-

faces to Data Intensive Systems UIDIS'99 (Edinburgh, 5-6 September 1999), N.W. Paton & T. Griffiths (eds.), IEEE Press, Los Alamitos, 1999, pp. 86-96.

[7] Lonczewski, F. and Schreiber, S., *The FUSE-System: an Integrated User Interface Design Environment,* in Proceedings of the 2nd International Workshop on Computer-Aided Design of User Interfaces CADUI'96 (Namur, 5-7 June 1996), J. Vanderdonckt (ed.), Presses Universitaires de Namur, Namur, 1996, pp. 37-56.

[8] McKirdy, J., *An Empirical Study of the Relationships Between User Interface Development Tools & User Interface Software Development,* Technical Report TR-1998-06, University of Glasgow, Department of Computing Science, March 1998.

[9] Poet Software. http://www.poet.com

[10] Puerta, A.R., *A Model-Based Interface Development Environment*, IEEE Software, Vol. 14, No. 4, July/August 1997, pp. 41-47. Accessible at http://www.arpuerta.com/pubs/ieee97.htm.

[11] Schlungbaum, E. and Elwert, T., *Automatic User Interface Generation from Declarative Models ,* in Proceedings of the 2nd International Workshop on Computer-Aided Design of User Interfaces CADUI'96 (Namur, 5-7 June 1996), J. Vanderdonckt (ed.), Presses Universitaires de Namur, Namur, 1996, pp. 3-17.

Chapter 13

MDL: A LANGUAGE FOR BINDING UI MODELS

R. E. Kurt Stirewalt

Department of Computer Science and Engineering
Michigan State University
East Lansing, Michigan 48824
stire@cse.msu.edu

Abstract   The model-based approach to UI design and synthesis is complicated by the need to bind behavior that is specified in one model to corresponding behavior in another model. In the MASTERMIND project, the problem concerns the binding of user-task and presentation models. We designed a powerful task language called MDL, and we compile MDL models into code that reifies the structure of a task model. The structural symmetry between models and code allows binding to be performed at many levels of granularity. We believe that such flexibility is required for model-based approaches to gain widespread acceptance.

Keywords: model based, user-interface software, binding

1.   INTRODUCTION

The model-based approach to UI design and implementation provides multiple, separate models of different facets of the UI (Bodart et al., 1994; Wilson et al., 1993; Neches et al., 1993; Elwert and Schlungbaum, 1995; Puerta, 1996). This approach is complicated by the *multi-model binding problem*, which concerns how a designer is able to *bind* behavior that is described in one model to correspond with behavior that is described in another model. This paper presents our solution to the binding problem in the MASTERMIND project.

In MASTERMIND (Neches et al., 1993), designers use a task model to specify the tasks that a user may perform (Browne et al., 1997) and a presentation model to specify the graphical design of the UI (Castells et al., 1997). Task and presentation models are compiled into executable code components independently of one another; however, functionality described in one model may overlap or be dependent upon functionality that is described in another. A but-

159

ton, for example, is specified in a presentation model, but the behavior of the button influences behavior in other models, such as when pressing the button signals the initiation of some task. The binding problem concerns the mechanism for specifying how features in one model should compose with features in another model and the reification of this mechanism into code that coordinates the independently generated components.

This paper addresses the need to specify binding at different levels of granularity. Whereas a coarse-grain binding combines an entire presentation model with an entire task model, a fine-grain binding combines parts of a task model with parts of a presentation model, opening the question of how these "part compositions" affect the overall composition of the two models. To specify fine-grain binding, a designer requires a language in which to articulate *what* facets of which models should be bound together. This language should be defined so that it does not limit the independence of existing modeling notations, and the run-time reification of the features of this language should be efficient.

The MASTERMIND Dialog Language (MDL) has a syntax for specifying task models and additional features for binding tasks with presentations. The meaning of an MDL model is defined in terms of an action calculus that combines operators from LOTOS (Bolognesi and Brinksma, 1987) and the User Action Notation (UAN) (Hartson and Mayo, 1994). In addition to these task-modeling operators, MDL provides a clean semantic definition of binding. MDL models can be compiled into an efficient run-time dialog component that coordinates a run-time presentation component. We synthesize a layered dialog component from a toolkit of hierarchical components, each of which implements a different MDL operator. Consequently, the modular structure of a dialog component is symmetric with the structure of a task model.

The symmetry of design-time models and run-time implementations is crucial to fine grain binding because binding is both a design-time operation and an operation over code components. The symmetry allows a designer to express task-presentation bindings at any level of task granularity and for the bound component to be integrated without modification into the larger run-time dialog component. After introducing some background terminology (**Section 2.**), we present MDL (**Section 3.**) and illustrate its use on a concrete example (**Section 4.**). We then show how MDL is compiled into an efficient run-time dialog component (**Section 5.**).

2.   BACKGROUND AND TERMINOLOGY

MASTERMIND was a joint effort of the Graphics, Visualization, and Usability Center (GVU) of the Georgia Institute of Technology and the Information Sciences Institute (ISI) of the University of Southern California. It was designed to explore the hypothesis that by separating the user-interface from the

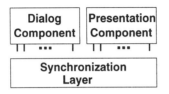

Figure 1.1   Architecture for separation and conjunction.

underlying application functionality, designers could address each concern with a narrowly focused and highly declarative modeling language (Neches et al., 1993). MASTERMIND describes interactive systems using three declarative models. *Presentation models* represent the appearance and behavior of the user interface; *Application models* represent functional and data resources; and *Task models* represent end-user interactions, how they are ordered, and how they affect the presentation and the application. As a graduate student at Georgia Tech, the author worked on the task modeling language and code generator; the presentation modeling language and code generator were developed at ISI. At the end of the project, the code produced by the task and presentation models could be integrated by hand, but the integration could not be performed automatically.

In (Stirewalt and Rugaber, 1998), we presented the MASTERMIND architecture, which supports coarse-grain binding. In this architecture, a *synchronization layer* coordinates activity between independently generated dialog and presentation components (**Figure 1.1**). Both dialog and presentation components execute by performing *actions*, which are atomic computational steps that can be observed and influenced by the other component. The pins that are shown emanating from each component are called *gates*; they represent the interface to a mechanism for observing and influencing actions within a component. By plugging into the synchronization layer, dialog and presentation actions that share the same gate are forced to execute in lock step. Consequently, a presentation action that corresponds to a task action can only be performed when the task action is ready to be performed and vice versa.

The facility for connecting components (depicted in **Figure 1.1** as pin connectors) is implemented using an hierarchical model of components (Batory and O'Malley, 1992). In this model, a layered component is *parameterized* by any lower-level components that it requires in order to implement its services. The global Dialog Component, for example, is parameterized by a set of Gate components each of whose services implement the synchronization of actions across multiple components. Layered components are "plugged together" by *instantiating* the higher-level component with the lower-level components. The Dialog component, for example, plugs into the global Synchronization Layer by being instantiated with gate components that reside within this layer. The

Table 1.1   High level syntax of MDL

$$module ::= \textbf{binding } bdecl \; [g_1, \ldots, g_n](x_1 : T_1, \ldots x_m : T_m)$$
$$\qquad\qquad \textbf{is hide } e_1, \ldots, e_j \textbf{ in } tdecl \; \| \; edecl_1 \; \| \; \ldots \; \| \; edecl_k$$
$$\qquad \textbf{end}$$
$$\qquad | \quad \textbf{extern } edecl \; [g_1, \ldots, g_n](x_1 : T_1, \ldots x_m : T_m)$$
$$\qquad\qquad \textbf{interface } anon\_action^* \textbf{ end}$$
$$\qquad | \quad \textbf{task } tdecl \; [g_1, \ldots, g_n](x_1 : T_1, \ldots x_m : T_m)$$
$$\qquad\qquad \textbf{is } process \textbf{ end}$$

same gate component can be used to instantiate both the Dialog and Presentation components; this is how we implement the sharing of a gate among actions in different components.

The user-computer dialog is specified indirectly through task models. The relationship between task and dialog models has been studied by other researchers. Our work was inspired by (Paternò, 1994) and also (Markopoulos, 1997), both of whom use process algebra to formally relate task models to the dialog of a user-interface component. Our work incorporates some of these concepts; however, we do not require our users to specify their UIs in LOTOS, which is difficult for a typical UI engineer to refine into a working UI. Early versions of MDL were described in (Szekely et al., 1996) and (Browne et al., 1997). We now describe the current version and show it can be compiled into layered dialog components that plug in to the MASTERMIND run-time architecture.

3.   MDL LANGUAGE

MDL is a deterministic notation for expressing task hierarchies and the binding of task and presentation models. The high-level syntax of MDL is a collection of *module* declarations (**Table 1.1**). The behavior of a module is specified as a *process*, which is a behavioral abstraction that defines the actions that can be observed of a module and the allowable sequencing of these actions. MDL processes are similar in many regards to the processes defined in a process algebra, such as LOTOS (Bolognesi and Brinksma, 1987). Whereas every MDL module defines a process, only processes declared using the syntax of **Table 1.1** qualify as modules.

MDL defines three categories of module, each of which represents a different technique for defining a process. In a *task*, a process is defined as a hierarchy of user tasks, the leaves of which denote actions. In an *extern*, a process is defined implicitly as a continuously available collection of anonymous actions, which

Table 1.2   MDL process operators.

Operator name	Syntax	Description
completion	**exit**	Successful completion of a process.
prefixing	$a;\ P$	Prefix P with action a.
enabling	$P_1 >> P_2$	P_1; then P_2.
choice	$P_1 \ [] \ P_2$	P_1 *or* P_2, but not both.
interleaving	$P_1 \ ||| \ P_2$	Interleave P_1 and P_2.
disabling	$P_1 \ [> P_2$	P_1; terminate P_1 by P_2.
interruption	$P_1 \triangle P_2$	P_1; interrupt/resume by P_2.
optional	P^{opt}	P zero or one time.
loop	P^*	P zero or more times.
symmetry	$P_1 \leftrightarrow P_2$	Alternate P_1 and P_2 until completion.

Table 1.3   Action declaration in MDL.

action $::=$ *identifier* (($'?'$ *identifier*) | ($'!'$ *expression*))*
anon_action $::=$ *identifier* ($'?'$ *type* | $'!'$ *type*)*

we define shortly. Finally, in a *binding*, a process is defined as the coordination of one task and one or more externs.

An underlying process calculus describes how to specify primitive processes and how to combine existing processes into new ones. **Table 1.2** describes the operators in this calculus that are used to specify task modules. Each operator combines one or two sub-processes (denoted either P or P_1 and P_2) into a new, more complex process. For example, the disabling operator $P_1 \ [> P_2$ combines sub-processes P_1 and P_2. The new process behaves exactly like P_1 unless P_2 begins execution, at which point P_1 is terminated. Two additional operators that are not shown in **Table 1.2**—synchronizing parallel composition $(|\ [g_1, \ldots, g_n]\ |)$ and hiding—may only appear in a binding.

Table 1.3 describes how to declare actions. An action specifies a *gate*, over which the action may synchronize with other actions, and zero or more *value offerings*, which are either inputs into a storage location, or outputs of the result of some expression. MDL distinguishes between two kinds of actions: Concrete actions (denoted *action* in the table) comprise fully elaborated inputs and outputs; whereas anonymous actions (denoted *anon_action*) comprise input and output prototypes. Anonymous value offerings are place holders for storage

task ManagePlane [commitLand, newPosition]   (1)
               (flight : **const string**, pos : **integer**)   (2)
is   (newPosition ? pos; **exit**)* >> (commitLand; **exit**) **end**   (3)

Figure 1.2   Task: managing a plane in flight.

locations and expressions that are assumed to be specified elsewhere (i.e., the presentation model). All that is known about an anonymous offering is the type of storage location or expression. Concrete value offerings, on the other hand, fully specify a named storage location for inputs and a full expression for outputs.

Externs may only declare anonymous actions, and they may not declare any structure on the sequencing of these actions. A task on the other hand may only declare concrete actions. When a task uses a sub-process that is declared to be another module, that sub-process must be either another task or a binding. The restrictions imposed by the syntax of Table 1.1 guarantee that extern modules do not specify the details of their respective actions. These details will be specified in another model.

4.   EXAMPLE

We illustrate the use of MDL on a small example from the air-traffic management domain. In this domain, new tasks are created and discharged dynamically as new flights enter and leave the airspace of an airport. We present here one task module, one extern module whose behavior is elaborated in a presentation model, and the corresponding binding. The full example is given in (Stirewalt, 1997).

Figure 1.2 lists the MDL description of a task called ManagePlane, which describes the actions that a controller performs when servicing a flight in the air. The task declares two gates, commitLand and newPosition, and two parameters, flight and pos. Actions labeled by these gates correspond to respectively choosing a plane from the many within the airspace and entering a new position for a plane. The first parameter is a constant string, which will contain the unique flight number of a flight; the second parameter is an integer, which will represent the position a plane within the airspace. Because flight is declared constant, its value is immutable during the performance of this task.

The process description that specifies the behavior of ManagePlane (line 3 in Figure 1.2) indicates that the controller may instruct the flight to change position zero or more times before instructing the flight to land. The enabling operator ($>>$) specifies sequential composition; we read it to mean that com-

extern Airplane [select, drag] (flight : **string**, pos : **integer**)   (1)
interface select, drag ! **integer**   **end**   (2)

Figure 1.3   MDL interface of an airplane presentation.

mitLand may be performed after zero or more performances of newPosition. Note that the input value to newPosition is deposited into the parameter pos.

Code for presentation objects, such as the graphical depiction of the airspace and the presentation of an individual plane, is generated from a separate presentation model (Castells et al., 1997). In this example, the controller indicates a change of position by dragging a particular plane graphic to another spot in a legal air-traffic lane, and he indicates the desire to land a plane by double-clicking on its corresponding graphic. These gestures, selection and drag-and-drop, represent actions which have meaning in both the presentation and the task world. It is, therefore, necessary that some aspect of the presentation model be represented for binding with the task model. We model the successful completion of these gestures as actions in MDL.

Figure 1.3 specifies an extern module whose interface names two actions, select and drag. This module corresponds to a presentation that represents a flight in the airspace of the airport. For simplicity, we modeled this presentation as a dragable button whose label displays the flight number. A more elaborate presentation might use a graphic that conveys more information about the flight, such as type of aircraft, country of origin, or direction of flight; however, even a more elaborate presentation could be described using the declaration in Figure 1.3.

The select action represents the result of double clicking on the button; whereas the drag action represents the result of dropping (after having dragged) the button onto a new location. The select action communicates only control; whereas the drag action communicates an integer that corresponds to a new position for the plane. When these specifications are realized in code, the communications will actually be initiated by an Amulet *interactor* (Myers et al., 1997), which manages input gestures and invokes methods at various points during the gesture.

Figure 1.4 defines the binding ManageFlight, which takes two parameters flight and pos (line 1). The binding behavior is expressed in line 3. An instance of the ManagePlane task is composed with an instance of the Airplane presentation through the synchronizing parallel operator. Because choose and move are specified as synchronizing gates, the Airplane and ManagePlane instantiations must synchronize any actions that use these gates. Observe that with this syntax, task and presentation modules can be bound together without

bind ManageFlight(flight : **const string**, pos : **int**)   (1)
is hide choose, move   (2)
   in ManagePlane[choose,move](flight,pos) |[choose,move]| (3)
     Airplane[choose,move](flight,pos)   (4)
end   (5)

Figure 1.4   Binding the manage plane task to the airplane presentation.

the modules having to explicitly reference one another. This property is very important to the separation of models in MASTERMIND.

The binding behavior is wrapped up in a larger declaration that begins with the **hide** keyword (line 2). Hiding allows one to make gates *unobservable* outside the scope of the **hide** declaration. Tasks within the binding (such as ManagePlane and Airplane) can synchronize on the gates, but tasks external to the binding cannot. We use hiding in bindings such as ManageFlight because there may be many run-time instantiations of this binding, and we do not want these separate binding instances to interfere with each other! The operation and utility of MDL should now be more clear. Designers can separately define tasks and the behavior of presentations and then bind these modules to specify the actual behavior of an interactive system.

5.   CODE GENERATION

Our approach to the fine-grain binding problem is to generate run-time components whose structure is symmetric with the structure of MDL models. We achieve this symmetry by organizing the global dialog component into a layered hierarchy in which each layer implements the dialog of a task in the task model. Both tasks and dialog layers are tree structures; consequently, the leaves of both structures correspond to actions (i.e., MDL actions in a task, and Action components in a dialog component that implements the task).

To simplify the construction of dialog layers from MDL tasks, we designed a library of parameterized components, one for each MDL process operator as shown in **Table 1.4**. The notation $c\,[X_1, \ldots, X_n]$ means that c is a parameterized component that must be instantiated with components $d_1, \ldots, d_n$, such that d_i implements the interface X_i. The name Dial refers to the set of *all* dialog components. Each component in this set implements an interface that allows a higher-level dialog component to observe and influence its behavior by receiving notifications of activity and invoking enable/disable services. Each component in **Table 1.4** exports this interface. Moreover, with the exception of compl, each component is parameterized by one or more Dials. The pref component is parameterized by an Action component, which is itself parameterized by a

Table 1.4   Control modules

Operator	Dial	‖	Operator	Dial
[]	alt [Dial, Dial]	‖	[>	dis [Dial, Dial]
↔	excl [Dial, Dial]	‖	△	int [Dial, Dial]
;	pref [Action, Dial]	‖	*	loop [Dial]
opt	opt [Dial]	‖	‖‖	par [Dial, Dial]
>>	seq [Dial, Dial]	‖	**exit**	compl

Gate component. Parameterized Action components are described in (Stirewalt and Rugaber, 1998).

Recall that the global Dialog component is itself parameterized by Gate components. Consequently, it is trivial to generate a Dialog component by stacking up components from **Table 1.4** on top of a layer of Actions, each of which is parameterized by a Gate. To demonstrate this synthesis, we use a component-layout notation called MTREE, which is an intermediate form in the MDL code generator. The MDL expression:

$(a;$ **exit** $[]$ $b;$ **exit**$)$ *

is transformed into the functionally equivalent MTREE:

task000 [a, b] **is** loop [alt [pref [action [a], compl]
                                 pref [action [b], compl]]]

This expression defines a new dialog component called task000, which is a machine generated name. The component takes two parameters, a and b, which are placeholders for Gates that will be provided when either: (1) we plug the global dialog component into the synchronization layer, or (2) we bind this task to a presentation. The top layer of this component is implemented by a loop component, which is instantiated by another component whose top layer is implemented by an alt component. This process continues until we reach Action and compl components.

As another example, consider the task ManagePlane from **Figure 1.2**. This task compiles into the following module:

task001 [commitLand, newPosition](flight : **const string**, pos : **integer**)
is   seq [loop [pref [action [newPosition](pos), compl]],
              pref [action [commitLand], compl]]

It should be clear that the generation of MTREE from MDL is a simple syntactic transformation. The generation of C++ from MTREE is a correspondingly simple transformation, which is described in (Stirewalt, 1997).

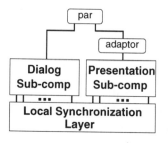

Figure 1.5   Binding to produce a dialog component.

Because task-generated dialog components are parameterized by Gates, we implement the additional operators associated with binding—hiding and process instantiation—using different patterns of parameterized-component instantiation. For example, when a binding combines a task and an extern and gates are hidden, we construct a new component that encapsulates the dialog component associated with the task and the presentation component associated with the extern. The hidden gates are compiled into Gate components in a local synchronization layer into which the encapsulated dialog and presentation components connect. This is shown schematically in **Figure 1.5**.

The reader should observe two features of **Figure 1.5**. First, this new component is a Dial because its top layer is a par component. Consequently, the new component can be incorporated as a layer of the global dialog component. Of course, unlike other dialog layers, the new component does not attach to the global Synchronization Layer. Second, we use a par component to coordinate the new component. We do this for technical reasons, because the par component allows its sub-components maximal independence. However, by using it, we need an adaptor component that translates requests from the par component into method invocations over the Presentation sub-component.

To illustrate the implementation of a fine-grain binding, consider the binding ManageFlight from **Figure 1.4**. Given the extern module pres001 [select, drag], which names a presentation component, we implement the binding as follows:

bind001 (flight: **const string**, pos: **integer**)
is   local   choose : **Gate**
      local   move   : **Gate**
      par [task001 [choose, move](flight, pos),
                   adaptor[pres001 [choose, move](flight, pos)]]

Observe that the hiding of actions over gates choose and move is accomplished by introducing components of type Gate as local parameters to the binding module and supplying these as parameters to the instantiations of task001 and pres001. These local Gates constitute the Local Synchronization Layer of **Figure 1.5**.

6.   SUMMARY AND DISCUSSION

This paper illustrates how fine-grain binding is expressed in MDL and implemented using parameterized components in an implementation toolkit. At the model level, a fine-grain binding is specified using parallel-composition with hiding, which is a well-known approach to modularity and layering in process algebras. The MASTERMIND implementation architecture supports parallel composition by synchronizing on common gate components. Model compilers generate components that are parameterized by the gate components that are required for composition. To implement hiding, we simply create wrappers that internalize gate components and then instantiate the components to be bound with these gates.

The example demonstrates how MDL is used to bind task and presentation modules. To support such high-level, declarative binding specifications, a presentation-model code generator must do three things. First, it must parameterize each observable presentation action by a gate component so that the action may be observed and influenced at run time. Second, it must emit an extern module interface as a result of compiling a presentation model. Third, it must generate presentation components with standard interfaces so that it is possible to construct generic adaptor components that interpret dialog-component commands, such as enabling and disabling, by invoking presentation-component methods.

These assumptions represent necessary conditions on the part of model-based code generators to support the separation of models. It is an open question as to whether these assumptions limit the freedom of expression in an individual modeling notation. It seems clear, for example, that the interaction with flight graphics in the ATM example is orthogonal to the action that is observed by the task model (e.g., newPosition). In this case, presentation designers are free to concentrate on issues such as layout constraints and the design of interim feedback objects. However, until we can fully automate the integration of dialog and presentation components, this question will remain open.

Our long term goal is to understand the fundamental issues of separation in the model-based approach so that we can pick and choose the right models and the right synthesis technology for the right kind of UI. Obviously, such a question is difficult to address without building a lot of systems and trying to integrate a lot of different modeling notations. However, we believe that notations such as MDL, that was designed to address a fundamental obstacle to model-based separation (i.e., binding), provide a robust data point from which to analyze these questions.

References

Batory, D. and O'Malley, S. (1992). The design and implementation of hierarchical software systems with reusable components. *ACM Trans. Softw. Eng. Meth.*, 1(4):355–398.

Bodart, F. et al. (1994). A model-based approach to presentation: A continuum from task analysis to prototype. In *Proceedings of DSV-IS'94*.

Bolognesi, T. and Brinksma, E. (1987). Introduction to the ISO specification language LOTOS. *Comp. Netw. ISDN Sys.*, 14(1).

Browne, T. P. et al. (1997). Using declarative descriptions to model user interfaces with MASTERMIND. In Paternò, F. and Palanque, P., editors, *Formal Methods in Human Computer Interaction*. Springer-Verlag.

Castells, P., Szekely, P., and Salcher, E. (1997). Declarative models of presentation. In *IUI'97: International Conference on Intelligent User Interfaces*.

Elwert, T. and Schlungbaum, E. (1995). Modelling and generation of graphical user interfaces in the tadeus approach. In *Proceedings of DSV-IS'95*.

Hartson, H. R. and Mayo, K. A. (1994). A framework for precise, reusable, task abstractions. In *Proceedings of DSV-IS'94*, pages 147–164.

Markopoulos, P. (1997). *A formal compositional model for the specification of user interfaces*. PhD thesis, Queen Mary and Westfield College, University of London.

Myers, B. A. et al. (1997). The Amulet environment: New models for effective user-interface software development. *IEEE Trans. Softw. Eng.*, 23(6).

Neches, R. et al. (1993). Knowledgeable development environments using shared design models. In *Intelligent Interfaces Workshop*, pages 63–70.

Paternò, F. (1994). A theory of user-interaction objects. *Journal of Visual Languages and Computing*, 5:227–249.

Puerta, A. (1996). The Mecano project: Comprehensive and integrated support for model-based user interface development. In *Proceedings of CADUI'96*.

Stirewalt, R. E. K. (1997). *Automatic Generation of Interactive Systems from Declarative Models*. PhD thesis, Georgia Institute of Technology.

Stirewalt, R. E. K. and Rugaber, S. (1998). Automating UI generation by model composition. In *Proceedings of the IEEE International Conference on Automated Software Engineering*, pages 177–186.

Szekely, P. et al. (1996). Declarative models for user-interface construction tools: the MASTERMIND approach. In Bass and Unger, editors, *Engineering for Human-Computer Interaction*. Chapman & Hall.

Wilson, S. et al. (1993). Beyond hacking: A model based approach to user interface design. In Alty, J. L., Diaper, D., and Guest, S., editors, *People and Computers VIII, Proceedings of the HCI '93 Conference*.

Chapter 14

VANISHING WINDOWS: AN EMPIRICAL STUDY OF ADAPTIVE WINDOW MANAGEMENT

Tunu Miah and James L. Alty
IMPACT Research Group, Department of Computer Science, Loughborough University, Loughborough, United Kingdom
[T.Miah, J.L.Alty]@lboro.ac.uk
Tel : +44-1509-222648 - Fax : +44-1509-211586

Abstract   One problem with windowing systems today is that the desktop quickly becomes cluttered with the number of windows in use, hindering users in the performance of their tasks. Users can become disorientated by the number of active and inactive windows, lose track of documents and spend time locating document and managing windows rather than working on application tasks. The Vanishing Windows approach aims to reduce the window manipulations required by the user and to aid the user in the performance of search activities. The technique gradually reduces screen real-estate requirements for inactive windows. The reduction of inactive window size progressively increases the overall visibility of windows. This paper briefly discusses the design of the system, based on empirical studies, and presents an evaluation comparing the approach to a Non-Vanishing Windows system using a search task.

Key words: Screen Clutter, Vanishing Windows, Cognitive Overload, Adaptive Window Manager and Screen Real Estate

1.   INTRODUCTION

A basic problem for a window manager is how to mediate between user and application about the screen area devoted to each application. In the early 80's, Xerox developed one of the first tiled window management strategies for its STAR [[17]] system where the display screen was tiled with non-overlapping windows. The Cedar [[20]] system followed a similar tiling strategy. Shortly thereafter, Apple developed a more flexible arbitrary over-lapping window management strategy in Finder 1.0 using guidelines which are still followed [[1]]. Since then, both strategies have evolved, and there have been no major significant changes in commercial window management systems.

Bly and Rosenberg [[3]], define two user requirements for a multi-window system:

- The ability of Windows to conform to their contents so as to maxi-mise the visibility of those contents, and
- The ability of the system to relieve the user of having to manage the size and location of the windows.

Overlapping window systems maximise the first user requirement, since the user has control over the placement of the window, i.e. moving, resizing and overlapping windows anywhere on the screen. However, such systems do little to aid the user in window management. *Tiled* window systems [5], in contrast, maximise the second user requirement. Most tiled systems at-tempt to satisfy the conformance requirement by using all of the available screen space, so windows often change size and location when other win-dows open or close. Tiled systems typically do little to conform to window contents and as the number of open windows increases, the size of each de-creases.

There is now renewed interest in window management in the research community. Important questions are - how do we make current window management more intelligent? What knowledge and inferencing techniques are required? What and how can we co-ordinate between multiple windows? [[16]].

2.   WINDOW SYSTEMS AND THEIR PROBLEMS

The window approach has been promoted because it supports the way that people really work. Bannon et al. [2] analysed the workflow of people using a traditional (non-windowing) computer system. They found that peo-ple seldom completed one task in a continuous time frame. Instead, they switched between applications in response to events from inside and outside the environment. The advantages of windowing systems also arise from how people manage their desks. Malone [11] investigated the way people ar-ranged papers on their desktops. He observed that people tended to position papers to reinforce the way they in which they categorised tasks. This helped them to structure their work, and served to remind them of unfinished tasks. Further, it was observed that users rearranged desktop materials to match changing priorities.

However, in any windowing system the screen can quickly become cluttered with the number of windows concurrently opened by the user. Funke et al. [[6]] define clutter as a condition involving highly dense and overlapping information, and there is already some evidence that clutter adversely affects user performance. As early as 1986, Bly and Rosenberg [[3]] found that, for a database management task, almost half of the users' time was spent in managing the window-based interface. Users also spend a substantial amount of their time moving, resizing, and scrolling windows [[4], [7]]. These tasks have added to the user's existing application domain tasks, and do not contribute to user productivity.

Originally it was felt that the advantages of windowing systems easily outweighed the additional burden imposed by window management. Research on this question, however, is not completely supportive of this belief. Bury, Davies and Darnell [[4]] investigated the impact of windowing systems on completion times for a series of information retrieval tasks. Contrary to the author's predictions, subjects took a significantly longer amount of time to complete the task in the windowing environment than in a non-windowing environment. A detailed analysis of the results suggested that the time spent on the task itself was indeed less in the windowing condition, but the extra time required by window management operations increased the overall time spent.

The above studies indicate that the advantages of window management systems are often offset by the resulting additional management operations that users need to perform. However, it is unknown whether an overall efficiency gain would result as users became more experienced, since extensive training may be necessary [[3]] before the users of a windowing system are able to recall and execute the management operations quickly and accurately.

This paper examines the design, implementation and evaluation of an Intelligent Window Manager which develops a concept called *Vanishing Windows*. It is based on the premise that, by freeing the user's cognitive resources from the task of managing the window aspects of the interface, more of these resources are available for application domain activities. As the problems and application tasks confronting the users become more complex and information intensive, the potential of this approach for improving overall human system performance should be enhanced.

3.   RELATED WORK: INTELLIGENT WINDOW MANAGEMENT SYSTEMS

An adaptive or intelligent window management system changes the window configuration in response to the environment. This adaptation can be informed either from a user model or from algorithms that determine user or system behaviour.

The CUBRICON Intelligent Window Manager (CIWM) [6], is a partially knowledge-based and algorithm-driven system that automates window operations. It automatically performs window management functions such as window creation, sizing, placement, removal, and organisation. The operations are accomplished without direct human input, although the system allows user override of CIWM decisions. The knowledge base contains information regarding the tasks and the different type of presentations that are available to CIWM, such as tables, maps, text, forms, graphs, and graphic illustrations. The system is task-dependent. A better approach would be to generate a knowledge base for generic tasks and adapt the system based on these generic tasks.

Stille et al. [[19]] have proposed an Adaptive Window Manager (AWM) based on their earlier work on Adaptive Automatic Display Layout (A^2DL) [[18]]. The system automates the layout of the windows on the display screen according to the current user, the current task domain and gradually learns the users' layout requirements.

Kandogan and Shneiderman [[8]] approached the problem of minimising user window management time from a different perspective. Rather than adapting the windows automatically, they provided rapid window management operations. For example, closing one application closes all related applications in the same context. They have also conducted an evaluation of their system [[9]], called *Elastic Windows* with an Independent Overlapping Windows system in terms of user performance times on task environment set-up, task switching and task execution times. They found a statistically significant performance difference in support of the Elastic Windows interface for most of the tasks. For some tasks, there was a ten-fold speed up in performance.

One interesting solution to the screen real-estate problem is a 3D Window Manager [[10]]. The system, MaW^3 , uses a 3D space with windows arranged in a tunnel. The user is positioned in the middle of the mouth of the tunnel looking toward the other end. The tunnel, and windows in it, are displayed with a perspective projection. Windows are essentially 2D, i.e. their work area is 2D. However, they have 3D frames, decorations and buttons. The 3D Window manager was designed to address the issue of "window thrashing" [[7]]. It addressed it in four main ways: window hanging, scaling, mouse reduction and transparency. However, extensive evaluation needs to be carried out on the 3D-window manager to quantify whether these techniques solve the window-thrashing problem. The problem is not as simple as reducing mouse movement but is more concerned with identifying required windows without the need for too many searches and switches between windows.

Any adaptive window management system needs to answer the following questions:

- What goal is adaptation trying to achieve?
- What do we want to adapt?
- How do we adapt the system?
- Under what conditions should adaptation take place?

The objective is to reduce user window management operations, so that the user is free to concentrate on the task at hand and not spend unproductive time managing the interface. The approach taken by the Vanishing Windows system is to progressively reduce the size of inactive overlapping windows. The technique minimises the screen real estate occupied by inactive windows and progressively reduces their size. Miah et al. [[14]] demonstrated a technique for reducing wasted workspace, in an application, by limiting the number of toolbars shown and adaptively displaying only the required toolbar based on user needs. Similarly, toolbars on inactive windows can remove themselves, as they serve no purpose when windows are inactive.

Two techniques for minimising screen real estate were developed and experimentally evaluated. The first technique involves progressively reducing the window and its contents in proportion. We call this SCALING. The user always sees the whole window content but at a reduced size. The second technique does not alter the size of the contents of the window, but simply reduced the window size from the bottom right hand corner (often referred to as clipping). We call this CROPPING. These experiments are presented in the next section. In both cases Toolbars were removed from inactive vanishing windows to increase window utilisation.

3.1   Experiment 1: Scaling Verses Cropping

The first experiment determined whether better identification of a target window containing a document was achieved when the document was presented using a scaled or cropped view. Also, investigated was the affect the window size had on user's ability to correctly identify a target document.

This pilot experiment examined the effects of reducing the window size and the presentation styles (cropping and scaling) on a user's ability to identify a target document. Software was written to select and display randomly one of four possible documents, at various window sizes and either of two presentation styles (cropped or scaled). To minimise the effect of learning, 200 samples were presented to each user in a random sequence. The software varied each of the samples in terms of the size of the window and the presentation style.

3.1.1   RESULTS OF ANALYSIS

Initial findings show that a slightly better performance was achieved for the cropped presentation style (detailed results of this experiment can be found in [[12]]). As expected, lower correct identification of the document was observed at low screen utilisation percentage (i.e. window size as a percentage of the desktop size). As the screen utilisation percentage increased so did the number of correct identification. In addition, an accuracy level of about 60% was reached for 30% screen utilisation. Beyond this point, the accuracy seems to be very close for both presentation strategies (Figure 1).

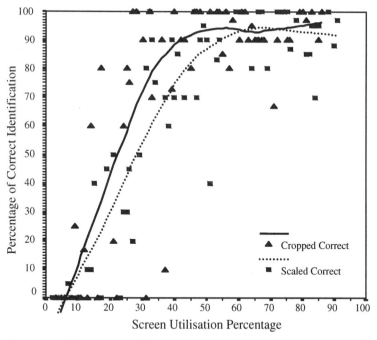

Figure 1. Screen Utilisation % Against Number of Correct Identifications for both Strategies

A comparison was carried out between the means of number of correct identification for the cropped and scaled reduction strategies for <30% screen utilisation using Student's t-test. A significant ($t(9)=4.34$, $p<0.001$, 1-tail) difference was found between the two groups.

3.2 Experiment 2: Adapting The Contents Of The Document

During the first experiment, subjects told us that they identified documents primarily by looking for keywords in the document (although they did use other properties such as font and layout, as well). At low screen sizes, the area available in the vanishing window is necessarily small and the number of defining words in the document may be reduced to a low level since other non-defining words will also be there. In order to improve recognition at low screen sizes, we developed a technique for increasing the proportion of defining words (or keywords) in a document. The frequency of a word in a document was compared with a standard corpus of English usage. If its frequency was significantly greater than its frequency in the corpus then this word was taken to be a keyword (i.e. a word that uniquely identifies the document).

Three methods for presenting these keywords in reduced documents were developed, which could enhance the visual cues at low screen size. These methods were *highlighting*, *listing* and *compressing* the keywords. The second experiment was therefore carried out to determine if higher identification rates could be achieved using one or more of these presentation styles.

A similar experimental procedure to that of experiment 1 was used. Subjects were asked to read a paper for 15 minutes. They familiarised themselves with the four possible techniques - Compressed, Highlighted, List and Normal - Normal being the standard Cropped presentation technique. A random sequence of 200 sample screens was presented to subjects. The software varied the screen size between 0-100 % screen utilisation and the presentation styles.

3.2.1 Results of Analysis

Eighteen subjects volunteered for the experiment. All eighteen subjects were presented with all 200 hundred samples (detailed results of this experiment can be found in [[13]]). The overall result shows that the compression presentation technique yields the greatest recognition (see Table 1). On average, 82.8% of the samples were correctly identified. The remaining three-presentation techniques are very close together in terms of the correct identification percentage. However, the incorrect and don't know percentages vary between these three styles. The normal presentation shows the highest incorrect responses. A repeat measure ANOVA shows that the mean number of correct identification is significantly different between the different adapted presentation styles; $F(3,537)=9.69$, $p<0.001$. It was concluded that increased performance in identification can be achieved by adapting the presentation styles particularly at the lower end of screen utilisation (that at less than 30%).

Table 1. Percentage of Correct, Incorrect and Dont Knows

	Correct	Incorrect	Don't Know
Compressed	82.8%	6.2%	11.0%
Highlighted	75.7%	2.5%	21.8%
List	76.5%	5.3%	18.2%
Normal	76.2%	7.5%	16.3%

Above 30% screen utilisation, subjects tended to score, on average, an 80% correct identification rate. Between 0-9% the compressed strategy showed a higher recognition rate and this was found to be statistically significant ($F(3,51)=2.95$, $p=0.041$). For the 10-19% ($F(3,51)=1.25$, $p=0.302$) and 20-29% ($F(3,51)=1.51$, $p=0.224$) screen utilisation groups the adapted presentation (compressed, highlighted, list) showed higher recognition than the normal. However, there was no statistical evidence to support that the distribution of the sample means were different.

Some subjective comments were also collated from subjects. They were asked to rank the four presentation styles (compressed, highlighted, list and normal) in the order they found easiest to identify the target document. An overall ranking made by subjects was determined by calculating the mode for each presentation styles (see Table 2).

Table 2. User Ranking of Presentation Styles

Style	Rank
Highlighted List	1 - easiest
Compressed	3
Normal	4- hardest

4. FINAL DESIGN OF THE VANISHING WINDOWS SYSTEM

Based on these results, a full Vanishing Windows system was implement. Firstly, the toolbars are removed from all inactive windows and put back on when the window becomes active. Secondly, the window contents are progressively cropped as the size of the window decreases, and finally, inactive window contents are transformed by highlighting keywords identified by the automatic process [13] and restores to the original content when reactivated.

5.   EVALUATING THE VANISHING WINDOWS SYSTEM

5.1   Experimental Design

An experiment was carried out on the final Vanishing Windows system using a within-subject counterbalanced design with 12 subjects. Each subject was tested on both windowing systems (Vanishing and Non-Vanishing). To minimise the effect the order in which a subject carried out the experiment, half of the subjects used Vanishing Windows first, while the other half used Non-Vanishing Windows first. Also, two data sets were used for the task. These data set were randomly assigned to each experimental condition.

There were two Independent variables: the *Windowing System* and the *number of windows contained in the search space* (we refer to this as the *Complexity Level*). There were three complexity levels LOW (4 Windows), MEDIUM (6 Windows) and HIGH (8 Windows). Two dependent variables were logged. *Search Time* – the time required to find the required window and *Number of Window Operations* performed to locate the required window. 'Activating', 'Moving', 'Resizing', 'Maximising' and 'Restoring' a Window, all constituted windows operations. Subjects were not allowed to minimise or close a window.

For each complexity level, five questions about the target paper were required to be solved using one of the systems. An example of a question is:
- Find the paper on "Expert Systems for Threat Analysis in Radar Warning Receivers"
- What is the title of figure 5?

Each subject answered 5 questions in each of the complexity levels, using both windowing systems. Two sets of documents and questions were used. Each set consisted of 8 documents and 15 questions (5 for each complexity level). These sets were assigned to each subject based on a schedule.

Prior to the experiment each subject was given 5 minutes training session of the Vanishing Windows system and 20 minutes to familiarise themselves with a set of eight documents. The subject then continued with the experiment using one of the windowing systems and complexity sequences assigned to them. Upon completion, they were given another set of eight documents to familiarise and then tested on the other windowing system. A short question was completed at the end of the experiment.

The experiment was carried out on a laptop, with a screen resolution of 600x480 pixels and the screen size was 25cm x 19cm. 12 subjects participated in the experiment and all were from the Computer Science Department. All the documents contained in the experiment were related to the computing field.

5.2   Results and Discussions

5.2.1   Search Times

Figure 2 shows the average search times (for 5 searches) to located the required window for different complexity levels and for the two windowing system (Vanishing and Non-Vanishing Windows). For the high complexity environment (i.e. 8 windows), subjects using the Vanishing Windows technique, on average, took less time to locate the required window. However, for the low and medium complexity levels, subjects on average took less time using the Non-Vanishing Windows System.

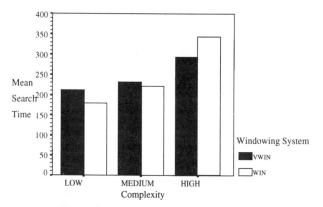

Figure 2. Average Search Times.

A Paired Sample t-test was carried out to determine if the difference in the means were statistically significant, between the Vanishing and Non-Vanishing systems. The result of the t-tests showed that the differences between the means were not statistically significant [Low - (t(11)=1.206, p=0.253, 2-tail); Medium – (t(11)=0.362, p=0.724, 2-tail); High – (t(11)=-1.130, p=0.282, 2-tail)] for any of the complexity levels.

The search time did not take into consideration the system performance differences between the two windowing system. The Vanishing Windows system had a slower system response time, which did affected the search time. As users switched between windows, they had to wait approximately 1 second for the system to process and adapt the windows. Therefore, the

Vanishing Window search times shown in Figure 2 are higher than what they should have been compared to Non-Vanishing Windows. We also examined the number of windows operation carried out during the search task. This was expected to be a more reliable measure for performance.

5.2.2   Number of Windows Operations

The average number of windows operation a subject used to located the desired window for each complexity level for the two windowing systems is shown in Figure 3. For all three-complexity levels, subjects used less windowing operations to locate the required window. As expected, the differences between the Vanishing and Non-Vanishing systems increased as the complexity increases. Since, in the medium complexity environment, the search space consists of 6 windows, and for the high complexity environment it is 8 windows, this has a direct bearing on Short Term Memory Effects [[15]]. As the number of Windows increases beyond 5, users will begin to experience difficulty in short-term memory and may forget where documents are located within the search space.

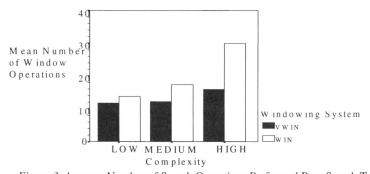

Figure 3. Average Number of Search Operations Performed By a Search Task

Again paired samples t-tests was conducted to check if the results were statistically significant. The results of the t-tests showed a high statistical significance in all three cases [Low – (t(11)=-1.414, p<0.01, 2-tail); Medium – (t(11)=-2.454, p<0.01, 2-tail); High – (t(11)=-3.031, p<0.01, 2-tail)]. The differences between the mean number of window operations required to locate the target window when using the Vanishing Windows system were lower for all complexity levels.

5.2.3   Results of the questionnaire

The questionnaire asked five very important questions.

Q1: Did you find the highlighted keywords on Inactive Windows helpful in identifying the document?
Q2: Did you find the removal of toolbars on Inactive Windows helpful in identifying the document you were looking for?
Q3: Did you find Vanishing Windows helpful?
Q4: Did you feel a loss of control when working with Vanishing Windows?
Q5: Did you find the automatic movement of Windows (i.e. Vanishing) disruptive?

The majority of the subjects found highlighting keywords and removing the toolbars on inactive windows helpful in completing their task. Majority of the subjects also found Vanishing Windows system to be helpful, however 2 subjects (17%) did find it unhelpful. The Chi-square tests performed for all questions show that there is evidence for a significant departure from equal choices.

42% of the subjects reported that they never felt that they had lost control when using the Vanishing Windows Systems. Another 42% indicated that they sometimes felt a loss of control. Both of these responses are reasonably positive results. Therefore, we can be concluded that on average subjects felt in control when using the Vanishing Windows System. The data indicates that the majority of subjects were not distracted or disrupted by inactive window size changing. The Chi-square test for both questions showed a statistically significant departure from equal choice (Q1,Q3,Q4; $p<0.05$, Q2,Q5; $p<0.01$).

6.   CONCLUSIONS AND FUTURE WORK

Our main experiment compared Vanishing Windows with a Non-Vanishing Windows system, in terms user performance times to locate a target window, and the number of windows operation needed to locate a target window. Statistically significant results were found in favour of the Vanishing Windows system in terms of the number of windows operation needed to locate a target window. In addition, as the complexity (number of windows in the search space) increased so did the performance differences between the systems.

Lower search time to locate a window in the Vanishing Windows system was observed for the high complexity case. However, this result was not statistically significant. Also for the low and medium complexity cases the Non-Vanishing Windows results showed better performance in terms of search times. Again, no statistical significance was found in favour of the Non-Vanishing Windows.

Because of the additional processing required by the Vanishing Windows the system response times, we can speculate that search times for the Vanishing Windows would have been lower, if the system performance of the Vanishing Windows to the Non-Vanishing Windows had been comparable. We aim to improve the performance and repeat the experiment.

Overall, subjects did not feel any loss of control when using Vanishing Windows, nor were they distracted from their tasks by automatic movement/resizing of inactive windows. However, this area of research can benefit with an extensive evaluation of how far the auto-adaptation idea can be carried out before users begin to feel real loss of control which causes disruption to current task activities.

REFERENCES

[1]   Apple Computer Inc., *Macintosh Human Interface Guidelines.* Addison Wesley, Reading, 1992.

[2]   Bannon, L., Cypher, A., Greenspan, S., and Monty, M.L., *Evaluation and analysis of users activity organisation,* in Proc. of ACM Conf. on Human Aspects in Computing Systems CHI'83, ACM Press, New York, 1983, pp. 54-57.

[3]   Bly, S.A. and Rosenberg J.K., *A comparison of tiled and overlapped windows,* in Proceedings of ACM Conf. on Human Aspects in Computing Systems CHI'86, ACM Press, New York, 1986, pp. 101-106.

[4]   Bury, K.F., Davies, S.R., and Darnell, M.J., *Window Management: a review of issues and some results from user testing,* IBM Report HFC-53, IBM Human Factors Center, San Jose, June 1985.

[5]   Cohen, E.S., Smith, E.T., and Iverson, L.A., *Constraint-Based Tiled Windows,* in Proceedings of the 1st IEEE International Conference on Computer Workstations (San Jose, 11-14 November 1985), IEEE Computer Graphics and Applications, Vol. 6, No. 5, 1986, pp. 2–11.

[6]   Funke, D.J., Neal, J.G., and Paul, R.D., *An Approach to Intelligent Automated Window Management,* Int. Journal of Man-Machine Studies, Vol. 38, No. 6, 1993, pp. 949-983.

[7]   Henderson, D.A. and Card, S.K., *Rooms: The use of multiple virtual workspaces to reduce space contention in a window based graphical user interface,* ACM Trans. on Graphics, Vol. 5, No. 3, 1986, pp.211-243.

[8]   Kandogan, E. and Shneiderman, B., *Elastic Windows: Improved Spatial Layout and Rapid Multiple Window Operations,* in Proc. of 3rd Int ACM Workshop on Advanced Visual Interfaces AVI'96 (Gubbio, 27-29 May 1996), ACM Press, New York, 1996, pp. 29–38.

[9]   Kandogan, E. and Shneiderman, B., *Elastic Windows: Evaluation of Multi-Window Operations,* in Proceedings of ACM Conf. on Human Aspects in Computing Systems CHI'97 (Atlanta, March 1997), ACM Press, New York, 1997, pp.250-257.

[10] Leach, G., Al-Qaimari, G., Grieve, M., Jinks, N., and McKay, C. *Elements of a three-dimensional Graphical User Interface*, in Proceedings of INTERACT'97, S. Howard, J. Hammond and G. Lindgaard (eds.), Chapman & Hall, London, 1997.

[11] Malone, T.W., *How do people organise their desk? Implications for the design of office automation systems*, ACM Trans. on Office Information Systems, Vol. 1, 1983, pp. 99-112.

[12] Miah, T. and Alty, J.L., *Vanishing Windows: A Technique for Adaptive Window Management*, Interacting with Computers, Vol. 12, 1999, to be published.

[13] Miah, T. and Alty, J.L., *Visual Recognition of Windows: Effects of Size Variation and Presentation Styles*, in *Proceedings of OzCHI'98*.

[14] Miah, T., Karageorgou, M., and Knott, R.P., *Adaptive Toolbars: An Architectural Overview*, in Proc. of 3rd ERCIM Workshop on User Interfaces for All (Obernai, November 1997), ERCIM, 1997, pp 157-163.

[15] Miller, G.A., *The magical number seven, plus or minus two: Some limits on our capacity for Processing Information*, Psychological Review, Vol. 63, 1956, pp. 81-97.

[16] North, C. and Shneiderman, B., *A Taxonomy of Multiple Window Coordinations*, Technical Report, University of Maryland, Dept of Computer Science. CS-TR-3854, 1997.

[17] Smith, D.C., Irby, C., Kimball, R., and Harslem, E. *The Star User Interface: An Overview,* in Proc. National Computer Conference, 1982.

[18] Stille, S., Minocha, S., and Ernst, R., *A^{2}DL- Adaptive Automatic Display Layout System,* in *Proc. of 3rd Ann. IEEE Symp. on Human Interactions with Computer Systems (HICS'96),*. IEEE Computer Press, Los Alamitos, 1996.

[19] Stille, S., Minocha S., and Ernst, R., *An Adaptive Window Management System*, in Proc. INTERACT'97, S. Howard, J. Hammond and G. Lindgaard (eds.), Chapman & Hall, London, 1997.

[20] Teitelman, W.A., *A Tour Through Cedar,* IEEE Software, Vol. 1, No.4, April 1984.

Chapter 15

ADAPTIVE LAYOUT CALCULATION IN GRAPHICAL USER INTERFACES: A RETROSPECTIVE ON THE A²DL-PROJECT

Stefan Stille

Steinhoff Competence Center, Langebrügger Straße 5, D–26655 Westerstede, Germany

Stefan.Stille@steinhoff.de

Rolf Ernst

Technical University Braunschweig, Institute of Computer Engineering,

Hans–Sommer–Straße 66, D–38106 Braunschweig, Germany

ernst@ida.ing.tu-bs.de

Abstract   The aim of our project A²DL (Adaptive Automatic Display Layout[1]) was to develop concepts for the usage of layout algorithms for adaptive automatic window management. With the basic objective of minimizing the user's involvement in window management activities, our emphasis has been to relieve the user from explicitly specifying any parameters for layout algorithms. Instead, an adaptive layout system is expected to learn the layout requirements from a user's manual corrections of the layouts presented by the system and automaticly adapt its layout calculation accordingly. In this paper, we present basic results of the A²DL–project.

Keywords: Adaptive User Interfaces, Adaptive Layout Calculation, Task Modeling, Windowing Systems, Neural Networks, Combinatorial Optimization.

Introduction

The extended availability and complexity of information that users have to work on with current graphical user interfaces (GUIs), often results in a situation Kahn und Charnock [12] called 'Windowitis': there are so many windows opened on the desktop that users are not able to get an overview of the information displayed in them. The visual chaos that users perceive causes significant cognitive overhead since current windowing systems mainly provide single–window layout operations which are an answer to the needs of

---

[1]The A²DL–project was supported by German Research Foundation (DFG) under grant no. Er 168/7–1/2

80's applications [13]. The results are dramatically extended task completion times and dissatisfaction of users.

In our previous work [16], [17], [18], we have proposed an approach of Automatic Display Layout (ADL), wherein it has been suggested that layout algorithms could be used to automatically organize the windows on the screen and assist the user in his current activity. The problem of ADL has been formulated as a graph layout problem by abstracting graphical objects as nodes and semantic relationships between them as edges. The layout problem was then treated as a combinatorial optimization problem [19], [20].

In practice, however, it turned out to be a problem that the user has to specify many input parameters for the ADL layout algorithms (e.g. the optimization criteria). The user is thus, expected to know about the intricacies of the layout computations that take place in the background. This is obviously not acceptable from the software–ergonomic point of view.

In our current research [31], [32], we have propounded the concept of A^2DL (Adaptive Automatic Display Layout) where our aim was to extend the usage of layout algorithms for adaptive automatic window management in state of the art multi–window environments. With the basic objective of minimizing the user's involvement in window management activities, our emphasis, in the notion of A^2DL, has been to relieve the user from explicitly specifying any parameters for the layout algorithms. Instead, the layout system was expected to learn the layout parameters directly from a user's manual corrections of the layouts presented by the system.

1.   THE FRAMEWORK FOR ADAPTIVITY

The layout requirements of users are generally related to the current task a user performs. Our first approach to task recognition based on the working set model described in [9] and [2]. This model states that users use distinguishable sets of windows to perform their tasks. We chose to analyze the keyboard focus to detect the current working set of windows [31]. The window getting the keyboard focus for a considerable amount of time is an indication of its usage. Provided that the working sets are detected, we classified a vector consisting of the attributes of all windows in the working set using an ART1 neural network [3]. Its output (i.e. a unique class identifier) was interpreted as a symbolic description of the task currently being performed. This approach turned out to be inadequate [33], mainly for two reasons. At first, the keyboard focus can not be solely taken as an indication of window usage because windows were used without having the focus (e.g. for read–only activities). This usage can generally not be observed by the layout system because of the limited bandwidth of the information available. Secondly, the use of neural networks for this kind of task recognition is generally prone to errors since they do not allow a detailed analysis of their behavior in a complex environment [5]. In particular, an ART1 network builds up complex dependencies between its class prototypes and the input vectors considered members of the class. The granularity of its classifications could therefore hardly be adjusted.

Consequently, we developed the AW model (for a complete description see [33]; the model gets its name from the modeling concepts described below) that describes the applications and windows needed for the execution of users' external ('real world') tasks. We presume that, in contemporary computer systems, users define their external tasks keeping the applications and windows provided by the system in mind (cf. [24]). We therefore assume that main tasks are first decomposed into 'application level tasks' (ALTs) which allow users to determine the application(s) they have to use in order to perform a given main task. ALTs are further decomposed into 'window level tasks' (WLTs) which directly correspond to a set of windows on the screen. The windows of a WLT are, from the layout system's point of view, a semantic unit [33]. The attributes of the windows corresponding to a WLT are defined in an AW description. At runtime, the layout system can recognize the WLTs a user *is able to perform with the currently open windows*, by comparing the attributes of these windows with those in an AW description.

The real time task switching behavior of users is not specified in an AW description since it is inherently unpredictable in a windowing system. However, the AW model defines the activation states which WLTs can have during parallel task execution taking results from cognitive psychology into accout (cf. for example [1], [23]). Only one WLT at a time can be in 'active' state (i.e. consciously be performed) due to the limited capacity of short term memory [22]. All other WLTs are either 'backgrounded' (i.e. performed by the system under 'unconscious attention' from the user [23]) or 'stopped' (i.e. not performed at all). As a consequence of their limited cognitive resources, users coordinate their external tasks [10], i.e. change their activation states. It can be concluded that user oriented window operations can only be realized by supporting these task switches efficiently. Hence, in A^2DL, WLT objects (i.e. task objects with a mapping to the related windows) and coordination operations for WLT ob-

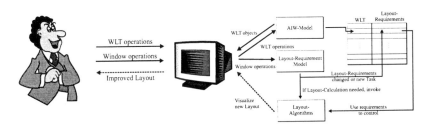

Figure 1   Basic approach to adaptivity in A^2DL

jects are added as GUI concepts. This enables users to directly communicate with the layout system in terms of the external tasks they want to perform. The layout system on the other side can exactly determine the currently active task and nows the context for layout calculations and the adaptation of layout requirements (figure 1).

2.   A²DL'S BASIC LAYOUT STRATEGY

We decided to use overlapping windows rather than a tiled windows approach (cf. [4], [30]) which was also used in ADL [19] . The most important reason for our decision is that overlapping windows provide better support for parallel display of information [6], which is one of the main concerns of our research. In addition, all contemporary commercial window systems use the overlapping layout strategy [13] so that the concepts of A²DL can be applied to them.

Another basic layout principle in A²DL can be derived from the user's fundamental layout requirements for windows corresponding to WLTs with specific activation states. The windows of the active WLT have to be clearly arranged on the screen since they are needed by the user for his current activities. Windows of backgrounded WLTs should be arranged as clearly as possible since the user has to check for results from time to time and then probably switch to this task. It is obvious that the windows of the active WLT have higher priority than those of backgrounded WLTs. To match these fundamental requirements, we introduce primary and secondary layout areas as shown in figure 2. Windows of stopped WLTs need not be displayed on the screen, so they can be removed (not destroyed!) by the layout system because their WLT objects still remind the user of the unfinished task[2]. For this reason, we do not use any icons for single windows in A²DL.

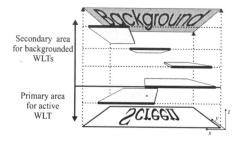

Figure 2   Separation of z–dimension into main and secondary area. This basic layout strategy allows to place the windows of the active WLT with higher priority than those of backgrounded WLTs. The number of slots in the main area is always adjusted to the number of windows of the active WLT.

---

[2]This is a basic requirement for window systems [23], [2], [14], [21] (see also Norman's principle of 'knowledge in the head and in the world' [27])

3.   IDENTIFYING LAYOUT EXAMPLES

The layout system must be able to determine the layout wishes of users by analyzing their normal windows operations (cf. figure 1). The following operations for windows are presumed to exist in a windowing system (cf. [25]): Move, Resize, Maximize/Minimize (bring to full screen size/original size), Lower/Raise (bring window to back/front of window pile). Provided that the currently active WLT is known from WLT operations, these operations are interpreted as follows:

- *Move* indicates that the current layout is not clearly arranged. The resulting layout is to be interpreted as a layout example.

- *Resize* at first indicates that the size of a window is inadequate. But it is also possible that the user thought that the layout is not clearly arranged and tried to solve this problem by changing a window's size. Therefore, the resulting layout is to be interpreted as a layout example.

- *Maximize* and *Minimize* are only used to temporarily change window sizes (maybe because of some special window contents). It is therefore assumed that these operations are used to actually work on a task and do not reflect changed layout wishes.

- *Lower* and *Raise* are also used to work on a task without changing the context because the framework for efficient task switching is given by WLT operations. Therefore, these operations do not reflect changed layout wishes.

4.   COST FUNCTIONS IN A²DL

In ADL, cost functions for layout calculation were proposed [20]. Static cost functions quantify characteristics of the current layout (e.g. overlap of windows/window titles, changes of shape/size of windows from their desired size/shape, etc.). Dynamic cost functions, on the other hand, quantify changes of the current layout relative to the last layout arranged on the screen – also called a 'reference layout' – (e.g. changes of absolute and relative positions of windows). They are important because the topological consistency of subsequent layouts is a substantial ergonomic requirement for all layout calculations [26], [31], [4].

In A²DL, each cost function now exists in two versions: one that takes only windows in the primary area into account and one that takes windows from both areas (primary and secondary) into account. This diversification is necessary because of the high importance of windows in the primary area which raised the demand for an explicit control of their layout characteristics.

To analyze the distribution characteristics of cost functions, we generated stochastic layouts by randomly modifying the characteristics of given graph abstractions of screen contents. More specifically, a significant number (10000) of random, valid layouts were generated and the results of all cost functions were logged for each graph. For dynamic cost functions, we repeated these tests with a number of different reference layouts.

We found that all cost functions (static and dynamic) are approximately normal distributed over the whole solution space of the layout calculation. Given that $N(c) = \frac{1}{\sigma\sqrt{2\pi}}e^{-\frac{(c-\mu)^2}{2\sigma^2}}$ is the density function of a cost function, we were able to show that mean μ and standard deviation σ depend on the graph structure (i.e. the number and size of nodes and the number of edges between them).

5.   ABSTRACTION OF STATIC LAYOUT REQUIREMENTS

Given that a user provides a layout example by arranging the windows on the screen, we calculate the values $c_{d,\text{stat},i}$ (called 'desired costs') of all static cost functions $C_{\text{stat},i}$. The resulting vector $\vec{c}_{d,\text{stat}} = (c_{d,\text{stat},1}, \ldots c_{d,\text{stat},n})$ quantifies all (static) layout characteristics that are considered in A^{2}DL and is therefore a sufficient abstraction of user requirements. It is obvious that the user will not be able to perceive every deviation from the desired costs in a calculated layout. We therefore assume that a deviation of $\pm\Delta c_{\text{stat},i}$ from the desired costs is acceptable.

The probability $N(c_{d,i})$ of the desired costs $c_{d,i}$ for a specific static cost function C_i allows to estimate how hard the user must have tried to arrange a layout with these costs. If $N(c_{d,i})$ is small, only few layouts with the desired characteristics exist. Consequently, the user has focused on improving[3] this layout characteristic and will most likely only accept a small Δc_i. On the other hand, if $N(c_{d,i})$ is large, many layouts with the desired characteristics exist. The user did obviously not care about this characteristic and will therefore accept a larger Δc_i.

As a measure for the importance, the desired costs c_d have for the user, we use the following function:

$$I(c_d) \stackrel{\text{def}}{=} \frac{N(c_d)}{N(\mu)} = \frac{\frac{1}{\sigma\sqrt{2\pi}}e^{-\frac{(c_d-\mu)^2}{2\sigma^2}}}{\frac{1}{\sigma\sqrt{2\pi}}e^{-\frac{(\mu-\mu)^2}{2\sigma^2}}} = e^{-\frac{(c_d-\mu)^2}{2\sigma^2}}. \tag{1}$$

---

[3]Due to the symmetry of $N(c_{d,i})$, low probabilities also exist for $c_d \rightarrow c_{\max}$. This means that the user tried hard to generate a 'bad' layout (for example a layout where all windows overlap completely). From our practical experience, however, we can exclude this case and will ignore it for the rest of our argumentation.

The maximum of I is obviously 1 for $c_d = \mu$. In addition, it is $I(c_d) < 1$ for all $c_d \neq \mu$. So I is actually a reciprocal measure for the importance.

The acceptable deviations from the desired costs for static cost functions are described by $\Delta c_{\text{stat}}(c_d)$ which is defined as:

$$\Delta c_{\text{stat}}(c_d) \stackrel{\text{def}}{=} \max(I(c_d) \cdot (k_{\text{stat}} \cdot \sigma), \Delta_{\min}). \tag{2}$$

The parameter $\Delta_{\min}$ denotes the cost difference, the user can not perceive at all. It depends on the implementation of a cost function and is inherently small compared to μ and σ. The largest deviation $(k_{\text{stat}} \cdot \sigma)$ depends only on μ and σ and will be accepted when $c_d = \mu$.

From the qualitative considerations in this section, we can not completely define what deviations users will find acceptable. We therefore introduce the constant k_{stat} that allows to further customize the absolute deviation. It can only be determined in practical tests which evaluate user feedback for layout calculations with different values for k_{stat}. For reasons we give later in this paper, we have not performed these tests yet.

Putting all these considerations together, the formal description of the static characteristics, a calculated layout L must have, is given by:

$$\forall i : C_{\text{stat},i}(L) = c_{d,i} \pm \max(e^{-\frac{(c_{d,i}-\mu_i)^2}{2\sigma_i^2}} \cdot (k_{\text{stat}} \cdot \sigma_i), \Delta_{\min,i}). \tag{3}$$

6.   ABSTRACTION OF DYNAMIC LAYOUT REQUIREMENTS

Generally, a layout example does not allow conclusions about the dynamic costs that a user is willing to accept. The reason is that the user manipulates the layout by successively moving or resizing windows and therefore does not care about topological consistency. Hence, we presume that the dynamic costs should be as small as possible and define that

$$\Delta c_{\text{dyn}} \stackrel{\text{def}}{=} \max(c_{\min}, (\mu - (k_{\text{dyn}} \cdot \sigma))) \tag{4}$$

is the upper bound of costs that are acceptable for a dynamic cost function C_{dyn}. The maximum function just simply guarantees that the upper bound can not be less than $c_{\min}$, the minimal cost value for a given layout. Like k_{stat}, the constant k_{dyn} can only be determined in practical tests. The formal description of the dynamic characteristics, a calculated layout L must have from the user's point of view, is thus given by:

$$\forall j : C_{\text{dyn},j}(L) \leq \max(c_{\min,j}, (\mu_j - (k_{\text{dyn}} \cdot \sigma_j))). \tag{5}$$

7.   THE OPTIMIZATION GOAL IN A²DL

We define the optimization goal using equations (3) and (5):

$$C_{\text{total}} = \sum_i \bar{C}_{\text{stat},i} + \sum_j \hat{C}_{\text{dyn},j} \quad \text{with} \tag{6a}$$

$$\bar{C}_i = \begin{cases} 0 & \text{if } c_{r,i} \in c_{d,i} \pm \max(e^{-\frac{(c_{d,i}-\mu_i)^2}{2\sigma_i{}^2}} \cdot (k_{\text{stat}} \cdot \sigma_i), \Delta_{\min,i}), \\ |c_{r,i} - c_{d,i}| & \text{otherwise.} \end{cases}$$

$$\tag{6b}$$

$$\hat{C}_j = \begin{cases} 0 & \text{if } c_{r,j} \le \max(c_{\min,j}, (\mu_j - (k_{\text{dyn}} \cdot \sigma_j))), \\ c_{r,j} - (\max(c_{\min,j}, (\mu_j - (k_{\text{dyn}} \cdot \sigma_j)))) & \text{otherwise.} \end{cases} \tag{6c}$$

The parameters $c_{r,i}$ denote the values calculated by the cost functions for a temporary layout and are called 'raw costs'. The optimization goal only depends on the cost functions' distribution characteristics which are to be calculated for the current layout structure at runtime and on the cost vector $\vec{c}_{d,\text{stat}}$ which is learned by the system. The global minimum of C_{total} is 0. It will be reached if and only if a layout has the required layout characteristics and the required degree of topological consistency. It can be concluded that the layout algorithms must be able to find the global optimum even if there are only few layouts which have the required characteristics.

8.   LAYOUT ALGORITHMS FOR A²DL

As mentioned before, manual changes of z–positions of windows are to be considered as an indication of a user's work on his task. In principle, layout algorithms can not support users in actually performing a task. Hence, no changes of z–positions have to be made and the 3–dimensional solution space of the overlapping layout strategy can be reduced to 2 dimensions (x and y) for layout calculation.

Layout calculations are performed in two phases with reduced solution spaces to save time. This principle was successfully introduced in ADL as a consequence of the fact that a layout calculation based on the full solution space requires calculation times of several minutes [20]. The layout algorithms are fully described in [33], a brief summary is given in figure 3.

The simulated annealing optimization strategy [15] is used for both layout phases. Control parameters define whether a temporary layout is accepted or rejected and whether the algorithm should stop because no further improvement can be expected. The annealing schedule, which specifies how the control parameters should be adapted, is therefore crucial for the quality of the algorithms. For our algorithms, we use an adaptive annealing schedule proposed in [28], which adapts the annealing process automaticly to the strucure of C_{total}.

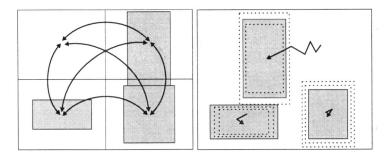

Figure 3 In the global layout phase, a coarse grid is defined for the placement area to reduce the complexity of the solution space. In an initial step, each node is placed on exactly one grid point. Global layout changes are performed by stochastically exchanging grid positions of nodes in order to improve the overall costs of the layout. The local layout phase takes the grid based layout and calculates the final layout. Only local changes of node positions and small changes of node geometry are stochastically performed to further improve the overall costs of the layout.

Results

We performed various tests to analyze quality and behavior of our layout algorithms in practical use. For brevity, we only give the main results in this paper. For a given graph abstraction of an actual layout consisting of 6 windows with 4 semantic relationships between them, a layout L_{wish} should be calculated with static layout characteristics given by different cost vectors. The vectors were calculated from different layout examples that we manually arranged on the screen. This guarantees that at least one layout L_{wish} really exists. The cost vectors were selected based on the number of optimal layouts that are expected to exist, i.e. based on the complexity of the layout problem defined by them[4]. We simplified the layout problem further by taking the layout example as the reference layout for the dynamic cost functions. This guarantees that at least one layout L_{wish} exists even if total topological consistency (i.e. $\forall j : C_{\text{dyn},j}(L_{\text{wish}}) = c_{\text{min},j}$) is demanded.

As mentioned before, the constants k_{stat} and k_{dyn} were not known at the time of the experiment. We therefore chose k_{dyn} from $[-2.0, 1.0]$ and k_{stat} from $[0, 3.0]$. For dynamic cost functions, this means that between 15,87% ($k_{\text{dyn}} = 1, 0$) and 97,72% ($k_{\text{dyn}} = -2, 0$) of all layouts are considered optimal during our tests. For static cost functions, the accepted deviation ranged between 0 (for $k_{\text{stat}} = 0$ and small $N(c_d)$) and σ (for $k_{\text{stat}} = 3, 0$ and $c_d = \mu$, i.e. maximum $N(c_d)$). In the latter case, the cost function is practically ignored during optimization.

---

[4]The measure we used to determine the complexity of the layout problem is derived in [33].

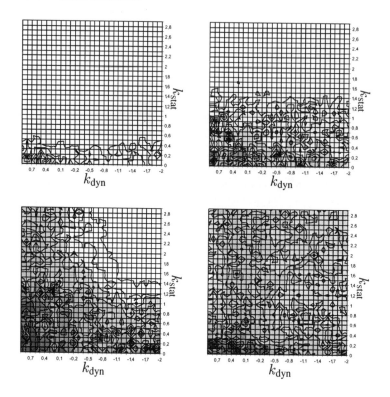

Figure 4   Final costs for four different cost vectors.

For each pair (k_{stat}, k_{dyn}) 100 layout calculations were performed. In figure 4, the average final costs C_{total} of the layout calculation are given for each parameter pair and four different cost vectors. Dark areas reflect high costs, white areas reflect that the layout goal $C_{total} = 0$ was reached in all 100 calculations. The complexity of the layout problem rises from the left top to the bottom right diagram.

Our experiment clearly shows that even the complexity of a relatively simple real world window layout problem is so high that it can not reliably be solved by the proposed layout algorithms. The reason is that the simulated annealing approach to optimization tends to 'get stuck' in local minima if the complexity of the layout problem gets too high. Assumed that it is possible to find an upper boundary for the complexity of real world layout problems, the calculation times for a simulated annealing algorithm with an adequate slow annealing schedule will be far from being acceptable for interactive use. Even in our simple test environment, the average calculation time for a single layout was nearly 20 seconds on an UltraSparc with a 300 MHz CPU.

Conclusions

The contribution of the A^2DL project is at first a framework which allows to realize an adaptive windowing system. The task recognition problem can now be solved by describing the relationship between external tasks and windows in an AW model and providing WLT objects and operations for an adaptive windowing system. The semantics of manual layout operations were analyzed in the context of this model giving a detailed description of how a A^2DL–system should react opon their occurence. Currently, however, an AW model must be manually generated by the user. This is relatively easy but surely not acceptable for every user. Therefore, it should be considered to build the bridge from design time models for task oriented GUI design (like TKS [11] or MAD [29]) to a runtime model like the AW model. The designer's analytical knowledge about window usage of an application could be used to automaticly build up a runtime description for adaptive layout management.

The second major contribution of the A^2DL project is that the problem of adaptive window layout was formulated as a combinatorial optimization problem that allows to take user requirements into account. Two optimization algorithms based on the simulated annealing strategy were proposed to solve this problem. However, it turned out that the complexity of real world layout problems is so high that it can not be solved in reasonable time by those algorithms. Somewhat surprising, this result brings us to questions similar to those treated in the ADL project in which appropriate optimization algorithms for automatic display layout were sought. Candidates to be examined for adaptive display layout are for example genetic algorithms [8] or the tabu search paradigma [7].

References

[1] John R. Anderson. *Kognitive Psychologie.* Spektrum Lehrbuch. Spektrum Akademischer Verlag, Heidelberg, Berlin, Oxford, 1996.

[2] S. K. Card, M. Pavel, and J. E. Farrell. Window-based computer dialogues. In *Proceedings of IFIP INTERACT'84: Human-Computer Interaction,* Dialogue Interaction / Analysing Interactive Dialogues, pages 239–243, 1984. Reprinted in Baecker & Buxton, 1987, p. 456.

[3] G. A. Carpenter and S. Grossberg. The art of adaptive pattern recognition by a self–organizing neural network. *IEEE Computer,* pages 47–88, March 1988.

[4] E.S. Cohen, E.T. Smith, and L.A. Iverson. Constraint–based tiled windows. *IEEE Computer Graphics and Applications,* 6(5):35–45, May 1986.

[5] G. Dorffner. *Konnektionismus: Von Neuronalen Netzen zu einer 'natürlichen' KI.* Teubner, Stuttgart, 1991.

[6] Douglas J. Funke, Jeannette G. Neal, and Rajendra D. Paul. An approach to intelligent automated window management. *International Journal of Man–Machine Studies*, 38:949–983, 1993.

[7] F. Glover. Tabu Search – Part1. *ORSA Journal on Computing*, 1(3):42–51, 1989.

[8] Goldberg, D. *Genetic Algorithms in Search, Optimization and Machine Learning*. Addison–Wesley, 1989.

[9] D. Austin Henderson and Stuart K. Card. Rooms: The Use of Multiple Virtual Workspaces to Reduce Space Contention in a Window–Based Graphical User Interface. *ACM Transactions on Graphics*, 5(3):211–243, July 1986.

[10] Michael Herczeg. *Einführung in die Software–Ergonomie*. Addison–Wesley, Deutschland, 1994.

[11] H. Johnson and P. Johnson. Task knowledge structures: Psychological basis and integration into system design. *Acta Psychologica*, 78:3–26, 1991.

[12] M. J. Kahn and E. Charnock. How to prevent "windowitis" in your graphical interface. In *Proceedings Silicon Valley Ergonomics Conference & Exposition, ErCon '95*, pages 18–25, 1995.

[13] E. Kandogan and B. Shneiderman. Elastic windows: Improved spatial layout and rapid multiple window operations. Technical Report CS–TR–3522, Human–Computer Interaction Laboratory, University of Maryland, College Park, MD 20742-3255, USA, September 1995.

[14] E. Kandogan and B. Shneiderman. Elastic windows: Evaluation of multi-window operations. Technical Report CS–TR–3695, Human–Computer Interaction Laboratory, University of Maryland, College Park, MD 20742-3255, USA, October 1996.

[15] S. Kirkpatrik, C. D. Gelatt jr., and M. P. Vecchi. Optimization by Simulated Annealing. *Science*, 220(13):671–680, 1981.

[16] P. Lüders and R. Ernst. The dynamic screen – beyond the limits of traditional graphical user interfaces. In *Proceedings of 13th IFIP World Computer Congress, Hamburg, Germany*, pages 109–114, Amsterdam, The Netherlands, September 1994. Elsevier Science Publishers.

[17] P. Lüders and R. Ernst. Improvement of the user interface of multimedia applications by automatic display layout. In *Proceedings of Multimedia and Networking Conference, San Jose, CA*. Multimedia and Networking Conference, San Jose, CA, February 1995.

[18] P. Lüders and R. Ernst. Improving browsing in information by the automatic display layout. In *Proceedings of the IEEE Symposium on Infor-*

mation Visualization, Atlanta, Georgia, USA, pages 26–33, Los Alamitos, California, USA, October 1995. IEEE Computer Society Press.

[19] P. Lüders, R. Ernst, and S. Stille. An approach to automatic display layout using combinatorial optimization algorithms. *Software – Practice & Experience*, 25(11):1183–1202, November 1995.

[20] Peter Lüders. *Ein Beitrag zur Verbesserung der grafischen Benutzungsschnittstelle durch das automatisierte Bildschirmlayout.* Fortschritt–Berichte VDI. VDI Verlag, Düsseldorf, 1995.

[21] Thomas W. Malone. How Do People Organize Their Desks? Implications for the Design of Office Information Systems. *ACM Transactions on Office Information Systems*, 1(1):99–112, January 1983.

[22] G. A. Miller. The magical Number Seven, Plus or Minus Two: Some Limits on our Capacity for Processing Information. *Psychological Review*, 2(63):81–97, 1956.

[23] Y. Miyata and Norman D. A. Psychological issues in support of multiple activities. In D. A. Norman and S. W. Draper, editors, *User Centered System Design*, pages 265–284. Lawrence Erlbaum Associates, Publishers, Hillsdale, NJ, 1986.

[24] Thomas P. Moran. Getting into a system: External-internal task mapping analysis. In *Proceedings of ACM CHI'83 Conference on Human Factors in Computing Systems*, Interface Design 2 – The Design Process, pages 45–49, 1983.

[25] Brad A. Myers. A taxonomy of window manager user interfaces. *IEEE Computer Graphics and Applications*, 8(5):65–84, September 1988.

[26] F. Newberry-Paulish and W. F. Tichy. EDGE: An Extensible Graph Editor. *Software – Practice & Experience*, 20(6):63–88, July 1990.

[27] D. Norman. The design of everyday things, 1990. Doubleday: New York, NY.

[28] R.H.J.M. Otten and L.P.P.P. van Ginneken. *The Annealing Algorithm.* The Kluwer International Series in Engineering and Computer Science. Kluwer Academic Press, Boston, Dordrecht, London, 1989.

[29] Suzanne Sebillotte. Methodology guide to task analysis with the goal of extracting relevant characteristics for human–computer interfaces. *International Journal of Human–Computer Interaction*, 7(4):341–363, 1995.

[30] Ben Shneiderman. *Designing the user interface: strategies for effective human–computer interaction.* Addison–Wesley, 3. edition, 1998.

[31] S. Stille, S. Minocha, and R. Ernst. A^2DL–An Adaptive Automatic Display Layout System. In *Proceedings of the IEEE 3rd Annual Symposium on Human Interaction with Complex Systems (HICS 96)*, Dayton, OHIO, USA, August 1996. IEEE Computer Society Press.

[32] S. Stille, S. Minocha, and R. Ernst. An adaptive window management system. In *Proceedings of the 6th IFIP Conference on Human-Computer Interaction*, Sydney, Australia, Juli 1997.

[33] Stefan Stille. *Adaptive Layoutberechnung zur anwendergerechten Layoutgestaltung in Grafischen Benutzungsoberflächen*. PhD thesis, Technische Universität Braunschweig, 1999.

Chapter 16

SEMANTIC DIFFERENCES BETWEEN USER INTERFACE PLATFORMS
Relevance to design and re-design of user interface

Morten Borup Harning
Department of Informatics, Copenhagen Business School,
Howitzvej 60, DK-2000 Frederiksberg, Denmark
harning@cbs.dk
Tel: +45 3815 2400 – Fax: +45 3815 2401

Abstract   This paper shows how user function diagrams can be used to describe some of the important semantic differences found between common user interface platforms. The differences described can be difficult to communicate and hence to address if described at a more detailed level as is often the case in descriptions of user interface standards such as the Windows-standard [1]. It is argued that the logical design which the user function diagram is part of is important both when designing and re-designing user interfaces. Especially if an existing user interface needs to be ported to a difference target platform.

Keywords: User interface design, user interface redesign, user interface platform, user interface standards, cross-platform design, multiple target platforms.

1.   INTRODUCTION

When designing a user interface for a given target platform it is important for the interface designer to know the details of the user interface standard that constitutes the look and feel of that specific standard. The description of the Microsoft Windows95/NT standard [1] is between 500 and 600 pages long, most of which contain small but important details. It is difficult for designers to grasp and understand all of the details. Hence many designers tend to study only concrete examples readily available to them or to extend skeleton programs instead of trying to follow the standard as described.

When designing based on examples it is fairly easy to come up with a design that looks right, it is much more difficult to capture the feel of the interface standard. Most graphical user interfaces look very similar, but tend to differ more at the semantic level.

2.   USER FUNCTION DIAGRAMS

The notation used in this paper, called *user function diagrams*, has been developed as part of a structured user interface design method called Software User Interface Engineering (SUIE) [2,3].

In a user function diagram, such as the one in figure 1, a box is used to depict a logical window presenting information related to a specific concept and circle to depict a user function. A dotted line indicates temporary information as opposed to permanent or stored information. Arrows to and from a logical window is used to indicate that a user function reads or modifies information related to the concept being presented. An arrow with a small circle indicates that the user function replaces what was previously stored. A complete description can be found in [2].

3.   AN EXAMPLE OF SEMANTIC DIFFERENCES BETWEEN INTERFACE PLATFORMS

The following examples illustrate some of the semantic differences found between common user interface platforms such as the Window95/98/NT platform and the Macintosh platform.

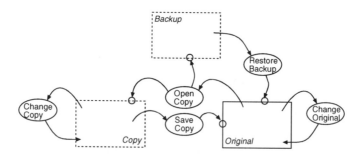

Figure 1. A *user function diagram* describing three generic user functions, that can be used to explain the semantic differences between functionality for changing, saving, applying and cancelling provided by most graphical user interface platforms

The generic functions in figure 1 describe how the user can work with the following three versions of some information. The *original* is the currently stored version of the information, the *copy* is a working copy that allows user to make changes without affecting the original. The *backup* is a copy of the stored information that can be used to restore a previous version.

The user function *OpenCopy* makes a copy of the currently stored information and makes it available as a working copy. If the platform make use of the backup, then *OpenCopy* will also update the backup. *SaveCopy* replaces the currently stored version with a copy of the working copy. *RestoreBackup* is similar to *SaveCopy* but replaces the original with a copy of the backup version. Depending on the platform, changes can be made directly to the currently stored version or to the working copy, but both approaches will typically not be allowed.

3.1   Interface platforms using a working copy

Figure 2 illustrates the differences between the user functions an application, designed for the Windows95/98/NT platform and the Macintosh respectively, needs to provide.

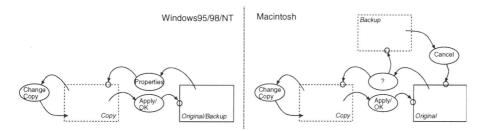

Figure 2. The figure shows the differences between the way the Windows95/98/NT and the Macintosh platform facilitate changing information related to a concept.

The differences described in figure 2 are not reflected in the "look" of the two platforms, that in this case appears to be almost identical. The differences however make a big difference to the user. Using an application following the Macintosh platform standard the user will assume, that *Apply* (*SaveCopy* in the generic diagram) allows him to see if the changes made have the intended effect, while maintaining a backup copy of the original values. Had the application used the Windows95/98/NT platform standard however, the user would have had to make a backup copy of the original manually before making the changes in order to perform the same test.

The example illustrates that what might appear to be subtle differences, can have catastrophic consequences for the user. This might well be the case if an application designed for the Windows platform is ported to the Macintosh platform without the appropriate redesign

3.2   Interface platforms that change the original directly

Figure 3 illustrates a very different approach typically used in devices
with a custom made user interface, e.g. with a LCD display and a number of
custom made buttons used to change information. In such cases modifying
the original directly will be preferable, because it is simple to implement and
because it can be implemented with fewer buttons than would otherwise be
the case.

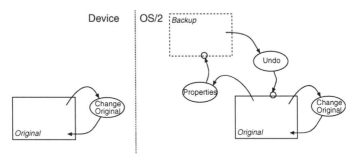

Figure 3. The figure shows a significantly different approach to those described in Figure 2
where the original is modified directly

Figure 3 also shows the semantics of the model used in the OS/2 CUA
platform standard [4]. As the figure shows the model used in OS/2 is in fact
closer to the device model, than to those found in the more common GUI's
described in Figure 2.

It might be somewhat surprising to find that OS/2 CUA differs so much
from the approaches described in Figure 2. The underlying assumption is
however that the simpler model will be more intuitive for the user, while
maintaining the advantages found in Macintosh platform standard. The
downside of this argument is of course that approach will be confusing to the
users accustomed to the Windows or Macintosh platform.

4.   THE LOGICAL DESIGN – AN IMPORTANT
PART OF THE DESIGN METHOD

Figure 4 shows the design steps in SUIE where the design of user functions is part of logical design used to describe the semantics of the user interface. A description of the user interface semantics, such as the logical design
in SUIE, seems to be important when describing the differences and similarities between different user interface platforms, such as different graphical
user interfaces, web-based interfaces and palm based interfaces etc. The experience from development projects and design courses where SUIE have

been used also suggest that the logical design is a valuable tool when designing or redesigning a user interface. Not least when an existing user interface or parts of it needs to be moved to different target platform, e.g. when making legacy systems available through a web-based interface.

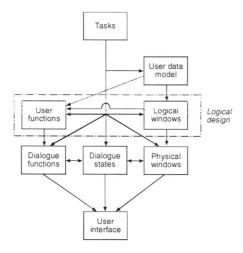

Figure 4. The design steps used in Software User Interface Engineering [2]

5. IMPLICATIONS FOR COMPUTER-AIDED DESIGN TOOLS

All computer-aided design tools supporting design for multiple platforms (e.g. most 4GL's where the applications can be executed on a number of different target platforms) ought to address issues such as the semantic differences described in this paper. Ideally user interfaces designed using such tools should be adapted to the semantics of the target platform, contrasting what is often seen today, where the adaptation is merely a question of mapping a generic set of widgets into the widget set available on the target platform.

One of the central questions is however in these situations whether the semantics of the user interface produced should remain the same across platforms (making it easier to use the same application on several platforms) or if it should be consistent with native interfaces designed for the target platform.

When dealing with the kind of semantic differences discussed in this paper. It would seem possible in case of 4GL's to perform the necessary adaptations automatically because these tools tend to be geared towards designing user interfaces *similar in type*. It will hence be possible to describe how this type of interface should be implemented for each of the supported target platforms. In general however, performing such adaptation automatically will be difficult without some kind of human intervention.

5.1 When the available interaction techniques change

When moving a user interface design from one GUI to another it is usually safe to assume that information can be changed using entry fields, radio buttons, check boxes etc. However the move towards using smaller specialised devices to perform certain tasks away from the desktop has made the challenge of multi-platform design even more challenging [6]. In these cases not only screen-size and available GUI widget change. It might well be the case that the keyboard, the mouse or other standard selection mechanisms will need to be substituted with a small number of function keys. In such cases, even the number of available user functions might need to be adapted because it will be infeasible to implement all function with a small number of buttons. To support this process the design tools need to make it possible for the designer to select the most important tasks, and hence the user functions that need to be implemented.

REFERENCES

[1]   *The Windows Interface Guidelines for Software Design*, Microsoft Press, Redmond, 1995

[2]   Harning, M.B., *Software User Interface Engineering – a structured method for designing user interfaces* (in danish), Ph.D. series 5.97, Copenhagen Business School, 1997.

[3]   Lauesen, S. and Harning, M.B., *Dialogue design through modified dataflow and data modelling*, in G. Grechenig and M. Tscheligi (eds.), *Proc. of Vienna Conference on Human Computer Interaction* VCHCI'93 (Vienna, September 1993), Springer-Verlag, Berlin, 1993.

[4]   *Systems Application Architecture Common User Access Advanced Interface Design Reference*, SC34-4290-00, IBM, 1991.

[5]   Harning, M.B., *An approach to structured display design – coping with conceptual complexity*, in J. Vanderdonckt (ed.), *Proc. of the 2nd Int. Workshop on Computer-Aided Design of User Interfaces* CADUI'96 (Namur, 5-7 June 1996), Presses Universitaires de Namur, Namur, 1996, pp. 121-138.

[6]   Szekely, P., *Retrospective and Challenges for Model-Based Interface Development*, in J. Vanderdonckt (ed.), *Proc. of the 2nd Int. Workshop on Computer-Aided Design of User Interfaces* CADUI'96 (Namur, 5-7 June 1996), Presses Universitaires de Namur, Namur, 1996, pp. xxi-xliv.

Chapter 17

A FRAMEWORK FOR MANAGEMENT OF SOPHISTICATED USER INTERFACE'S VARIANTS IN DESIGN PROCESS
A Case Study

Pekka Savolainen[1] and Hannu Konttinen[2]
[1]*VTT Electronics, Kaitoväylä 1, P.O. Box 1100*
FIN-90571 Oulu Finland
Pekka.Savolainen@vtt.fi
http://www.ele.vtt.fi
[2]*Nokia Mobile Phones, Elektroniikkatie 13, P.O. Box 50*
FIN-90571 Oulu Finland
Hannu.Konttinen@nokia.com

Abstract   In modern electronic devices, the same basic functionality is presented in differing product variants that constitute a product family. Usually, the high-end of a product line offers better displays and an extended set of functions, but in principle the intended use of the products is the same throughout the whole product family. Thus the "look-and-feel" should also remain the same despite the differing hardware platform. This presentation describes a framework being built with this aim in mind, for the management of mobile phones' UI specifications at Nokia Mobile Phones (NMP). The solution is based on an idea to manage the phone UI's in the format of common UI specifications (CUIS) as structured documents, and be able to automatically generate the specifications of differing individual products. Basically, the CUIS releases integrate UI design data into a corporate UI knowledge repository for use starting with generation of new features to implementation and field testing of phone prototypes. Though examination is based on management of UI design data for mobile phones, this solution can be applied to management of UI specifications for any product when there is demand for product variants with differing features, user environments, or hardware platforms.

Keywords: automatic configuration, UI design, UI specification, structured documentation, SGML, XML.

1.   MANAGEMENT OF USER INTERFACE SPECI-FICATIONS

Design of the user interfaces (UI) of modern electronic consumer devices requires considerable development effort. Rapid development of competitive products in the market requires short development cycles—concurrent engineering—in bringing new features into the device. To compete in the market, a device must be easy to use, which on the international market presumes accommodation to local language and culture, so called localisation. In the case of complex products, there must be differing variants of the product to satisfy different market segments. While the product's environment changes and new standards emerge, the older versions of product, proven successful, may require inclusion of new features basic concept still remaining the same.

Modern electronic devices are complex with large set of features, and development of a competitive electronic device requires thorough specification. To accommodate to the described situation, the specifications must be accurate enough to describe each end product, yet at the same time there may not be delays in reflecting a change in the design to the other parts of the design it may affect. This brings on demands for fine-tuned version control for design tools of the distributed product development. As the products tend to form product lines, some of the changes affect the whole family of products. To keep the product lines consistent, changes to related designs must be automated; manual repetition of updates is too prone to errors, and besides frustrating to highly educated designers. We will demonstrate that the automation can be achieved with a formal presentation of product family's features and derivation of final products' features from this generic specification.

It is beneficial for both product developers and users that the UI's are alike over one family of products. This makes further development of complex products easier, and facilitates user's changing over to the new or more advanced products. The consistency over differing products presumes, in concurrent engineering environment, close co-operation between the developers of the products. Common design documentation, where product specifications are shared and the common parts of design are actually the same, forms good basis for collaboration. When the product development effort is focused on the common platform, from where the design of individual products can be derived, all the products can be developed further at once.

2.   PROJECT SCOUT

To develop and test a framework for management of generic UI specifications, project SCOUT, Structured Documentation for User Interface Specifications, has investigated the complexity of mobile phone UI specifications, with the aim to automate production of specifications at the end product level. Thus, only the common specification (platform) would be produced and maintained, together with the parallel detailed layout and localisation design. In this way, a database of UI specification knowledge would be created that could be used to produce up-to-date end product UI specifications. Figure 1 depicts the operations of UI design in respect to the design knowledge.

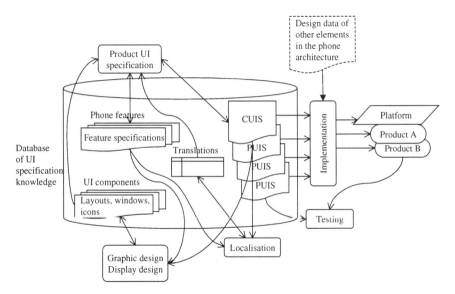

Figure 1. The links between UI design and UI specification knowledge.

The operation of specification management framework shown in figure 1 will be described in the following chapters. As shown in the figure, the UI specification of a product family is comprised of three separate specifications: phone features, in the form of feature specifications; display layouts and windows, called together with special graphics as UI components; and translations. UI designers manage all UI knowledge of the end products as a set of feature specifications (FS). In authoring the phone features they can use detailed information of display layouts, designed by display designers and graphical designers. Localisation contributes to the design by providing translations of all the display texts, for all the different products and markets.

UI designers are also responsible for compilation (described below) of the UI design knowledge into common UI specification (CUIS) releases and product UI specification (PUIS) releases. The releases provide a consistent view to the UI design knowledge, and are utilised by all designers participating in the UI design process—and by marketing and other parties interested in the features of forthcoming products. Implementation and testing use the CUIS and PUIS releases as the primary source of information, though implementation must also access the native translations and UI component data. (It may not be reasonable to include this detailed information into the CUIS and PUIS releases, if only implementation needs it and they can access native data directly and up-to-date in regard to the release.)

The following chapter describes the product UI specification process in detail.

3.   PRODUCT UI SPECIFICATION PROCESS

Mobile phones are under rapid development, new models substitute old ones with a production cycle less than a year. Central element in the market is the usability, and look-and-feel of the device. The usability is a sum of several implementation and usage environment factors, and only when all the design factors meet, will the final product be acceptable. The UI specification of a mobile phone can be several hundreds of pages in length, full of descriptions of detailed design decisions, being equivalent to several years of development work.

3.1   Logic of gathering the UI specification knowledge

As described above in Figure 1, the entire functionality of a product family is divided into a set of features that, when put together and adjusted (the adjustment will be described in detail below), form the look-and-feel of a product. When a new feature is thought up, its contribution is judged against the existing UI knowledge, represented by a CUIS release.

As a new feature is accepted, the knowledge base is augmented with this new feature and its premises. The augmentation includes describing the function of the feature as a feature specification, and fine-tuning the existing features in relation to the added functionality. This activity is iterative and contains formation of both the new and already existing features, managed with different specifiers.

As the UI specification evolves, modernised releases of the platform are introduced, where new features are added, and some old ones may be dismissed.

3.2   Logic of utilising the knowledge base

In order to the knowledge base to be useful, it must produce specifications for the designs of end products. Extraction of the UI specification for a
single product, i.e., PUIS comprises of the following steps: compilation of
the feature specifications and UI components into a CUIS release, picking of
the features the product should include, and subsequent adjustment, i.e., configuration of each selected feature. The meaning of configuration is to fine-
tune the features for the selected feature set to provide, in the given system
and hardware, a localised interface ready for implementation. The steps of
PUIS extraction are illustrated in Figure 2.

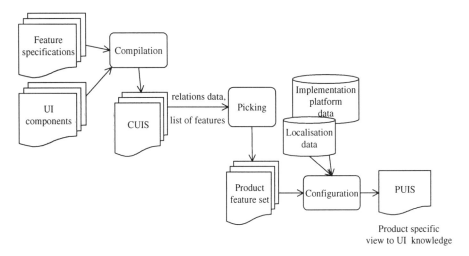

Figure 2. Generation of a PUIS consists of 1) picking up the product features and 2) subsequent configuration of the feature set to produce a consistent end-product UI specification.

CUIS release compilation collects the feature specifications and UI components accepted to this release into a CUIS release. The required version
and status information is included in the specifications. After this, the designer (or even marketing person) can start picking up the features for the
phone to be built. Picking of the features is based on the names of features
and utilises selection tool's knowledge about relations of the features: some
features require the existence of another feature, others reject each other.
This knowledge is recorded in the knowledge base, in the feature specifications, and exported to the selection tool prior to the picking. This knowledge
of feature relations, as all the knowledge base's content, is specific to the
current release of CUIS.

Not until in configuration are the discrete features united to form a conceptually integrated product UI specification. The UI includes a lot of functions (or consequences) not belonging to a single feature, but building up as a composition of several features. An example can be found in the feature Short Term Memories, which dictates the date and time of the call to be stored with a missed call. But the time can be stored only if the phone has feature Real-Time Clock and the date only if there is Calendar (and if the calendar date is set). This kind of shared function must be included into the feature specification they fit best, either as a single property description or several pieces of them, scattered into the specifications of related features. Thus, the feature Short Term Memories includes property sections describing the feature's behaviour together with features Real-Time Clock and Calendar, and the configuration application selects only the appropriated sections according to the picked body of features.

It is evident that this compilation of product UI specification works in close relationship to authoring of the features. Beside the interrelationships of the features, there are properties in the UI that depend on the hardware environment—the keypad, display, or system platform of the product. All these properties are described, and marked up, during authoring and traversed during product configuration. Also, the translation of interaction examples and substitution of variables with product-specific values are carried on during the product configuration process.

4.   IMPLEMENTATION

In order the product configuration to succeed, we needed a formal presentation for the features [1]. SGML (and soon XML) standard for structured text presentation provides this format and a basis for commercial tools to operate with documents conforming to the standard [2]. Adept Editor from Arbortext, Inc. was selected as the authoring tool. While Adept can be programmed, it is intended for on-line processing only. Therefore, another tool was needed to run the configuration process; OmniMark from OmniMark Technologies Corp. was selected.

For graphics presentation an equivalent standard does not exist yet. The late releases of standard Computer Graphics Metafile (CGM) would presumably provide the level of graphics control sophisticated enough for phone display modelling, but there are no tools yet supporting the standard to this extent. However, Visio from Visio Corp. provides structured management of vector graphics, and it can be used both interactive and batch, for mass-configuration.

4.1   Feature structure

Use of SGML requires a document structure to be specified. The structure must correspond to the actions required to produce the intended result document, in this case the configured product UI specification [3]. Thus, the features and their properties that form the basis of configuration had to be modelled as a document type definition, DTD. In this modelling, the existing specification documents, together with knowledge of the most experienced specifiers, proved to be invaluable to find the structure's building blocks. Special care was taken to model the interrelationships and product platform dependencies that are needed in the end-product configuration. The document structure dictates what kinds of configurations are possible: the UI interactions not authored in the first place cannot be derived either.

The DTD is common to all features, meaning that all feature documents obey the same document structure. Besides a body that describes feature's behaviour, the structure contains common document header and footer information, with change histories, glossaries and indexes, as depicted in Figure 3.

Each document begins with ID information that includes documents unique name for the configuration application to identify the feature. Data content of the features is structured as follows. An abstract of the features responsibility is given in an introduction; a more detailed description of feature's behaviour follows. Tables, lists, and graphics can be used among the ordinary text, and the content can be further divided into sections and subsections. The index and glossary entries are produced automatically from their declarations written during authoring, which is the normal procedure in structured documentation. Thus achieved document structure provides a skeleton for the configuration structure, explained in the next section, and location of configuration attributes.

Graphics included in the specifications can be either non-configurable, bitmaps of drawing tools used in the environment, or configurable Visio graphics. In Visio, stencils can be made that give the templates for display layouts. When initialising a layout to be used as a phone display illustration, designers must select a style for it, in order to pre-configure the common template to conform to the implementation platform. In this way, designers can draft sample displays, matching the real-world displays in layout detail level, to illustrate the written feature behaviour.

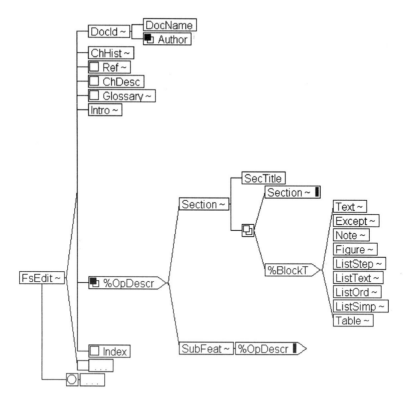

Figure 3. The structure of feature specification documents.

The selected style can be changed later (in PUIS configuration phase) to another style, for example to adjust the display examples to another graphic display with different size or resolution. The style change usually affects the sizes of windows (placeholders of texts and icons) in display, but contents of the windows readjust to the changes, as the style is their configuration parameter, also.

Figure 4. Menu screen for messaging in product Nokia 6110.

Figure 4 illustrates the need for figure configurability. The display image shows the menu screen for messaging in product Nokia 6110. 6110 has two keys below the display with the command names shown on the screen (in this example "Select" and "Back"). But for example product Nokia 5110 has only one key below the display. For this product the display image should only show one command (in this example "Select"). In Scout this kind of difference will be produced automatically at the configuration phase when the specifics of the product in question are known, i.e., the screen size and number of display keys.

4.2   Levels of configuration

During the DTD development process it was ensured that the required configuration could be established as selection and substitution of elements included in the product UI structure. In structured documentation the structure routinely reflects the layout to be produced, i.e., the titles, subtitles, paragraphs and lists can be located in the structure [3]. Above and beyond, the structure should resemble the cognitive logic comprising a feature, and furthermore also that comprising the common or product UI specification as a whole.

4.3   Configuration aspect to the structure

In SCOUT, the structural levels of configuration can be categorised to minor scale configurations i.e. substitutions and large-scale configurations i.e. selections. The minor scale changes are substitutions of general terms with their product-specific values, variables with their values set in the configuration, or translations of display texts in display examples according to the style and market area of the product. The large-scale configurations occur in two phases, as direct selections of features and sub-features (to be explained shortly), and as in-direct selections of property sections based on selection of another feature. Also the style differences are managed as large-scale configurations when a style incorporates additional or exceptional behaviour.

The property sections are marked parts (from section to paragraph in size) of a feature that are meaningful only with another feature. They are used to describe functions produced by two or more features together, when the combined effect would be too small for a full-scale feature.

In some occasions it may be reasonable to leave the joint effect out even if both the features are selected. In this case, the property section is named and included as an individual feature into the feature list—which turns the property section into a sub-feature. In case of collaborating features, the feature-picking tool needs to know the requirement for another feature. These requirements are expressed as attributes of the features or, in case of the sub-features, of the sub-features themselves.

5.   DISCUSSION

The product data extracted from the UI knowledge base will form the basis of e.g. implementation of the phone's UI and field testing of the prototypes. While the automatic UI generation described by Szekely [4] is years away, as the gap from design abstractions to implementation elements keeps on requiring human intervention, there is constant strive to automate the specific development processes, and to integrate the nascent islands of automation.

NMP is going to apply this method of product UI specification management in development of mobile phones' features. In time of writing, the project has proceeded to piloting phase. User training is in progress, sample features have been translated to SCOUT format, and configuration has been tested and fine-tuned. The production use has not been started yet, as there are some implementation tool specific issues to be answered, after which the workflow of authoring and product release configuration can be completed.

The major benefits that we are gaining with the described solution are:
1. The development of corporate UI knowledge is divided into chunks, feature specifications, which are small enough for individual designers to manage.
2. The same designs, or selected parts of them, are automatically—via the configuration—applicable in a variety of products.
3. The detail level design data, localisation information and style-specific variations, can be managed apart from the common UI design and applied to the products in batch.

Generally, the advantage is that designers are able to produce human-readable design information that is as such formal enough for automatic processing, also. Feature specifications in textual format can be easily disseminated, via Intranet, up-to-date to readers in remote locations, which is essential in concurrent engineering environment.

A technical benefit is that basing the specification management on standard SGML gives options to partial development of the specification environment. For example, the editor or dissemination strategy can be changed with no need to change the configuration process. Furthermore, the structure could fairly easily be converted into XML, which should offer an opportunity to more economical tools in the future. This helps with the one minus point of this solution: it requires a significant economical input to build a smoothly running SGML solution with the tools available today.

6.   FURTHER RESEARCH

The described method to produce re-usable UI specifications can be seen as an expedient to integrate the now separate islands of electronic product design. Further challenges include:

1. To study the integration of the described system and the design data management systems (PDM, Product Data Management Systems) used to manage other parts of product information (the closer the interaction with the implementation the better).
2. To study how the described approach fits to other specification needs of software design. The solution should be applicable to management of other mobile phone design data, but in that case the document structures (DTD) and management of graphics and other non-textual information need to be reconsidered. (Note that this and the previous item are alternative methods to design data integration.)
3. Integration with the virtual prototyping (VRP) tools, which could be used in demonstrating the interfaces.

REFERENCES

[1]   Freuder, E.C., *The role of configuration knowledge in the business process*, IEEE Intelligent Systems & their applications, July/August 1998.
[2]   Goldfarb, C.F. and Rubinsky, Y., *The SGML handbook*, Clarendon Press, Oxford, 1990.
[3]   Maler, E. and Andaloussi, J., *Developing SGML DTDs from text to model to markup*, Prentice Hall, New Jersey, 1996.
[4]   Szekely, P., *Retrospective and Challenges for Model-Based Interface Development*, in J. Vanderdonckt (ed.), Proc. of the 2nd Int. Workshop on Computer-Aided Design of User Interfaces CADUI'96 (Namur, 5-7 June 1996), Presses Universitaires de Namur, Namur, 1996, pp. xxi–xliv.

Chapter 18

GRASYLA: MODELLING CASE TOOL GUIS IN METACASES

Vincent Englebert
Jean-Luc Hainaut
University of Namur
Rue Grandgagnage 21
B-5000 Namur
Belgium
{ven,jlh}@info.fundp.ac.be
http://www.info.fundp.ac.be/~dbm

Abstract   Meta-CASEs are CASE (Computer-Aided Software Engineering) tool factories. For some years, much effort have been spent in this realm to propose a competitive alternative to the traditional CASE framework. Meta-CASEs now benefit from efficient and rich meta-repositories, they support several methods and are multi-user. However, all current meta-CASEs share the same approach of the Graphical User Interface modelling task. We analyze here the new challenges to take up and we propose a new graphical symbolic language (Grasyla) to model the CASE's GUI.

Keywords: MetaCASE, CASE tool, graphical symbolic language, meta-modelling, Grasyla

1.   INTRODUCTION

CASE tools are programs that support software engineers[1] activities during the software life cycle. They can automate some stages (code generation, metrics, model checking, . . .) or help the software engineers to follow/respect some methodologies. Meta-CASEs are high level compilers/interpreters that produce CASE tools that meet specific models and engineering processes. They use an abstract description of a CASE tool (i.e., its models, its behaviour, its processes, . . .) to produce a ready-to-use product. Of course, such products cannot be ex-

---

[1] Software engineers use CASE tools to build software.

pected to enjoy the same qualities than hand-coded dedicated CASE tools. The current situation exhibits an interesting dilemma. From one side, CASE tools become ineluctable. Indeed, the market is inundated with a plethora of models[2] and paradigms[3], so that programmers cannot keep using mere text editors or vendor-dependent IDE[4]. On the other side, as Lending and Chevarny [11] write: *"Few organizations use CASE tools [2, 16]; organizations abandon the use of the tools [2, 21, 23]; and organizations that do use CASE tools contain many systems developers who do not actually use the tool [14] "*.

Meta-CASEs attempt to reduce the distance between the programmers/analysts needs and the CASE functionalities. Indeed, meta-CASEs allow analysts to define their own models (i.e., meta-models), to visualize their specifications in accordance with their requirements, and to apply their processes (metrics, transformations, report generation, ...). Moreover, this technology is ideal to integrate independent meta-models and can act like an *enterprise's meta-model-warehouse*. Some research [7, 13, 24] concentrated on the knowledge representation aspect and deliberately left aside the graphical representation of the specifications, while other groups [1, 9, 18, 19, 20, 22] investigated the whole problem. In all the cases, the graphical representation plays a crucial role since it is often the only way to visualize and edit the stored specifications. It will also be a major criterion for deciding on a meta-CASE tool.

In order to generate/simulate the GUI[5] component of a CASE tool (i.e., the description of the CASE tool's GUI), every meta-CASE has its own GUI meta-model that allows method engineers[6] to specify the interface they want. The current research all share the same approach, that is, method engineers[7] associate, with each concept of a meta-model, a form built from the concept's characteristics. This form is described either with a formal text (MetaView [5]) or via a graphical editor (MetaEdit+ [9, 15], GraphTalk [19]).

In this article, we will review some important but still unexplored challenges. They are dictated by two goals: *a)* meta-CASEs GUIs should be as good as hand-coded CASE tools and *b)* they should be independent of the model of the meta-repository (i.e., the meta-meta-model). That is, whatever the way engineers will model a methodology, it should be possible to define any GUI over its meta-model.

We will present the Grasyla language: a graphical symbolic declarative language to define the graphical representation of a specification (i.e., an instance

---

[2]OSA, SADT, UML, OML, ERA, NIAM, ...
[3]Object Oriented Analysis, Distributed Systems, Workflow, Client/Server, Real Time, ...
[4]Integrated Development Environment
[5]Graphical User Interface
[6]Method engineers define the models and methodologies.
[7]The engineer who edits and defines the meta-models.

of a meta-model). One will present the motivations and the strengths of this approach with two case studies.

Section 2. will present a résumé of the main concepts of our meta-repository. The next section analyses the challenges of the graphical visualization task in meta-CASEs. Grasyla is presented in section 4. We will describe how Grasyla helps the method engineer and takes up the challenges. After a brief description of the implementation, a case study will be discussed.

2.   META-REPOSITORY PRESENTATION

The meta-repository stores information about both types and their instances. Because concepts stored in this meta-repository will describe CASE tools, we will call types and instances respectively *meta-classes* and *classes*. The example below shows the different levels of abstraction: `Customer` is the name of a class of the application domain, and is a component of the specifications built by the analyst; (``Smith'' is an instance of this class and concerns users only); `Customer` is an instance of meta-class `entity-type` that is a component of standard entity-relationship models.

``Smith'' $\rightarrow$ Customer $\rightarrow$ entity-type $\rightarrow$ meta_class

The $\rightarrow$ symbol denotes the *instance-of* relationship.

The meta-classes can have attributes (*meta-properties*) and participate in one-to-many relationships (*meta-relations*) with other meta-classes. Meta-classes can inherit characteristics from several meta-classes (*multiple inheritance*). Meta-classes are grouped together to define ontologies (*meta-models*). For instance, these sentences could describe very basic entity-relationship diagrams that are made up of entity-types and attributes:

```
meta-class <entity-type> {
    string:  <name>;                        ‡a meta-property
    owner of <has>;                         ‡ the ∞-role of a meta-relation
    local identifier = { <name> }};         ‡name identifies entity-type
meta-class <attribute-type> {
    string:  <name>, <type>;
    integer:  <min>, <max>;
    member of <has>;                        ‡the 1-role of a meta-relation
    local identifier = { <name>, owner of <has> }};
meta-model <ERA diagram> {                  ‡a meta-model
    string:  <name>;
    document:  <author>;                    ‡URL of the author
    list video:  <minutes>;                 ‡a multivalued video meta-property
    components = { <entity-type>, <attribute-type> }};
```

Some details have been omitted for simplicity sake. For instance, the meta-repository includes characteristics such as *1)* multivalued meta-properties and multimedia types[8]; *2)* meta-models are themselves meta-classes and share their

---

[8]`picture, audio, video, document.`

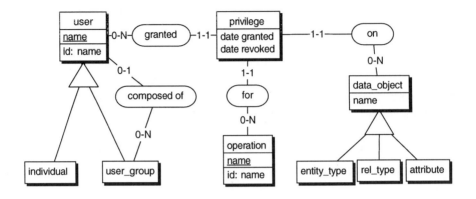

Figure 1.1 **[Database Security Diagram Meta-Model]** This schema models the access rights granted to users for operations on database objects such as *entity-types*, *attributes* and *rel-types*. A *user* is either a *user_group* or an *individual*. A group is itself composed of users.

semantics; *3)* the member roles can be mandatory and *4)* meta-models can share one or more meta-classes in their definitions[9]. The meta-repository and its semantics are described in [4].

The meta-CASE is endowed with a meta-language (Voyager 2) that allows the method engineer to define new functionalities [3, 4]. Voyager 2 is an object-oriented C/Pascal-like language with meta-types, predicative queries, garbage collected lists, GUI functions, dynamic linked libraries, I/O statements, communication with Windows programs and meta-homogeneity[10]. Each meta-class has predefined triggers and predicates that can be overloaded by the method engineer.

The ERA schema depicted in fig. 1.1 describes the meta-model of a *"Database Security Diagram"* (DSD). This example will be used throughout this article.

3.   THE CHALLENGES

The graphical representation of specifications is a crucial issue when building CASE tools. As for many programs, the graphical interface will be a major criterion (both subjective and objective) in a CASE tool evaluation and acceptance. Norman *et al* [17] argues that the *"customization without loss of functionality "* and *"customizable user interfaces "* were needed in CASE tools and should be investigated in the 1990's. Moreover, recent studies [8, 12] explain that this gap

---

[9]The components clause in the extract.
[10]The meta-meta-model can be queried in the same way as a meta-model.

is not yet filled "*A well-designed user interface should create a metaphor that bridges the conceptual gap between a computer system and human thinking. Such a metaphor is not the strength of current CASE tools*".

From our experience in the building process of the DB-MAIN tool [6], we observed these criticisms and we have deduced some important rules concerning the graphical user interface, and more specially the graphical representation:

1) One needs both textual and graphical views. Our experience leads us to consider two kinds of specification visualization: graphical diagrams (graph, tree, table, matrix, ...) and textual views (report, code, hypertext, ...). Software engineers often require several views of a same specification depending on the process to perform. Graphical views are preferred for teaching or for validation while textual views[11] are preferred to edit huge specifications. Meta-CASE tools have thus to offer these views.

2) The graphical representation of a concept is contextual. Its representation depends on its use. For instance, in ERA diagrams, attributes can be indented (resp. underlined) depending on their belonging to compound attributes (resp. to identifiers).

3) The shape of a concept is polymorphic. In OO meta-models, concepts are modelled by inheritance hierarchies. Although this graph denotes an atomic concept, its representation will depend on its position in the graph. For instance, if one encounters this case: "`weak-entity-type isa entity-type`" in a meta-model, software engineers will expect to have distinct shapes for them.

4) The graphical representations must evolve. Scientists have certainly not yet discovered the ultimate methodology; new ones appear every year. However, they generally share common ontologies like statecharts, static model (ERA/NIAM/class/. ..), use cases, ... Semantics change but the structural meta-model does not vary very much. The main changes we observed are about the graphical representation[12]. Moreover, in meta-CASEs, method engineers can specialize and edit the meta-models to adapt them to their company requirements. These modifications must often be reflected in the graphical representation.

5) CASE tools must support multimedia data. CASE tools must support informal processes[8] and must accompany the software engineer in its rigorous steps as well as in "softer" aspects of software development. Multimedia data can enrich specifications with informal information such as interviews, requirement documents, imported diagrams, ... and bridges a gap between CASE tools and non-standard tools[13] in the software engineer environment.

---

[11]Textual views can have facilities like: sort algorithms, cross-referencing, . . .
[12]For instance: the static diagrams in the Booch, OMT, UML and OML methodologies.
[13]Graphical editors, home-made tools, . . .

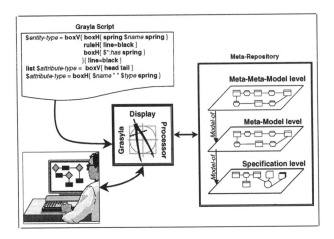

Figure   1.2   This schema shows how the Grasyla Display Processor interacts with the software engineer and the meta-repository.
Its behaviour is controlled by the script

6) The graphical requirements should not affect the meta-model definition. Meta-repositories often offer richer abstractions than usual DBMS in order to meet the peculiar needs of software meta-models. However, this quality would be useless if we had to change the meta-model definition each time we modify or add a new visualization.

This list discusses some of the main challenges the engineers should investigate when defining the GUI requirements of a meta-CASE.

4.   THE GRASYLA LANGUAGE

Grasyla is a graphical symbolic language that allows the method engineer to define the appearance of a specification through a display script. A Grasyla script defines which concepts the display processor will have to show as well as their graphical representation. Display processors manage all the interactions with the software engineer (contextual menus, click, drag&drop, selection, ...). The environment of the graphical processor is shown in fig. 1.2.

4.1   THE GRASYLA PRINCIPLES

Each meta-model can have several named Grasyla scripts; each one will correspond to a definite visualization of the specifications. Scripts are made up of three sections (directive, main and connection sections). The *directive section* selects the meta-classes to display. The *main section* associates with each meta-class an expression that explains how to display its instances. This section is a textual description of a function $: MetaClass × {single, list} × String → G-Expr. When the graphical processor will have to display one or several meta-class instances, it will use the $ function to retrieve the best expression to build the shape of this class. The first argument of $ denotes the type of the class. The second argument will be single (resp. list) for a single (resp. several) instance to display. The last argument denotes an identifier that will act as a switch and will be explained later. The section will be composed of constructs that will reflect the different kinds of argument of the $ function. The method engineer will have to edit one of these 4 patterns for each possible entry of the $ function:

---

1) $*name* = *Grasyla expression*

2)   list $*name* = *Grasyla expression*

3)   *Func* ($*name*) = *Grasyla expression*

4)   *Func* (list $*name*) = *Grasyla expression*

Grasyla expressions are symbolic descriptions of shapes built from the "semantics" of a concept/meta-class, i.e., its attributes, its roles, and its supertypes. The different kinds of expressions are

$*att* : where *att* is the name of a meta-property; graphical representation of a meta-property value.

$1 :*rel* : where *rel* is the name of a meta-relation; graphical representation of the meta-relation's owner.

$* :*rel* : where *rel* is the name of a meta-relation; graphical representation of the meta-relation's members.

Func (*exp*) : *Func* is an identifier; graphical representation of the *exp* expression in using the *Func* name.

boxH{$exp_1...exp_n${*args*} : arranges n graphical objects (described by the exp_i) horizontally in a box. Similar expressions exist for circles, round rectangles, diamonds, ... args is a list of parameters that specify the colour, the line width and other aspects.

boxV{$exp_1...exp_n${*args*} : same as both but for vertical order.

if *cond* then exp_1 else exp_2 : uses graphical expression exp_1 or exp_2 depending on the value of the *cond* expression.

head, tail : used when the argument denotes a list (patterns of lines 2 and 4); denote respectively the first element and the tail of the argument; makes it possible to define recursive graphical expressions.

spring : introduces in a shape an invisible compressed spiral spring that will stretch out between the neighbouring faces.

These rules give the general principles of the Grasyla expressions syntax. Other functions exist such as handles to hitch arrows, line separators, multimedia data, fonts, aggregate forms, graphical alignment and so on. The Grasyla principle is inspired by the TEX's boxes [10].

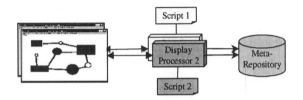

Figure 1.3 They are as many Display Processors as active displays. The events relative to a display are trapped and managed by its DP. DPs access the meta-repository only to read the classes description and to update their positions once the display is closed. Several DPs can process a same specification whatever their scripts. This makes possible several displays with distinct views of a same specification

Finally, the **connection section** will associate edges to meta-relations through such expressions as:

$name = connect{ *or-param* }{ *line-param* }{ *targ-param* }

The parameters are lists of values that specify respectively the form of the origin handle, the body of the line and the target handle. For instance, the following sentence

$*has*= connect{ outside_arrow{ size=5, fill=black, line=black }}
        { line=black }
        { bullet{ size=4, fill=white, line=black }}

will display the instances of the meta-relation has with this symbol: ○—▶ (the circle on the attribute side and the arrow on the entity-type side).

4.2   THE IMPLEMENTATION

The Grasyla architecture is depicted in fig. 1.3. Each "display" (window, printer, clipboard) is controlled by a *Display Processor* (DP). This machine has to display a specification with respect to a Grasyla script and must manage all the possible interactions with the software engineer. Every DP has its own memory, can access the meta-repository and can communicate via a common black-board with other DPs. The software engineer can ask for several displays of a specification whatever the script. He can thus visualize several parts of a huge specification in distinct windows simultaneously.

The meta-repository stores the (x, y) positions of the main objects only. Their shape description is automatically computed by the Grasyla machine. This independence makes it possible to keep the layout of a diagram even if its definition changes.

Each meta-model has a default DP to place and build the representation of their meta-classes. The behaviour of this default DP suits graph-like specifications very well. However, some views require special algorithms that cannot be modelled directly in Grasyla: Matrices, Tables, Browsers, Sequence Diagrams, Screen Layouts, …. For this reason, the meta-CASE architect[14] can implement hard-wired graphical processors dedicated to some meta-models acting like *meta-model-patterns*. This meta-model pattern can be specialized into other meta-models with their own graphical statements. Hence, the hard-wired DP will use user-defined statements to display the specifications. Hence, one could think of writing a DP to display graphical matrices, for instance a matrix with the pictures of the software engineer as x-axis and entity-types as y-axis. Cells of such a matrix could be a textual form of the respective rights granted (read/write/…).

4.3   TEXTUAL REPRESENTATION

Grasyla can also be used to define textual views in exactly the same way as discussed in the previous sections. Moreover, these views are active graphical displays where bitmaps, boxes, arrows, … have disappeared. This kind of textual representation is closer to hypertext than a passive ASCII text. This brings much more benefits. The modification of the text remains synchronous with the meta-repository and the software engineer can navigate through it via hyper-links. Nevertheless, the Voyager 2 language is much more suited to generate ASCII reports or code (RTF/IDL/HTML/…).

4.4   EXAMPLE

This example will illustrate the basic concepts of Grasyla on the "toy" ERA meta-model presented in Section 2. Let us imagine that entity-types are displayed as boxes with two compartments, their name being diplayed centered in the first one and attribute names left-justified in the second one. The compartments are separated by a line. The Grasyla script that defines this graphical layout is as follows:

```
1. $entity-type = boxV{ boxH{ spring $name spring }
2.                          ruleH{ line=black }
3.                          boxH{ $*:has spring }
4.                      }{ line=black }
5. list $attribute-type = boxV{ head tail }
6. $attribute-type = boxH{ $name " " $type spring }
```

| CUSTOMER |
| Name String |
| ID_code Integer |

– Output Sample –

When a DP will have to display an entity-type, it will use the first rule (lines 1–4), substitutes all the variables ($name and $*:has) by their respective values and proceeds with other rules depending on the type of the variables. The has meta-relation will be replaced by a list of attributes, and another rule (line 5)

---

[14]The engineer who define and implement the meta-CASE program.

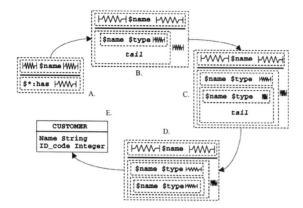

Figure 1.4   The *A* box denotes the Grasyla expression defined in lines 1–4. The *A* → *B* transition replaces the $*:has variable through the rule of line 5. The head has been substituted through the rule at line 6. The tail becomes empty at step *C* and variables are replaced with their respective values in transition *D* → *E*

will be used, and so on. The picture in fig. 1.4 shows the successive steps the DP will follow to display an entity-type with two attributes.

5.   CASE STUDY: A SECURITY META-MODEL

Let us examine the DSD meta-model (see fig. 1.1). Users are denoted by small bitmap icons topping their name, groups of users are represented by boxes comprising their composition tree. Each privilege is displayed as a labelled node linking a user with a data object. Figure 1.5 illustrates the graphical representation of a DSD specification excerpt. Items were positioned by the software engineer. The figure expresses facts such as: *a) colombo* and *kojak* are people, and form the *employees* group, *b)* group *staff* is made of groups *managers* and *employees*, *c)* members of group *managers* are allowed to *read* the *address* attribute and *d)* members of group *staff* are allowed to *read* entity type *customer* and to *delete* entity type *order*.

The Grasyla script that tells the display processor how to display each concept (*users, user_groups, data_objects, privileges,* ...) is given in fig. 1.6.

6.   CONCLUSION

This article has presented the main challenges that should be taken into consideration when defining a meta-model of a CASE tool graphical user interface. The Grasyla graphical language was defined to meet these requirements in order to reconciliate the software engineers with CASE tools that are sometimes too static and too formal. We showed on several examples that the language was as simple as possible. The graphical language is powerful enough to bootstrap two editors of the meta-case to edit the meta-models definitions and to define the Grasyla scripts, i.e., to propose a graphical counterpart of its textual representation. Figure 1.7 illustrates a screen-shot of the meta-CASE with several advanced views.

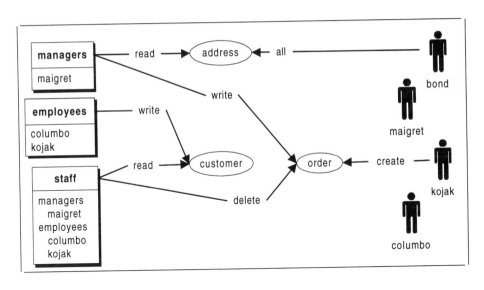

Figure 1.5   Graphical view of a DSD specification

```
01 root : user, data-object, privilege ;
02 $user_group= boxV{boxH{handle spring bold { $name } spring handle }
03                     ruleH
04                     boxH{in_group($compound_of) spring}
05                     }{frame=shadow colour=black}
06 $individual= boxV{boxH{handle spring bitmap("man.bmp") spring handle}
07                     boxH{spring $name spring}
08                     }
09 $privilege= boxV{boxH{spring handle spring}
10                   boxH{handle spring $about spring handle}
11                   boxH{spring handle spring}
12                   }{frame=simple colour=black}
13 $operation= boxH{handle $name handle}
14 $data_object= ovalH{handle $name handle}
15 in_group(list $user)= boxV{head in_group(tail) }
16 in_group($individual)= boxH{$name spring}
17 in_group($user_group)= boxV{boxH{$name spring}
18                         boxH{H(10pt) in_group($compound_of) spring}
19                         }
20 $granted = connect{ }{line=black width=2pt}{ }
21 $on = connect{outside_arrow{size=5}}{line=black width=2pt}{ }
```

Figure 1.6   **[Grasyla Script of the DSD Diagram]** The directive at line 1 expresses that all the instances of the user, data-object and privilege meta-classes must be displayed. Statements at lines 2, 6, 9, 13, 14, 15, 16 and 17 define how to display instances of the corresponding meta-classes in terms of geometrical forms (box, oval, line, ...), letters and their characteristics (properties and roles). Statements at lines 20 and 21 define the arcs denoting relations between classes. The use of the *in_group* name (line 4) allows the method engineer to use non standard Grasyla expressions for the *user* (and its subtypes) classes when they figure in *user_group* boxes

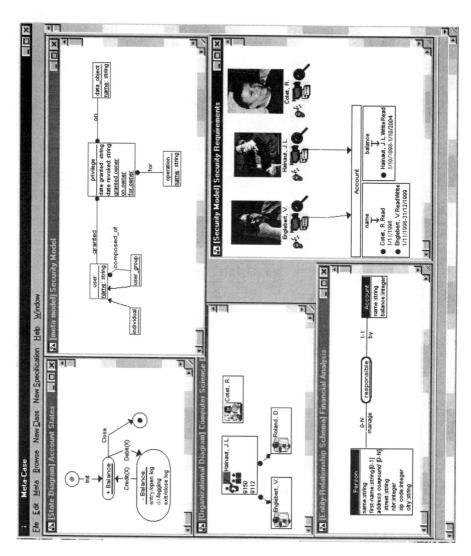

Figure 1.7 **[Screen Shot]** Four specifications and one meta-model definition are visualized in this screen shot. Windows denote respectively *1)* a state diagram *2)* an organisation diagram *3)* an entity-relationship schema *4)* a visualization of a DSD specification wrt. a richer Grasyla script than the one described in this article and *5)* the visualization of the DSD meta-model definition. In window *4*, the `account` entity-type is displayed as a table, and each column contains the grants (who, what and when). The arrows denote privileges on the whole table/entity type. Let us remark that the `account` concept is shared by specifications *3* and *4*, and that the `hainaut` person is itself shared by specifications *2* and *4*. Icons (sound/camera/magnifying glass) are active and a double click on them shows a multimedia document

References

[1] Jürgen Ebert, Roger Süttenbach, and Ingar Uhe. Meta-CASE in practice: a case for KOGGE. In A. Olivé and J. A. Pastor, editors, *Advanced Information Systems Engineering, , CAiSE'97*, number 1250 in LNCS, pages 203–216, Barcelona, Catalonia, Spain, June 1997.

[2] H. Elshazly and V. Gover. A study on the evaluation of CASE technology. *Journal of Information Technology Management*, 4(1), 1993.

[3] Vincent Englebert. *Voyager 2. Version 3 Release 0*. University of Namur - DB-MAIN, FUNDP, Rue grandgagnage 21. 5000 Namur. Belgium, 1998.

[4] Vincent Englebert and Jean-Luc Hainaut. DB-MAIN: A next generation meta-CASE. *Information Systems*, 24(2):99–112, 1999. Special Issue on MetaCASEs.

[5] Dinesh Gadwal, Pius Lo, and Beth Millar. EDL/GE users's manual. Technical report, University of Alberta and University of Saskatchewan, 1994.

[6] Jean-Luc Hainaut, Vincent Englebert, Jean Henrard, Jean-Marc Hick, and Didier Roland. Database reverse engineering : from requirement to CARE tools. *Journal of Automated Software Engineering*, 3(2), 1996.

[7] M. Jarke, R. Gallersdorfer, M.A. Jeusfeld, M. Staudt, and S. Eherer. ConceptBase – a deductive object base for meta data management. *Journal of Intelligent Information Systems*, 4(2):167–192, 1995.

[8] Stan Jarzabek and Riri Huang. The case for user-centered CASE tools. *Communications of the ACM*, 41(8):93–99, August 1998.

[9] S. Kelly, K. Lyytinen, and M. Rossi. MetaEdit+: A Fully Configurable Multi-User and Multi-Tool CASE and CAME Environment. In P. Constantopoulos, J. Mylopoulos, and Y. Vassiliou, editors, *Proceedings of the 8th International Conference CAiSE'96 on Advanced Information Systems Engineering*, volume 1080 of *LNCS*, pages 1–21, Heraklion, Crete, Greece, May 1996. Springer-Verlag.

[10] Donald Ervin Knuth. *The TEXbook*. Addison-Wesley, nineteenth edition, 1990.

[11] Diane Lending and Norman L. Chevarny. The use of CASE tools. In *SIGCPR'98. Proceedings of the 1998 conference on Computer personnel research*, pages 49–58, 1998.

[12] U. Leonhardt, J. Kramer, B. Nuseibeh, and A. Finkelstein. Decentralised Process Enactment in a Multi-Perspective Development Environment. In *Proceedings of the 17th International Conference on Software Engineering*, pages 255–264, April 1995.

[13] Fred Long and Ed Morris. An overview of PCTE: A basis for a Portable Common Tool Environment. Technical Report CMU/SEI-93-TR-1, Soft-

ware Engineering Institute. Carnegie Mellon University, Pittsburgh, Pennsylvania 15213, March 1993.

[14] M.P. Martin. The case against CASE. *Journal of Systems management*, 46:54–57, Jan/Feb 1995.

[15] MetaCase Consulting, Ylistönmäentie 31. FIN-40500 Jyväskylä. Finland. *MetaEdit+ 3 Method Workbench User's Guide. Version 3.0*, 1999.

[16] C.R. Necco, N.W. Tsai, and K.W. Holgeson. Current usage of CASE software. *Journal of Systems Management*, pages 6–11, May 1989.

[17] Ronald J. Norman, Wayne Stevens, Elliot J. Chikofsky, John Jenkins, Burt L. Rubenstein, and Gene Forte. CASE at the start of the 1990's. In *ICSE '91. Proceedings of the 13th international conference on Software engineering*, pages 128–139, Burlington, MA, USA, 1991. International Workshop on CASE.

[18] L. Beth Protsko, Paul G. Sorenson, Tremblay J. Paul, and Douglas A. Schaefer. Towards the automatic generation of software diagrams. *IEEE Transactions on Software Engineering*, 17(1):10–21, January 1991.

[19] Rank Xerox France, Direction Informatique Avancée et Génie Logiciel. 7 rue Touzet Gaillard. 93586 Saint-Ouen CEDEX. *GraphTalk Environnement objets de développement et d'utilisation d'atelier de génie logiciel*, 1991.

[20] Matti Rossi, Mats Gustafsson, Kari Smolander, Lars-Ake Johansson, and Kalle Lyytinen. Metamodeling editor as a front end tool for a CASE. volume 593 of *LNCS*, Manchester, May 1992. 4th International Conference CAISE'92, Springer-Verlag.

[21] J.A. Senn and J.L. Wynekoop. The other side of CASE implementation: Best practices for success. *Information Systems Management*, 12:7–14, 1995.

[22] Paul G. Sorenson, Jean-Paul Tremblay, and A. J. McAllister. The Metaview system for many specification environments. *IEEE Software*, 5(2):30–38, March 1988.

[23] M. Sumner. Making the transition to computer-assisted software engineering. In A.L. Lederer, editor, *1992 ACM SIGCPR Conference*, pages 81–92, New York, 1992. ACM Press.

[24] Unisys. *Universal Repository. Technical Overview. Release 1.2*. Unisys Corp., August 1996.

Chapter 19

USER DEFINED OBJECTS ARE FIRST CLASS CITIZEN[1]

Guillaume Texier and Laurent Guittet
LISI / ENSMA, Téléport 2, 1 Avenue Clément Ader
BP 40109, 86961 Futuroscope Chasseneuil Cedex
{texier, guittet}@ensma.fr
Tel : +33-5-49.49.80.67 - Fax : +33-5-49.49.80.64

Abstract   The improvements originated from the end users of an application lead to a better adaptation of the user specific needs. We propose to use the programming by demonstration and the parametric modelling techniques to permit an end user to define new classes. To integrate this new classes in the system interface dynamically, dialogue specific tools are used. These tools are obtained by the reification of the elements described in the H_4 architecture model. The TexAO system is a graphical application that uses the techniques described in this paper in order to offer the end user the possibility to define and to integrate new classes.

Keywords: End User Programming, Programming by Demonstration, User Interface, Application Extension.

1.   INTRODUCTION

Computer Aided Design systems (CAD) productivity largely depends on the possibility to adapt them to the specific design processes of the company where they are used. One desirable adaptation would consist in integrating, in the system company, specific objects with their specific behaviour. This adaptation has the disadvantage of requiring a great competence in the computer science area that rarely has problem domain specialist (it is seldom to

---

[1]   This paper is a short version. The long version can be found at http://www.lisi.ensma.fr/ftp/pub/documents/papers/99/Cadui99.doc

see a car designer able to modify his/her CAD system). The purpose of this paper is to show that progress in terms of end user programming and of user interface permits designing systems that allow end users to adapt an application to their domain.

In order to permit end users to define and to integrate new object classes in a graphical application, three objectives have been extracted. The first one consists in defining a method to record the building process of an object without any explicit programming. The second one concerns the definition of the attributes of the objects (e.g. the centre of a circle, the height of a table, etc...) and their computation functions without explicit programming as well. Finally, the last one is to consider these new classes as native classes from instantiation and interrogation points of view.

In the second part of this paper, two different existing methods allowing an end user to capture a program are discussed. The first method resulting from the human computer interaction research area, is called programming by demonstration [6] (PbD). The second method is issued from the CAD technology. This approach, known as parametric geometry [18], consists of recording the building process of each geometrical entity in order to allow further modification of its parameter values and new evaluations of its CAD representation. In the third part of this paper, we survey two well-known methods for developing user interfaces, Model-Based Generation Systems and Toolkits. In the last part of this paper, we suggest solutions to allow an end user to integrate new classes of objects he/she has described. These solutions are presented with the TexAO system that is a graphical application supporting end user extensions. Concerning new class definitions, the TexAO system is based on a parametric model extended to accept the addition of attributes to geometrical entities. The programming by demonstration abstraction mechanism is used to create new object classes from parametric model entities. Regarding the problem of dynamic integration of the new classes, the TexAO system uses a specific set of elements that are as dynamic as presentation elements are but which correspond to dialogue specifications.

2.   CAPTURING PROGRAMS

To define a new object class from the description of one of its instances, the system has to record a program that corresponds to the building process of the chosen instance. This program is called each time the end user defined class is instantiated. Two slightly different approaches have been developed to capture a program without explicit programming. The first one is the programming by demonstration; the second one is called parametric geometry.

2.1 Programming by demonstration

The programming by demonstration technique has been introduced to permit end users to create programs without explicit programming. These systems are able to generate macros that automatically execute some user's actions. For example the Topaz system [12] creates macros that can generalise some treatment on drawings. Other systems are able to generate programs in neutral language that can be used on other systems. For example the EBP system [16] generate FORTRAN for exchanging CAD geometry.

Programming by demonstration means creating a program using an example of its execution. An important notion brought by the programming by demonstration technique is the abstraction method. In classical programming languages, the program manipulates variables within their names. In the opposite, PbD allows the "program" to directly manipulate variables within their values. The link between names and values is made in a table of symbols, called the context [15]. Thus, all the variables of the program are referenced without ambiguity regardless of their values. Creating a program, that deals only with values, from an example of its execution needs to associate a variable name with each value. This is the task of the *dynamic context*. For each created value in the example, a new variable name (whose data type is defined by the value) is added in the dynamic context. These variable names may be used in the generated program.

Capabilities to specify the program parameters shall also be provided by programming by demonstration systems. There are two main approaches to define the parameters of a program created by demonstration. The *implicit manner* described by Bauer [3] consists of creating several examples of the same program. Then, the system automatically infers the parameters after an analysis of the different examples. With the *explicit manner*, the PBD user has to define which values are program parameters. The other values are considered by the PBD system as constants. This paper will follow the second approach.

The programming by demonstration permits the creation of a program representing the building process of an object without explicit programming. The two main advantages of this approach are the program abstraction and the parameter definition. For our purpose, PBD might be a good approach; for example, Mondrian [10] allows end-users to create new objects and to include them as native objects in the interactive system. However, it does not allow the user to define parts or attributes onto the designed objects.

2.2   Parametric geometry

The parametric geometry comes from the CAD field. In this area, geometrical objects are often made by constrained constructs; for example a line can be explicitly parallel to another line [18, 19]. The goal of parametric geometry is to permit the dynamic modification of geometrical entities; for example if a circle is created using the intersection of two lines as centre (Figure 1), the modification of one of these lines leads to moving the circle.

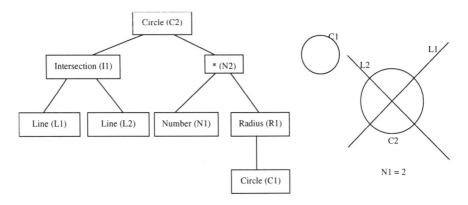

Figure 1. Building tree in a parametric construct.

Figure 1 shows an example of a parametric construct of a circle whose radius is an expression of an another circle radius and whose centre corresponds to the intersection of two lines.

In parametric geometry, each entity records the sequence of functions that were used for its creation. This sequence of functions can be seen as a building tree like in Figure 1. To create a program representing the building process of an object, this sequence of functions could be used. But, most of the CAD systems using parametric geometry do not have the necessary tools to abstract a program like in PBD. In parametric geometry, there is no notion of parameters and constants, all the leaves of the tree can be modified and then the objects depending on the modified leaves are re-evaluated.

The main advantage of this approach regarding the program generation is that it is so ergonomic that in most cases the user do not know that he/she creates a program when he/she builds a geometrical entity. But, this method has two drawbacks. The first one concerns the abstraction of the program. The possibility to extract an independent program from the recorded sequence of functions is rarely given to the user. The second one is that few systems offer the possibility to define program parameters.

As in PBD, in parametric geometry, there is no way to express the characteristics of a designed object are accessed.

3.   DIALOGUE SPECIFICATION

The dynamic integration of end user classes is crucial to improve the productivity of graphical systems. It is important for end user comfort to handle in the same way the native objects and the instances of the classes he/she has defined. There are two well-known families of tools that a designer can use to create the interface of an interactive system: the interface generators and the Toolkits.

These two families are studied in this part, and particularly the way they permit the modification of the interface of the system in order to add end user defined classes.

3.1   Model-based interface generators

Model-based interface generators are also called top-down generators. They permit describing the application interface using the specific language associated to some underlying model. Then, this description is compiled; the result of this compilation is used to generate the interface. The TRIDENT system [4] offers three models to describe the user tasks, the presentation, and the functions of the application. MECANO [17] defines a meta-model to create a task model, a domain model and a presentation model, which are used by specific tools to generate the application.

The specification approach of this method allows the designer to easily modify the interface of a system because the specification usually takes into account only the important aspects of the interface and deduces the other ones. However, the problem is that the model-based systems are not yet dynamic. The generated applications cannot be modified through a dynamic modification of their model because once the application is generated there is no link between the application and the models used to create it. For example, the JANUS [1] system generates C++ code, which is completely independent from its model. When a designer wants to modify its application, he/she has to modify the model and has to use the generator to re-create the application. So a modification of the model cannot be taken into account on the fly.

3.2   The toolkits

The toolkits are essentially presentation element libraries like the MFC [9] or Tcl/Tk [13]. These elements are called widgets. They are used to define the presentation of the application. They have their own behaviour (e.g. opening a menu) and have an elementary mechanism for the application control: the callback. An activation of a widget calls automatically one or several functions of the domain component.

The creation of the interface by the bottom-up method can be divided in three parts: the first step consists of realizing the domain component. Then, the designer creates the presentation with widget instantiations. At last, he/she links the presentation to the domain component functions by using callbacks. A lot of tools (like Microsoft Visual C++ or Visual Basic) permit a designer to easily describe the presentation of the application and they facilitate the creation of the link between the application functions and the widgets.

The widgets can be dynamically instantiated (e.g. the modification by the end user of the toolbar in MS-Word). But, as Myers says [11], it is a problem to define the control of a real application only with callbacks because in a real system there are often hundreds of callbacks, which make the code hard to modify and to maintain. So, it is difficult to modify dynamically an interface created using the bottom-up approach.

4.   THE PROPOSED SOLUTION : TEXAO

A solution to integrate dynamically end user defined classes in the interface has been developed. It consists of creating a specification, not with a language based approach like in model based systems but, by instantiating the different elements described in the model we suggested. This solution is put into practice in the TexAO system with a dialogue tool set. This tool set is obtained by reification of elements described in the H^4 architecture model [14].

TexAO is a graphical application that supports constraint constructs. It has a parametric model that permits an easy definition of the programs. It uses specific tools to define the dialogue that permit the dynamic integration of end user classes. This application has been created using the CAS.CADE (Matra DataVision) geometric library and the MFC toolkit to create the interface.

In the following, the parametric model is described first. The second part of this section deals with the dialogue tools. Finally, an example of the use of our technique is shown to explain how to create a new class and how to dynamically integrate it in the application.

4.1   Parametric model

The Parametric model of the TexAO system is shown on Figure 2 using the EXPRESS-G formalism [7] which proved efficient to describe an object oriented model.

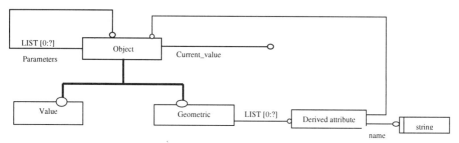

Figure2. Object of TexAO's parametric model.

In the EXPRESS-G formalism the classes are represented by rectangles (e.g. the object class), the thin lines characterise class attributes (Current_value is an attribute of the Object class), the thick lines represent inheritance relation (Geometric and Value inherit from Object).

Figure 2 shows that each class of the parametric model of TexAO have a link to a value that depends on the class (the current_value attribute): a circle will refer to a CAS.CADE circle, a number will refer to a C++ real value. The "parameters" attribute is the list of the parametric model instances used to create an instance, thus each instance of the parametric model knows its parameters and each of them knows its own parameters, etc. This attribute is used to create the building tree of each object.

The attribute "derived attribute" of the geometric object characterizes the list of the characteristics defined for this instance. An attribute is defined by its name and contains a parametric model object. Only the geometric objets may have attributes. This model allows each object to remember exactly how it is built. The "derived attributes" are objects of the parametric model, so they record not only their values but also the way these values are computed.

The main rule of our model is that a class represents each constructive function of the application. Each class inherits from the class describing the output type of the function (for example the circle_by_centre_and_one_point class inherits from the circle class); we call these super classes the base classes.

4.2   The dialogue tool set

The dialogue tool set is a set of gadgets that permit a designer to create a dialogue component (respecting the Arch [2] architecture model and based on the elements defined in H^4 [14]) by the same way he/she makes the presentation component using widgets.

The Tokens are the information units used to capture, at various levels of abstraction the user input (e.g. number, position, circle, and line...) in the dialogue tool set.

The Questionnaires represent the user tasks. They link the dialogue component with the specific domain component. They are defined by the command used by the user to activate the task they represent, by the types of the tokens used by the task to call functions of the specific domain component and by the types of the returned tokens when the task returns a result. The call of the specific domain component function is made in a function called "questionnaire implementation" which is in charge of the transformation of the tokens in data usable for the specific domain component functions and to transform into tokens the result of these functions.

The Interactors organise the different questionnaires of the application in abstraction levels. All the questionnaires dedicated to the creation of geometric entity are brought together in the "creation" interactor. The "Calculator" Interactor is shaped by the questionnaires dealing with arithmetic's operations. Interactors contain ATN [8] that aggregate tokens to call a questionnaire implementation.

The Monitor manages all the interactors. It recovers the tokens coming from the presentation and sends them to all the interactors from the lower abstraction level to the higher abstraction level.

The dialogue tool set has a tool that permits the generation of the presentation component of the application.

The following example shows the creation of a system that has three tasks: create a circle by its centre and radius, compute the centre and compute the radius of a circle.

The symbols { } represents lists, the word between "" represents characters, a sentence behind the symbol // is a comment. The syntax of the dialogue tool set elements instantiations is CLASSNAME instance_name (parameters);

The first things to describe are the tokens. The parameters of the class constructor are a string representing the token type. Three types of token are needed:

> **TOKEN point ("point");** *// represents a position coming from the presentation or computed by the system*

TOKEN number ("number"); // *represents a number coming from the presentation or computed by the system. Like a point or a circle, a number is an object with an identity and not a simple value type*

TOKEN circle ("circle"); // *represents a Circle of the data base*

Now we can create a representation of user tasks with the questionnaires. The parameters of the questionnaires are a string representing the command name which calls the questionnaire, a list of string representing the list of tokens types needed to call the questionnaire and an optional string representing the result type of the questionnaire execution.

QUESTIONNAIRE Circle ("Circle", {"point", "number"});

QUESTIONNAIRE Radius ("Radius", {"circle"}, "number");

QUESTIONNAIRE Centre ("Centre", {"circle"}, "point");

The parameters of the interactor constructor are the list of allowed questionnaires.

INTERACTOR Creation ({Circle});

INTERACTOR Calculator ({Centre,Radius});

The list of interactors a monitor manages represents parameters.

MONITOR MiniApp ({Creation,Calculator})

The Creation Interactor is the highest in hierarchy level because it uses the result computed in the Calculator Interactor. The dialogue controller defined upper allows users to create concentric circles and circles having the same radius.

The instantiation of dialogue tool set elements represents the specification of the user tasks of the application. This specification can be changed dynamically by instantiating new questionnaires corresponding to new user tasks and integrating them in the existing interactors or creating new interactors to manage them. A specific class of token, called dynamic token, exists in order to permit the definition of new token types. A string gives the type of the dynamic token at creation time. The data transported by this kind of token are pointers on the object they represent.

4.3   An example of use

The way the TexAO system works is explained in a small example. Assume that the end user wants to make a class to create "dump-bell" (Figure 3). This class has a constructor which has two points representing the centre of the two spheres and a number for the radius of the spheres. This class has one attribute representing the distance between the two spheres.

Figure 3 shows on the one hand the dump-bell associated with the name of the object, which compose it and on the other hand the building tree of the dump-bell. Thanks to the "parameter" attribute of each object (Figure 2) the link between the different parametric model object is made.

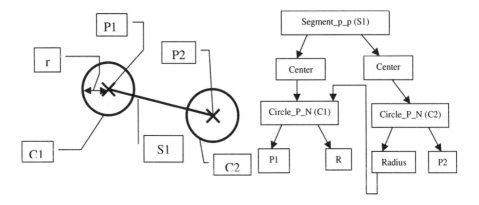

Figure 3. Example of TexAO use, a dump-bell.

The parameter definition could be done at two moments in the class description process. The first solution consists of defining the parameters before using them. For example, defining a position as a parameter and using it to create a circle. The second solution is to distinguish between parameters and constants once the building process is terminated. The user selects the objects of the building tree which will represent parameters for the class generation. For example the user selects the centre a circle for parameter once the circle is created by selecting the centre in its building tree. The first solution has been chosen in TexAO because the CAD users know the parameters of the piece they build before the building process begins.

To create a new parameter, the user selects the command "make parameter" and gives a name and a value representing the parameter's current value. Then, a button representing this parameter is created in the presentation. This button is used to select the parameter and to use it in a construct.

Once the parameters are defined, the building process can begin. The user creates all the elements used to make a dump-bell. All these elements are linked by the building tree as shown in Figure 1.

To add an attribute to the example and then to the class, the command "make attribute" is selected and a string representing the attribute name is provided by the user. Then, the system waits for two entities: 1) the geometrical object whose building tree will be used to create the class constructor and 2) an object representing the value of the attribute. The second object is an instance of the parametric model so it records its building tree that will be used to create the computation function of the attribute. This object representing the attribute and its name is added in the "derived attribute" list (see Figure 2) of the first object given by the user. In the example, the user creates an attribute representing the distance between the centres of two circles and calls it "D".

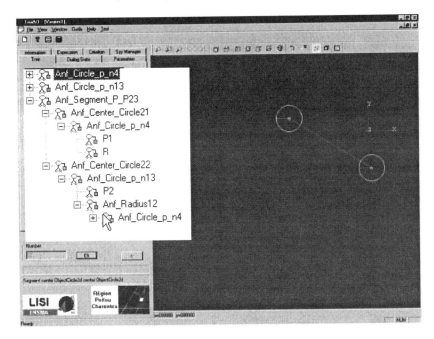

Figure 4. Building tree representation in TexAO.

The TexAO system is now able to generate a class to make dump-bells. The user selects the command "make class" and he/she gives a string representing the class name and selects the object containing the building tree representing the building process of the new class instances. In the example, the user gives the name "dump-bell" to the class and selects the segment_p_p S1 (see Figure 3) which contains the building process of the dump-bell. The building tree is copied in the tree database represented by an array linking a tree with a name. Here, a copy of the tree that constructs the line S1 is associated to the name "dump-bell". The copying process copies not only the tree but also the list of the "derived attributes" contained in the object S1.

The system generates the different dialogue elements necessary to handle the new class. First, it creates an instance of questionnaire able to call the class constructor. Its name is the same as the class ("dump-bell" in the example). A mapping process permits the recovering of the input tokens from the parameter type. A new token type is created to represent dump-bells in the dialogue. It is used to create the questionnaires in charge of querying the attributes.

The new dialogue gadget added in the dump-bell example can be described as:

```
Questionnaire Dump-bell ("Dump-bell", {point, point,
    number});
Questionnaire D_Dump-bell ("D", "dump-bell", number);
```

The questionnaire D_Dump-bell returns a token number corresponding to attribute D of the dump-bell object in input. The Dump-bell questionnaire is added to the interactor creation because it corresponds to a new geometrical object creation. The D_Dump-bell questionnaire is added to the information interactor gathering the questionnaire computing attributes (the questionnaire in charge of computing the centre of a circle is also placed in this interactor). The addition of these two questionnaires leads to the creation of buttons in the presentation, these commands allow the user to indicate to the system that he/she wants to create a new dump-bell or he/she wants to use the attributes.

When the user wants to create an instance of a new class, he/she indicates the class using the command representing the class in the presentation. He/she gives the parameters values of the constructor. To create an instance of a dynamic class, the system has to find the building tree in the tree database with the name of the class given by the command name. It copies this tree and changes the objects representing parameters by new objects contained in the tokens with respect to their type and their order. Then, the new created tree is evaluated to create a new instance. It is important to notice that all the attributes are copied in the instance and re-computed. This instantiation method is called prototyping [5] in object oriented paradigm. It consists of copying an existing object and changing its parameters rather than creating an instance from a class.

When an instance of the dynamic class is selected, a dynamic token is instantiated to represent this object in the dialogue component. For example when the user selects a "dump-bell", the system creates a dynamic token with the string "dump-bell", and links it to the selected dump-bell.

To recover the value of attribute, the user selects the command that corresponds to the attribute name and the object for which he/she wants the attribute value. Then, a specific questionnaire is used to extract the attribute value from the object by finding it in the "derived attribute" list using the attribute name. It creates a token that corresponds to the attribute type and that carries a link to the object that describes the attribute.

5.   CONCLUSION

Adding new classes by end users in existing systems is a major challenge. It would permit increasing the productivity by specialising a system. To reach this goal, the application has to: 1) record the building process of an instance and abstract it to a class 2) associate to this class some query functions for accessing some internal characteristics and, 3) integrate this new class in the dialogue in order to permit the user to handle such instances as native objects. There exists in computer graphics domain two methods to record the building process of an object. The first one is the Programming by Demonstration technique that creates a program from an example of its execution. This method offers the possibility to define parameters and to abstract a program from an example but there is no way to access internal characteristics of the designed object. The second one is given by the parametric geometry, which preserves the building process together with any object used in the design. This approach is so ergonomic that the user often ignores that he/she is implicitly building a "program". But, it is not possible to separate the building process from a particular instance. Thus, it is difficult to abstract a (class constructor) program from parametric instance. Moreover, no parametric system, to our knowledge, provides for associating several methods with the same parametric object. Therefore, no accessible attribute may be associated with a parametric object.

In this paper we have proposed an approach that allows an end-user to define new classes of objects without any explicit programming activity. This approach consists in abstracting a class from one of its instances. To capture the class constructor the system uses a parametric model that records the building process of the instance. Techniques coming from the programming by demonstration area enable the user to choose the parameters of the constructor. To describe class attributes, the user builds their values by means of references to entities of the parametric model instance. The building process of these values is used by the system to abstract the computation functions of these attributes.

To integrate the end-user defined classes in the interface, the proposed method consists of using the advantages of the two approaches. The first one is the top-down approach where the interface is generated from its specification. This approach has the advantage to ease the modification of the specification and so the modification of the generated interface. But, it is rarely dynamic. The second approach, called the bottom-up method, generally uses a set of elements to create the presentation component. These elements are associated with special functions that call the domain component functions. This approach is more dynamic than the first one but an interface created by this approach is hardly modifiable. In this paper, our proposed approach is based on dialogue component elements that describe the interface like in the top-down approach but which are as dynamic as presentation elements are. So, this approach permits the dynamic modification of the interface by dynamically instantiating dialogue elements.

These two proposed approaches have been implemented in the TexAO system. This system provides all the required capabilities allowing an end user to specialise a general purpose CAD system towards a particular application. In the current version, the user interface to access these new objects is almost identical to the interface provided to access pre-existing objects.

REFERENCES

[1] Balzert, H., *From OOA to GUI : The JANUS-System*, in Proc. of 5th IFIP TC 13 Int. Conf. on Human-Computer Interaction INTERACT'95 (Lillehammer, 27-29 June 1995), Chapman & Hall, London, 1995, pp. 319–324.

[2] Bass, L., Pellegrino, R., Reed, S., Sheppard, S., and Szezur, M., *The Arch Model : Seeheim revisited*, in Proc. of User Interface Developper's Workshop, 1991.

[3] Bauer, M., *Programming by Examples*, 1979.

[4] Bodart, F., Hennebert, A.-M., Leheureux, J.-M., Provot, I., B. Sacré, and Vanderdonckt, J., *Towards a systematic building of software Architectures: the Trident Methodological Guide*, in Proc. of 2nd Int. Workshop on Design, Specification, and Verification of Interactive Systems DSV-IS'95 (Bonas, 7-9 June 1995), Springer-Verlag, Vienna, 1995, pp. 262–278.

[5] Cohen, B. and Murphy, G.L., *Models of Concept*, 1984.

[6] Cypher, A., *Watch What I Do: Programming by Demonstration*, The MIT Press, Cambridge, 1993.

[7] EXPRESS, *The EXPRESS language reference manual*. ISO, 1994 ISO 10303-11.

[8] Green, M., *A Survey of three Dialogue Models*, ACM Trans. on Graphics, Vol. 5, 1986, pp. 244–275.

[9] Kain, E., *The MFC Answer Book*, Addison Wesley, Reading, 1998.

[10] Lieberman, H., *Mondrian: a Teachable Editor*, in Cypher, A. (ed.), *Watch What I Do: Programming by Demonstration*, The MIT Press, Cambridge, 1993, pp. 341–360.

[11] Myers, B.A., *User Interface Software Tools*, ACM Trans. on Computer-Human Interaction, Vol. 2, 1995, pp. 64–103.

[12] Myers, B.A., *Scripting Graphical Applications by Demonstration*, in *Proc. of ACM Conf. on Human Factors in Computing* Systems CHI'98 (Los Angeles, 18-24 April 1998), ACM Press, New York, 1998, pp. 534–541.

[13] Ousterhout, J.K., *Tcl and the Tk ToolKit*, Addison-Wesley, Reading, 1994.

[14] Pierra, G., Girard, P., and Guittet, L., *Towards precise architecture models for computer graphics: the H4 architecture*, in Proc. of 2nd Int. Workshop on Design, Specification, and Verification of Interactive Systems DSV-IS'95 (Bonas, 7-9 June 1995), Springer-Verlag, Vienna, 1995.

[15] Pierra, G., Potier, J.-C., and Girard, P., *The EBP system : Example Based Programming for Parametric Design*. J. Texeira and J., Rix (eds.), *Modelling and Graphics in Science and Technology*, Springer-Verlag, Vienna, 1996.

[16] Potier, J.-C., *Conception sur exemple, mise au point et génération de programmes portables de géométrie paramétrée dans le système EBP*, Ph.D. thesis, Université de Poitiers, Poitiers, 1995.

[17] Puerta, A., *The MECANO project : comprehensive and intégrated support for Model-Based Interface development*, in J. Vanderdonckt (ed.), Proc. of the 2nd Int. Workshop on Computer-Aided Design of User Interfaces CADUI'96 (Namur, 5-7 June 1996), Presses Universitaires de Namur, Namur, 1996, pp. 19–35.

[18] Shah, J.J. and Mäntylä, M., *Parametric and Feature-based CAD/CAM: Concepts, Techniques and Applications*, John Wiley, New York, 1995.

[19] Zalik, B., *An Interactive Constraint-Based Graphics System with Partially Constrained Form-Features*, in J. Vanderdonckt (ed.), Proc. of the 2nd Int. Workshop on Computer-Aided Design of User Interfaces CADUI'96 (Namur, 5-7 June 1996), Presses Universitaires de Namur, Namur, 1996, 229–245.

Chapter 20

THE VISUAL TASK MODEL BUILDER

M. Biere, Birgit Bomsdorf and Gerd Szwillus
Universität - GH Paderborn, Fachbereich Mathematik/Informatik
D-33095 Paderborn, Germany
{kne, szwillus}@uni-paderborn.de
Tel : +49 5251 60-6624

Abstract   The Visual Task Model Builder (VTMB) tool enables the user to create and modify rich task models. These contain a hierarchical task structure, temporal relations between tasks, conditions of task execution, and objects involved while performing a task. Based on precise semantics the model can be simulated for validation with the future user and the user interface designer. Additionally, it provides the basis for the transformation of the task model into a working dialogue model.

Keywords: Task-based design, model-based approahc, Model Builder.

1.   INTRODUCTION

Knowing the user's tasks is essential for the designer to construct user interfaces adequately reflecting the tasks' properties [[5]]. The importance of task models has increased in the user interface design process, and the need to create, modify, and verify task models has come up. The term task model is not used coherently in the literature; we found, however, that there is a consensus on the following issues:

(1) There exist two distinct task models: the **current task model** describes a work situation as is; the **envisioned task model** describes the work situation assuming the new system to be in operation. Parts of the second task model are close to the dialogue model, hence, it can be seen as a specification for the dialogue implementation.

(2) A task model contains a **task hierarchy**, where the subtasks are linked by temporal relations, such as sequence, selection, do-in-parallel, etc.

(3) Task performance is additionally influenced by **pre- and postconditions**, meaning conditions to hold before the execution may begin or end, as well as effects of the task execution.

(4) Tasks operate on **objects** which are created, used, modified, or deleted during their performance.

Task models represent the task analyst's knowledge of the user tasks. It is important that the model is correct in itself and reflects the user's current or future task properly. To help in developing task models our tool allows a **simulation** of the task model. This enables the designer to check the model for all kinds of inherent inconsistencies, such as dead ends, unreachable parts, inadvertent loops and decisions etc. If made available to the user of the future system, it can help to find out, whether the analysis result is correct and reflects the real work done by the user adequately; also it enables the user to evaluate the future tasks to be performed. Using this type of tool for task analysis, paves the way to further use of the task model in the design process, namely to create the framework of the dialogue design, and to support a smooth transition from the envisioned task model to the dialogue model of the user interface.

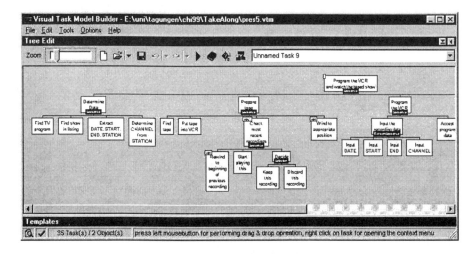

Figure 1. The Visual Task Builder.

We started working on executable task models with some studies [[3]], discussing the general idea. ADEPT [[5]] allows the animation of a task hierarchy, reflecting temporal relations and to some extent the objects worked upon; our model, however, seems to be more detailed and less informal than the task knowledge structure (TKS) used in that approach, thus leading to a more "exact" behaviour. Also ADEPT provides an animation [[12]] of the task tree, while our simulation displays only the active tasks and objects at a time, thus leading to a more comprehensive behaviour. Other work of this type includes task specifications with LOTOS [[7]] and with Petri nets [[6]], leading to executable systems as well, but aiming primarily at formal verification rather than simulation and validation. The task model editing tool Euterpe [[11]] was developed recently by van Welie; this is richer in terms of information collected in the task model, but has no precise semantics for allowing execution. Similar to our approach, DIANE+ [[10]]allows the expressive specification of temporal relations and conditions as well as linking of objects to the model; it aims, however, at user interface generation and not at interactive testing of task models at an abstract level of description. Within the TADEUS system [[8]] a simulation of task models is provided as well, but a task is seen more technically, functional-oriented in this system, as an algorithm is entered for every task which is then used for generation of a running system.

2. CREATING TASK MODELS

Task models tend to get big, so working with pen and pencil is out of question. To support the creation and modification of task models, the VTMB provides a graphical editor for this purpose.

2.1 Creating the Task Hierarchy

The **task hierarchy** is built up visually as a graphical tree structure. The user does not have to care about the layout of the tree; this is created automatically from the hierarchical relations. When the editor is opened for creating a new model, it contains exactly one task node, which then is used as root for a new task tree. Adding a subtask is done with the help of a context menu showing up when selecting an arbitrary node of the tree. The figure on the previous page shows a situation while creating a big task hierarchy in the editor. The user can zoom the representation easily with the slider on the top left, giving him, for example, the magnified view on a part of the task model (Figure 2).

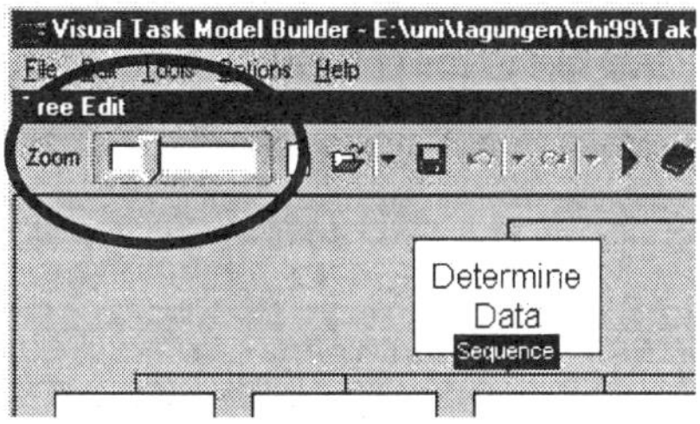

Figure 2. Magnified view.

Also, the user is able to collapse the visual representations of subtrees individually, to keep an overview of the whole tree and still be able to work on the details of a sub-branch. The tree can be manipulated with intuitive drag-and-drop operations, allowing easy restructuring operations, such as copying a complete subtree to another node.

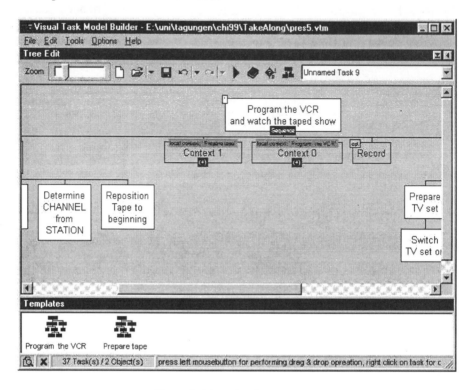

Figure 3. Selected task components.

Finally, the tree editor allows the creation of subtrees, referred to as templates, as sketched out above. Any arbitrary branch of the task tree can be defined as being a separate unit, to be stored in a file or within the tool and then re-used within the same or other task models. Using this feature the designer can create re-usable sub-task models and incorporate them into later designs. Overall, the tree editor of VTMB allows for an easy way of creating and manipulating tree structures representing task hierarchies.

2.2   Task Properties

When adding subtasks to a node or calling the task properties dialogue box (see figure on the right), several properties of the task can be specified. Apart from specifying a name for the new task, one of the most important properties the user can define is the temporal relation of the new task to its subtasks. VTMB provides the following possibilities:

- Unrestricted: the subtasks can be executed in any temporal order.
- Sequential: the subtasks must be executed one after the other in the order given in the tree.
- Random Sequence: the subtasks must be executed one after the other, but in an arbitrary order.
- Selection: one of the subtasks is to be selected for execution.
- Parallel: the subtasks are executed in parallel

These temporal relations have a well-defined semantics, such that the time behaviour of task execution can later be simulated. A task can be specified of being a user task or a system task. A user task is assumed to be performed by a human operator of a system, while a system task is considered to be work carried out by the system. During the simulation of the task model, a system task will not wait for input from the user, but will perform automatically. To create a more realistic time behaviour, the designer can specify a time delay to be active while the system task is executed.

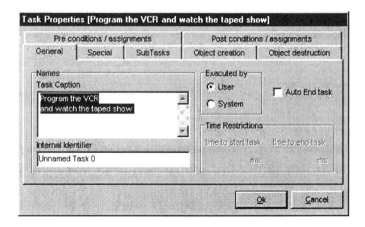

Figure 4. Task properties.

2.3 Conditions

All task models incorporate external ("world") **conditions** influencing the execution of tasks. Conditions can be included in the system as

- pre-conditions for tasks, needing to be fulfilled before the task can be executed,
- post-conditions (or effects) of tasks, being fulfilled after the task was executed, and
- iteration or skip conditions, specifying information which causes a task to iterate or to be skipped.

To use a condition in VTMB it has to be specified in the condition list and given a unique name. If he wants, the designer can create new conditions as logical expression from existing ones, thus allowing a clearer representation of facts; this can be done in the "Mapped To" column in the screen below.

Condition declaration and -mapping		✕
Condition	Location	substituted with / mapped to
ShowWasCancelled	Project	
StationSignalOK	Project	
TapeExists	Project	

Figure 5. Condition declaration and mapping.

Once introduced, a condition can be used as a pre-condition, post-condition, iteration condition or skipping condition of a task, by specifying it in the appropriate place in the task property sheet (see example above). When simulating the task model, the conditions can be dynamically set by the user, thus influencing the task model execution. So, the designer can check the effect the conditions have on the task model dynamics.

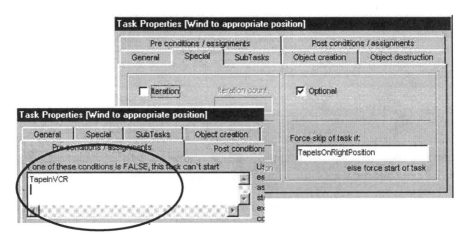

Figure 6. Task properties.

2.4   Task Objects

Tasks typically modify objects of the "world" they operate in. VTMB allows to incorporate the task objects into the model. A class editor (see figure on top of next page) allows the definition of simple object classes to be used within the task model. A class consists of members, i.e. static attributes of a class of certain simple data types. The model is not particularly rich, but this was done on purpose as we did not create an object-oriented programming language here. The intention was to provide some possibilities for modelling object stuctures within the task model, not to allow their technical implementation.

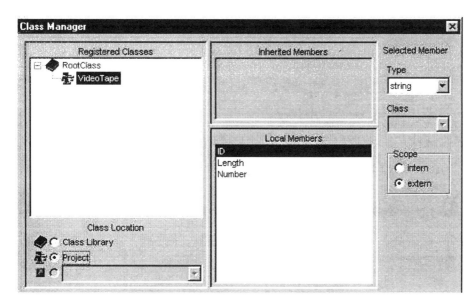

Figure 7. Class manager.

Once an object class is defined the designer can use objects within the tasks. First, a task can be specified as creating object instances of a given object class, also allowing initialisations of the instance's attributes (see figure on the right). On the other hand, objects can be specified as being destroyed by a task as well. The most important relation between objects and tasks, however, is the possibility for tasks to have effects on objects, i.e. change the values of object attributes. This is specified, as for conditions, in the task property sheet describing effects (see figure above).

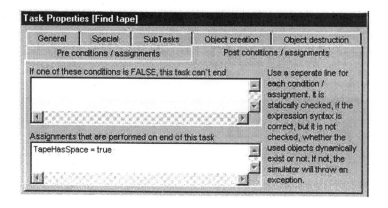

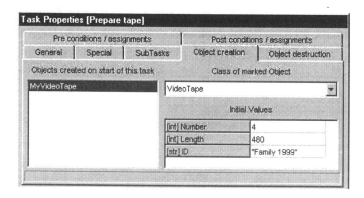

Figure 8. Task properties.

In general, the distinction between object attributes and conditions is blurred: expressions containing object attribute values can also be used as conditions. Overall, the execution of tasks can depend on properties of objects and conditions, and can modify both elements as well. Technically, conditions and object attributes can be mixed freely; hence, object attribute values can also be used in the "Mapped To" field of the condition definition. The integration of the object hierarchy and the influence of objects to the task model, allows for partially modelling the functionality of the future system and thus arriving at a much more realistic task model simulation. When making use of these features one must keep in mind, however, that their purpose is not the implementation of a running system - their functionality should only be used as a coarse **model** of the task modifications on the object world. VTMB does not provide enough power to do the "real thing".

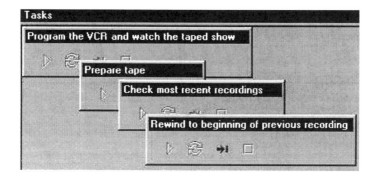

Figure 9. Tasks linking.

3. SIMULATING TASK MODELS

As our task model has precise execution semantics, it can be simulated by interpretation. The simulation shows at any time the "next possible" tasks to be performed according to the temporal relations and conditions specified. A "possible" task is shown (see figure above) as a small dialogue box, containing the task name, and four buttons, influencing the task performance:

- The Go-Button representing the beginning of the task execution,
- The Done-Button representing the ending of task execution,
- The Repeat-Button representing the possibility to execute the task once more, and
- The Skip-Button representing the possibility to skip the task.

At any time in the simulation, only those actions of the four mentioned above are enabled, which are possible with respect to the specification in the task model. So, during the simlulation the designer can check, whether this model contains the correct conditions, temporal relations, and object dependencies. Overall, in a situation several task buttons are typically visible and shown to be selected and "performed". The conditions, are shown in a separate part of the screen. They depict their current state; conditions, which are not mapped to elements of the model, also have a toggle button, allowing the user to dynamically toggle the condition state between "true" and "false".

Figure 10. Tasks status.

The setting of conditions immediately influences the simulation, thus changing a condition typically enables or disables task action buttons. The

objects are also represented on the screen in simple text windows showing
the current values of all attributes as text entries (see figure on the right).

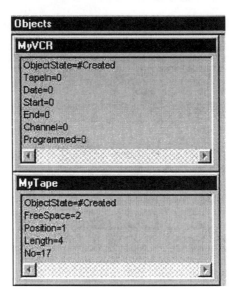

Figure 11. Objects.

Watching these entries, the designer can inspect the effect taks execution
has on the object properties. The visualisiation of the objects is very simple
and straightforward - not very intuitive - and we are currently working on
improving object representation, to come closer to a user-oriented visual
picture of the task object world. The figure below shows a complete screen,
with conditions and objects displayed, during a more complex task model
simulation. Overall, when performing the task model simulation, the designer and maybe the future user can discover the behaviour of the task
model in an abstract representation, which does not contain any user interface design decision. Technically, we perform this simulation by translating
the task model into the object-oriented dialogue modelling language ODSN
[[9]] and then use its interpreter for executing the model, with VTMB interpreting the runtime information from ODSN and then creating the visualization.

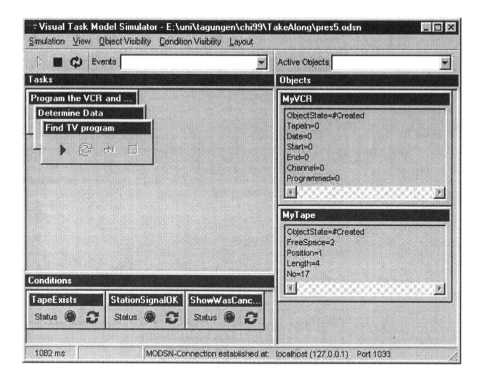

Figure 12. A typical screenshot.

4. CONCLUSION

As a tool to be used by designers, working on task models, we think VTMB lacks still some important features. We mentioned already the inadequate object representation. Also, the task representation as simple box with text can be improved, as tasks could be visualised in a more intuitive way as appropriate graphical representations. Furthermore, the dynamical layout of the task boxes during the simulation was done in a very simple way, with certain negative effects, such as task boxes being hidden by others, although being active. The object model is not truly dynamic, such that we cannot "really" create new objects, which is a problem in modelling highly dynamic systems. We will address all these issues in the near future.

Also, we see VTMB as a starting point for supporting the (non-trivial) transition from the task model to the dialogue model. Starting conceptually with a simulation as provided by VTMB, there could be a tool allowing the stepwise introduction of **user interface objects** into the model, and then supporting the transition of control from the task boxes to these user interface objects. Also, the task objects could gradually be transformed into user interface objects. A tool supporting this type of stepwise development from task model to dialogue model could be a substantial help in creating user interface design which conform with the underlying task model.

REFERENCES

[1]   Biere, M., Bomsdorf, B., and Szwillus, G., VTMB Tool, University of Paderborn, 1999. Available under http://www.uni-paderborn.de/cs/Gerd.Szwillus.html.

[2]   Biere, M., Bomsdorf, B., and Szwillus, G., *Specification and Simulation of Task Models with VTMB*, CHI'99 Extended Abstracts, ACM Press, New York, 1999, pp. 1-2.

[3]   Bomsdorf, B. and Szwillus, G., *Early Prototyping based on Executable Task Models*, CHI'96 Conference Companion, ACM Press, New York, 1996, pp. 254-255.

[4]   Bomsdorf, B. and Szwillus, G., *From Task to Dialogue: Task-Based User Interface Design*, SIGCHI Bulletin, Vol. 30, No. 3, 1988.

[5]   Johnson, P., Johnson, H., and Wilson, S., *Rapid Prototyping of User Interfaces Driven by Task Models*, in "Scenario-Based Design", J.M. Carrol (ed), John Wiley & Sons, 1995.

[6]   Palanque, P. and Bastide, R., *Petri Net based Design of user-driven Interfaces using the Interactive Cooperative Objects Formalism,* in Proc. of 2nd Eurographics Workshop on Interactive Systems: Design Specification and Verification DSV-IS'95, Springer Verlag, Vienna, 1995.

[7] Paterno, P. and Mezzanotte, M., Analysing Matis by Interactor and ACTL, *Amodeus II 7040 Project Report sm_wp36,* 1994.

[8]   Stary, C., *Task- and Model-Based Development of Interactive Software,* in Proc. of IFIP'98 World Congress, Vienna, 1998.

[9]   Szwillus, G., Object-Oriented Dialogue Specification with ODSN (In German: Objektorientierte Dialogspezifikation mit ODSN), in Proc. of Software-Ergonomie'97, Dresden, Germany, 1997.

[10] Tarby, J.-C. an Barthet, M.-F., *The DIANE+ Method*, in Proceedings of 2nd Workshop on Computer-Aided Design of User Interfaces CADUI'96 (Namur, 4-6 June 1996), J. Vanderdonckt (ed.), Presses Universitaires de Namur, Namur, 1996, pp. 95-119.

[11] van Welie, M., Euterpe 0.1 beta, 1999. Accessible at http://www.cs.vu.nl/~martijn/gta/.

[12] Wilson, S. and Johnson, P., *Empowering users in a task-based approach to design*, in Proceedings of ACM Symposium on Designing Interactive Systems DIS'95, ACM Press, New York, 1995, pp. 25-31.

Chapter 21

COMPUTER-AIDED ANALYSIS OF COOPERATIVE APPLICATIONS

Giulio Ballardin, Cristiano Mancini, Fabio Paternò
CNUCE-C.N.R., Via S.Maria 36
56126, Pisa, Italy
f.paterno@cnuce.cnr.it
Tel : +39-050 593289 - Fax : +39-050 904052

Abstract   In this paper we discuss how tool-support can be useful for designers who apply task modelling. We focus on how tools can help designers during the development, analysis, and management of task models for cooperative applications. In particular, we introduce how CTTE, a set of tools that we have developed, provides support for the development and analysis of task models of multi-user applications specified in ConcurTaskTrees.

Keywords: Task Models, Cooperative Applications, Tool-support for Design, Formal Methods for HCI.

1.   INTRODUCTION

The importance of task models in design, development and evaluation of interactive applications has generally been recognised. However, the use of such task models has strongly been limited by the lack of automatic tools supporting them and a need for such a tool-support has been highlighted also in recent workshops [3]. Indeed, as soon as designers have to address realistic applications they immediately feel the need to have some tools that allow them to analyse the result of their modelling work, to modify it later on, to show it to other people or to use it to implement concrete software-based artefacts that support the tasks identified. The lack of tool support has been pointed out even for successful approaches such as GOMS [6] and UAN [7].

Tools for supporting environments for the design based on task models would also allow designers to overcome limitations of most current development tools, such as Visual Basic, that allow developers to rapidly obtain user interfaces by direct manipulation techniques but do not provide any suggestion concerning how to structure the user interface and to select the interaction and presentation techniques in such a way as to support effectively the activities indicated in the task model. We can notice that just a few proposals (such as [11], [9]) have been put forwards to overcome such limitations and there are various issues that still need to be solved.

Besides, when tools have been developed to support the design of interactive applications starting from task models (examples are Mobi-D [11] or Trident [2]), they have mainly addressed the design of single user interfaces. Even when they have considered the possibility of different type of users, this was done on the assumption that these types of users do not access the same data at the same time to cooperate through them synchronously. For example, in [11], a tool supporting the design of a user interface for different types of users (sergeant, captain, ..) is described. We too had some experience in designing adaptable interfaces [10]. In that case the problem addressed was to design an interactive application able to support different presentations or interactions depending on current user type and allowing dynamic change of the user type supported directly on request from the user. This gave more flexibility to our approach. However we have recognised that there is an additional issue that in the near future will become always more important: the possibility to support groupware or in other words, applications where multiple users can interact at the same time. This opens a new challenge to model-based approaches that have neglected this issue: how to provide high-level support for designing the specific features of multi-users applications that are becoming more and more common. A need for these new approaches is also motivated by the current toolkits for multi-users interfaces development: even when they address innovative solutions [12], they provide rather low-level constructs to designers and developers.

As described in [5] a groupware system covers three domain specific functions: production, coordination and communication. The *production* space denotes the set of domain objects that model the multi-user elaboration of common artefacts such as documents, or that motivate a common undertaking such as flying an airplane between two places. Typically, shared editors support the production space. The shared artefacts that we can consider are, for instance, orders and product descriptions. The *coordination* space covers dependencies among activities including temporal relationships between the multi-user activities. For instance, in ERP (Enterprise Resource Planning) applications the coordination should define, for example, how salesmen and clients can communicate and when each of them can perform their tasks. The *communication* space supports person-to-person communication. Email and media spaces are examples of systems designed for supporting computer-mediated communication either asynchronously or synchronously. In particular, coordination seems to be a crucial part in designing cooperative applications.

Generally speaking, we can find applications inherently cooperative such as air traffic control that have always been based on the successful cooperation of different persons and the introduction of software technology allows designers to create environments where this coordination is better supported; and applications, such as ERP applications, that so far have provided low support to cooperations but that could be strongly improved for this purpose thus creating more flexible and interactive environments. We believe that a strong need for redesigning existing applications will arise by the request of better support of cooperation among multiple users.

In this paper we want to report and discuss our experiences in developing an environment that supports the development of task models for cooperative applications specified by the ConcurTaskTrees [8] notation. Such tools are developed within the GUITARE R&D European project (http://giove.cnuce.cnr.it/guitare.html) which aims to improve the design of interactive applications, with particular attention to ERP applications, using task models.

In the paper, we introduce how in ConcurTaskTrees it is possible to describe cooperations among multiple users, next we discuss the tool support required to analyse such cooperations. Then, a more detailed description of our tool, also considering an example of application in the domain of ERP applications is provided and finally some concluding remarks are given.

2. DESCRIBING COOPERATIONS IN CONCURTASK-TREES

The ConcurTaskTrees notation [8] allows designers to specify task models hierarchically structured with the possibility to indicate temporal relationships among tasks, objects that they manipulate, how their performance is allocated and so on. Besides, it is possible to specify cooperative applications where different roles are involved. For this purpose there is a part dedicated to the cooperative aspects that allows designers to indicate relationships among activities performed by different users using the same notation. When developing a task model for cooperative applications, designers first have to identify the roles involved. A role is defined by a set of tasks and a set of relationships among such tasks. Each role has a cardinality indicating the number of users that can be active with that role during an application session. The cardinality can be one, a fixed predefined number or a variable number (in this case the number of users with the considered role will depend on the dynamic evolution of the application). In case of variable number it is possible to indicate a maximum number of users in that role that can be active at the same time.

Then we have a task model according to the ConcurTaskTrees syntax for each role. In addition there is a cooperative part. In the cooperative part we have cooperative tasks structured in a hierarchical manner. A task is cooperative when it implies actions from multiple users. For example, *Negotiating an order* is a cooperative task because it implies actions from both the salesman and the client. These cooperative tasks are decomposed in a hierarchical way until we reach tasks performed by single users. Thus the leaves of the cooperative part are only tasks performed by single users and in addition to the task name there is the indication of the relative role.

A task can occur in different points of the hierarchy. Each occurrence can manipulate either the same objects or different instances of objects of the same class. If a task occurs again in the subtree that it originates then we have a recursive task. If the task that occurs in different places of the task model has a relative subtree then it is sufficient to expand it only once in the task model and it is not required to expand it again in all its occurrences.

The leaves of the cooperative part then are also included in the task model of the corresponding role, thus creating a connection among the two parts. In the single user task tree they can occur in any part. Thus if they are not leaves in the single user part it means that they can be further refined in subtasks performed by the user of that role.

The purpose of the cooperative part of the overall task model is not only to identify cooperative tasks but also to indicate their temporal relationships, these have the effect of defining additional constraints for the tasks relative to each role. In Figure 1 we provide a simple example to introduce our approach (>> is the sequential operator). Above we have the cooperative part and below the two simple task models associated with the two roles.

If we considered the two roles without the cooperative part we would have at the beginning task1 and task3 enabled to be performed. However the cooperative part adds the additional constraint that task3 can be performed only after task1, thus at the beginning only task1 is enabled.

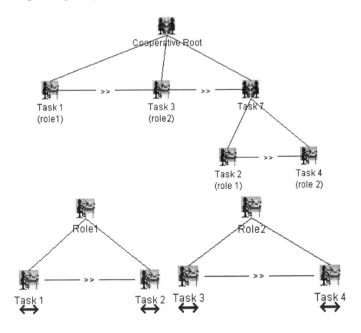

Figure 1. An example of the parts of a simple task model for a cooperative application.

As it is easy to understand the cooperative part allows designers to provide a declarative specification of session managers that control when enabling and disabling the interaction techniques available for each user depending on the state of the cooperation among them. Designers can need to specify other information. Thus, for each basic cooperative task (a cooperative task which is no longer decomposed into other cooperative tasks), they can specify the following information:

- Task name,
- Roles of users involved,
- names of the sub-tasks which have to be performed by each type of user
- the objects which are manipulated to perform the task, they can be either presentation or application objects, in case of application objects it is possible to specify for each role involved whether it has right access to modify it,
- roles cardinality (how many users for each role are involved in the cooperative task) ,

- some additional informal comments that can be added to further describe the task or some of its main features.

3.   TASK MODELLING IN CTTE

We have seen how ConcurTaskTrees allows designers to obtain modular specifications where the various parts can be developed in a consistent way. The resulting specification allows designers to focus on both the behaviour of specific classes of users and the cooperations among the various roles involved clearly indicating their relationships. The tool (CTTE – ConcurTaskTrees Environment) supporting the development of ConcurTaskTrees task models (available at http://giove.cnuce.cnr.it/ctte.html) provides various types of functionalities:

- *to allow designers to input and edit the information requested by the notation*: tasks and their attributes (name, category, type, related objects, …), temporal relationships among tasks and other information;
- *to help designers in improving the layout of their specification*: supporting automatic lining up, movement of levels or subtrees of the task model, cut and paste of pieces of task model, folding and unfolding of subtrees, possibility to add tasks as sibling or as child of the current task, etc....;
- *to check completeness of the specification*, for example it is possible to automatically detect whether temporal operators among tasks at the same level are missing or whether there is a task with only one child.
- *to save the specification or parts of it in various formats,* the tool also supports functionalities such as inserting other task models in the current one or saving images containing the task model or part of it so that they can easily included in reports or documents, saving the task model in XML format to easily export it in other environments.
- *to simulate the cooperative task model,* this is useful both in the development of the model and once the result is satisfying, as an interactive documentation of design decisions.

The tool gives also some useful statistical information on the task model: number of levels and of basic tasks, number of iterative and optional tasks, number of tasks for each category (the category of a task indicates how its performance is allocated, to the user or to the application or to their interaction), number of occurrences of each operator used to describe the temporal relationships.

When there are mistakes in the specification detected by the tool it is possible to select one error and then automatically the tool highlights the related part of the specification.

4. AN EXAMPLE OF SESSION USING CTTE

In this section we consider a use case [4] concerning the interaction between a Customer and a Sales Representative to describe how to build the relative cooperative task model associated by using our tool. We first introduce the use case and then we discuss how the tool can be used to develop the related task model.

A Customer visits the Web Page of a Sales Organisation and enters his name and/or Customer ID in order to get in contact with a Sales Representative of the Sales Organisation. The system identifies the Customer and links this customer on-line to the appropriate Sales Representative. Once the connection is established, both the Customer and the Sales Representative can communicate about a shared object via a chosen communication channel, which is in this case a 'chat' program. The shared object is a Draft (for a Sales Order). It is not known beforehand whether this Draft can be converted into a Quotation or an Order, since this depends on the wish of the Customer.

The goal of the Sales Representative is to identify the needs of the Customer, make a sound deal on price and delivery dates and finally be able to convert a Draft into a Quotation or an Order. The goal of the Customer is to get the correct products just in time at the right place, and for a good price.

The Sales Representative has access to the appropriate data for selling products, while the Customer can only see or enter data that is provided by the sales organisation/or sales person. In fact, the Sales Representative's task of entering the Draft is the basis of the co-operation with the Customer. During the interaction, the Sales Representative and the Customer are totally free in determining the order of entering the data, although only one value can be entered at a time.

The Customer's wishes are the basis for the actual working order, while the Sales Representative has all the 'power' on the task's functionality. When the Customer and Sales Representative agree on the Draft, the Sales Representative can trigger the conversion of the Draft into a Quotation or an Order. There is also a possibility for the Sales Representative to save the Draft temporary for later conversion.

Next to the 'standard' situation of having the Draft as basis of the cooperative interaction, there is also the possibility to interact about a Quotation or an Order as shared object between Sales Representative and Customer. In these cases, the Sales Representative opens these objects. The Sales Representative can only edit the Quotation attributes and convert the Quotation into an Order.

Once the tool is started it is in "single user" modality. In this case we can build only Task Models without cooperative behaviour. By selecting the "Cooperative mode" option in the "Tools" menu we are able to starting a new cooperative Task Model.

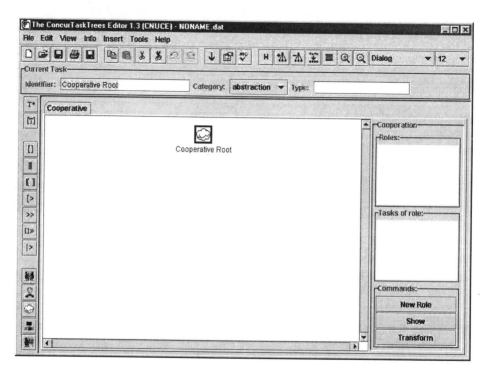

Figure 2. The CTTE tool in Cooperative mode.

In Figure 2 we can see CTTE, in cooperative modality, at the beginning of a session. Initially designers have only the Cooperative Tab Panel associated with the Cooperative part of the global task Model. The designer can either start to model the cooperative part or the task model associated with the roles involved in the application, "Sale Representative" and "Customer" in our example. In the latter case s/he has to select the "New Role" button in the "Commands" panel.

We prefer to start to build the task model associated with the two roles of the use case that we consider in our example, and during this developing phase switch to the "Cooperative" part to insert cooperative tasks involving multiple roles whenever we identify a need for their inclusion.

To explain how to build a generic task model associated with a role we can consider the "Sales Representative" role.

From the textual representation of the use case we identify the main tasks of the role considered and we start to insert them in the tree structure (for example, *Receive message, Manage Draft, Mange session, Manage conversion*). We can insert a new task in the tree structure as sibling, child of parent of the current task selected. We can insert a temporal relationship between task siblings representing the temporal order among them (for example, the salesman transforms a draft int a quotation only after that s/he receives an explicit request from the customer). The current task is identifiable because it is represented with a blue frame around the corresponding icon indicating the category of the task. The insertion can be made by the drag and drop feature from the category icon visible in the left side of the editor main window to a generic task visible in the tree. How the new task is inserted depends on where the cursor is when dropping the icon of the selected task.

It is possible at any time to switch to the view of the task model associated with another role or the cooperations part. The tool provides standard editing operation: it is possible to copy, cut and paste a task sub tree or a task selected, it is possible to undo and redo operations if the designer makes mistakes. It is also possible to move a single task (mouse left button) or a sub tree (mouse right button) in the work area to enhance the layout of the tree view. It is possible use the "Justify" features, zoom operations or unfold a sub tree to reduce the space used to draw the tree structure when the task model reach big dimensions. For each task, designers can specify some additional information not provided during the development of the tree structure. For example, they can provide a textual description of the task useful to describe more in details the task features, the task type, the task frequency and specify the objects used to perform the task and the relative actions. The tool can specify if a task of a specific role is involved in a cooperative task annotating it with a blue double arrow under the task name. Figure 3 shows the tool during the developing of the task model corresponding to the use case considered.

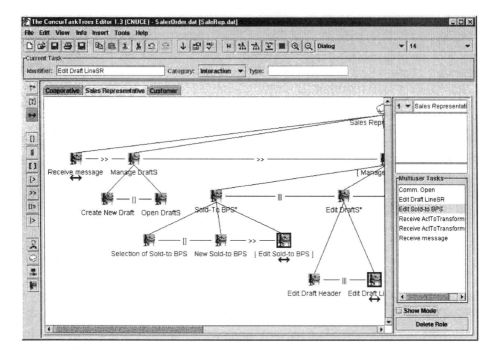

Figure 3. The CTTE tool in an advanced state of task model developing.

To build the cooperative part of the task model we have to select the "Cooperative" tab panel. Once we have identified some tasks part of cooperative tasks for each role (task with blue double arrow) it is possible to group them with the relative temporal constraints in the cooperative part. To prevent designers from making mistakes during this phase and to help them to find rapidly the task involved in cooperations, the tool shows the list of all tasks involved in cooperation belonging to each role.

Figure 4 shows the task model relative to the cooperative part. The tool allows designers to browse the complete task model. There is the possibility to interactively select a basic task in the cooperative part and then ask an automatic presentation (by the "Show" button) of the single user task model where that task occurs. There is also the automatic check of correctness to identify some mistakes in the Task Model structure. For example, if some temporal operators are missing or if in the cooperative tree designers have not specified all tasks part of a cooperative task that have been indicated in the task models associated with each role (or vice versa). Moreover, some semantic errors in the temporal relationship can be detected: for example, it is not possible to have an iterative task followed by the enabling operator (infinite cycle that would never enable the next task).

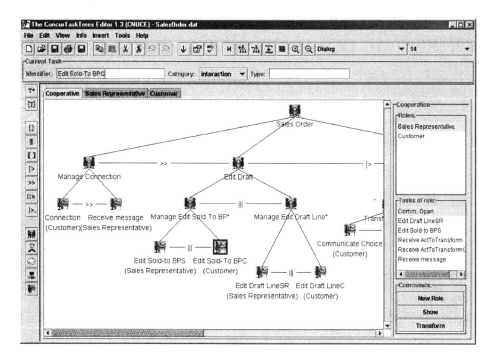

Figure 4. The specification of temporal constraints in the cooperative part.

5. SIMULATING COOPERATIVE TASK MODELS

Some simulators for task models have already been proposed [3]. However, they have mainly been developed for single user task models whereas multi-user application would particularly benefit from them. The resulting behaviour of an interactive cooperative application can be difficult to precisely understand without any support because it is the result of various parts interacting with each other. Thus, some tool support to simulate the behaviour of the cooperative task model can give additional information and allows the designer to check that the specification models the desired behaviour. Such a support can also be useful to discuss with other persons (such as end users) how tasks can be performed in an application so it is also a useful additional interactive documentation.

In our environment, when the simulator is activated there is a panel on the right side listing the tasks enabled. These are the tasks whose preconditions are satisfied and that are ready to be performed, according to the task model. In the central area the designer can interactively select one part of the overall task model and the tool presents the related hierarchical structure with temporal operators. Enabled tasks are highlighted by specific frames.

The designer can interactively select one of the enabled tasks and asks the simulator to perform it, then the simulator updates the state of the task model and shows an updated list of enabled tasks. It is possible to know also what the active tasks are. An active task is a high level task that has at least one subtask performed and has not been completely terminated. In this manner designers can see if the behaviour of the task model built satisfies their expectations. If the behaviour is different with respect to that expected designers can stop the simulation at any time and change the task model structure of a particular role or the cooperative part.

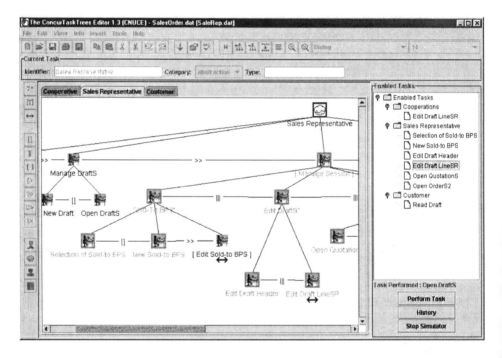

Figure 5. The Task Model Simulation in action.

The tool gives also the possibility to store the history of tasks performed during a simulation. This is a high-level indication of a scenario supported by the task model considered. That can be executed again also on a different task model for example to check whether it is able to support it. At any time the designer can stop the simulation and move to the editor to modify the original task model if it has shown some limitations or errors.

In Figure 5 we can see the Task Model Simulation in action. Once simulation is started the list of the enabled tasks appears at the right side of the main window of the tool. So at any time we can see which are the tasks enabled to be performed.

6. CONCLUSIONS

In this paper we have discussed how it is possible to help designers during the development of task models of cooperative applications and their analysis. In particular, we have focused on how to model cooperative applications in ConcurTaskTrees and the support that can be obtained by CTTE, the relative automatic tool. The tool described (the editor and the simulator of cooperative task models) is publicly downloadable at http://giove.cnuce.cnr.it/ctte.html.

We now plan to use our environment to support the design and development of ERP applications and to develop an empirical study for better evaluating the support that our tool gives to designers and developers.

ACKNOWLEDGMENTS

We gratefully acknowledge support from the GUITARE R&D Esprit Project (http://giove.cnuce.cnr.it/guitare.html) and comments from Marnix Klooster.

REFERENCES

[1] Biere, M., Bomsdorf, B., and Szwillus G., *Specification and Simulation of Task Models with VTMB*, Proceedings CHI'99, Extended Abstracts, ACM Press, New York, 1999, pp.1-2.

[2] Bodart, F., Hennerbert, A., Leheureux, J.-M., and Vanderdonckt, J., *A Model-based approach to Presentation: A Continuum from Task Analysis to Prototype*, in F.Paternò (ed.), Interactive Systems: Design, Specification, and Verification, Springer Verlag, Berlin, 1995, pp.77-94.

[3] Bomsdorf, B. and Szwillus G., *Tool Support for task-Based User Interface Design*, Proceedings CHI'99, Extended Abstracts, ACM Press, New York, 1999, pp.169-170.

[4] Breedvelt-Schouten, I., *Guitare Use Case*, Requirements and Use Case for CSCW-ERP, GUITARE Project Working paper, 1999.

[5] Calvary, G., Coutaz, J., Nigay, L., *From Single-User Architectural Design to PAC*: a Generic Software Architectural Model for CSCW*, Proceedings CHI'97, ACM Press, New York, 1997, pp. 242-249

[6] Card, S., Moran, T., and Newell, A., *The Psychology of Human-Computer Interaction*, Lawrence Erlbaum, Hillsdale, 1983.

[7] Hartson, R. and Gray, P., *Temporal Aspects of Tasks in the User Action Notation*, Human Computer Interaction, Vol.7, pp.1-45.

[8] Paternò, F., *Model-Based Design and Evaluation of Interactive Application*, Springer Verlag, Berlin, 1999, ISBN 1-85233-155-0.

[9] Paternò, F., Breedvelt-Schouten, I., and de Koning, N., *Deriving Presentations from Task Models*, Proceedings EHCI'98, Creete, Kluwert Academic Publisher, September 1998.

[10] Paternò, F. and Mancini, C., *Developing Adaptable Hypermedia*, in Proceedings of ACM Symposium on Intelligen User Interfaces IUI'99, ACM Press, New York, 1999, pp. 163-170.

[11] Puerta, A., Cheng, E., Ou, T., Min, J., *MOBILE: User-Centred Interface Building*, in Proceedings of ACM Conf. on Human Aspects on Computing Systems CHI'99, ACM Press, New York, 1999, pp. 426-433.

[12] Roseman, M. and Greenberg, S., *Building Real-Time Groupware with GroupKit, A Gropware Toolkit*, ACM Transaction on Computer-Human Interaction, Vol 3, n°1, March 1996, pp. 66-106.

[13] van der Veer, G., Lenting, B., and Bergevoet, B., *GTA: Groupware task analysis - Modelling complexity*, Acta Psychologica, Vol. 91, 1996, pp.297-322.

Chapter 22

METHODOLOGICAL AND TOOL SUPPORT FOR A TASK-ORIENTED DEVELOPMENT OF INTERACTIVE SYSTEMS

Anke Dittmar and Peter Forbrig

University of Rostock, 18051 Rostock, A.-Einstein-Str.21, Germany

Summary. In this paper, a model-based approach is introduced which allows beginning with the development of task and domain models a semi-automated generation of prototypes of user-interfaces.

1 Introduction

There are a lot of methods in order to support the design of more usable interactive systems ranging from more technical specification methods like [2], [4], or [1] to task analysis methods, such as ADEPT [8] and MUSE [5].

However, many methods consider only a few aspects of system design. In this paper a broader model-based approach is introduced which demands the modelling of users tasks and of the environment in which they act now and in the future. Based on these models the requirements for the interactive system can be derived and stored in an application and a dialogue model. Dialogue models allow a semi-automated generation of user interface prototypes. Thus, a participation of users in the early design steps is facilitated.

2 The Design Process

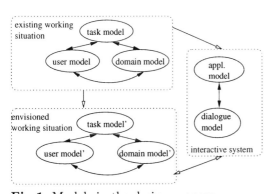

Fig.1. Models in the design process

We want to emphasize that the design and introduction of new interactive software is not only a technical problem. It can change the whole working situation. The approach distinguishes between the existing and the envisioned working situation as the situations before and after the introduction of the designed interactive system.

271

A thorough analysis of the existing situation is necessary to make reasonable suggestions for the envisioned one, and in particular for the interactive system. The results of the analysis and design step are described in the formal models visualized with their relationships in Fig.1. The participation of users is not directly visible in the models but in the design process itself which has to be seen as an argumentative process (e.g. [7]).

3   Models in Use - An Overview

A *task model* gives an impression of how people act to achieve certain goals. It describes both the hierarchical structuring of user tasks into subtasks and possible orders of subtasks to perform a task (sequential task structure). The environment in which a user has to act is described in an object-oriented *domain model*. It contains classes with attributes and methods and relations between them. Concepts like inheritance, association and aggregation well-known from object-oriented analysis and design methods (e.g. [6]) can be used. The *user model* refers to some characteristics of the people working together to fulfil tasks (e.g. roles they have to play).

There are several relations between the models in use. For example, within the context of a task an object (as an instance of a class in the domain model) can be considered as an artifact or a tool. The term *artifact* is used to refer to parts of the environment which are intended to be changed by performing a task, a *tool* refers to things which are intended to be used during task execution. A goal of a task can be expressed by a state of the involved artifact.

The suggested approach is a unified strategy of structured and object-oriented ideas. Hence, the design process is to be seen as a loose order of specification activities and mutual adaptation procedures in and between the different models. We think that this combination of modelling techniques is more natural and can contribute to better models.

4   How to get User Interfaces ?

Users perform tasks by applying tools to artifacts. How is this basic assumption reflected by interactive software ? The only thing a user can do is to input some data and to get some output of data. In fact, it is a specific feature of interactive systems that things we want to manipulate share the same media with things we have to use for that purpose. A mapping of concepts like task, tool, and artifact to appropriate concepts of a user interface specification is needed. In this approach the task dependent parts of user interfaces are specified by using *dialogue models* ([3]) consisting of *navigation graphs* and *processing dialogues*. A node in a navigation graph represents a (dialogue) view. Each view has three special attributes defining its activity, visibility, and manipulability and can represent a senseful context for a task or similar tasks and related objects of the domain model. We do not support an auto-mated grouping of subtasks into views. This decision is left to the designers. The edges of a navigation graph model sequential and concurrent transitions between views. In many cases the type of a transition can be derived from the sequential task structure. Dialogue views are refined to *processing dialogues* containing the *dialogue forms* data input, function call, navigation, and data output as abstractions. The leafs of a task tree (basic tasks) are mapped to function calls, non-basic tasks to navigations, a representation of the state of an application object to data output and domain knowledge users need to control the task execution to data input. Temporal relations between task model and constraints to object behaviours define temporal relations between dialogue forms. A stepwise semi-automated generation process as illustrated in Fig.2 can supply prototypes of user interfaces.

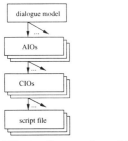

Fig.2. Generation of UI

In the first generation step the dialogue model is transformed to a set of *abstract interaction objects* (AIOs) which are transformed in the second step to *concrete interaction objects* (CIOs). AIOs and CIOs are described by terms of algebras. The process is controlled by rules of a knowledge base. In the last step the CIOs are translated in a script of an existing UIMS (e.g. ISA-Dialog Manager) as the final prototype. The stepwise transformation has several advantages.

For example, it is easier to change the UIMS. An enrichment of a user interface description on various abstraction levels is possible by applying the knowledgebase and by inputs of the designer.

5 An Example

A short example illustrates only some aspects described above. It has to be designed a 'bibliography management system' (BMS) for a research group which allows the members access to all references used in the group. As a constraint the users do not want to change their text editors (Latex and Word

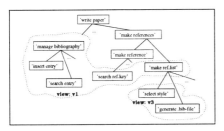 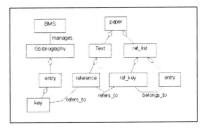

Fig.3. Parts of the task and the domain model

Fig.4. UI prototype

in this case). Fig.3 visualizes parts of the models of a possible envisioned working situation for Latex-users. We concentrate on the subtasks 'manage bibliography' and 'make references' which are mainly influenced by an intended use of the BMS. Views v1 and v2 are sketched for the development of a navigation graph. In Fig.4 a possible prototype is to be seen.

6   Conclusion

The design of an interactive system has to start with a precise analysis of the existing situation. The results can be used in the design process to develop both the application core and the user interface of the software system which has to be embedded in the envisioned working situation. We consider design processes as activities which have to involve not only software developers but also users. Prototypes of user interfaces are generated semi-automatically by stepwise refinement on the basis of abstract dialogues. In the future some improvements are possible. For example, dialogue pattern could be studied in more detail for the generation process of user interface prototypes .

References

1. H. Balzert. From OOA to GUIs: The JANUS system. *Journal of Object-Oriented Systems*, (2):43–47, 1996.
2. D. deBaar, J. Foley, and K. Mullet. Coupling Application Design and User Interface Design. In *CHI'92 Human Factors in Computing Systems*, pages 259–266. ACM, 1992.
3. T. Elwert and E. Schlungbaum. Dialogue Graphs - A Formal and Visual Specification Technique for Dialogue Modelling. In J. C.R. Roast, editor, *Formal Aspects of the Human Computer Interface*. Springer Verlag, 1996.
4. C. Janssen, A. Weisbecker, and J. Ziegler. Generating User Interfaces from Data Models and Dialogue Net Specifications. In *INTERCHI'93 Human Factors in Computing Systems*, pages 418–423. ACM/IFIP, 1993.
5. K. Lim and J. Long. *The MUSE Method for Usability Engineering*. Cambridge University Press, Cambridge, 1994.
6. J. Rumbaugh. *Object-Oriented Modeling and Design*. Prentice Hall, 1991.
7. S. Shum. Design Argumentation as Design Rationale. *The Encyclopedia of Computer Science and Technology*, 35, 1996.
8. S. Wilson, P.Johnson, C. Kelly, J. Cunningham, and P. Markopoulos. Beyond Hacking: A Model-Based Approach to User Interface Design. In *HCI'93*, pages 418–423, 1993.

Chapter 23

MODELING WORK: WORKFLOW AND TASK MODELING

Hallvard Trætteberg
Dept. of Computer and Information Sciences, Norwegian University of Science and Technology
7491 Trondheim, Norway
E-mail: hal@idi.ntnu.no
Tel : 73 59 34 40- Fax : 73 59 44 66

Abstract   In this paper, we motivate integration of workflow and task modeling, present
               and compare workflow and task modeling concepts and suggest benefits of
               integrating them. We show how a workflow model can be utilized when mod-
               eling the tasks of a workflow participant and propose that task enactment can
               be a practical result of workflow and task model integration..

Keywords: End User Programming, Programming by Demonstration, User Interface, Ap-
               plication Extension.

1.   INTRODUCTION

An organization's IS must support work being performed at three levels: the organizational, group and individual levels. *Workflow* modeling languages are often used for describing the former two, while *task analysis* and task modeling are used for describing and formalizing that latter. The boundary, however, is blurred and in this paper we look at integration of workflow and task modeling *language* and *model*s, having the following hypotheses:

- At the *language* level, workflow modeling concepts can be used for task modeling.
- At the *model* level, workflow models can provide a useful context for task models.

- At the *enactment* level, an integrated approach to workspace design and user interface execution may result in better human workplaces.

Section 2 will introduce important workflow concepts and interpret them in the context of task modeling. Section 3 will show how workflow models might influence task modeling. In section 4 turn to how an integrated machinery for workflow enactment and user interface execution might benefit the end user.

2. ASPECTS OF WORK AND ITS DESCRIPTION

Marshak [2] identifies four dimensions for describing work: the *action structure*, the *actors* that perform the work, the *tools* that are used and the *information* (sources) that are needed. These concepts are presented below and exemplified in Figure 1. The **action** is the building block for actions structures. An action is enabled by certain implicit and explicit pre-conditions, e.g. the availability of necessary information. The pre-conditions of an action may depend on other actions, giving a dependency structure. Dataflow, explicit pre-conditions and control flow are used to define *necessary* constraints on action sequences, while speech acts[3] based on institutionalized dialog patterns, gives more *restrictive* pre-conditions and constrained action sequences. Composite actions and action hierarchies help to reduce complexity. Actions can be abstract, by defining the external characteristics and leaving the internals unspecified.

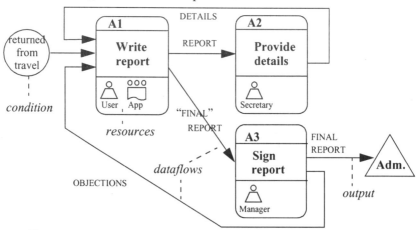

Figure 1. Write travel report workflow: USER must write a report upon return from a travel, supported by the SECRETARY and MANAGER roles and a software tool (APP) that we want to design. USER interacts with the others to fill in details and gather and respond to objections.

Task interpretation The action concept corresponds to the task concept, and the action hierarchy to the task/subtask structure. At the model level, we believe low-level work-flow actions may correspond high-level tasks. Most task modeling languages are based on explicit sequencing primitives. Hence, it is not explicitly expressed whether a sequence is due to necessary (e.g. data flow) or social conditions.

Actors are the intentional beings performing the actions. Technically, actors can be viewed as resources with certain characteristics and abilities that are required by the actions. By listing the needed characteristics, like rights and abilities, actions implicitly define who can perform them. Sets of actors can be defined extensionally, by listing their members, or intentionally, by defining their common characteristics, giving **groups** and **role**s, respectively. An actor can be part of several groups and play several roles, although not necessarily for all actions or in all contexts.

Task interpretation The actor and group concepts correspond to users and user groups, which refer to concrete individuals, while roles' counterpart are user stereotypes. The former tow is typically used when describing current practice, while the latter is introduced when there is a need for more than a single "generic user".

Objects are the material, mental or representational things that actions are performed on, as well as useful contextual information used by actors. The objects granularity and detail can be from whole databases and documents to records and words.

Task interpretation Most task models assume there is a model of the domain or the application data, that task are defined in terms of. As for workflow, the level of formality and detail may vary, although it is common to use object oriented or similar models with concepts, relations and attributes. We expect workflow objects, if further detailed to a relevant level, to be directly usable in task models.

A **tool** is a kind of resource, which in workflow models typically are applications or components. A tool can be concrete application like 'Eudora' or abstract like 'email client'. In addition, tools can be composite by listing several applications (classes) or components in a suite or referring to the suite as a whole, e.g. 'Internet access tools'.

Task interpretation Tools are software elements supporting the performance of actions, which at the granularity of user tasks correspond to *dialog elements* or *user interface objects*. The tool concept provides the link from the *specification* of the user interface functionality to the user interface *design* elements providing it.

Table 1 summarizes our analysis of the *action*, *actor* and *tools* concepts, indicating their correspondences with and opportunities for task modeling. The ontology or metamodel for task modeling presented in [4] seems to support our analysis. Paterno's ConcurTaskTrees [5], embodies the idea that co-operation and coordination can be handled by including a level above individual task models, which is consistent with our view.

3.   WORKFLOW AND TASK MODELING

Our suggested integration of workflow and task modeling languages is based on the idea that workflow and task models essentially describe the same domain, but at different levels. By using the workflow model as a context for the task modeling, we should gain two important advantages: 1) The relevance of the task structure should be ensured, since it is motivated by organizational goals. 2) In addition to using the low-level actions as the top-level tasks, most of the elements of the task model, like roles, information and tools are already identified.

Table 1. Workflow and task modeling concepts.

Generic	Abstract	Composite	Task interpretation
Action: basic unit of work, data flow or speech act based	Delayed definition, action template parameter	Provides hierarchical composition, also called process, job, activity	Task, task/subtask hierarchy • Data availability defines necessary pre-conditions • Work practice as additional constraints
Actor: intentinal beings performing actions	**Role:** Intentionally defined set of actors, based on actor characteristics	**Group:** Extensionally defined set of actors	User, user group, stereotype • Multi-user task models • Multiple work practices • Design targeted at different user groups
Tool: software supporting actions	Application class	Application suite, integrated components	Dialog element • Links spec. and design • Task based enactment • Component composition

The APM[1] example in figure 1 illustrates our point. USER performs one low-level action, A1, which can be used as the top-level task. The three ways of starting and resuming this task, are defined as sub-tasks, as shown in Figure 2. The data initiated tasks are decomposed into tasks for sending, receiving and handling the relevant information. We see that the workflow model can provide both initial task model elements and opportunities for further refinement. The communication task suggests that communication tools should be included in the design.

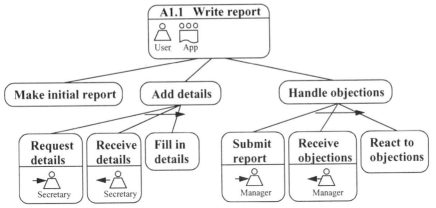

Figure 2. Task model for USER based on the workflow model example.

4. CONCLUSION AND FURTHER WORK

We have shown that Marshak's four dimensions[2] for describing workflow have natural correspondences in the task modeling domain. Suggestions for how these can be used in task modeling have been presented, and we how shown how a workflow model can be used as a context and starting point for a task model. A strong motivations for workflow modeling is the process enactment In moving from modeling to enactment, the tool resources of the actions must be refined. At some point, workflow enactment will have to be in terms of tasks and the supporting user interface elements, and this *task enactment* is an exiting direction for further research. This requires the ability to reference the dialog elements indirectly through the task dimension and motivates a stronger coupling between task and dialog models.

REFERENCES

[1]   Carlsen, S., *Action Port Model: A Mixed Paradigm Conceptual Workflow Modeling Language*, in Proceedings of CoopIS - Cooperative Information Systems '98.

[2]   Marshak, R.T., *Workflow: Applying Automation to Group Processes,* in D. Coleman (ed.), "Groupware - Collaborative Strategies for Corporate LANs and Intranets", Prentice Hall, 1997, pp. 143-181

[3]   Searle, J.R. and Vanderveken, D., *Foundations of Illocutionary Logic,* Cambridge University Press, Cambridge.

[4]   Van Welie, M., Van der Veer, G.C., and Eliëns, A., *An Ontology for Task World Models,* in P. Markopoulos & P. Johnson (eds.), Proceedings of the 5th Eurographics Workshop on Design, Specification and Verification of Interactive Systems DSV-IS'98, Springer-Verlag, Vienna, pp. 57-70.

[5]   Paternò, F., Mancini, C., and Meniconi, S.: *ConcurTaskTrees: A Diagrammatic Notation for Specifying Task Models,* Proceedings of Interact '97, Chapman & Hall, London, 1997, pp. 362-369.

Chapter 24

A GENERIC FRAMEWORK BASED ON ERGONOMICS RULES FOR COMPUTER AIDED DESIGN OF USER INTERFACE

Christelle Farenc and Philippe Palanque
L.I.H.S., Université Toulouse I, Place Anatole France, F-31042 Toulouse Cedex, France
E-mail:{farenc, palanque}@univ-tlse1.fr

Abstract   Ergonomic rules are supposed to help developers to build UI respecting human factor principles. Unfortunately, studies carried out with designers show that guidelines are difficult to apply at design time. The difficulties encountered by designers is mainly due to the structuring of the guidelines and the way they are formulated. This is due to the fact that, at the origin, ergonomic rules were dedicated to people with skill knowledge in cognitive science and ergonomics. At present time these rules are widely available and developers want to use them. This paper presents a method for structuring ergonomic rules in order to make them usable by developers. This method can be used for any set of ergonomic rules and is applied on an example

Keywords: Ergonomic rules, usability evaluation.

1.   INTRODUCTION

Incorporating Human Factors in the development process of interactive systems has been the corner stone of human computer interaction research for many years.

One possible way for such an incorporation is an explicit use of Human Factors expressed in terms of ergonomic rules. These ergonomic rules (also called guidelines, human-computer interaction principles, design rules or maxims) correspond to the explanation of the ergonomic knowledge dedicated to interactive systems.

Ergonomic rules are numerous and distributed among different sources: recommendation papers [1], design standards (e.g., [2]), style guides which are specific to a particular environment (e.g., [3]), design guides (e.g., [4], [5]) and algorithms for ergonomic design (e.g., [6]).

An ergonomic rule can be considered as a principle that has to be taken into account for the building or the evaluation of user interfaces (UI) in order to respect cognitive capabilities of users. The scope of these principles is usually not general and vary according to the "context of use" that can be as different as tasks, user models, user environment (organisational aspects),...

An example of taking into account context in ergonomic rules is extracted from [7]: "Give key assignments for frequently used functions in order to take into account the user's level of experience".

Ergonomic rules are supposed to help developers to build UI respecting human factor principles. Unfortunately, studies carried out with designers show that guidelines are difficult to apply at design time:

- average search time for a guideline in a design guide lasts 15 minutes [1];
- about 58% of designers succeed in finding guidelines relevant to their problem [1];
- designers do not respect about 11% of guidelines [8];
- designers experience interpretation problems for 30% of guidelines [8].

The difficulties encountered by designers is mainly due to the structuring of the guidelines and the way they are formulated. Indeed, most of the developers consider a UI in terms of input/output whatever the development methodology used, and thus need to have recommendations structured according to the components used for building the UI. On the opposite, ergonomic rules are expressed in terms of ergonomic criteria, cognitive principles, etc. This discrepancy between ergonomic knowledge expression and developers' needs is at the basis of difficulties found by developers in order to embed this knowledge in UI. This is due to the fact that, at the origin, ergonomic rules were dedicated to people with skill knowledge in cognitive science and ergonomics. At present time these rules are widely available and developers want to use them.

This paper presents a method for structuring ergonomic rules in order to make them usable by developers. Indeed, in order for an artefact to be usable, it must be designed according to the way users use it [9], thus this structuring organises ergonomic rules according to developer's use. The next section of the paper presents the method for structuring ergonomic rules. This method is then applied to build a full evaluation method called Ergoval. Ergoval structures ergonomic rules according to user interface objects. Section 3 describes on a simple example how Ergoval can be used for evaluating the ergonomic of a given user interface. Section 4 presents a discussion about the possibility of using Ergoval for automatic evaluation of user interfaces. The interests and the scope of this automatic evaluation is discussed.

2.   PUTTING ERGONOMIC RULES AT DEVELOPERS' DISPOSAL

The aim of this section is twofold:
- first to propose a set of rules for structuring ergonomic rules in order to make them usable by developers with limited knowledge in ergonomics or cognitive science ;
- then to present an evaluation method Ergoval structured according to the previous rules. Ergoval is dedicated to the evaluation of WIMP user interfaces.

2.1   Rules For Structuring Ergonomic Rules

2.1.1   The first rule

In order to provide information to developers in a way they can handle it, it is mandatory to structure it according to developers' knowledge. The first rule is thus to produce a structure of the knowledge of the developers. The main part of developers' knowledge that can be embedded in ergonomic rules concerns the interaction objects (IO), thus structuring developers' knowledge consists in organising IO.

2.1.2   The second rule

This rule is to use the canvas produced by the first rule in order to structure ergonomic rules. This only corresponds to rephrase and instantiate rules according to the IO structure produce in the previous phase.

2.1.3   The third rule

This rule must be considered at a different level form the previous ones. Its aim is not to organise or structure information but at the opposite to structure the evaluation process in order to provide results that will be usable directly by developers. This means that the recommendations have to concern IO and not any more usability criteria. This rule can be applied directly by interpreting the previous structuring.

These three rules for structuring and using the ergonomic rules can be applied to any set of ergonomic rules. However as stated in rule one, these rules heavily rely on interface presentation and thus the products of these rules cannot be considered as general. For example the same rules cannot be applied for user interfaces with direct manipulation or WIMP dialogue styles.

2.2   The ERGOVAL Method

We have applied this method for structuring ergonomic rules for WIMP interfaces and built an evaluation method called Ergoval. This method is dedicated to the evaluation of Graphical User Interface developed in the Windows environment. The method has been designed according to the rules presented in section 2.1. Other aspects of the method such as evaluation process and implementation optimisation are introduced.

2.2.1   The first rule

We first have to build a representation of the UI in terms of the interaction objects of the norm CUA [3] that we call *the decomposition of graphical objects.*

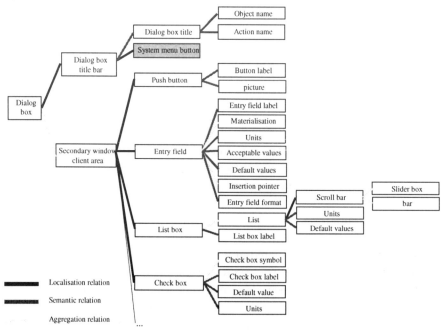

Figure 1. Extract of the structural decomposition.

The inclusion mechanisms is at the basis of this decomposition thus all the objects are linked according to the relation *composed of*. Objects may also entertain other kind of relationships such as: *activation, chaining, aggregation, localisation and semantics*. A subset of the structure of all the IO is presented in Figure 1.

This structure is hierarchical, so greyed out boxes are decomposed in a more precise structure. White boxes correspond to elementary object and thus cannot be decomposed further.

The main principle of building this structure is only to take into account all the interaction objects even though there is no ergonomic rule that can be applied to them. Indeed, this is out the scope of this stage.

It is important to notice that part of the interface will be represented within objects by attributes. For instance, the title of a menu option has an attribute *opening* which value is "..." if a dialogue box will be opened when the option is selected.

2.2.2   The second rule

This stage aims at refining ergonomic rules according to the IO structure built at the previous stage. Thus each ergonomic rule is associated to a set of IO. As input we have gathered ergonomic recommendations coming from different research work that can be found in the literature: [5], [10], [11].

These recommendations were selected according to two main criteria:
- a good level of accuracy i.e. these recommendations are refined enough and are thus close to IO,
- a good covering of the various elements involved in ergonomic expertise, namely: the diversity of objects involved: lexical, syntactic, pragmatic, semantics, levels and ergonomic design principles. As for the pragmatic level, only guidelines that do not require in-depth analysis of the task were incorporated. However, this is only due to the fact that automation of the evaluation is considered. Otherwise, such rules would have been introduced.

All the ergonomic rules have been reformulated (and can be found in [12]) according to the IO structure. This reformulation process consists in:
- *finding all the IO* of the decomposition that are concerned by the ergonomic rules;
- *verifying that ergonomic recommendations are not redundant*. This verification is very important as ergonomic recommendations come from different guidelines;

- *verifying that ergonomic recommendations are not conflicting.* Conflicts only occur when high level rules are considered. When refinement is done (for example by clarifying context) conflicts are removed.

2.2.3   The third rule

As this rule concerns the evaluation process, we have decided (in the Ergoval method), to define another knowledge structuring. All IO concerned by the same set of recommendations are grouped together into classes of objects: *the typology of graphic objects.*

2.2.3.1   Optimisation problem

This typology has been done by grouping (in classes) all the objects that are interested in the same set of rules. The resulting typology consists in several levels of abstraction, the graphical objects being the leaves of this typology. Fig. 2 presents an extract of this typology. The entire typology can be found in [12].

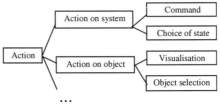

Figure 2. An extract of the typology.

The links presented in Figure 2 are *types of* links which have hierarchical properties, i.e. each type inherits attributes from the parent type and associated rules. In this way, the *action on system* type inherits attributes from the *action* type and the *command* type inherits attributes from the *action on system* type.

An object may belong to several types. For instance, an object icon-button (called *graphic key* in the CUA terminology) belongs both to the *command* and *choice of state* types and therefore inherits attributes from those types. By structuring objects and rules it this typology allows:
- to reduce the design deviation search time - all rules associated to types to which the object under evaluation does not belong are not explored;
- the completeness and cohesion of the base to be improved by matching types to rules;
- at implementation level the maintainability of the rule base to be increased, particularly by reducing the number of rules to be implemented - rules are only implemented once, at the highest possible level of abstrac-

tion of the typology, and are then inherited by lower level graphical objects.

As far as the development of the rule base is concerned, it is assisted by the typology which offers two entry points - graphical objects and ergonomic recommendations.

2.2.3.2 Implementation

In order to make implementation of the rule reformulated by the rule 2 easier we have defined a new implementation structure called the *table of transformed ergonomic rules*.

For each recommendation examined, the table contains:

- the *design criterion* or criteria to which the ergonomic rule relates;
- the *object type or object* concerned by the ergonomic rule;
- the *attribute* to which the ergonomic rule relates;
- the *reference value* of the attribute;
- if necessary, the *context* for applying the ergonomic rule.

The attributes of both object types and objects, define all the evaluation variables. The reference values of the attributes are derived from ergonomic recommendations and may be numeric, boolean or symbolic.

2.2.3.3 Evaluation procedure

The Ergoval evaluation procedure consists in two sequential tasks:

- preparing the evaluation process which consists in gathering general information on the evaluation context (stage of development of the software, hardware and development environment, etc.) so as to limit the applicable knowledge field to relevant information;
- the evaluation process itself based on the identification of design deviations - i.e. interface design options which do not adhere to the ergonomic recommendations.

The evaluation process consists in the following stages, relating to the various stages of the reasoning of the ergonomics experts, thus for each IO:

- *Select* the object to be evaluated and the relevant attributes of the object to carry out this evaluation;
- For each rule associated to the IO:
- *Specify1* i.e. to find in the rule base the reference value of the object's attributes;
- *Specify2* i.e. to find on the interface of the application being evaluated the value of the attribute,
- *Compare* to compare the value of the attribute with the reference value for this attribute (a difference in these values indicates an error in the design);

The strategy embedded in the evaluation process presented above is an objcct-bascd strategy which permits in-depth analysis of the interface. However a transversal strategy must be followed in order to apply directly evaluation according to criteria (i.e. criteria whose reference value depends on the value of the attributes of other objects).

3.   ILLUSTRATIVE EXAMPLE

This section fully presents the use of the Ergoval method on an illustrative example. The example chosen is an editor for information about customers stored in a relational database table. This editor allows adding new customers into the database, deleting customers, selecting customers from those already stored and changing their values. The overall look of the interface is shown on Figure 3. Three different areas can be distinguished in that window:
- The editing area, in which the attributes of a selected customer may be edited through the use of standard interface components (radio buttons, simple-line entry field);
- A command zone in which database operations (creation, deletion, etc.) may be launched by clicking on command pushbuttons;
- A scrollable list (list box) shows the customers in the table. Items in this list may be selected by clicking on them with the mouse.

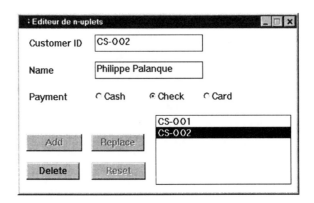

Figure 3. The customer edition window.

Graphical objects to evaluate
The decomposition of the graphical objects is shown on Figure 4. This figure presents a part of the graphical objects hierarchy of a GUI, instantiated according to the objects of the dialog box.

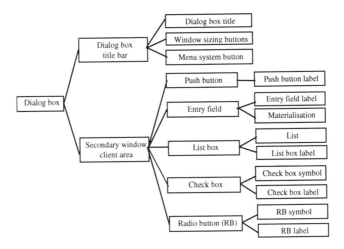

Figure 4. Dialog box decomposition.

3.1   Evaluation

For evaluating the application, we directly apply the evaluation process presented in section 2.2. Thus, the evaluation of the dialog box consists in evaluating all the graphical objects that compose the dialog box. For each graphical object, different rules must be evaluated:

- rules associated to the object type of the graphical object. According to the principle of ergonomic rules inheritance in the « typology », ergonomic rules associated to the object type are those associated directly to the type and those associated to parent-type of the object type;
- rules associated to the graphical object.
- Push button is a *Command* type object, ergonomic rules that must be evaluated are:
- rules associated to Action, Action on system and Command types: R16, R8, R18, R19, R20, R36,
- rules directly associated to push button: R15, R34, R55, R78.

For the list box, no rule is directly associated to this object. As a result the rules that must be verified are rules associated to Action, Information entry, Data entry and Data selection types: R16, R4, R3, R6bis, and R31.

Figure 6 presents the list of ergonomic rules that must be verified for a push button and a list box. The first column shows the graphical object concerned by the rule, the second column specifies whether or not the rule is directly associated to the graphical object The fact that a rule can be directly applied is depicted by a *, the third column presents the number of the rule that is applicable and the last column presents the text of that rule.

Table 1. Ergonomic rules that applied to the graphical objects.

Graphical Object	Direct rule	N° rule	Text of the rule
Push button	*	15	When a push button is pre-selected, this pre-selection must be graphically displayed.
	*	34	Access to push button, radio button, list box, dynamic list box, combination box, dynamic combination box, check box, entry field, menu option, spin button must be possible through a mnemonic contains in their label.
	*	55	If a pull-down option menu. Or push button opens a dialog box an ellipsis (...) must be added to their label.
	*	78	A push button concerning a box or a window must be placed at the bottom of this window. When concerning a specific object it must be placed on the right of this object.
		8	Any unavailable command or choice of state must be greyed.
		16	Any user action on a IO must be graphically displayed.
		18	Any command must have a visible result.
		19	When the result of a process activated by a command is displayed in more than 2 seconds and less than 6 seconds the mouse pointer must become a waiting pointer (hourglass, clock).
		20	When the result of a process activated by a command is displayed in more than 6 seconds a progress indicator box must be displayed
		36	When a command might lead to loss or modification of data or to a long process a message box requiring confirmation of the command must be displayed (warning message).
List box		3	If the data to be entered (typed or selected) consists in measures, units must be displayed.
		4	Any time data must be entered (typed or selected) by the user or restituted by the system, the nature of this data must be indicated by a label.
		6bis	When a default selection is displayed by the system, this selection must be relevant for the user.
		16	Any user action on a IO must be graphically displayed
		31	Any time data must be entered (typed or selected) by the user or rendered by the system, the unit displayed must be the one commonly used by the user.

The complete evaluation of the dialog box needs the evaluation of 85 ergonomic rules. This important number proves that it is necessary to automate this evaluation.

Besides, the evaluation of the dialog box shows that it is not possible to evaluate it using only its static presentation as several rules concern the behaviour of the dialog box. For example rule 45bis "dialog box, message box, progress indicator must have non-sizable window borders." This rule can not be verified only using the presentation part of the dialog box.

Finally, we observe that ergonomic rules are not always a good help for the development of UI. For example rule 99: "In a set of radio buttons, a radio button must be default preselected." This rule does not specify which button is to be selected by default.

The result of the dialog box evaluation correspond to the list of non respected rules:

- For the *dialog box*, rules 45bis and 45ter are not respected: a dialog box must have non-sizable window borders because some IO can disappear when the dialog box is resized. Moreover, the dialog box must not have window sizing buttons (CUA norm).
- For the *push buttons*, rules 34 and 36 are not respected: it must be possible to select a push button using shortcuts. When an element of the database is deleted, this action must be confirmed by the user in a warning message box.
- For *radio buttons*, rules 34 and 99 are not respected: mnemonics must be supported on radio button labels and one of these radio buttons must be preselected.
- For *check box and entry field*, rule 34 is not respected.
- For *check box label*, rule 50 is not respected: this label must be placed on the right of the check box symbol.
- For *the Secondary window client area*, rules 14bis, 33bis and 42 are not respected: push buttons must be horizontally aligned and the dialog box must contain a Cancel push button and a Help push button.

4. DISCUSSION

The example presented in the previous section shows that the evaluation process is very precise and can be time consuming when applied to a with large scale application. For these reasons we have considered the possibility to make the process as automated as possible. The main difficulty is to collect in an automated way the values of the graphical objects. Thus we have considered several ways for gathering this information: to use software spies; to exploit resource files; to analyse the source code. The advantages and disadvantages of each option are explained in [14].

Another limitation of using automated tools is that only a subset of all the rules defined in the Ergoval method can be exploited. Indeed, information related to the pragmatic level (related to context or tasks) cannot be collected automatically. We have shown in [13] that only 78% of the rules implemented in Ergoval can be evaluated in an automated way. The tool for automated evaluation has been built [13] but we are now considering and interactive tool for allowing evaluators to enter pragmatic information that cannot be automatically found by the tool. Another extension of this work is to use ergonomic rules in a proactive way together with a formal notation during the design phase [14].

REFERENCES

[1]   Smith, S.L., *Standards Versus Guidelines for Designing User Interface Software*, in Handbook of Human-Computer Interaction, M. Helander (ed.), North-Holland, Amsterdam, 1988, pp. 877-889.

[2]   ISO/WD 9241, *Ergonomic requirements for Office Work with Visual Displays Units*, International Standard Organization, 1992.

[3]   *IBM Common User Access Guidelines, Object-Oriented Interface Design*, Document SC34-4399, IBM Corp. Publisher, 1993.

[4]   Scapin, D.L., *Guide ergonomique de conception des interfaces homme-ordinateur*, Research report INRIA N°77, INRIA, Le Chesnay, 1986.

[5]   Vanderdonckt, J., *Guide ergonomique des interfaces homme-machine*, Presses Universitaires de Namur, Namur, ,1994, ISBN 2-87037-189-6.

[6]   Bodart, F. and Vanderdonckt, J., *On the Problem of Selecting Interaction Objects*, in Proceedings of HCI'94 (Glasgow, 23-26 August 1994), Cambridge Univ., Cambridge, 1994, pp. 163-178.

[7]   Alonzo, *Ebauche d'une méthode de conception orientée tâches pour une interface de contrôle aérien*, INRIA Report, 1994.

[8]   De Souza, F. and Bevan, N., *The Use of Guidelines in Menu Interface Design: Evaluation of a Draft Standard*, in Proceedings of INTERACT'90 (Cambridge, 27-31 August 1990), Elsevier Science Publishers, Amsterdam, 1990, pp. 435-440.

[9]   Norman, D.A., *The psychology of everyday things*, Harper and Collins, 1988.

[10] Smith, S.L. and Mosier, J.N., *Guidelines for designing user interface software*, Report EDS-TR-86-278, The MITRE Corporation, Bedford, 1986.

[11] Bastien, C. and Scapin, D. L., *Critères ergonomiques pour l'évaluation des interfaces utilisateurs: définitions, commentaires, justifications et exemples*, Research report INRIA, November 1991.

[12] Farenc, C., *L'évaluation Ergonomique des Interfaces Homme-Machine*, PhD thesis, January 1997.

[13] Farenc, C., Liberati, V., and Barthet, M.F., *Automatic Ergonomic Evaluation: What are the Limits?*, in Proceedings of 2nd Int. Workshop on Computer-Aided Design of User interfaces CADUI'96, Presses Universitaires de Namur, Namur, 1996, pp. 159-170.

[14] Farenc, C., Palanque P., and Bastide R., *Embedding Ergonomic Rules as Generic Requirements in a Formal Development Process of Interactive Software*, in Proc. of 7th IFIP Conf. on Human-Computer Interactop, INTERACT'99 (Edinburgh, 30 August – 3 September 1999), A. Sasse and Ch. Johnson (eds.), IOS Press, Amsterdam, 1999, pp. 408-416.

Chapter 25

CMF: A COHERENT MODELLING FRAMEWORK FOR TASK-BASED USER INTERFACE DESIGN

Birgit Bomsdorf and Gerd Szwillus
Universität Paderborn, FB 17, Fürstenallee 11, D-33102 Paderborn, Germany
{kne, szwillus} @uni-paderborn.de
Tel : +49 5251 60-6624

Abstract　　User interface design should be strongly guided by the user's tasks to be executed with the system. One practical way of achieving this is the explicit support of the transition from task modelling to dialogue modelling. Here, the integration of the models plays a central role. The models to be used are still under discussion and the adoption of their meta-models becomes an increasing requirement of tools supporting task-based user interface design. To cope with these aspects and as a first step towards modelling explicit links between task models and dialogue models we propose a theoretical modelling framework, called *Coherent Modelling Framework CMF*, supported by a general modelling tool. This framework can house task models as well as dialogue models, thus integrating them and enabling a smooth transition between the two. In fact, the approach is even more general, covering virtually any type of discrete modelling structure. The approach covers the single models, allows expressing links between the models, and enables the designer to modify the meta-models, i.e. the models describing the models used. In this paper we discuss the modelling framework and briefly describe a proof-concept-version of a tool supporting it.

Keywords:　　Modelling framework, task-based design.

1.　　INTRODUCTION

Task-based user interface design is based on the analysis and modelling of the user's tasks, and the transfer of the information gained to the user interface design process. To cope with the various aspects a lot of different models are used. In task modelling, for instance, there exists a variety of dif-

293

ferent approaches using different elements of modelling; however, hierarchical task structures, temporal relations, pre- and post-conditions, and task objects are elements used almost everywhere. A similar situation with an even richer variance applies to user interface modelling.

As the single models are already complex enough in themselves, let alone their mutual dependencies, tool support is essential for enabling the designer to cope with the models and the links between them. Actually, tools to support task-based design are still non-existent, or currently under development. There exists limited support for task modelling in tools such as *Euterpe* [13] and the *Visual Task Model Builder* [1,2], but these tools do not support the transition to the dialogue model. On the other hand, model-based approaches dealing with this transition (a lot of examples can be found in [7]) are strongly oriented towards the future dialogue in the user interface, and thus restricted to the non-creative and more technical part, suitable for immediate generation purposes. There are indeed cases where design decisions can systematically be transferred from one model to the other - in these cases tool support can substantially help in the process. Transferring knowledge from one model to another, however, is generally accepted as a highly creative and complicated process, founded primarily on the designers' experience [12]. Ultimately, a powerful tool should ease tedious or mechanical parts [4], with the possibility to influence the degree to which parts are automatically generated [9, 14].

Two approaches of ongoing work deal with explicit links between different models. Within the VISTA system [5], links between hierarchical task models, UAN-models, and abstract data models can be established; the approach is only used, however, to visualise and document the links. Within TADEUS [10] a task is seen more technically, functional-oriented, as an algorithm is entered for every task which is then used for generation of a running system.

If task-based user interface design is to be supported, the different models must be **integrated** within a tool. The models themselves must be specified, together with links between models from the same design phase, as well as links between models from different design phases. Currently, a discussion is going on as to which models are to be supported at all. Additionally, special design situations (e.g. special application areas) necessitate the customisation of the models used. Given this situation, a general tool supporting various models and their integration should enable the designer to define the ontology of the models (i.e. the terms, elements, concepts, and relations used within the models) to be used.

In this paper we propose the integration of models on the basis of the *coherent modelling framework CMF*. CMF is defined formally and is used as a theoretical foundation, as well as the underlying basic structure for implementing tool support for this approach. CMF was created following three basic modelling requirements:

- Support and integrate all models needed within the single design phases.
- Support the integration of models from different design phases.
- Support modelling of meta-models for any design phase.

The result of CMF-based modelling is the creation of one big integrated model containing the single models as submodels. A first version of a tool supporting CMF, provides basic editing and display capabilities, allows the creation of arbitrary, flexible views on the integrated model, and contains sophisticated navigation methods.

2. CMF: THE COHERENT MODELLING FRAMEWORK

To allow the integration of different models, we define a formal framework, which allows the specification of single models and their interrelations within one coherent model. Such a model can contain elements, which can be any thing of our awareness, for instance a task or an object modified by a task, and relations e.g. between a task and an object. In analogy to the concept of object orientation, the model explicitly supports the basic concepts classification, generalisation, specialisation and aggregation.

2.1 Elements and Relations

The underlying structure principle is represented by a non-directed graph, referred to as *ERG* (Element-Relation-Graph), as it contains two types of nodes, namely element nodes and relation nodes. In Figure 1 an abstract representation of a small part of an ERG is shown, denoting that a task is carried out in a special situation resulting in a new situation. In all figures of this paper only subparts of the whole graph are shown. Actually, they are interrelated by relation nodes and edges integrating them into one coherent ERG.

Elements, such as Task, TaskEvent and TaskState are represented as round nodes; *relations*, such as pre_sit and post_sit are depicted as rectangles. If an element plays a *role* in a relation this is depicted by a connection between the element node and the relation node, with the name of the role given as inscription of the edge. Hence, in Figure 1 for example, Task plays the role of a process while TaskState plays the role of a state in the relation pre_sit representing a situation. TaskEvent takes an event-role only in a pre-situation as a task event defines a noteworthy change in state causing an actor to perform a task.

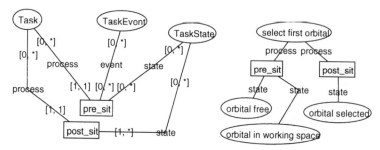

Figure 1. General description of a task.   *Figure 2.* Example description of a task.

Additionally, we can specify quantitative properties of relations. The cardinality specification between an element node and the role name defines how often an instance of the element can play the given role. As an example, the specification of [0,*] says that for every task no or an arbitrary number of situations can be defined. The second cardinality specification constrains the number of the given roles in the relation. The specification [1,1] at the process-edges, for instance, limits the number of the process-role linking a pre_sit node to a task-node to exactly one, i.e. each situation should be modelled for exactly one task. The cardinal numbers [0,*] at the state-edge, however, define that for every pre_sit relation no or an arbitrary number of states can be defined.

In Figure 2 an application of this general task description is shown. This example is taken from a project we are currently working on. The objective of this project is to implement an editor for constructing molecular structures in 3D. The pre-situation of the defined task select first orbital is characterised by the two states orbital free and orbital in working space while the post-situation consists of the state orbital selected.

The ERG allows arbitrary relations to be specified within the graph. Additionally, important basic relations, such as *classification* (clas), *specialisation/generalisation* (s/g), and *aggregation* (agg) are predefined. These have well-defined semantics and can be used to structure the models.

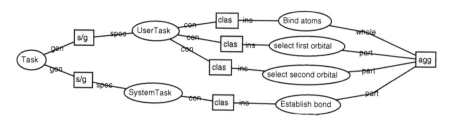

Figure 3. Basic relations.

CMF: A coherent modelling framework for task-based
user interface design
297

In the ERG of Figure 3, for instance, on the left it is shown that UserTask and SystemTask are specialisations of Task. The semantics imply, for instance, that UserTask is defined by pre_sit and post_sit relations, even if this is not specified for UserTask but for Task shown in Figure 1. The clas relations defines Bind atoms, select first orbital (already introduced in Figure 2) and select second orbital to be user tasks and Establish bond to be a system task, i.e. functionality provided by the system. By the agg relation, select first orbital, select second orbital and Establish bond become subtasks of Bind atoms. All graphs depicted in Figure 1 to 3 are different subparts of the whole even bigger ERG describing a general task and its application.

2.2   Concepts and Relations

An important property of the ERG is its capability to describe its own structures. This property is based on the distinction between *concepts* and *instances*. A concept describes properties of a set of "things", while an instance of this concept is one individual "thing" of that sort. In terms of object orientation this corresponds to the difference between an object type and object instances. As we describe here a more general approach, we stick to the terms *concept* and *instance*. Both concept and instance nodes are represented as elements in the ERG; the instantiation relation between the two is expressed by a clas relation in the graph. In the ERG of Figure 3 the element select first orbital   is defined as an instance of the UserTask concept. As such, situations can be defined for it, as this is specified for the concept UserTask, which is a specialisation of the concept Task. Figure 2 shows, that this is indeed the case. To summarise, the relations an instance (e.g. select first orbital) has to fulfil are defined by the specification of relations defined for its related concept (e.g. UserTask).

In general, the neighbouring nodes of a concept node define the pattern of relations, all its instances must fulfil. The cardinal numbers given with the roles (not shown in the figure) contain additional information about **how many** element nodes with certain roles need to be linked. In consequence, this means that the ERG describes its own substructures.

3.   META-MODELLING

The decision to model the distinction between a concept and its instances in a very general way in the ERG opens the possibility to incorporate models on arbitrary abstraction levels. The ERG in Figure 4 shows different abstraction levels, denoted as L1 to L3 and visually separated through the dotted lines. On level L1 the structure of a general, predefined meta-kernel-model (MKM) of task and dialog models is defined - the figure shows only a part of the complete specification. Level L2 shows specific task and dialogue models. The task model is the one we used in the 3D-project; the dialogue model is based on the dialogue specification notation ODSN [11] - again only small and simplified parts of the models are shown. On level L3 these are instantiated to an application-specific task and dialogue model.

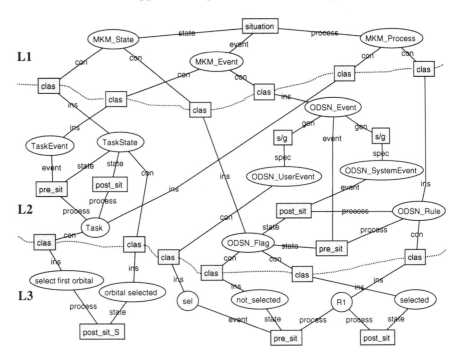

Figure 4. Meta-Modelling within CMF.

Based on the self-description property, a concept level defines, how the instance level "below" has to be built. The relation between concept and instance, however, is relative to the viewpoint: In Figure 4, L2 contains instances of concepts defined on level L1. The L2-elements, however, are used as concepts for the instances on level L3. Hence, every level defines the meta-model of the level below, which implies that all the concepts and relations defined in the meta-model can be used in the related instance level. For example, on level L1 the meta-kernel-model defines the situation relation between MKM_Process, MKM_Event and MKM_State in a very general way.

Both the task model and the dialog model are instances of the MKM. Hence, all elements and relations defined by the MKM can be used, i.e. instantiated, to specify the meta-models of a task and dialogue model. In the

figure this is shown for the situation example. The relations pre_sit and post_sit
are specialisations of the situation relation. Specialisations of relations are also
described by means of the ERG but not discussed in this paper. Hence, on
level L2 the elements Task and ODSN_Rule are linked to pre_sit and post_sit relation nodes - but used differently. The meta-task model corresponds to the
one in Figure 1. Using the language ODSN the designer describes the behaviour of a dialogue using production rules. The meta-model of ODSN defines the left and right side of rules by means of situation relation, stating that
both sides can consist of flags denoting states - defined by the state edge.
Additionally, at the left side of a rule the designer can define events which
can be either a user or an internal system event. At the right side, however,
only system events are allowed. Level L3 shows example applications of the
task and ODSN-model. This small example shows how the MKM elements
and relations can be used to specify different models, e.g. the task and
ODSN model. In the same way the ERG can specify other meta-task and
meta-dialogue models leading to different concepts for describing domain
specific task and dialogue models on level L3.

4.   INTEGRATION BY LINKS BETWEEN MODELS

4.1   Models and Meta-Models

Every model, apart from the top level model, owns "its" meta-model, describing its construction principles. The links between the levels are defined
through classification relations (clas). In Figure 4 it is shown that a task
model as well as a dialogue model are instances of the MKM. As a consequence, there must exist an initial, universal start-ERG, which provides elementary concepts for the whole modelling process. This graph, however,
contains only general modelling concepts, which are not dedicated to a special field, such as task modelling or dialogue modelling. Instead, it defines
the basic modelling concepts, such as the concepts element and relation, of the
CMF framework in general.

4.2   Structure and Behaviour

Within task modelling and within dialogue modelling the developer has
to specify the structure of the objects as well as their dynamic behaviour.
Both aspects are highly interrelated to each other. In an ERG these depend-

encies are described by relation nodes linking element nodes of the "static model" to element nodes of the "dynamic model".

Figure 5 shows examples of static-dynamic-link descriptions within the ODSN model and instances of it. In ODSN a flag describes state information of an object; this is specified in the example by a state_info relation. The executed relation between the element nodes ODSN_Object and ODSN_Rule specifies each rule to be executed by an object. By means of these concepts at the next level R1 and the flag selected are linked to the object Orbital. In the same way aspects of the structure and of the behaviour described in the task model are linked, e.g. by the relation use in Figure 6.

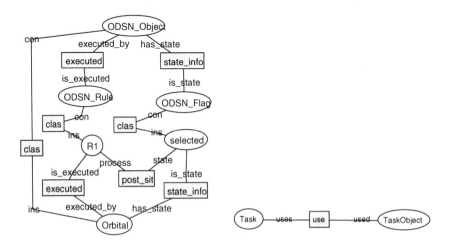

Figure 5. Linking structure and behaviour   *Figure 6.* Structure-behaviour-link
within the dialogue model   within the task model

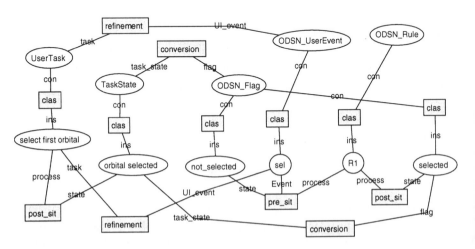

Figure 7. Linking task model and dialogue model

4.3   Task Model and Dialogue Model

To meet the requirements implied by the task model necessitates explicit decisions by the designer of which and how elements and relations of the dialogue model relate to the elements and relations of the task model. Within an ERG these interrelations are introduced by means of relation nodes on the level of the meta-models linking the concepts of a task model and a dialog model to each other. In Figure 7 one can see, for instance, that UserTask is linked to ODSN_UserEvent while TaskState is linked to ODSN_Flag. Hence, on the instance level user tasks are refined into user events, e.g. select first orbital into sel, and task states are converted to flags, e.g. orbital selected to selected. In this examples the concepts are related to each other very directly. However, in an ERG elements cannot only be converted to other elements but also linked to relations, which is not discussed in this paper.

5.   TOOL SUPPORT FOR CMF

Already the size of the models under consideration is a problem in itself – enforced by the integration of several models into one even bigger model. In a practical situation, where task model and dialogue model are combined within CMF, this contains the application-specific task model, object models, dialogue model, their corresponding meta-models, and the even more general meta-kernel-model. Hence, tool support is essential for this approach to be applied successfully to a realistically sized project.

The underlying concept of the undirected graph was chosen as a universal and powerful basis for modelling structures, as it provides easy access to view definition and navigation procedures. Technically spoken, this functionality is based on the construction of subgraphs and paths through the graph structure. The ERG is not intended to be visualised directly to the user, for example as shown in the figures above. We use these visualisations within this paper to explain the principles of CMF only. Within a tool based on CMF more sophisticated representations are needed.

The first tool version we created to support CMF incorporates three different views, referred to as template, tree, and map view respectively. Using the **template view** (see Figure 8), the user can inspect, modify and link single elements of the model; however, one can not get an overview of link structures or hierarchies; templates provide a very local view. **Tree views** are used to display structures such as task hierarchies or object hierarchies. The display looks like the well-known tree structures as used for representing e.g. file system hierarchies, and provides the commonly applied techniques of folding subtrees and drag-and-drop-operations for tree manipulation. **Map views** show concrete views of arbitrary substructures which can be modified according to the different meta-models defined in the ERG; also, in map views the physical representations of nodes and edges can be modified by the user. As shown in Figure 8 the representation of a map results in a graph structure - which is not identical with but visualising the underlying structure of the ERG.

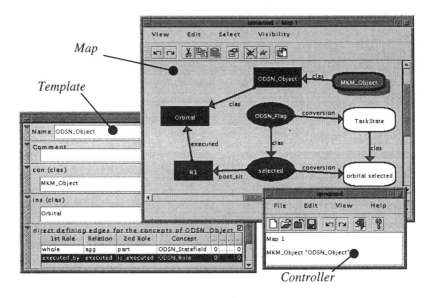

Figure 8. First version of a tool supporting the CMF.

All views can easily be called from each other. Based on the graph structure the user can navigate not only within one map, but also freely between several maps and other views; he can inspect single elements via templates, and their positions in hierarchies with tree views. Hiding and showing operations only influence the visual representation, not the underlying ERG. At any time as many views of any type may be opened and visible as the user likes. This helps him in getting an individual, customised view on the model. Real editing operations on the graph are reflected immediately in all open views. To handle the multiple window situation a controller providing a window list is available.

The views allow the typical editing operations, such as inserting a new node as instance of a given concept, inserting relations between existing nodes, deleting of nodes and relations, and renaming. As these operations are available on all levels of the model with the model containing the meta-level as well. This implies that the meta-model can be manipulated in the same way. The core part of the initial starting graph can not be modified, as some of the semantics had to be hard-coded; apart from that, however, the designer has complete freedom to redefine the models he wants to use. Modifying the meta-model is as easy as modifying the application-dependent models themselves. When introducing completely new concepts these get a standard representation first; this can then be modified as needed.

6.   DISCUSSION

Our approach can be considered to be model-based. Our goal, however, is not the generation of user interface design from the specified models, but to support the creative transition from task model to dialogue model. Some parts of this effort might be good candidates for an automated process; we think, however, that it is more important for the designer to be able to keep track of links within and between models.

The underlying ERG is a formal system; the information stored, however, is not formalised - hence, our approach can be considered to be semi-formal in its nature. In other work [1,2,3,4,] we follow the idea of early testing of task models, hence, we add formal semantics to task models, and then execute them. The two approaches should and will grow together in the future. In the resulting tool we will also incorporate transformation rules for the links between the task model and the dialogue model supplying them with concrete semantics. Hence, in contrast to VISTA [5], within the executable system the links will be used to test a dialogue model in the context of its task model.

The self-description concept allows the coherent specification of models and meta-models within a single structure. Subgraphs are used as "construction rules" for other parts of the same graph. This principle allows for highly flexible modifications of the models and their "language", i.e. the meta-models. Our approach is similar to others dealing with meta-models but in contrast to e.g. KOGGE [[6]], it takes arbitrary numbers of levels of meta models into account. ConceptBase [[8]], though dealing with unlimited levels of meta-models, treats transitions differently, and is oriented towards support for software-engineering models in general. In contrast to this, CMF allows more complex transformation rules between different models, i.e. crossing meta-layers and consisting of a sub-graph of its own. Additionally, we explicitly focus on task models and dialogue models and the transition between them.

The underlying ERG is basically a flat graph structure. Technically, it is implemented as a structure of nodes and edges, with "higher" structures being introduced as interpretation rather than as implementation basis. This enables highly flexible view and navigation operations. The basic modelling relations, such as classification and aggregation, are treated like all other relations in the model. This also enables the easy addition of new relations.

The first version of the tool we implemented showed the feasibility of the approach. Especially, we wanted to prove that an editor enabling the designer to work with several models and their meta-models in an integrated way, can be built. Hence, we concentrated first on the support of the underlying CMF structures, and then on implementing the three representations mentioned in this paper. Ongoing work will improve the interface, the representations, and the visualisation techniques of the tool. We plan to implement more sophisticated visualisation techniques, such as fish eye views, lens techniques, or additional layout algorithms, to deal more efficiently with large models.

REFERENCES

[1]   Biere, M., Bomsdorf, B., and Szwillus, G., *Visual Task Model Builder*, in this Volume, 1999.

[2]   Biere, M., Bomsdorf, B., and Szwillus, G., *Building and Simulating Task Models with VTMB*, CHI'99 Extended Abstract, ACM Press, New York, 1999, pp. 1-2.

[3]   Bomsdorf, B. and Szwillus, G., *Early Prototyping based on Executable Task Models*, CHI'96 Conference Companion, ACM Press, New York, 1996, pp. 254-255.

[4]   Bomsdorf, B. and Szwillus, G., *From Task to Dialogue: Task-Based User Interface Design: A CHI'98 Workshop*, SIGCHI Bulletin, Vol. 30, No. 4, 1998, pp. 40-42.

[5]   Brown, J., Graham, N., and Wright, T., *The Vista Environment for the Coevolutionary Design of User Interfaces*, in Proceedings of the ACM Conference on Human Aspects in Computing Systems CHI'98, ACM Press, New York, 1998, pp. 376-383.

[6]   Carstensen, M. and Ebert, J., *Ansatz und Architektur von KOGGE, Projektbericht 2/94* (in German), Universität Koblenz-Landau, Institut für Softwaretechnik, Koblenz, 1994.

[7]   *Computer-Aided Design of User Interfaces*, Proceedings of the 2nd Int. Workshop CADUI'96, J. Vanderdonckt (ed.), Presses Universitaires de Namur, Namur, 1996.

[8]   Jeusfeld, M.A. and Johnen, U.A., *An executable meta model for re-engineering of database schemas*, in Proc. of Conf. on Entity-Relationship Approach ER'94, Manchester, December 1994.

[9]   Puerta, A., *Issues in Automatic Generation of User Interfaces in Model-Based Systems*, in [7], pp. 323-325.

[10] Stary, C., *Task- and Model-Based Development of Interactive Software*, in Proc. of IFIP'98 World Congress, Vienna, 1998.

[11] Szwillus, G., *Object-Oriented Dialogue Specification with ODSN* (In German: Objektorientierte Dialogspezifikation mit ODSN), in Proc. of Software-Ergonomie '97, Dresden, Germany, 1997.

[12] *Task Analysis for Human Computer Interaction*, Diaper, D. (ed.), Ellis Horwood, 1989.

[13] van Welie, M., van der Veer, G.C., and Eliens, A., *Euterpe: A Task Analysis Environment*, http://www.cs.vu.nl/martijn/gta/

[14] Wilson, S., *Reflection on Model-Based Design: Definitions and Challenges*, in [7], pp. 327-333.

Chapter 26

TOWEL: REAL WORLD MOBILITY ON THE WEB

Simon Harper, Robert Stevens, and Carole Goble
University of Manchester, Oxford Road, Manchester M13 9PL, UK
E-mail: {sharper, crstevens,cgoble}@cs.man.ac.uk
Tel: +44 (0)161 275 61{38,95} - Fax: +44 (0)161 275 6236

Abstract   The 'Towel' project seeks to find solutions to problems encountered by both visually impaired and sighted users when travelling in the World Wide Web. Drawing similarities between real-world travel metaphors of visually impaired people and web-based travel metaphors of both visually impaired and sighted people, enhances an understanding of the problem and therefore enables solutions to these travel problems to be more easily identified. By likening web-travel to real-world travel in terms of mobility, navigation, orientation, and mapping, and by fitting web-travel into a real-world travel framework a number of similarities can be identified, and problems characterised. These problems have solutions in the real-world and so these real-world solutions may be of use in addressing web-based travel problems.

Key words: Visually Impaired, WWW, Mobility, Travel, Navigation, Orientation, Adapt-ability, Tools.

1.   INTRODUCTION

Browsing the World Wide Web (WWW) can be a complex and difficult task, which is further complicated if the user happens to be visually impaired because the richness of visual navigational cues presented to a sighted user are not appropriate or accessible to a visually impaired user [16].

Web browsing and searching suggests a degree of travel as well as reading, and while there are a number of WWW Browsers that support the reading task for visually impaired people, few support the task of travelling around a page, a web site or indeed the WWW in general. Many such browsers are concerned with the 'sensory translation' of visual information to

305

auditory information, and are not concerned with enhancing web mobility [15]. In a survey, carried out by email, a marked difference can be seen between the navigational speed of sighted users and that of visually impaired users when asked to perform a series of navigational tasks using the 'Internet Movie Database' as the reference site. This survey illustrates how a major part of the www experience, namely movement within a page, from page-to-page and site-to-site, is unsupported in many browsers.

Research already undertaken suggests that these issues need to be addressed with regard to all web users and not just visually impaired people [15]. Current research divides movement through the Web into landscape metaphors [7] and path metaphors [12]. It is however asserted here that such a separation is unhelpful as real world travel is accomplished with no such segregation.

It is then the aim of this paper to apply holistic real world travel task metaphors encountered in the blind mobility field to web based mobility as it is believed that there are a number of similarities between the tasks and problems encountered in both. It is thought that this transfer from the real to the web-based world will enhance the discourse on travel through the WWW and therefore provide novel solutions to the problems faced by all web travellers, and particularly those with a visual impairment. These solutions would include tools to aid the design and integration of travel components into web design methodologies to aid mobility based on these real world metaphors. They would also include a degree of adaptability in the user interface to enhance the provision of mobility components based on the incoming information.

2. MOBILITY PRIMER AND TERMINOLOGY REFERENCE

Many important lessons can be learnt from knowledge gained in assisting visually impaired travellers in real world situations. This knowledge can be applied to both visually impaired and sighted web travellers.

Travel can be thought of as the whole experience of moving from one place to another regardless of whether the destination is known at the start of travel or if the journey is initially aimless. In this context a successful journey is one in which the desired location is easily reached. Conventionally, travel or mobility can be separated into two aspects, those of Navigation and Orientation [6].

- Orientation – can be thought of as knowledge of the basic spatial relationships between objects within the environment [1]. It is used as a term to suggest a comprehension of a travel environment or objects that relate to travel within the environment. How a person is oriented for travel is crucial to successful travelling. Information about position, direction, desired location, route, route planning etc. are all bound up with the concept of orientation.

* Navigation – in contrast, suggests an ability of movement within the local environment [11]. This navigation can be either by the use of pre-planning using maps or fore-knowledge, or by navigating 'on-the-fly' and as such a knowledge of immediate objects and obstacles, of the formation of the ground (holes, stairs, flooring etc.), and of dangers both moving and stationary are all required.

3.   EGOCENTRICITY

Because navigation entails some form of mapping and knowledge storage, an understanding of how information is stored and processed in the brain can be useful in mobility research. Cognitive or mental mapping is an abstraction of the real world, covering the mental abilities that allow us to collect, organise, store, recall, and manipulate information about the spatial environment and real world surroundings [10]. In the context of travel, this means everyday spatial environments. Thus information is stored to make sure navigation is possible, ('how to get there'). In addition, other cognitive knowledge is used to discover 'where to go' [8].

There are additional features of mobility by visually disabled people that are pertinent to web travel. These features mainly relate to cognitive mapping and how visually impaired people mentally visualise the world, and as such are useful for inclusion in any mobility model as feedback can be tailored to enhance these mental visualisation characteristics [10]. Many visually impaired people have a tendency to think of the real world in a 'egocentric' manner, such that descriptions of distance and journey become associated with the traveller and not the environment [10]. A sighted person may say "walk to pedestrian crossing and then continue on to the bank" where as a visually impaired person may say "walk 20 metres ahead, then from the tactile surface walk 10 metres to the North West of that position and you are at the Bank". It can be seen that the specification of distance and direction is far more exacting and the traveller relies on a limited amount of external information to reach the destination. Visually impaired travellers also break their journey into shorter stages and orientate themselves within the journey a greater number of times. On average a visually impaired traveller orientates themselves every 40 metres compared to a sighted travel who does so every 100 metres. The mental maps created by visually impaired travellers therefore have a tendency to be egocentric, exact, and divided into smaller more manageable steps. Tailoring feedback to enhance these traits would therefore enhance the mapping process for visually impaired (and sighted) travellers [10].

4.   PARALLELS BETWEEN REAL WORLD MOBIL- ITY FOR WEB MOBILITY PROBLEMS

4.1   Preview and Probing

In real world blind mobility, a lack of preview of upcoming information is one of the major issues to be addressed. Consequently, this preview is supported by both electronic and non-electronic means and travel aids range from the conventional cane and long cane through to laser obstacle detectors. However, in all cases the travel aid performs a 'probing' task such that a limited amount of preview is given [5]. This amount is limited because in travel experiments complex information was found to not be easily assimilated by non-visual means and therefore too much information was found to be as unhelpful as too little [4].

In a web-mobility context, the lack of previews of both upcoming hyperlinks and information relating to movement on the web page itself suggests that some degree of 'probing' must be implemented so that a limited preview can be obtained [15]. Indeed if a user is observed traversing the web, they can be seen to select a hyperlink, preview the contents (by clicking or placing the caret over the link to see the destination) and return if the contents are not applicable. This probing is continued until each hyperlink is previewed, and interesting contents are found [9]. Therefore, too much information may be the presentation of the entire page, when probing, and too little may be the presentation of just the hyperlink.

4.2   External Memory

Blind mobility solutions exist to accomplish obstacle avoidance and are based on both enhancing preview (as described above), planning to avoid obstacles through knowledge of the environment (orientation), and on navigating oneself around obstacles based on a knowledge of ones orientation within that environment [13]. Planning[1] to avoid obstacles suggests a certain knowledge of an end goal to be achieved, while this is true in many cases it is not always known at the outset and related travel information may be used in transit as the goal becomes more evident. These problems are addressed in

[1] In real world mobility.

blind mobility by the provision of electronic or tactile maps, by using knowledge gained from previous travellers of the area (similar to a guide-book) [2] or by the provision of information points giving complex informa-tion about an area, and by in-route guidance systems such that location within an area is pin-pointed to a finer or courser granularity [3].

This is also the case in web mobility where a search for a specific goal may be instigated at the outset or where a user may choose to browse with-out much idea of a goal until well into browsing. Therefore, to find and avoid obstacles (like Feints - options that are not available can be thought of as obstacles) encountered 'on-the-fly'. A web traveller, therefore needs some form of preview. They also need to be supplied with fore knowledge of an area, or be supplied with it in-route, and have some knowledge of ones ori-entation within an environment. These obstacles like feints, graphics, and frames may also change with the context and task being performed, a graphic while an obstacle in the context of information searching, may be useful as a marker in the context of navigation.

4.3   Cueing

Orientation or 'where-ness' (detecting cyclic behaviour, direction and distance) is important in blind mobility as it enables travellers to navigate with some degree of accuracy. However, problems exist for visually im-paired travellers, because they do not have the luxury of visual cues to base these judgements on. Therefore, the environment must be updated such that cues are provided in an appropriate manner, giving explicit orientation in-formation such that navigational information can be detected. This is accom-plished using tactile surfaces' or by using audible road signals, and by the placement of specific electronic devices known as 'waypoint' markers [3], so that this explicit information can be given.

The similarities between real-world and web mobility for visually dis-abled people suggests that the provision of some form of explicit, appropri-ate, orientation method (such as waypoint devices) would be an advantage when travelling in the virtual web environment. This would mean that a user can make a choice as to whether they want to be at the current location and if not how to best attempt to get to their perceived destination [16]. Visited hy-perlinks change colour giving a visual cue that is not present when travelling the web as a visually impaired person.

4.4   Feedback

Supporting the general mobility task by providing appropriate explicit feedback, returned implicitly from many objects, is also undertaken by many real world travel aids. This functionality is mainly included as an addition to a travel aid fulfilling a different task. The premise of these additions is that much feedback is implicit and can be assimilated at speed, if the recipient is sighted. This is not the case however, if the recipient has a visual impairment as the cues, and complexity of the cues, often depend on the recipient having vision and being able to assimilate this complex visual information at a fast speed [14]. A long cane is an obstacle detection device that enables a limited tactile preview of upcoming obstacles, however by tapping it against obstacles, auditory feedback is created such that the user has a more complete picture of an object. This multiple feedback is replicated in electronic devices such as the "VA-Bionic Laser Cane" which gives different tones to signify distance and direction. It can be seen that these travel aids provide explicit feedback (sometimes using sound, sometimes speech) such that feedback appropriate to the user is given.

Therefore, when making any web journey an analysis of all implicit feedback should be taken, and this information should be expressed in an appropriate and explicit way so that the general task of movement is supported [16,17]. It should also take into account the natural mental mapping methods[2] for individuals with a visual impairment or sighted individuals with temporarily restricted vision, and be speedily assimilate-able regardless of complexity. Progress bars, moving 'Netscape' graphics, and percentage-loaded notifications all employ visual feedback mechanisms that are not usable by visually impaired people.

5.   PROPOSAL FOR FUTURE RESEARCH

Applying knowledge about real world mobility to web based mobility problems can enhance the travel experience for visually impaired users. Because all users share some of the characteristics of visually impaired travellers when travelling off the viewable area these enhancements can also be applied to sighted users too. The use of egocentric description, accurate journey information, and more frequent orientation points are directly related to the lack of preview found in real world travel, which is also encountered frequently in web based journeys.

By analysing real world travel solutions for visually impaired people, in the context of web travel, a framework can be generated. This framework will enable a critique of web design and design methodologies to be facilitated such that lessons learned with regard to web mobility can be incorporated into design methods and practice. Browsers can then include a mobility

---

[2] As described in the previous section.

model that takes on board these lessons and applies them to web mobility. By doing this, solutions established for visually impaired travellers in the real world are applied to all web travel thereby solving problems faced by all web travellers, sighted or unsighted. It is envisaged that this mobility framework will be practically applied by using a set of XML-DTDs and a browser plug-in to implement the framework once suitably defined such that accurate testing can be accomplished. Tools that automatically enhance the travel information provided in web pages and over web sites can then be created so that any automatically generated output is tailored to fill the spaces in the mobility information left by manually designed output.

REFERENCES

[1]   Bentzen B. L., *Orientation Aids*, in Foundations of Orientation and Mobility, R.L. Welsh et al. (eds.), AFB, 1979, pp. 291-355.

[2]   Blenkhorn P. and Evans D.G., *A System for Reading and Producing Talking Tactile Maps and Diagrams*, in Technology and People with Disabilities, Proceedings of CSUN'94, Los Angeles, 16-19 March 1994.

[3]   Blenkhorn, P. and Evans, D.G., *A System for Enabling Blind People to Identify Landmarks: the Sound Buoy*, IEEE Transactions on Rehabilitation Engineering, Vol. 5, No. 3, 1997, pp. 276-278.

[4]   Blenkhorn, P., Pettitt, S., and Evans D.G., *An ultrasonic mobility device with minimal audio feedback*, in Proceedings of the Twelfth Annual International Conference on Technology and Persons with Disabilities, Los Angeles, March 1997.

[5]   Brabyn J.A., *Mobility Aids for the Blind*, Engineering in Medicine and Biology Magazine, IEEE, December 1982, pp. 36-38.

[6]   Brambring, M., *Mobility and Orientation Processes of the Blind*, in Electronic Spatial Sensing for the Blind: Contributions from Perception, Rehabilitation and Computer Vision, D.H. Warren and E.R. Strelow (eds.), Proceedings of the NATO Advanced Research Workshop on Visual Spatial Prosthesis for the Blind, Lake Arrowhead, Dordrecht, Nijhoff in co-operation with NATO Scientific Affairs Division, 1985, pp. 493-508.

[7]   Chen, C., *Structuring and Visualising the WWW by Generalised Similarity Analysis*, in Proceedings of the Eighth International ACM Conference on Hypertext and Hypermedia, ACM Press, New York, 1997, pp. 177-186.

[8]   Collins, C.C., *On Mobility Aids for the Blind*, in Electronic Spatial Sensing for the Blind: Contributions from Perception, Rehabilitation and Computer Vision, D.H. Warren and E.R. Strelow (eds.), Proceedings of the NATO Advanced Research Workshop on Visual Spatial Prosthesis for the Blind, Lake Arrowhead, Dordrecht, Nijhoff in co-operation with NATO Scientific Affairs Division, 1984.

[9]   Cool, C., Park, S, et al., *Information Seeking Behaviour in New Searching Environments*, in Integration in Perspective, P. Ingwerson and N. Ole Pors (eds.), Proceedings of CoLIS 2, The Royal School of Librarianship, Copenhagen, 1996.

[10] Dodds, A.G. et al, *The Mental Maps of the Blind*, Journal of Visual Impairment and Blindness, S. Shively (ed.), January, Vol. 76, 1982, pp. 5-12.

[11] Farmer L.W., *Mobility Devices*, in Electronic Spatial Sensing for the Blind: Contributions from Perception, Rehabilitation and Computer Vision, D.H. Warren and

E.R. Strelow (eds.), Proceedings of the NATO Advanced Research Workshop on Visual Spatial Prosthesis for the Blind, Lake Arrowhead, Dordrecht, Nijhoff in co-operation with NATO Scientific Affairs Division, 1984, pp. 357-402.

[12] Furuta, R., Shipman, F.M., Marshall, C.C., Brenner, D., and Hsieh, H-W., *Hypertext Paths and the World Wide Web: Experiences with Walden's Paths*, in Proceedings of the Eighth International ACM Conference on Hypertext and Hypermedia., ACM Press, New York, 1997, pp. 167-176.

[13] Gollege, R.G., *Tactual Strip Maps as Navigational Aids*, Journal of Visual Impairment and Blindness, September 1991, pp. 296-301.

[14] Jaffe, D.L. et al, *Responsive Environment Project – Transparent Navigation Assistant*, in Proceedings of International Conference RESNA International '92, 6-11 June 1992, RESNA, pp. 176-178.

[15] Jones, S. and Cockburn A., *A Study of Navigational Support by Two World Wide Web Browsing Applications*, in Proceedings of the Seventh International ACM Conference on Hypertext and Hypermedia., ACM Press, New York, 1996, pp. 161-169.

[16] Petrie, H., Morley, S., and Majoe, D., *Initial Design and Evaluation of an Interface to Hypermedia Systems for Blind Users*, in Proceedings of the Eighth International ACM Conference on Hypertext and Hypermedia, ACM Press, New York, 1997, pp. 48-56.

[17] Spink, A., *Feedback during Information Retrieval: A Third Feedback Framework*, in Integration in Perspective, P. Ingwerson and N. Ole Pors (eds.), Proceedings of CoLIS 2, The Royal School of Librarianship, Copenhagen, 1996.

Chapter 27

TOOL-BASED SUPPORT FOR USER-DESIGNER COLLABORATION IN DISTRIBUTED USER IN-TERFACE DESIGN AND EVALUATION

Jarmo Sarkkinen

Department of Information Processing Science, University of Oulu
P.O. Box 3000, FIN-90401 Oulu, FINLAND
jarsa@rieska.oulu.fi
Tel : +358 8 553 1979 - Fax : +358 8 553 1890

Abstract   The purpose of this paper is to suggest a tool supporting distributed user inter-face design and evaluation in asynchronous collaboration. First a set of problems is identified related to collaboration tools. One narrative is provided to illustrate a collaboration situation based on the use of the tool. Finally discussion shows how tool-centredness needs to be supplemented by deeper understanding of collaboration in the future studies.

Keywords: Asynchronous collaboration, User interface design and evaluation

1.   INTRODUCTION

A tool presented in this paper is based on a technical solution drawing on so-called tool/technique-centredness. Tool/technique-centredness can be regarded as an approach stressing the use of tools or techniques as the participatory design (PD) school has done (see for example [3] and [6]). The concept of user-centredness was an underlining design idea in constructing the first prototype. To define user-centredness, a few general design principles suggested by the PD school [1] were considered as an eligible outline. In this case one pilot test was carried out to reform the implementation of the prototype, and some improvements were committed as a result of it. Two other tests were also undertaken but improvements are not yet implemented.

As the PD school acknowledges, there is a need for both user and designer knowledge in systems development [1], calling for co-operation based on differentiation and combination of specialities [4]. Based on this view it can be said that one has the skills the others do not have. A set of problems was identified as a result of finding implementations intended to support collaboration between users and designers. Striving for different time/place collaboration is preferred since designers cannot influence users. CARD [3], PICTIVE [3] and PictureCARD [6] techniques share a notable assumption. The use of them calls for physical presence (same time/place) of participants (users and designers). By introducing TelePICTIVE technique, [2] made it possible for participants to collaborate remotely in a synchronous manner (same time/different place). Nevertheless one problem remains. It is still required to gather in a computerised meeting conducted over distance and dictated by a predefined schedule. The aim of this study is to overcome time and space restrictions related to geographically distributed and collaborative user interface design and evaluation (different time/place).

2.   LITE PROTOTYPE: ARCHITECTURE, CHARACTERISTICS AND DESIGN RATIONALE

The architecture of the client/server system unfolds as follows. There is one client (web page browser) used by a set of users. Also there is a server harbouring contents, both functional (Common Gateway Interface script, CGI script) and accessible one for both retrieval done by File Transfer Protocol (FTP) programs and web page browsers. In the case of FTP programs designers handle user feedback as well as transfer or replace World Wide Web (WWW) pages on a server. The use of web page browsers refers to users who evaluate designs proposed by designers. In addition to this, designers utilise email programs in order to inform users about representations to be evaluated.

The user interface (LITE tool) visible for users and especially representational aspect of it merits special concentration. Paying attention only either to formality or information flows cannot be seen as satisfactory in participatory design [1]. When LITE prototype was being built, the principles were concerned. The fabric of the tool was designed so that it pays special attention to use situations.

Through a web page browser users can see a collection of scenarios (task scenarios), each of them describing a sequence of unfolding computerised tasks (use scenarios) presented so that there is an envisioned user performing tasks by using the sketched software. Each of those scenarios is divided into subparts to represent distinct stages in which a user is performing something.

Textual and pictorial versions of a scenario are represented in parallel. Evidently, pictorial representations render users as evaluators more competent to understand textual scenarios. Each of the web pages represents one of the stages of a scenario. Within one web page or a stage of a scenario it is possible to find answers to what, who and why questions (task scenario). User interface questions or details related to screen design correspond to how-to-do questions (use scenario). The use of symbols in underscoring dynamics of representations stems from what was said by [4] about directing attention with embedding cues such as marking particular items or highlighting. In images of pictorial scenarios there are red diagonal strikethroughs stressing that something is not allowed to do, green circles saying something's chosen, black arrows indicating movements as well as blue text sections emphasising recently added text sections. Figure 1 illustrates one of the stages of an example LITE representation.

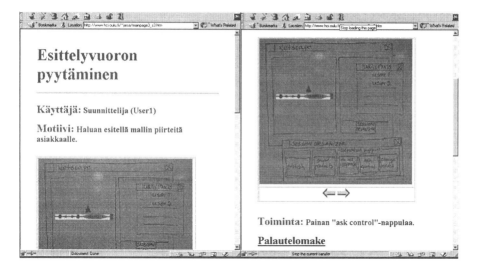

Figure 1. One stage of an example scenario.

Users are provided with links to questionnaires situated right after images so that users can easily shift from scenario representation to the corresponding questionnaire and fill it in with comments on user interface or functionality. It is possible for designers to add to these questionnaires both open-ended questions and fields with explicitly stated questions. Filling in questionnaires done by users and providing users with representations are good means for participants to converge each other or combine their interpretations. There are also some instructions for evaluators as well as the description of a target software to be evaluated in the beginning of scenarios on the main page of the tool.

3.   COLLABORATION OVER DISTANCE - A NARRATIVE

The collaboration in this situation draws on reciprocal interdependence [5] in which designer's outputs can be seen as inputs from the viewpoint of user and vice versa. There are also two other salient concepts in this case. Collaboration can be divided into two stages. First there is a phase in which either designer or user is immersed in completing his/her task based on differentiation [4], having appropriate skills to succeed in it. The other stage lies on combination of participants' skills. In the course of asynchronous user interface design and evaluation, act modes based on differentiation or combination alternate as is illustrated in figure 2 by juxtaposing stages of different kind. Designers are immersed in concretising ideas and proposing tangible proposals whereas users are more competent in comparing and evolving proposals to their work situations.

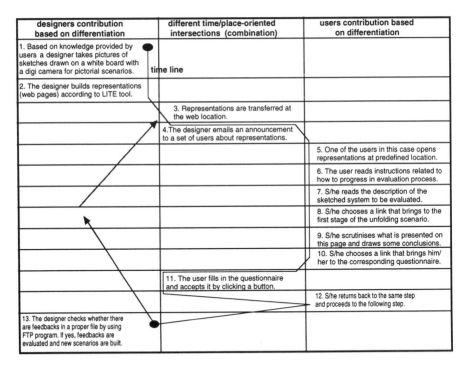

Figure 2. The diagram depicts how collaboration emerges in the case of geographically distributed asynchronous user interface evaluation. The steps 5-12 relate to only one stage in the scenario.

4.   DISCUSSION

Based on one pilot test and two usability evaluations it can said that in terms of usability LITE can be regarded as a possible solution for the presented problem. Nevertheless, only usability aspect from the viewpoint of users is scrutinised. There is an evident need to carry out some field studies involving designers in real design situations having geographically distributed and collaborative settings. In its current implementation, LITE is not integrated in any working protocols. Especially collaboration over distance entails complexity. By providing scenarios like the above-scrutinised narrative, it is possible for us to assess in advance how things unfold in reality, and based on that kind of view, in theory collaboration can be relied on. There is a clear need to study how articulation work between participants actually happens. For example it could be a good idea to make it possible for participants to trace back historically evolved design rationale.

REFERENCES

[1] Ehn, P. and Kyng, M., *The Collective Resource Approach to Systems Design*, in Computers and Democracy, G. Bjerknes, P. Ehn, and M. Kyng (eds.), Avebury, Aldershot, 1987, pp. 17–58.

[2] Miller, D.S., Smith, J.G., and Muller, M.J., *TelePICTIVE: Computer-Supported Collaborative GUI Design for Designers with Diverse Expertise*, in Proc. of the ACM Symposium on User Interface Software and Technology UIST'92, Monterey, 15-18 November 1992, ACM Press, New York, 1992, pp. 151–160.

[3] Muller, M.J., Tudor, L.G., Wildman, D.M., White, E.A., Root, R.W., Dayton, T., Carr, R., Diekmann, B., and Dykstra-Erickson, E., *Bifocal Tools for Scenarios and Representations in Participatory Activities with Users*, in Scenario-Based Design: Envisioning Work and Technology in System Development, J.M. Carroll (ed.), John Wiley & Sons, New York, 1995, pp. 135–164.

[4] Schmidt, K., *Mechanisms of interaction reconsidered*, in Social Mechanisms of Interaction, K. Schmidt (ed.), COMIC Deliverable 3.2, Lancaster, 1994, pp. 15–122.

[5] Thompson, J.D., *Organizations in Action. Social Science Base of Administrative Theory*, McGraw-Hill, New York, 1967.

[6] Tschudy, M.W., Dykstra-Erickson, E.A., and Holloway, M.S., *PictureCARD: A Storytelling Tool for Task Analysis*, in J. Blomberg, F. Kensing, and E. Dykstra-Erickson, (eds.), Proc. of the Participatory Design Conference PDC'96, Cambridge, Massachusetts, 13-15 November 1996, Computer Professionals for Social Responsibility, Palo Alto, 1996, pp. 183–192.

Chapter 28

AN APPROACH OF COMPUTER-AIDED CHOICE OF UI EVALUATION CRITERIA AND METHODS

André Nendjo Ella[1], Christophe Kolski[1], Fabrice Wawak[2], Catherine Jacques[3] and Pascal Yim[4]

[1] *Laboratoire d'Automatique et de Mécanique Industrielles et Humaines*

LAMIH-UMR CNRS 8530, Le Mont Houy, BP 311, F-59304 Valenciennes Cedex, France

{anendjo, kolski}@univ-valenciennes.fr

[2] *Laboratoire I3D, Bat. P2, University of Lille I*

59651 Villeneuve d'Ascq cedex, France

[3] *Centre Lillois d'Etudes et de Recherches Sociologiques et Economique*

CLERSE-URA CNRS 345, USTL, 59655 Villeneuve d'Ascq, and

Institut Fédératif de Recherche sur l'Economie et les Sociétés Industrielles (IFRESI)

2, rue des Canonniers 59800 Lille, France

C.JACQUES@ifresi.univ-lille1.fr

[4]*Ecole Centrale de Lille, LAIL URA CNRS 1440 - BP 48*

59651 Villeneuve d'Ascq cedex, France

yim@ec-lille.fr

Abstract   Interactive system evaluation is the source of many difficulties for human-machine communication specialists as well as for non specialists. The quality of the evaluation depends on many parameters which are often contradictory. A major problem which project managers (and even human evaluators) are confronted with is the choice of criteria and methods appropriate for the evaluation. Given the international context linked with the situation of use, social and cultural aspects must also be considered in certain cases. Our research is oriented towards the design of a Decision Support System (DSS) for computer-aided choice of UI evaluation criteria and methods. It is based on Fuzzy sets. A first prototype is implemented with PrologIII.

Keywords: Decision Support System, Evaluation, User Interface, Fuzzy Sets.

319

1.   INTRODUCTION

For the evaluation of interactive systems, two main families of criteria are often distinguished [15]: they concern (1) pratical acceptability which comprises several very different criteria, such as compatibility, cost, system reliability but also the usefulness ; (2) social acceptability. The usefulness is composed of two main sub-criteria: utility (technical or functional dimension) and usability (ergonomic dimension). For instance, concerning the ergonomic dimension, Bastien and Scapin [2] propose a classification with 18 sub-criteria.

Several dozen evaluation methods are described in the literature (see for instance [3,6,9,15,18]) and concern one or more of these evaluation criteria. For instance, some of these methods concern essentially human workload evaluation. The choice problem concerning these criteria and methods is very complex for the non-specialists, and even for the specialists.

What is more the social criteria are never really taken into account, and yet in certain countries, the social considerations become as important as the utility and usability constraints. For example, when the interactive part of a system designed by a western company is intended for Developing Countries (in Africa or Asia), it can lead to a freezing situation or rejection phenomenon when some social and/or cultural requirements (specific shapes, gestures, colors, signs...) are not taken into account [14,17]. In conclusion, in many situations, the evaluation must check not only the practical requirements (utility, usability, induced costs...) which are the source of many difficulties, but also social and cultural criteria [13]. For this reason, a computer-aided choice of evaluation criteria and methods can in many cases be particularly important. Such an approach is described in this paper. It is based on Fuzzy sets and implemented with PrologIII.

2.   RELATED WORK CONCERNING COMPUTER-AIDED EVALUATION

Many computer-aided approaches for helping the evaluators of interactive systems are described in the literature. The aid principles are various:
- automatic evaluation of interaction objects using a knowledge base containing ergonomic rules, like with Synop [10], KRI [11] or ERGOVAL [5];
- consideration of a task model for helping the evaluation, such as in EMA [3] or Chimes [8];
- Automatic capture of user actions, such as in EMA [3], Playback [12] or in the system proposed by Hammontree et al. [7];

- Automatic analysis of visual strategies [1];
- Advice concerning the evaluation methods to use [4];
- and so on.

Most of the tools dedicated to computer-aided evaluation help the evaluators to perform only partial evaluations. The evaluation is partial insofar as the evaluators can only check a part of the criteria set: in other words, at present, any given tool for computer-aided evaluation can help the evaluators to check only few criteria such as "efficient to use" or "subjective pleasing" (the same tool would be for instance ineffective for other criteria such as "easy to learn").

We adher to the logic of these tools existing for computer-aided evaluation, but in an overall perspective, carrying out a tool for computer-aided evaluation. It is called ADHESION (in French: **A**ide à la **D**écision **H**umaine pour l'**E**valuation des **S**ystèmes **I**nteractifs et leur validati**ON**; translation: Decision Support System for Interactive System Evaluation and Validation). Its main objective is to propose and explain the appropriate set of criteria and methods, usable for the "complete" evaluation (i.e. not only based on usability criteria) of a human-computer interface. To our knowledge, such a system does not have an equivalent in the literature. The principles on which it is based are described now.

3. FIRST PROTOTYPE OF THE ADHESION DECISION SUPPORT SYSTEM

3.1 General principles

The analysis of a Decision Support System (DSS) requests the specifications of the elements which take place in the system. First, we must define the set of alternatives on which will be based the decisions. Secondly, we should study the criteria which will be taken into account. This information will be sorted out and processed by a predefined decision-making approach in order to deduce the choice of the best alternative [16], Figure 1. In our case, the result concerns the adequate HCI evaluation criteria and methods to be used for the given situation. The possible decision criteria are numerous:

- About the situation: quality of the available information, Type of data (qualitative/quantitative), type of application (supervision, electronic commerce, business system...), presence of representative users, stage in the development process, human resources, available financial resources, location (country), product nature (prototype, paper version...), type of human-computer interaction (menus, virtual reality, hypermedia...), tem-

poral resources (number of days, weeks or months), required knowledge (psychology, sociology, computer scientist...)...
- About the potential performance of the evaluators: ability, experience, current workload...

The result (i.e. the choice) concerns:
- Evaluation criteria to consider in priority: social acceptability (ethical, social and cultural criteria), practical acceptability (environmental, economical, utility and usability criteria). Each criterion can be decomposed into sub-criteria. For instance, concerning the cultural dimension, in several countries, the system can give the advice to focus the evaluation on shapes or colours. About the usability criteria, sub-criteria are well defined in the literature: see for instance Bastien and Scapin [2].
- Evaluation methods to use in priority: many evaluation methods and variants exist. Each method can be described with several characteristics: name, concerned criteria, necessity of presence of users, and so on.

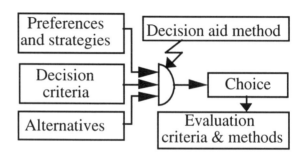

Figure 1. General principle (adapted from [16]).

3.2   Software architecture

The ADHESION DSS is composed of two main modules: a first module automatically selects and proposes evaluation methods and criteria; the Command Module (CM) is used for the control of the system.

The user (which can be a project manager, a student in HCI or an unskilled evaluator) operates on the CM by using a specific human-computer interface (Figure 2). The CM integrates the different elements intended to assist the human decision process. The user operates on the CM, in order to draw up a set of modifications necessary to compensate for unsatisfied suggestions.This first prototype is developed with the PrologIII langage. The choice of this language is justified by its ability to manipulate objectives and subjectives data, to model constraints, and to reason on them.

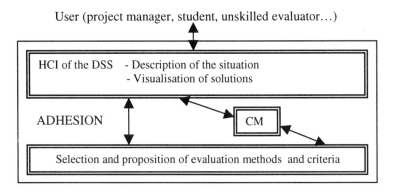

Figure 2. DSS Architecture.

3.3 Overall description of the approach based on Fuzzy logic

Our approach integrates Fuzzy rules and the concept of expert's preferences (Figure 3). One possibility could consist of working only with the Fuzzy rules, but the characteristics of our problem force us to use that combination. This way is encouraged when it is matter of a new or complex problem where well defined production rules do not exist [19]. The main stages followed in our approach are resumed in Figure 3, and progressively explained.

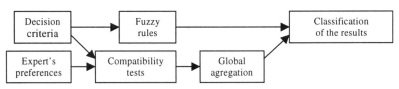

Figure 3. Main stages for decision aid in HCI evaluation.

The modelling of expert's preferences (aiming to build the knowledge base of the ADHESION DSS) can be illustrated with the following example. Let us consider the « human resources » criterion: to adjust this criterion, the expert prefers that another criterion (« available financial resources ») should be « rather good ». We know that the action concerned is « to adjust the human resources » (adjusting human resources consists in reducing or increasing the number of evaluators, seen as actors in the evaluation process) in relation with the criterion: « available financial resources ». The linguistic variable « L » to be used is denoted « expert's preferences » concerning the action « to adjust the human resources » in relation with the criterion: « available financial resources »; the expression which must be evaluated is « rather good ». In the literature, the term « good » is called a « describing term » and « rather » is called a « modifying term ».

The production rules to be used for the expression are :

    (1) $S \rightarrow T$ good

    (2) $T \rightarrow$ rather

Concerning the semantic to be associated to this linguistic variable, the variable is defined by a scale by 100, representing the percentage of the evaluators' workload or the maximum of the budget that one can not exceed. We must express what the expert means by « good » and « rather ». In this context, it becomes pertinent to use a Fuzzy approach [20], which, for example, can make easier the expression of the following expertise:

> Between 60 and 100% of the overall budget allocated to the evaluation, the expert estimates that the criterion « available financial resources » should be « good » to adjust the criterion « human resources ». Thus, from 50 to 60% of the overall budget, the action « to adjust » becomes less possible. Under 50 %, the adjustment becomes impossible.

A Fuzzy rule r_m can be written such as :

> « IF C_1 is A_{1m} … AND C_n is A_{nm} THEN a_j is DCF_m » (A_{im} and DCF_m are Fuzzy sets), that is to say that the C_i criteria respecting the A_{im} sets, we want to obtain DCF_m for the a_j action. »

Considering the same kind of example one can write :

> IF the C_1 criterion « available financial resources » is 0.8 AND IF the C_2 criterion « presence of an expert in ergonomics » is 0 AND IF the C_3 criterion « dimension to be evaluated » = "usability" THEN the (a_j) action is « to adjust the human resources » is 0.9.

That can be read like that: if the criterion « available financial resources » represents 80 % of the overall budget allocated to the evaluation and if there is no expert of ergonomics (0) in the evaluation team and if the criterion « dimension to be evaluated » is the usability, then the action « to adjust the human resources » is recommended at 90 %. That is to say, in practice that the system will suggest to adjust the « human resources ». One can also note that the evaluation criteria and methods suggested by the DSS must be adapted to the types of evaluators present in the evaluation team. For instance, if the evaluators are computer scientists, it would be not pertinent to offer them evaluation methods requiring a strong ergonomic practice.

4. CASE STUDY: ADVICE ABOUT EVALUATIONS FOR THE SAME HCI TO BE USED IN TWO DIFFERENT COUNTRIES

To illustrate our approach, it is important to show (1) the impact of taking into account socio-cultural problems in certain countries, (2) the influence of situational constraints. Note that the system takes into account certain social and cultural differences concerning 212 countries and islands. This knowledge is issued from a collaboration with sociologists (IFRESI Laboratory).

For instance, in two different projects, we suppose that the same situational constraints characterize these projects concerning the same type of HCI to be used in different countries (Pakistan and France). In each case, the role of the user is first to describe the situation. Figure 4 is relating to the HCI to be used in Pakistan; we suppose that, for the HCI used in France, the only one difference is the selection of this country (left corner, at the top).

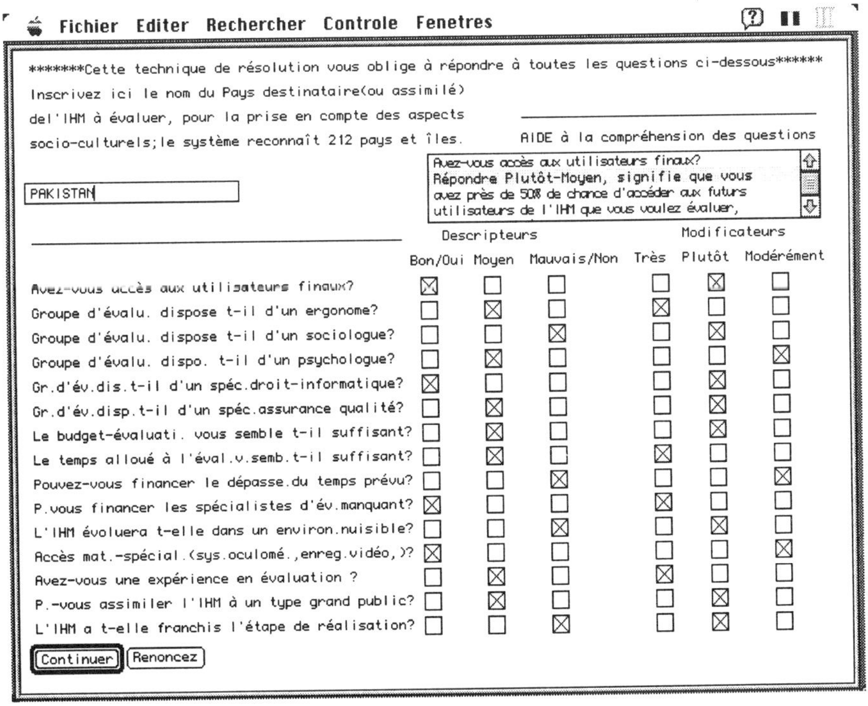

Figure 4. Data describing the constaints of the evaluation situation
for an HCI planned to be used in Pakistan.

On the screen (Figure 4), one can distinguish a list of questions (written in French in this first version). The answers are not binary (yes/not): by using three « descriptors » (Bon/Oui – Moyen – Mauvais/Non; translation : Good/Yes – Middle – Bad/No) and three « modificators » (Très – Plutôt – Modérément ; translation : Very – rather – Moderately), the ADHESION DSS is able to propose solutions taking into account the uncertainty or the imprecision of the user). Figures 5 and 6 show parts of propositions (solutions) provided by the ADHESION DSS.

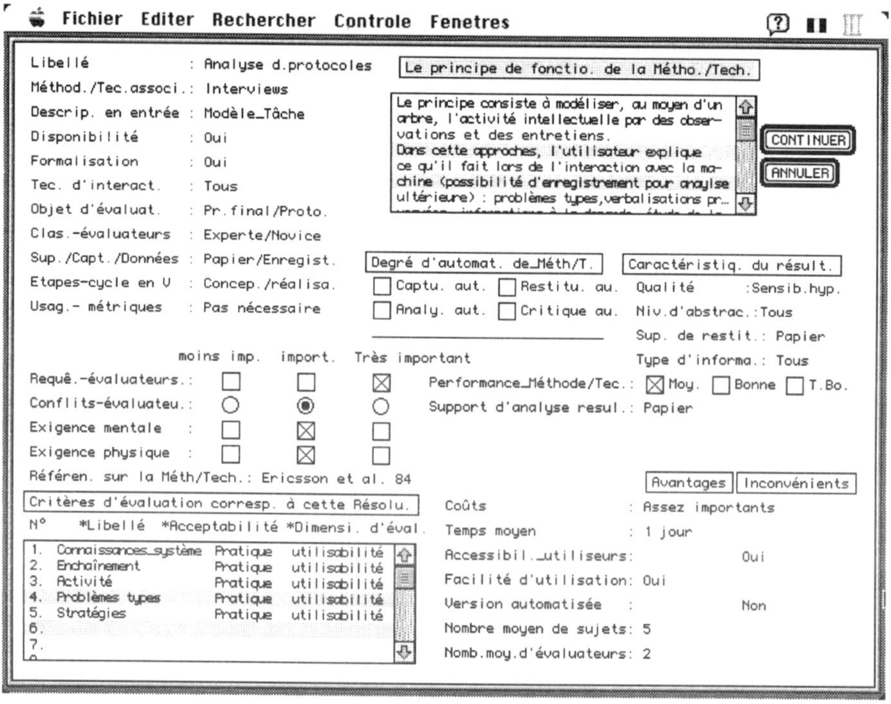

Figure 5. Propositions provided by the ADHESION DSS about the HCI planned to be used in France.

In the two cases, it has proposed several evaluation criteria and methods. For the evaluation of the HCI to be used in Pakistan, Figure 6, one can distinguish (left corner, in the bottom) that the DSS proposes to take into account some criteria concerning usability, but also criteria concerning social aspects. For the evaluation of the HCI to be used in France, the propositions are more focussed on usability aspects, Figure 5. The evaluation methods proposed by the system can be different in the two cases, according to the evaluation criteria to consider. Note that one to five complementary evaluation methods are automatically proposed. Each criterion or method is also described; for instance, about a proposed method: (1) name, (2) development stage in which the method will be useful, (3) approximative duration required to perform the evaluation, (4) its availability (a method can be validated on very simple tasks only, and not directly usable in more complex situations), (5) references, (6) existence of a software version, and so on.

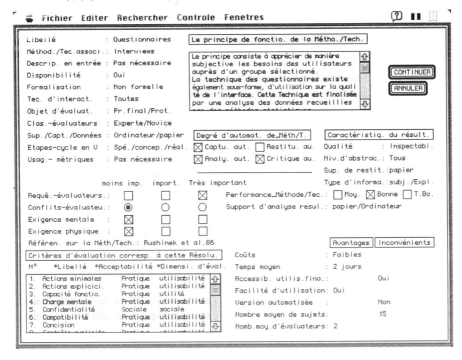

Figure 6. Propositions provided by the ADHESION DSS about
the HCI planned to be used in Pakistan.

5.   CONCLUSION AND PERSPECTIVES

Our approach can bring an original contribution to computer-aided evaluation of interactive systems. Indeed it becomes possible to assist automatically the choice of HCI evaluation criteria and methods adapted in each situation. A DSS called ADHESION is currently developed with the Prolog III language. The first results are encouraging in terms of expertise modelling and the solutions that it provides. The perspectives are numerous, according to: (1) the development of the software modules, (2) the expertise to integrate in its knowledge base, (3) the tests of this DSS, according to evaluation scenarios during real or simulated projects.

REFERENCES

[1]   Abed, M. and Angue, J.C., *Using the measure of eye movements to modelize an operator's activity*, Proceedings Ninth European Annual Conference on "Human decision making and manual control", Varese, Italy, 10-12 September 1990.

[2]   Bastien, C., and Scapin, D., *Evaluating a user interface with ergonomic criteria*, International Journal of Human-Computer Interaction, Vol. 7, No. 2, 1995, pp. 105-121.

[3]   Balbo, S., *Évaluation ergonomique des interfaces utilisateurs: un pas vers l'automatisation*, Ph.D. Dissertation, University of Grenoble, France, 1994.

[4]   Denley, I. and Long, J., *A planning aid for human factors evaluation practice*, Behaviour and Information Technology, Vol. 16, No. 4/5, 1997, pp. 203-219.

[5]   Farenc, C., *ERGOVAL: une méthode de structuration des règles ergonomiques permettant l'évaluation automatique d'interfaces graphiques*, Ph.D. Dissertation, University of Toulouse I, France, 1997.

[6]   Grislin, M. and Kolski, C., *Évaluation des Interfaces Homme-Machine lors du développement des systèmes interactifs*, Techniques & Sciences Informatiques, Vol. 15, No. 3, 1996, pp. 265-296.

[7]   Hammontree, M.L., Hendrickson, J.J., and Hensley, B.W., *Integrated data capture and analysis tools for research and testing on graphical user interfaces*, in Proceedings of ACM Conf. on Human Factors in Computing Systems CHI'92, ACM Press, New York, 1992, pp. 431-432.

[8]   Jiang, J., Murphy, E., Bailin, S., Truszkowski, W., and Szczur, M., *Prototyping a knowledge based compliance checker for user interface evaluation in Motif development environments*, in Proceedings MOTIF'92 Second Annual International Motif Users Meeting, Bethesda, Open Systems, 1992, pp. 258-268.

[9]   Kolski, C., *Interfaces Homme-Machine, application aux systèmes industriels complexes*, Editions Hermès, Paris, 1997.

[10]   Kolski, C. and Millot, P., *A rule-based approach to the ergonomic " static " evaluation of man-machine graphic interface in industrial processes*, International Journal of Man-Machine Studies, 1991, pp. 657-674 .

[11]   Lowgren, J. and Nordqvist, T., *Knowledge-based evaluation as design support for graphical user interface*, in Proceedings of ACM Conf. on Human Factors in Computing Systems CHI'92, ACM Press, New York, 1992, pp. 181-188.

[12]   Neal, A.S. and Simon, R.M., *Playback : a method for evaluating the usability of software and its documentation*, in Proceedings of ACM Conf. on Human Factors in Computing Systems CHI'83, A. Janda (ed.), ACM, North-Holland, 1983, pp. 78-82.

[13]   Nendjo Ella, A., Grislin, M., and Kolski, C., *Towards a global approach to solve social aspects of usability and acceptability, especially in Developing Countries*, in Proceedings of XVth European Annual Conf. on Human Decision Making and Manual Control, Soesterberg, The Netherlands, 10-12 June 1996.

[14]   Nielsen, J., *Designing user interfaces for international use*, Elsevier, Amsterdam, 1990.

[15]   Nielsen, J., *Usability engineering*, Academic Press, Boston, 1993.

[16]   Ozenoi, V.M. and Gaft, M.G., *Multicriterion decision problems*, in Conflicting objectives in decision, D.E. Bell, R.L. Keeney and H. Raiffa (eds.), John Wiley, 1977, pp. 17-39.

[17]   Russo, P. and Boor, S., *How fluent is your interface? Design for international users*, in Proceedings of ACM Conf. on Human Factors in Computing Systems INTERCHI'93, Addison-Wesley, Morristown, 1993, pp. 342-347.

[18]   Senach B., *Evaluation ergonomique des interfaces homme-machine : une revue de la litttérature*, Research report No. 1180, INRIA, Sophia Antipolis, March 1990.

[19]   Wawak F., *Elaboration d'un système d'aide à la décision pour la supervision en téléopération: Approche basée sur les théories des sous-ensembles flous et des possibilités*, Ph.D Dissertation, University of Lille, 1996.

[20] Zadeh, L.A., *The concept of a linguistic variable and its application to approximative reasoning*, Information Sciences, No. 8, pp. 301-357, and No. 9, pp. 43-80, 1975.

Chapter 29

CONSIDERATING SUBJECTIVITY IN SOFTWARES EVALUATION
Application for teachware evaluations

Olivier Hû, Philippe Trigano, and Stéphane Crozat
UMR CNRS 6599 HEUDIASYC
Université de Technologie de Compiègne - BP 20529
60206 Compiegne Cedex - France
phone : 03-44-23-44-23 / 47-68
e-mail: {olivier.hu}{philippe.trigano}@utc.fr

Abstract   Software evaluation is a hard problem: utilisability, robustness, graphics quality as many aspects to considerate for a global vision of the software quality.
In traditional evaluation methods, influence of users general feelings is ignored. In our context, the teachwares evaluation before use, subjectivity is
particularly relevant: the motivation, the empathy, for example, are key elements of all training processes. In other words, a good evaluation should provide an objective evaluation of the software and the perception that the user
had of this teachware. We proposed a method (called EMPI), for an evaluation
help of multimedia teachwares, proposing this duality. This method is proposed to teachers to help them in to certificate or to choose a teachware.
Mainly based on a hierarchical questionnaire with variable depth, this method
allow evaluator to capitalise his subjective opinion and to mark instinctively
any aspect of the teachware, in parallel with the questionnaire itself.

Key words: Software evaluation, Subjectivity evaluation, Teachware, Questionnaire.

1.   INTRODUCTION

There are many methods to evaluate the interface or the technical quality
of the software, but a dimension that we consider important often misses: the
subjective perception which has the user. These feelings can condition the
acceptance or the rejection of the software by the user [1]. In our evaluation
context, we want to provide a method to help a teacher, or any education ad-

visors, to choose, to certify or simply to correctly analyse, the multimedia teachware that they want to use.

Some distinctive features of our context favorise a better consideration of subjective point of view. First of all, students constitute a difficult population for motivation, attention and effectiveness. Nevertheless these problems can be solved with the use of environments or scenarios, to stimulate the pleasure of application use. Next, the teaching situation can be enough complex to avoid any evaluation before use: so it's important to consider the evaluator subjective opinion to judge the relevance of such software characteristics. At last, users of our method are not specialists and it's probably impossible to provide them a method to detail all the characteristics of any teachware. Because we allow them to deliver an opinion on software characteristic, we increase our chances to detect a fault. The problem is to find right balance between an evaluation of software objective characteristics and the required consideration of subjective criteria.

2.   AN EVALUATION HELP METHOD

In our case, the evaluator is the prescriber: a professor, a manager of a CD-library or someone who wants to learn himself. We directly evaluate the software and not its impact on users or students and we work on finished products. Our goal is not to improve the evaluated software but to give to the users a help for the choice, the certification or the discovery of their tools.

As we said, the method is presented as a structured questionnaire. We divide the global field in five themes: Technical quality, Ergonomics aspects, Multimedia documents, Scénarisation and Pedagogical tools. These topics are divided in criteria, sub-criteria and questions [2,3]. To elaborate this list, we had to explore various domains: ergonomic criteria [4,5], pictures semantic, textual theory [6], navigation, fiction, pedagogical evaluation [7], interaction process [8].

We obtain a hierarchical structure that allows a variable depth inspection: the evaluator has the choice between going thoroughly into a concept or passing to the following one. Then he can adapt the questionnaire to his competencies or his needs.

3.   CONSIDERATION OF SUBJECTIVE OPINION

Our questionnaire allows, on one hand, to check the principal teachware characteristics, and on the other hand, to offer an objective evaluation thanks to the precision and the structure of the questionnaire. Now we will see two characteristics of our method that permit to considerate evaluator subjective opinion: general feelings and instinctive marks.

3.1   General feelings

The goal is to capitalise, at the beginning of the evaluation, the impressions that the evaluator had during the use of the software. We propose to him some couples of impressions which he will able to give a ruling on : Reassuring/Disconcerting ; Luxuriant/Moderate ; Playful/Serious ; Active/Passive ; Simple/Complex ; Innovating/Traditional.

This list comes from an evaluation database that was analysed by a document indexing method [9]. We also compare this result with theoretical approaches: for example, visual perception theory [10].

These impressions show several characteristics:

- They are instinctive: users provide them without any assistance
- Describable: users are able to describe them with a few adjectives
- Homogeneous: they are concordant between users
- Persistent: they endure in time and influence further use.

This list allows the evaluator to provide a description of his impressions. He indicates what he feels for each couple of impressions. For example: very diverting, diverting, reassuring or very reassuring. There is no "neutral" evaluation to incitate the evaluator to give an opinion.

3.2   Instinctive marks

For any themes, criteria or sub-criteria, the evaluator could give a mark know as "instinctive" on the scale "- -; -; +; ++". Because the evaluators do not have the required competences in all evaluated fields, a help must be provided. This help is divided in three parts: a reformulation; an illustration and a deepening. We obtain a capitalisation of the perception of reality by the user. This result could be compared with the objective evaluation of this same reality by the questions themselves.

3.3   Final marks

As we already said, our objective is to help an evaluator and not to judge for him. So, and contrary to other approaches [7] the final mark will be only proposed by the method, the evaluator could modify it if he wishes. To help him in this step, some marks and indications are proposed to him for each theme, criterion and sub-criterion (Figure 1):

- A calculated mark: it results from the questions themselves.

- An instinctive mark: it corresponds to the instinctive mark given to this level by the evaluator. A more global instinctive mark is also given, it is an average between the instinctive mark of this level and lower levels ones.
- A correlation index: it measures the similarity between instinctive mark and calculated mark.
- A coherence index: it measures the coherence of instinctive marks between a level and its lower levels.
- A final mark: it is calculated with calculated mark, global instinctive mark and coherence index. Weaker the coherence index is, more the final mark is closed to the calculated mark.

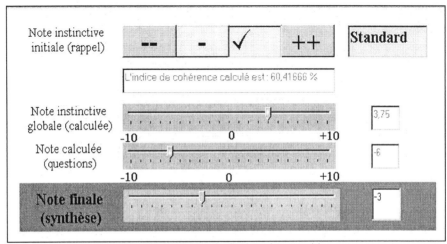

Figure 1. Example of a final mark proposition.

With all these marks and indexes, the evaluator will be able to fix for each theme, criterion and sub-criterion, the final mark that he is considering as being the right one.

4.   VALIDATION AND RESULTS

In addition to the iterative development of the method, we made some specific validations. We will develop the comparative evaluations which we carried out and confrontations we had with designers of some of the evaluated teachwares.

4.1   Several evaluations

In order to improve the range and the quality of our evaluation, we made two principal comparative evaluations:
- About fifty evaluators working on the same software: evaluators were students from the University of Technology of Compiegne. The goal of this validation was to test the evaluation stability and questionnaire utilisability.
- Several evaluators evaluated three software of the same type (languages training). Here, the objective was to determine the interest of the results provided by the method in software comparison.

A lot of data resulting of these evaluations are still to be analysed and other validations are already started. Nevertheless several remarks can already be done. When we compare the results of the evaluations made with or without instinctive marks, we can notice a slight increase of evaluations divergence. This effect was expected as accepting more subjectivity increase necessarily evaluations diversity. With regard to the results comparison, it appears that the classification of the software by the method corresponds to the classification that we had established after having studied in detail each software. But the current form of the results (tables and graphics) doesn't seem the best for a comparative study.

4.2   Confrontation with designers

In addition to the evaluation help used for validation or choice, it was important to know if the designers could use our results. They allow several interesting considerations for development. The initial general feelings give information on the potential users of the software: a description of feelings with a restricted list of key words, provided a clear vision of the natural population (users who will be finally interested in this software). The distinction between calculated mark and instinctive mark show the difference between reality and perception that the user has. For example, this distinction makes possible to examinate the software modification priorities: according to the development strategy, it will be better to examinate first all good aspects but badly judged by the users.

5.   CONCLUSION

This method of evaluation help permit to considerate more subjectivity without losing our target: to provide an evaluation as closed as possible to the reality. So, questions must be as precise as possible, and involve all the software aspects. If the possibility is offered to the evaluator to deliver his opinion on a criterion, a structured help is provided to contribute to his full comprehension. Moreover these instinctive marks will be considerate in the final mark only if they are coherent. It's only with these precautions that we ensure coherent results with a humanisation of evaluation.

A first software prototype version of the method is currently available. Results seem satisfactory, but several points are still to be improved:

- Presentation of the results, or how to distinguish the software characterisation from its evaluation. We work on edition of descriptive report of the software which would accompany marks and graphics.
- Results stability, which remains to be improved. We will make a specific effort in the redaction of the questions and their help.
- Improvement of the results comparison. It would be necessary to develop some tools allowing an effective comparison between software.

ACKNOWLEDGEMENTS

This search is financed by the Picardie area.

BIBLIOGRAPHY

[1]   Kolski, C., *Interfaces Homme-machine : application aux systèmes industriels complexes*, Ed. Hermès, Paris, 1997.
[2]   Hû, O., Trigano, Ph., and Crozat, S., *E.M.P.I.: une méthode pour l'Evaluation du Multimédia Pédagogique Interactif*, in Proceedings of NTICF'98, Rouen, 18-20 November 1998.
[3]   Crozat, S., Hû, O., and Trigano, P., *A method for evaluating multimedia learning software*, in Proceedings of ICSCM'99, Florence, 8-11 June 1999.
[4]   Bastien, J.M.Ch. and Scapin, D.L., *Ergonomic Criteria for the Evaluation of Human-Computer Interfaces*, Technical report No. 156, INRIA, June 1993.
[5]   Vanderdonckt, J., *Guide ergonomique des interfaces homme-machine*, Presses Universitaires de Namur, Namur, 1994.
[6]   Goody, J., *La raison graphique : La domestication de la pensée sauvage*, Les Editions de Minuit, 1979.
[7]   MEDA, *Evaluer les logiciels de formation*, Les Editions d'Organisation, 1990.
[8]   Vivet, M., *Evaluating educational technologies : Evaluation of teaching material versus evaluation of learning ?*, in Proceedings of CALISCE'96, San Sebastian, July 1996.
[9]   Lamrous, S. and Trigano, P., *L'organisation des espaces documentaires : vers une exploitation optimale*, Document Electronique, Ed. Hermès, Vol. 1, No. 4, December 1997.
[10] Gibson, J.J, *The ecological approach to visual perception*, Lawrence Erlbaum Associates, London, 1979.

Chapter 30

KALDI: A COMPUTER-AIDED USABILITY ENGINEERING TOOL FOR SUPPORTING TESTING AND ANALYSIS OF HUMAN-COMPUTER INTERACTION

Ghassan Al-Qaimari and Darren McRostie
Department of Computer Science,
RMIT University
Melbourne, Victoria, 3001, Australia
[ghassan,mcrostie]@cs.rmit.edu.au

Abstract   In this paper we describe the design and implementation of a Computer Aided Usability Engineering (CAUsE) tool built to automate many of the tedious and time consuming aspects of empirical usability testing. The tool presented, called KALDI, is tightly integrated with the Java graphical toolkit and uses only software techniques to record precise user actions as well as to capture a video-like recording of the user interface being tested. It also allows for the detailed analysis of the recorded user actions through the use of a sophisticated visualisation of data. The KALDI tool has many advantages over other techniques, including the ability to conduct tests without using specialised equipment, visually represent user actions at different levels of detail, record user performances from remote locations, perform automatic classification of abstract event data into user actions and the synchronised display of video-like playback with an indication of the corresponding recorded action/event. Furthermore, we propose in this paper that integrating this class of CAUsE tool in future graphical toolkits and User Interface Management Systems (UIMS) will provide many benefits to software designers and usability specialists. These benefits include helping to encourage usability testing throughout the development lifecycle, as well as providing a basis for interactive system designers and usability specialists to make sound design decisions more efficiently.

Keywords: CAUsE Tools, Usability Evaluation, Cognitive Walkthrough, GOMS.

1.   INTRODUCTION

The benefits of conducting usability evaluations throughout the development lifecycle of a software product have been well demonstrated through many case studies [14]. These benefits include increasing productivity of the users, increasing the likelihood of a product being used to its full potential, reducing training costs and increasing the marketability of a product.

Usability testing can be achieved by carefully examining and video taping a number of test users attempting to accomplish a pre-determined series of tasks using the interactive software (or a mock-up of the software) to be tested. The video recording is then analysed by logging the actions the users perform as well as the time each action takes. From this detailed study, the analyst can choose the best approach to take in an interface design, and can identify key problem areas in the usability of the system [22,26].

This technique provides good results if undertaken correctly, but requires a number of sample users, specialised video equipment for both recording and playing back (with accurate time information), and takes a significant amount of time for a skilled usability specialist to analyse [8,22]. Because of the expense in both time and equipment required to undertake this form of empirical user testing, other techniques have been devised for faster, cheaper evaluations. These techniques fall into two categories: analytical and inspection.

Analytical techniques rely on a skilled usability expert to understand and simulate the way a user would attempt to accomplish tasks using the interface under test [25]. Two such techniques are Cognitive Walkthrough [4,16] and GOMS [1,6,15]. The Cognitive Walkthrough evaluates systems by analysing the mental processes required of users. This technique helps determine how easy it is to explore and learn a system, identifies potential problems and reasons for these problems. The technique is useful for evaluating the usability of systems which users have not yet seen. It reveals how successfully a particular design guides the unfamiliar user through to the completion of their task. GOMS attempts to evaluate how efficient an interface will be by looking at the actions required to achieve goals and summing the estimated duration for each action. This technique helps decide between different interface options and can detect potential problems, however it does not identify the reasons behind these problems. GOMS methods are applicable in cases where users have already become familiar with the system, and they have the required cognitive skill [6].

Inspection techniques [13, 21], on the other hand, use a set of guidelines or rules with which an interface design is compared, and are usually performed by one or more usability experts. One such technique is a Heuristic (or Expert) evaluation, in which a number of evaluators compare the interface to a set of nine heuristics or design principles. This technique can uncover potential usability problems and the reasons for these problems, but it does not effectively reveal user confusion, nor does it measure user speed of performance.

Although faster and cheaper, analytical and inspection techniques have two main problems: Firstly, neither of the techniques utilises test users, instead relying on a simulation of the user. This may lead to problems if the usability expert did not fully understand the users of the system, which may lead to major problems being undetected. Secondly, they both require the use of skilled usability specialist whose time and availability is usually limited [19].

Due to the expense and difficulty involved in conducting usability activities, usability evaluation of any kind is often left out of the software development lifecycle or performed only towards the end of the cycle where its usefulness is limited. For usability evaluations to have a significant affect on the quality of an interactive system, they must be conducted throughout the entire software development lifecycle, whenever crucial design decisions must be made.

Currently, there is a recent trend towards developing automated tools for making usability analysis methods and empirical testing more effective. These tools are termed Computer Aided Usability Engineering (or CAUsE) tools. In this research work, we introduce KALDI[1] (**K**eyboard/mouse **A**ction **L**ogger and **D**isplay **I**nstrument), developed to combine an event logging and screen recording tool which forms part of the Java™ Abstract Windowing Toolkit (AWT) [9] with a Java based analysis and playback tool. The analysis tool displays the logged events in a graphical notation showing the description and duration of the recorded user action, which is combined with a linked video playback of the program output and mouse movements. KALDI demonstrates that usability testing can easily and cheaply be conducted at any stage of the development lifecycle, giving the developers the ability to measure the performance and detect the problems of an interactive system.

Further more, we will also propose in this paper that CAUsE tools such as the one we developed should be integrated in future graphical toolkits and UIMSs in order to reduce the gap between design/implementation and usability evaluation. This integration would promote active and ongoing usability assessment during the entire development lifecycle.

---

[1] According to legend, Kaldi was an Abyssinian goat herder who learned of the effects of the coffee bean when he noticed that his normally docile heard had become lively for no apparent reason. On further inspection he noticed that the goats had been nibbling on some bright red berries of a nearby plant, and so coffee was discovered [2].

The paper is organised as follows: section 2 contains background information; section 3 reviews existing CAUsE tools; section 4 provides a detailed description of the KALDI tool, and summarises its advantages and limitations; section 5 presents our conclusions.

2.   USABILITY AND USER CENTRED DESIGN

According to the International Standards Organization, ISO 9241-11 [13], usability is defined as "the extent to which a product can be used by specified users to achieve specified goals with effectiveness, efficiency and satisfaction in a specified context of use." Effectiveness refers to the accuracy and completeness with which users achieve specified goals. Efficiency refers to the resources (time, money, mental effort etc.) expended in relation to the accuracy and completeness with which users achieve goals. Satisfaction refers to freedom from discomfort, and positive attitudes to the use of the product. Context of use refers to the users, goals, tasks, equipment (hardware, software and materials), and the physical and social environments in which a product is used.

Producing highly usable interfaces on the first attempt (even when the most skilled usability specialists are involved) is rare. An iterative and user-centred approach is usually required, with the results of usability evaluations being fed back into the development process, steering the development effort towards an acceptable level of usability [12,22].

Traditional software development methods, such as the waterfall and spiral lifecycles, do not allow for this type of user-centred and iterative process [3,12,24,25,27]. Users are typically involved in contributing to the early stages and late delivery/acceptance stages of the cycle, while the steps from specification to delivery are treated as a linear progression of development, with only limited iterations between adjacent stages. With such a methodology, an incomplete assessment of the users needs during the specification or design stages will not be detected until the product is delivered and the users find it does not fit their tasks.

In HCI literature, user-centred design and development methodologies, such as the Star lifecycle [12], have been proposed for interactive systems. The Star lifecycle is highly iterative and self-correcting through placing usability evaluation in the centre of the lifecycle, and emphasising the importance of prototyping. Therefore, usability activities become an integral part of the development process. The Star lifecycle is also multi-disciplinary, as it recognises the need to involve different skills, such as human factors and instruction theory, in the design and development process.

The task of design involves a complex set of processes. Design is a goal directed process in which the goal is to conceive and realise some new thing.

But, with some training and a lot of practical experience, the accuracy of performance increases and people become or are labelled as 'experts'. Central to this notion is that there is a positive correction of accuracy and performance. There is a vast range of definitions of expert used in the literature and the definition of novice also varies widely. Most studies use experience as an operationalisation of expertise rather than actual performance. One approach to defining expert and novice is to take less experienced performers and more experienced performers and call the former novices and the latter experts. In many skill domains the distinction between experts and novices is clear: experts perform far better than novices do. First there are significant differences in domain knowledge, second there are differences in problem representation, third there are differences in problem perception, and fourth are differences in problem solving. As training and experience increase, people become significantly more accurate and so are labelled expert [7]. Research shows that these differences in expertise are accompanied by changes in cognitive processes: experts know more than, represent and perceive problems differently from, and have different ways of solving problems from novices [28].

A major problem in research in investigating the transition from novice to expert status, is research design and measurement. In laboratory-based studies, much behavioural data used to investigate cognitive processes have little ecological validity, and may not capture the expertise in the performance of expert subjects. How faithful is the laboratory task to the real thing? Self report data however may not reliably reflect the cognitive processes of subjects especially expert subjects. First their validity depends on high self-insight and second, the ability of the method to be uninvasive. These are just some of the issues in research methodology and measurement which are posed in studies of novice/expert designs in HCI. The present investigation attempts to address these issues by automating the process of user testing to produce more reliable data.

3.   CAUSE TOOLS

There is currently a trend towards improving the effectiveness of the different usability evaluation techniques, discussed earlier, by using computer-based tools to automate repetitive aspects and provide means of viewing the detailed and complex usability data in a simple and meaningful way [18,23]. There are few of these Computer Aided Usability Engineering (CAUsE) tools in existence. In this subsection we review three of the more notable ones.

3.1   DRUM

DRUM (Diagnostic Recorder for Usability Measurement) is a video logging and video player control tool [17]. It is a commercially available product that runs on an Apple Macintosh computer and is capable of driving several high-end video tape players (with computer interface cards). DRUM as-
sists in the mark-up and logging of video taped sessions. The usability tester
plays the videotape (which is controlled and monitored by the computer) and
logs the start and end of tasks or critical actions. These log entries are stored
along with a videotape index number that allows the computer to cue or re-
wind the tape to the exact log position.

Once a session has been manually logged by the usability tester, analysis
and metric calculation routines can be activated which provide useful statistical information regarding the logged tests. The logs can be viewed and
analysed, but the system does not provide for a graphical view of the information (text based time log only). It is suggested that DRUM is much more
efficient than manual video logging. This is because the statistical calculations and overhead of marking up video tape and measuring elapsed times
are automated - two to three hours per hour of tape, as opposed to manual
logging which often takes ten hours per hour of video [18]. However, the
actual mark up is manual, needing an experienced usability specialist to
mark start and end of user actions, with little scope for automation. Determining the start and end times of actions is also error prone and reliant on
the accuracy of the video recorder, amount of tape stretch and the diligence
of the human operator.

DRUM uses specialised equipment that requires careful set up and cali-
bration for both the recording and analysis of the usability testing session.
This increases the cost and means that the equipment must be available and
configured before a usability evaluation can be undertaken, which in turn reduces the likelihood of regular testing.

3.2   UsAGE

UsAGE (User Action Graphing Effort) is an operating system event-
logging tool that graphically displays and compares the logs [29]. It is a
prototype tool which aims to automate the analysis of an empirical usability
test and presents the results in a graphical representation. The tool takes a
different approach to DRUM. Instead of using a video recording and manual
logging, it directly logs the UIMS events as they are generated, and stores
them with a time stamp.

UsAGE attempts to automate analysis by graphically comparing the recorded event logs of expert and novice users. The expert actions are dis-

played as a graph of nodes that extend horizontally across the display. Novice events are displayed as a sequence of nodes that are matched to expert events, with arcs displaying the sequence of the events. Matched events are placed vertically below the expert event, with unmatched events being placed below previously matched events. In UsAGE, nodes are labelled with the UIMS event name, and the events displayed are at a very low conceptual level, making it hard for the analyst to understand how the events relate to the actual operation of the application. To overcome this, UsAGE allows the recorded events to be fed back into the application user interface, which replicates and displays the recorded user's actions.

The UsAGE tool overcomes some of the limitations of pure video tape analysis tools (DRUM for example), and provides a means of graphically viewing and comparing logged actions, and ensures very accurate time information. However the tool has some limitations. As UsAGE displays all logged events, understanding what the user was attempting to accomplish can be missed due to being overwhelmed by large volumes of data.

Although this tool requires no specialised equipment to record and playback the test session, it does require that a copy of tested software is available, with any other supporting data. This may be a problem where the data used by the system is changing in nature (like Internet applications and database systems) or with interfaces that might show unpredictable behaviour as a result to a given action, as is the case with intelligent interfaces.

3.3   Integrated Data Capture and Analysis Tool

The Integrated Data Capture and Analysis tool described by [11] is a combination of an operating system event logger and video player control tool. It combines the advantages of video based logging tools, as in the case of DRUM, with the benefits of UIMS event loggers, as in UsAGE. The tool uses filters to aggregate the user-generated events into meaningful classifications of the user's actions. This converts verbose system based event records into more useful and simple descriptions of the user's actions. The tool also can be used to control a video tape player, using the time stamped system events as index points on the videotape. This allows the usability tester to easily see how the filtered events relate to the actual application.

This tool removes the need for manual videotape logging while retaining ability to play back, search and quickly retrieve logged events. It also keeps accurate system level logs of the user interaction and presents the data at a higher conceptual level which is more useful to the usability analyst.

Although this tool makes a good attempt at combining the advantages of event logging and video techniques, it still has some limitations. Firstly, it relies on specialised video equipment with a computer-controlled interface. Secondly, it does not present the log data in a graphical way, and it does not allow the usability tester to change the level of detail of the log view to suit the current analysis task. Finally, the tool does not support the concept of hierarchical classifications of user actions, which may lead to the automatic classification presenting the high level user action without the low level actions that contributed to it.

3.4   Summary

The development of CAUsE tools is a new trend, and we can expect to see many more tools in the coming years. The three tools described above are representative of existing CAUsE tools that aim to assist empirical usability testing. They are also representative of the limitations of current tools.
Limitations of video logging tools include:
- Do not possess accurate and precise measurement of time.
- It is possible to miss actions performed by the user that are not highly visible.
- Automation of the classification of actions is very difficult.
- The tools require expensive specialised videotape equipment.

Event logging and automatic filtering tools, on the other hand, possess the following limitations:
- Difficult to conceptually understand how the raw events relate to the interface.
- Difficult to communicate and demonstrate usability problems once they are detected.
- Events capture without automatic filtering generally produces a volume of data, which is difficult to analyse.
- Events capture with automatic filtering can possibly obscure finer interaction details, which may be of importance.

4.   KALDI

In this section we present our CAUsE Tool, known as KALDI, which has been developed to address many of the limitations mentioned above. KALDI is a hybrid tool that both logs system events and records the interface display. The tool is designed to graphically display the logged events and allow them to be displayed at different levels of conceptual abstraction. The tool does not use videotape, but stores screen images directly to the hard drive, and therefore does not limit the frequency of usability tests due to specialised equipment. The tight mapping between the event visualisation and the video-like playback of captured events gives context to otherwise abstract events. KALDI is implemented using SUN SWING SET [10], and is applicable for currently emerging interface technologies, such as collaborative network based applications. The tight integration with the graphical toolkit provides KALDI with the means of recording internal program state information, as well as the visible program output, which would assist in evaluating and improving adaptive and intelligent interfaces. The KALDI is a suite of three individual tools: *the live capture tool*; the *live monitoring tool*; and *analysis tool*. The design of each tool within the suite is described in the following subsections.

4.1   The Live Capture Tool

It forms part of the Java Abstract Windowing Toolkit (AWT), and involves monitoring events, taking screen shots, if necessary, and transmitting the data along the network connection. Events in Java are objects that contain information regarding the event, including a reference to the widget that the event is targeting. The live capture tool reads this event information as it is generated and transmits it over the network along with a date-time stamp. A screen shot is taken whenever an event occurs that might have caused the screen to update. To take a snapshot, a blank in-memory image is created and the widget targeted by the event is "printed" into the image. The image is then converted to a byte array and transmitted over the network. The live monitor tool has no user interface of it's own as it forms part of the Java core library, and is invoked remotely from the monitor tool.

4.2   The Monitor Tool

The monitor tool (Figure 1) is a small interactive program that is used by the usability specialist while a test session is being recorded. This tool invokes the capture tool and receives the event and screen capture information, which it displays to the usability specialist and saves to permanent storage. As the screen capture playback is being displayed, the usability specialist can insert comments and categorise the user's interaction with the software under test by grouping the events into tasks and actions. The monitoring tool is not fully implemented yet. The current prototype version is capable only of receiving the network connection, saving the data displaying the live video capture.

After a few test recordings, it became obvious that the saved events and screen captures would consume considerable disk space during lengthy recordings. Compression is applied to the data as it is being saved (using the

GZIP algorithm) which reduces the size of the save file by approximately 95%. For example, a one-minute recording of a small sample application produces a save file consuming 2.43 megabytes, which is reduced to 24.6 kilobytes after compression is applied.

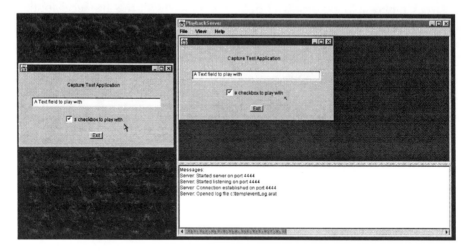

Figure 1. The monitor tool interface recording a sample application beside it.

4.3   The Analysis Tool

The analysis tool is used by the usability specialist after the recording of a test session. It gives the usability specialists the ability to classify the user's interaction with the system, compare user performance and analyse results. This component allows for the playback of recorded screen capture data, the reclassification of raw event data into hierarchical actions and tasks, and provides the usability specialist with an easy way to see how a user performed.

The analysis tool interface is divided into three functional areas (Figure 2): the *event viewing area* (top right-hand side sub-window), where the raw events, action groups, and tasks are displayed graphically; the *playback area* (bottom right-hand side sub-window) in which the recorded sessions are played back; and the *index area* (left-hand side sub-window) in which tasks can be easily selected for display or playback in the opposite two areas. The following sub-sections describe the three areas.

Event viewing area: It is in this part of the interface that the usability tester classifies the raw events into user actions and tasks. Classification of events is achieved by creating an action group and encapsulating the events (or other action groups) within the new action group. The usability specialist assigns a description to each action group and the encapsulated events are removed from the display and replaced with the action group. Action groups can be expanded by the usability specialist to examine and modify the contents if necessary.

Action groups give meaning to a series of seemingly unrelated raw events. For example, a series of events consisting of: mouse pressed, mouse moved to (x0,y0), mouse moved to (x1,y1), mouse moved to (x2,y2), mouse released, may be encapsulated in an action group with the description "Drag and Drop." Action groups may also contain other action groups. This allows the usability specialist to create higher-level action groups such as "Delete file" (which may consist of "open browser window," "select file icon," "drag and drop" action groups).

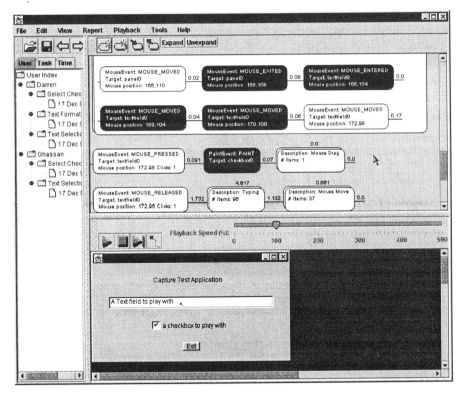

Figure 2. The analysis tool.

Events and action groups are encapsulated into a high-level group called a Task. Tasks behave in a similar way to action groups in that they contain other items and may be expanded to show that containment. Tasks are identified with a name, specified by the usability tester, and are also associated with the test user who performed the task.

Both tasks and action groups may be expanded to display their contents. This is achieved by double clicking the task/action group representation or by using the toolbar or menu. When a task/action group is expanded, its box grows and the encapsulated action groups and raw events are displayed inside the expanded task/action group. Once expanded, the encapsulated items can be selected and manipulated (Figure 3). Toolbar buttons associated with the event viewing area exist for the following operations:

- Creating a new action group and placing all selected items within the new group.
- Creating a new task and placing all selected items within the new group.
- Expanding (showing the contents) or contracting (hiding the contents) a selected action group or task.
- Moving adjacent or contained items into, or out of, an action group or task.
- Editing the properties of an action group or task (such as the action name).
- Playing the video-like screen captures for the selected items.

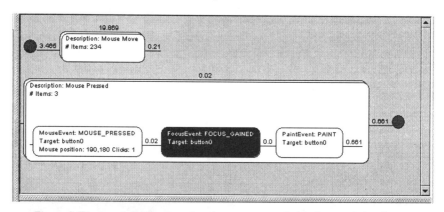

Figure 3. The event display area showing an unexpanded and expanded action group. The blue highlight indicates the currently selected event.

Playback area: The playback area displays the captured screen images and displays the recorded location of the mouse, providing a smooth full motion playback of the recorded session. As each frame is displayed, the corresponding event in the event viewing area is highlighted. In the event display area, the blue highlights signify selected events, while the green highlight shows the event being played back in the playback display area. This synchronised event view/playback display gives the usability tester immediate understanding of the event display, and provides important context information about the interface as a whole.

The playback area displays each recorded frame in sequence, beginning with the first event selected in the event viewing area, ending with the last event selected (or the last displayed event if only one event was selected). The display pauses for an amount of time equal to the difference between the time stamps of the currently displayed event and the next event, multiplied by the user specified playback speed factor, for each playback frame. A "ghost" mouse pointer is displayed in the playback area to show the recorded location of the mouse pointer during playback, and by changing colours, the recorded state of the mouse buttons.

The usability tester can display the historic location of the mouse pointer by toggling a mouse tail option. The mouse tail shows where the mouse has been by displaying a series of dots on the playback area. The size of the tail is limited by elapsed time, which gives the effect of a tail that follows the mouse around, growing longer as the pointer moves faster, and growing shorter as the pointer slows. This playback enhancement gives a simple and effective historic record of the mouse movements.

Toolbar buttons associated with the playback area exist for the following operations:

- Starting the playback from the item (event, task or action group) selected in the event view area. The playback will stop at the last item selected (if more than one item is selected) or the last item in the event view area.
- Stopping the playback. If the playback is started again, it will commence from the first selected item.
- Pausing the playback. If the playback is started again, it will continue from the last displayed event.
- Changing the playback speed.
- Changing the length of the mouse tail.

Index area: The index area (Figure 2, right-hand side sub-window) gives the usability specialist the ability to quickly find and display recorded tasks. It does this by presenting the task names, grouped by associated user names and recording times in a tree structure. Once the desired task is located, it can be selected and displayed in the task view area as well as replayed in the playback area.

The index allows the usability specialist to find all tasks performed by a given user, all users who performed a given task or a list of all tasks in chronological order. The index is automatically generated from the manipulated recording, and is updated as new tasks are added or removed.

The index area shows a tree with all the tasks displayed on first level branches. Once a branch is expanded, the names of all users who attempted the task are displayed on the second level branches. Expanding a user name branch displays a date and time for each occurrence of the expanded task commenced by the expanded user. Alternatively, another index can also be displayed which places the user name on the first level branches and the task names on the second level branches. This allows for finding all tasks performed by a specified use.

A third index is available which is displayed in a table form, showing all tasks, user names and date/time of the task's commencement, sorted by date/time. This index view is useful for locating tasks by the date/time they were started and for scheduling future experiments.

4.4   Action Display Notation

Display of event information as a textual event log can be tedious to read, and it is difficult to communicate the hierarchical nature of the action groups and tasks. A graphical notation is more compact, allows for direct manipulation, is easier to read and captures the hierarchical nature of action groups and tasks by having one representation graphically contain another.

The items in the notation represent the start and end of a recording session, raw events, action groups and tasks, and consist of a series of boxes connected with arcs. Each box contains textual information identifying and qualifying the item it represents, and if the item has duration, it is displayed above the box (in seconds). Each arc is labelled with the time difference between the end of the first item and the start of the second item, which are connected by the arc.

Raw events are represented in the notation as rounded boxes (Figure 3). Text within the box identifies the class and type of event (e.g. MouseEvent: MOUSE_PRESSED), the target for the event (e.g. button0), and (if available) the coordinate of the event.

Action groups are represented in the notation as two stacked events. Text within the box shows the action group description and the number of items contained within the action group. A label above the box shows the number of seconds between the start of the first and the end of the last contained item. Action groups may be expanded to show the contained items. When expanded, the box is enlarged and all contained items are displayed below the text within the box.

A task is represented in the notation as a bevelled box. Text within the box shows the task name, the name of the user who attempted the task, and the date/time that the task commenced. Tasks also show the duration and may be expanded.

Filled circles mark the start and end of a single contiguous session. An arc (and the time difference label) does not connect start and end markers.

4.5   Automatic Classification Filters

For the event log, video playback and timing information to be accurate, all events need to be captured. These results in a large volume of information being displayed in the event display area, making it difficult for the usability tester to determine what the user was attempting. Mouse movements in particular generate a large number of events, which can be represented more usefully as a single action group.

Two prototype filters were designed for this work. The first filter groups mouse movement events as well events that occur as a consequence of the mouse moving around the interface. These events included MouseMove events (which are generated very rapidly as the mouse moves over the interface), MouseEntered and MouseExited events (which are generated as the mouse enters or leaves a control on the interface).

The second filter groups events related to typing, which are generated as keys are pressed and released, as well as when the contents of a control (edit field for example) changes due to keyboard input.

The two example filters were designed to demonstrate the utility of automating event grouping, and is invoked by selecting an automatic filtering option from the main application menu bar.

4.5.1   Summary of Advantages and Limitations

The advantages of our approach over current video taping and event logging techniques include:
- Flexibility in use, allowing for testing on multiple platforms using multiple styles of empirical testing.
- Practicality in use, by reducing the need for specialised and expensive equipment or complex, time consuming set up.
- Precision in its ability to measure events and the time they occurred.
- Transparency to the test user, with little impact on the software being tested, and no intimidating video cameras or usability testers.
- Ability to archive and compare results of multiple test performances, as well as the ability to easily copy and share results (via e-mail for example).
- Remote usability testing, allowing a greater base of test users, with only a small additional cost.
- Tightly integrated quantitative data (through event logging) and qualitative data (through the video-like screen capture playback).

The visualisation of events described within this work provides the usability specialist with a means of managing the data presented. The main advantages to the visualisation approach used in this work include:

- Viewing the data at various levels of complexity, with the ability to reveal details of interesting sections of data.
- The tight mapping between the event visualisation and the video-like playback of captured events, giving context to otherwise abstract events.
- The ability to nest event classifications and record the hierarchical nature of user actions and tasks.

We have also demonstrated in this work the importance of integrating a CAUsE tool with the graphical toolkit, which we believe, is a trend that will continue in the future. The close association between the CAUsE tool and graphical toolkit makes the tool more accessible throughout the development of interactive software, giving the interface designers a ready means of evaluating and improving interface design decisions. Tight integration with the graphical toolkit provides KALDI with the means of recording internal program state information, as well as the visible program output, which would assist in evaluating and improving adaptive and intelligent interfaces. KALDI is still an evolving tool, and as such, is limited in its current functionality. We intend to implement the following components and enhancements in order for the tool to be fully utilised:

- Provide the ability to monitor multiple windows and multiple applications.
- Provide facilities in the live monitor tool to categorise events and insert comments as the data is being received.
- Provide the ability to display multiple tasks at the same time and compare them.
- Modify the graphical display of events to communicate not only the user actions and the interface feedback, but also the state of both the interface and the underlying model after every action.
- Add the ability for the tool to measure machine performance, so that test results will not be biased by machine lag.
- Provide statistical reporting on the event data.
- Evaluate the applicability of the tool to test multiple users in collaborative environments.

Informal software and usability evaluations were conducted throughout the development of KALDI. Further studies are to be undertaken in the future to formally evaluate the usability and utility of KALDI and the visual representations it supports.

5.   CONCLUSIONS

Usability analysis methods and empirical user evaluations are the standard accepted techniques for developing usable systems. It is widely agreed that these techniques, which are inherited from Human Factors, do indeed work when carefully applied [8]. However, many HCI researchers have agreed (e.g., see [5,20,21]), that empirical user testing is too slow and expensive for modern software development practice, especially when hard-to-get domain experts are the target user group. In this research work we discussed usability analysis and testing activities, and described the design and implementation of KALDI, a prototype CAUsE tool developed to automate these activities.

KALDI is still an evolving prototype. It was developed to demonstrate the advantages of automating usability activities using purely software techniques. The tool helps by integrating usability testing into the development lifecycle. It enhance the collaboration between interactive systems developers and usability specialists, and consequently improves their ability to make sound design decisions.

The recent trend towards implementing CAUsE tools to support usability evaluation represents a significant development in this area. In this paper we demonstrated the benefits of integrating such tools in future graphical toolkits and UIMSs to reduce the gap between design/implementation and usability evaluation. This integration would promote interactive and ongoing usability assessment during the entire development lifecycle.

ACKNOWLEDGEMENT

The authors wish to thank Dr. Janice Langan-Fox for her invaluable comments and continuous support.

REFERENCES

[1]   Baskin, J.D. and John, B.E., *Comparison of GOMS Analysis methods*, in Proc. of ACM Conf. on Human Aspects in Computing Systems, Summary CHI'98, Los Angeles, 18-23 April 1998, Addison-Wesley, New York, 1998, pp. 261–262.

[2]   Baxter, J., *The Book of Coffee - The Conoisseurs Handbook*, Quintet Publishing Ltd., 1995.

[3]   Boehm, B.W., *A Spiral Model of Software Development and Enhancement*, IEEE Computers, Vol. 21, No. 5, 1988, pp. 61–72.

[4]   Bradford, J., Franzke, M., Jeffries, R., and Wharton, C., *Applying Cognitive Walk-throughs to more complex user interfaces: Experiences, Issues and Recommendations*, in Proceedings of ACM Conf. on Human Aspects in Computing Systems CHI'92, Monterey, 3-7 May 1992, Addison-Wesley, New York, 1992, pp. 381–388.

[5]   Butler, K.A., Bennett, J., Polson, P., and Karat, J., *Report on the workshop on analytical methods: Predicting the complexity of human-computer interaction*, SIGCHI Bulletin, Vol. 20, No. 4, 1989, pp. 63–79.

[6]   Card, S., Moran, T., and Newell, A., *The Psychology of Human-Computer Interaction*, Lawrence Erlbaum, Hillsdale, 1983.

[7]   Chi, M.T.H., Glaser, R., and Farr, M.J., The Nature of Expertise, Lawrence Erlbaum, Hillsdale, 1988.

[8]   Crellin, J., Horn, T., and Preece, J., *Evaluating Evaluation: A case study of the use of novel and conventional evaluation techniques in a small company*, in Proc. of 3rd IFIP Conf. on Human Computer Interaction INTERACT'90, Cambridge, 27-31 August 1990), North Holland, Amsterdam, 1990, pp. 329–335.

[9]   Geary, D..M., *Graphic Java 2 Mastering the JFC Volume I: AWT*, Prentice Hall, New Jersey, 1999.

[10] Geary, D.M., *Graphic Java 2 Mastering the JFC Volume II: Swing*, Prentice Hall, New Jersey, 1999.

[11] Hammontree, M., Hendrickson, J., and Hensley, B., *Integrated Data Capture and Analysis Tools for Research and Testing on Graphical User Interfaces*, in Proc. of ACM Conf. on Human Factors in Computing Systems CHI'92, Monterey, 3-7 May 1992, Addison-Wesley, New York, 1992, pp. 431–432.

[12] Hix, D. and Hartson, H.R., *Developing User Interfaces: Ensuring Usability through Product and Process*, John Wiley, New York, 1993.

[13] ISO: *Ergonomic Requirements for Office Work With Visual Display Terminals (VDTs) - Part II: Guidance on Usability (DIS 9242-11)*, International Standards Organisation, Geneva, 1997.

[14] Karat, C., *Cost-Justifying Usability Engineering in the Software Life Cycle*, in M. Helander, T.K. Landauer, and P. Prabhu (eds.), Handbook of Human-Computer Interaction, Elsevier Science Publishers, Amsterdam, 1997, pp. 767–778.

[15] Kieras, D., *A Guide to GOMS Model Usability Evaluation using NGOMSL*, in M. Helander, T.K. Landauer, and P. Prabhu (eds.), Handbook of Human-Computer Interaction, Elsevier Science Publishers, Amsterdam, 1997, pp. 733–766.

[16] Lewis, C., *Cognitive Walkthroughs*, in M. Helander, T.K. Landauer, and P. Prabhu (eds.), Handbook of Human-Computer Interaction, Elsevier Science Publishers, Amsterdam, 1997, pp. 717–732.

[17] Macleod, M., Bowden, R., Bevan, N., and Curson, I., The MUSiC Performance Measurement Method, Behaviour and Information Technology, Vol. 16, No. 4/5, 1997, pp. 279–293.

[18] Macleod, M. and Rengger, R., *The Development of DRUM: A Software Tool for Video-assisted Usability Evaluation*, in Proc. of BCS Conference on People and Computers VIII HCI'93, Loughborough, 8-10 September 1993, Cambridge University Press, Cambridge, 1993, pp. 293–309.

[19] Newman, W. and Lamming, M., *Interactive System Design*, Addison-Wesley, New York, 1995.

[20] Nielsen, J., *Usability Engineering at a Discount*, in G. Salvendy and G. Smith (eds.), Proc. of Third Int. Conf. on Human Computer Interaction, Designing and Using Human Computer Interfaces and Knowledge Based Systems, Elsevier Science Publishers, Amsterdam, 1989, pp. 394–401.

[21] Nielsen, J., Finding Usability Problems Through Heuristic Evaluation, in Proc. of ACM Conf. on Human Aspects in Computing Systems CHI'92, Monterey, 3-7 May 1992, Addison-Wesley, New York, 1992, pp. 373–380.

[22] Nielsen, J., *Iterative User-Interface Design*, IEEE Computer, November 1993, pp. 32–41.

[23] Nielsen, J., *Usability Engineering*, Academic Press, Boston, 1993.

[24] Norman, D.A. and Draper, S.W., *User Centered System Design: A New Perspective on Human Computer Interaction*, Lawrence Erlbaum, Hillsdale, 1986.

[25] Preece, J., Rogers, Y., Sharp, H., Benyon, D., Holland, S., and Carey, T., *Human-Computer Interaction*, Addison-Wesley, New York, 1994.

[26] Rubin, J., *Handbook of Usability Testing*, John Wiley & Sons, New York, 1994.

[27] Ryan, C. and Al-Qaimari, G., *The Orbital Model: A Methodology for the Development of Evolving Interactive Software Systems Based on Complex Domains*, Submitted for publication, 1999.

[28] Soloway, E., Adelson, B., and Ehrlich, K., *Knowledge and Processes in the Comprehension of Computer Programs*, in M.T.H. Chi, R. Glaser, and M. J. Farr (eds.), The Nature of Expertise, Lawrence Erlbaum, Hillsdale, 1988.

[29] Uehling, D. and Wolf, K., *User Action Graphing Effort (UsAGE)*, in Proc. of ACM Conf. on Human Aspects in Computing Systems CHI'95, Denver, 7-11 April 1995, Vol. II, Addison-Wesley, New York, 1995, pp. 290–291.